Fundamentals of International Migration

Fundamentals of International Migration

Compiled by:

Deniz Yetkin Aker

Z. Banu Dalaman

M. Gökay Özerim

Deniz Eroğlu Utku

Ibrahim Sirkeci

TRANSNATIONAL PRESS LONDON

2021

Custom Textbooks: 2

Fundamentals of International Migration
Compiled by Deniz Yetkin Aker, Z. Banu Dalaman, M. Gökay Özerim, Deniz
Eroğlu Utku, Ibrahim Sirkeci

Copyright © 2021 Transnational Press London

First Published in 2021 by TRANSNATIONAL PRESS LONDON in the United Kingdom, 12 Ridgeway Gardens, London, N6 5XR, UK.

Transnational Press London® and the logo and its affiliated brands are registered trademarks.

Requests for permission to reproduce material from this work should be sent to:
admin@tplondon.com

Paperback

ISBN: 978-1-80135-036-5

Digital

ISBN: 978-1-80135-037-2

Cover Design: Nihal Yazgan

Cover image:

www.tplondon.com

CONTENTS

ACNKNOWLEDGEMENT

Chapters included in this book have been previously published as follows:

Agustín, Ó. G., & Jørgensen, M. B. (2013). Immigration and civil society New ways of democratic transformation. *Migration Letters*, 10(3), 271-276.

Aker, D. Y. (2020). Introduction. In *Citizenship and Naturalization Among Turkish Skilled Migrants*. London: Transnational Press London. 1-6.

Bauder, H. (2018). Westphalia, migration, and feudal privilege. *Migration Letters*, 15(3), 333-346.

Bauhn, P. (2019). Universalist Rights and Particularist Duties: The Case of Refugees. *Migration Letters*, 16(2), 145-153.

Bendel, P. (2005). Immigration Policy in the European Union: Still bringing up the walls for fortress Europe?. *Migration Letters*, 2(1), 21-32.

Biffl, G., & Martin, P. L. (2018). Migration and Integration: Austrian and California Experiences with Low-Skilled Migrants. *Border Crossing*, 8(1), 30-39.

Brettell, C. B. (2006). Wrestling with 9/11: Immigrant Perceptions and Perceptions of Immigrants. *Migration Letters*, 3(2), 107-124.

Cohen, J. & Sirkeci, I. (2016, 1 August). A record 65.3 million people were displaced last year: What does that number actually mean? The Conversation. https://theconversation.com/a-record-65-3-million-people-were- displaced-last-year-what-does-that-number-actually-mean-61952

Cvajner, M. (2019). International Mobility, Erotic Plasticity and Eastern European Migrations. *Migration Letters*, 16(4), 513–520.

Féron, É. (2020). Embracing Complexity: Diaspora Politics as a Co-Construction. *Migration Letters*, 17(1), 27-36.

Heim, D. (2016). "Old" natives and "new" immigrants: beyond territory and history in Kymlicka's account of group-rights. *Migration Letters*, 13(2), 214-227.

Iosifides, T., & Sporton, D. (2009). Biographical Methods in Migration Research. *Migration Letters*, 6(2), 101-108.

Koca, B. T. (2019). Bordering Practices Across Europe: The Rise of "Walls" and "Fences". *Migration Letters*, 16(2), 183-194.

Marshall, R. (2014). The case for a foreign worker advisory commission. *Migration Letters*, 11(1), 65-78.

Martin, P. L. (2016). Europe's migration crisis: an American perspective. *Migration Letters*, 13(2), 307-319.

Massey, D. S. (2015). A missing element in migration theories. *Migration Letters*, 12(3), 279-299.

Mata-Codesal, D., Kloetzer, L., & Maiztegui-Oñate, C. (2020). Strengths, Risks and Limits of Doing Participatory Research in Migration Studies. *Migration Letters*, 17(2), 201-210.

Pusch, B., & Sirkeci, I. (2016). Introduction: Turkish migration policy at a glance. *Turkish Migration Policy*, London: TPLondon, 9-22.

Schwarz, T. (2016). Naturalisation policies beyond a Western focus. *Migration Letters*, 13(1), 1-15.

Scissa, C. (2020). Fleeing from the Global Compact for Migration: A missed opportunity for Italy. *Border Crossing*, 10(2), 155-174.

Sirkeci, I. (2009). Transnational mobility and conflict. *Migration Letters,* 6(1), 3-14.

Sirkeci, I. (2016). It is all about being happy in search of security. A pledge for equal treatment of refugees and economic migrants. 2016. *Völkerrechtsblog*. 10.17176/20180522-200536

Sirkeci, I. (2017). Turkey's refugees, Syrians and refugees from Turkey: a country of insecurity. *Migration Letters*, 14(1), 127-144.

Sirkeci, I. and Yüceşahin, M. M. (2020). Coronavirus and migration: Analysis of human mobility and the spread of COVID-19. *Migration Letters*, *17*(2), 379-398.

Sirkeci, I., & Esipova, N. (2013). Turkish migration in Europe and desire to migrate to and from Turkey. *Border Crossing*, *3*(1), 1-13.

Ullah, A. A., Hossain, M. A., Azizuddin, M., & Nawaz, F. (2020). Social Research Methods: Migration in Perspective. *Migration Letters*, 17(2), 357-368.

Unutulmaz, K. O. (2017). Integration of Syrians: Politics of integration in Turkey in the face of a closing window of opportunity. In *Turkey's Syrians: Today and Tomorrow* (pp. 213-236). Transnational Press London.

Yazgan, P., Utku, D. E., & Sirkeci, I. (2015). Syrian crisis and migration. *Migration Letters*, 12(3), 181-192.

Yüceşahin, M. M., & Sirkeci, I. (2017). Demographic gaps between Syrian and the European populations: What do they suggest. *Border Crossing*, *7*(2), 207-230.

PART 1: INTRODUCTION TO MIGRATION STUDIES

Essential Reading:

Cohen, J. & Sirkeci, I. (2016, 1 August). A record 65.3 million people were displaced last year: What does that number actually mean? The Conversation. https://theconversation.com/a-record-65-3-million-people-were-   displaced-last-year-what-does-that-number-actually-mean-61952

Sirkeci, I. (2016). It is all about being happy in search of security. A pledge for equal treatment of refugees and economic migrants. 2016. *Völkerrechtsblog*. 10.17176/20180522-200536

Martin, P. L. (2016). Europe's migration crisis: an American perspective. *Migration Letters*, 13(2), 307-319.

Scissa, C. (2020). Fleeing from the Global Compact for Migration: A missed opportunity for Italy. *Border Crossing*, 10(2), 155-174.

Further Reading:

Efe, S. S. (2020). *Rights of Migrant Workers: An Analysis of Migration Policies in Contemporary Turkey*. London: Transnational Press London.

Kakosimou, V. (2018). Asylum Under Pressure: international Deterrence and access to asylum. In *Migration Policy in Crisis* (pp. 95-102). London: Transnational Press London.

Sirkeci, I. (2011). "The Turks are coming", *Inner Circle Magazine*, Issue 3, July 2011 (Regent's College London), pp.12-13.

Sirkeci, I., & Cohen, J. H. (2015). Measuring impact and the most influential works in Migration Studies. *Migration Letters*, 12(3), 336-345.

Cohen, JH and Sirkeci, I (2011). "The Growth of Migration: Mobility, Security, Insecurity" In *Cultures of Migration. Global Nature of Contemporary Human Mobility*. Austin: University of Texas Press.

CHAPTER 1

A Record 65.3 Million People were Displaced Last Year: What Does That Number Actually Mean?

Jeffrey H. Cohen and Ibrahim Sirkeci

We continue to witness violent attacks – bombings and murders in France, Germany, Turkey, Afghanistan and Iraq; fighting in South Sudan and the continued civil war in Syria. These conflicts have renewed interest in the global refugee crisis and the movements of displaced persons around the globe.

The United Nations Human Rights Council announced in June that 65.3 million people were forcibly displaced from their homes in 2015. This is a record number and is equal in population to the U.K. or France. People who have been forced to leave their homes, their nations and occupation against their will are often referred to as "displaced." And 65.3 million is a lot of displaced people.

They are found across the globe in response to crises that range from the social to the environmental, and include Syrian refugees fleeing civil war, Central American children crossing international borders to reach family and security in the U.S., Colombians moving internally to avoid warfare and violence and Filipinos who are forced to relocate in response to changing climates and environmental disasters. The UNHRC's report identifies important global patterns that we must acknowledge. But, the overwhelming size of the displaced population reported confounds a complex issue and creates new fears. The numbers overwhelm and make it difficult to define potential solutions.

Conflict, insecurity and migration

In our book, "Cultures of Migration," we argue that all migrants, including refugees, face conflicts and insecurities. Conflicts and insecurity can be physical and violent as in the Syrian civil war or nonmaterial and discriminatory and based in social and cultural differences. These nonmaterial challenges included those faced by migrants and refugees as they settle in Europe and the U.S. Insecurity complicates migration, and migration is no longer a decision made to in response to finding a good job or access to high wages.

Migration, forced or otherwise, is complex and challenging. There is no guarantee of success, and over time new conflicts and insecurities arise.

Displaced people, like all migrants, balance conflicts and insecurities at places of origin and of destination. Two examples help illustrate our point. Since 2011 Syrian refugees have fled violence and civil war. Yet their desire to leave has a long history, and reflects dissatisfaction with the Assad regime, restrictive national laws and a weak economy.

In Sudan, refugees fled their homelands to escape violence during more than 40 years of civil war between South and North over food, natural resources, religion and political control.

In 2013, a new civil war in the south brought a crisis, creating more than one million refugees fleeing the violence associated with the political struggles between competing strongmen.

Big numbers

Thinking in large numbers abstracts the challenges, conflicts and insecurities that displaced people face. About half of the world's refugees are living under the UNHCR's mandate and protection in Afghanistan and Somalia. Nevertheless, it is people fleeing smaller crises like the coup in Turkey, the drought in Central Asia and religious persecution in Myanmar among others that make up many of the displaced. In addition, more than 40 million refugees remain within their native homelands, including Colombians, Iraqis and South Sudanese who are fleeing their villages to escape violence, warfare and religious persecution.

How do we comprehend 65.3 million displaced people when they have little in common? It is hard to envision so many displaced people. The mathematician Spencer Greenberg notes we have no problem thinking in small numbers. Even 100 things – a large crowd, for example – is manageable. Nevertheless, "when we're talking about millions of things our ability to visualize completely fails."

To cope, we use metaphors in place of statistics. Often, displaced people are described as waves crashing upon the beach or spreading like a cancer.

Critics who exaggerate the numbers of displaced people and refugees overwhelm and terrify their audience. Donald Trump, the U.S. Republican presidential nominee, warns U.S. citizens to lock their doors, lest they fall victim to terror. Milos Zeman, the Czech president, describes the movement of refugees to Europe as an "organised invasion." These arguments deny the realities that the displaced and refugees face and prey on a shared fear of outsiders.

Good, bad and the morality of migration

One way to confront our fears of large numbers is to reduce them to discrete, manageable categories. However, categories typically carry judgments and create expectations. And too often in the discussion of refugees the categories divide people into "good" and "bad" groups based in shared perceptions, and what Stephanie Pappas calls our "caveman instincts."

"Good" refugees are the people who flee their homelands to avoid violence and seek shelter and a new way of life. "Bad" refugees threaten our shared values and lifestyle. The differences that define "good" and "bad" refugees misrepresent the conflicts that motivate movement. The need to divide "good" from "bad" renders the civil, social and environmental insecurities that drive migrants and refugees to move moot.

Beyond the numbers

Victoria Armour Hileman writes, "if the world measures a refugee according to the worst story, we will always excuse human suffering, saying it is not yet as bad as someone else's."

Knowing the numbers of displaced people globally captures the size of the crises driving people from their homes. However, it is more important to focus on the conflicts and insecurities that define specific crises. By identifying the causes of forced relocation, we can better address the outcomes and build toward solutions.

CHAPTER 2

It Is All About Being Happy in Search of Security

Ibrahim Sirkeci

Migration recently has been discussed in a very negative context. As Europe and the US moved towards right, we have to rethink human mobility and push for informed debates. Terminology used to describe migration and refugees is old, out dated and problematic. They were largely designed for the Cold War era and for a special category of people. The 1951 Geneva Convention had set the ground rules for treating refugees. Then, economic growth was the dominant character with clear need for foreign labour as Germany and other European countries signed multiple bilateral labour exchange agreements with the countries in the South to recruit millions of "guest workers" from the 1950s till the early 1970s.

Nevertheless, today, these countries are marked by after effects of a recent global financial crisis and characterised by very slow growth and limited employment opportunities. Although there is still great need for foreign labour in certain sectors and shortage occupations, the demand is very limited. At the same time, relatively peaceful period after the WWII has long gone. There are major armed conflicts on going in many parts of the world such as in Afghanistan, Syria, and Iraq while at the same time significant economic and political inequalities, which are evident in many countries have added fuel to migration pressures. Hence a new thinking is needed to understand and address the challenges today.

Numbers grew but remained negligible

Although the number of international migrants including refugees has almost tripled since the 1960s, 244 million migrants represent still just about 3.3% of the world population of 7.3 billion as of Summer 2016. At the end of 2015, the number of displaced people had peaked at 65.3 million, 21.3 million of whom were refugees. Despite the grave and urgent need for humanitarian protection in the case of refugees and internally displaced persons, there is no reason to separate them from international migrants as they share the same needs such as shelter, food, job, opportunities, education, health and so on. Thus the dichotomy of refugee versus economic migrant is a false one. People move in search of security. Whether it might be economic, political, cultural, environmental, or personal security.

Terminology matters

When Jeffrey Cohen and I set to write our book Cultures of Migration in 2005, one pressing concern for us was the negative connotations associated with the mainstream migration terminology. A decade later, immigrant and migration are still representing the "evil" against good. Anti-immigration and racist discourses are common on both sides of the Atlantic.

The terminology suffers from a neo-liberal fallacy about human mobility. The problem here is that once you place too much emphasis on the individual agent as a rational decision maker who often focused on economics of the origin and destinations, you are likely to get a distorted picture of contemporary human mobility. In this perspective, migration is often described with a focus on positive outcomes tied to destinations such as higher wages, quality education, welfare benefits and so on. It is true that people who move do want to be happy or happier. Since they often go through and face negative circumstances, which they perceive as insecurity at the origin and this is what drives mobility rather than positive outcomes at the destination. "While many movers typically talk about their hopes and dreams, their decisions are often made around a present that they are trying to escape as well as a future that they cannot describe". Hence people only begin thinking about destinations and what can be available there for them once they are clearly convinced of the environment of insecurity at home.

Cultures of Migration and Conflict Model

The conflict-migration nexus is more obvious in cases like Syria today, however, as we define conflict in a very wide sense here, it applies to most migration decisions. The model originally draws upon research on migration from Turkey, migration from Iraq, migration from Mexico, and more recently it is clearly applicable to Syrian migration. It also integrates the cumulative causation model of Doug Massey.

The key premises of the cultures of migration and conflict model of migration are as follows:

1. Nobody moves when they are comfortable where they are and contempt with what they have. Population movements are almost always triggered by some discomfort, tension, disagreements, conflicts, absence or paucity of resources and/or opportunities, wars and the like.

2. When there are armed conflicts, civil wars and/or wars, mass movements occur.

3. Environment of insecurity is what individuals, households or groups perceive in a subjective fashion. Therefore, even if we can identify many conflicts and issues in a given place, it does not necessarily mean all people living in that place would be moving.

4. Even when there is a clear perception of an environment of insecurity, only some people move because human mobility is a self-selective and costly process and only those able and with necessary means can move. These qualifiers can be categorised into (a) human capital, (b) social capital, (c) financial capital, (d) physical and psychological ability to move.

5. Migration experience is often built within households, communities, groups, and places. This means, even when the initial triggers of migration disappear out-migration can continue. In fact, over time, migration corridors turn to carry two way flows and transnational living arrangements emerge. Cultures of migration emerge and influence the ways in which

9

people move.

Moving away from pejorative meanings of migration, immigration, migrants and the like is easy to understand. The rest of the story is more complicated and nuanced. Mobility and movement are neutral terms and they reflect the dynamic nature of human migration. This is clearer within the conflict model, as people move and continue to move at the face of conflicts, which change, appear and fade away over time and space.

CHAPTER 3

Europe's Migration Crisis: An American Perspective

Philip L. Martin

Introduction

The United States is a nation of immigrants unsure about the best migration policy for the future. With almost five percent of the world's people but 20 percent of the world's 244 million international migrants, the US is the major country of immigration. The UN reported 47 million international migrants in the US in 2015, four times more than Germany and Russia, which each had 12 million migrants (UN DESA, 2015). The US is alone among high-income countries in having a quarter of migrants who are unauthorized, some 11.3 million in 2014. What to do about these unauthorized foreigners has dominated policy debates over the past two decades.

The foreign-born are 14 percent of US residents. The US has a higher share of foreign-born residents than most European countries, but a lower share than Australia and Canada, where over 20 percent of residents were born outside the country.[1] The major sources of migrants to the US are different from other industrial countries as well. Over half of US migrants are from Latin America and a quarter are from Asia, while over half of migrants to Australia and Canada are from Asia.

Most Americans think that immigration is good for the US, but more want immigration reduced than increased, although the gap has narrowed in recent years. Pollster Gallup also found that most Americans believe it is "very important" or "extremely important" for the government to take steps to reduce illegal migration and to deal with the unauthorized foreigners in the US. Congress has held hearings and debated bills on how to accomplish these goals, but none became law, allowing illegal migration to take center stage when Republican presidential contender Donald Trump made the issue the centerpiece of his campaign in summer 2015.

This article explains the three major doors through which foreigners arrive in the US, the debate over what to do about unauthorized migration, and responses to the largest wave of newcomers in a century. Immigration is a federal responsibility, but there is unlikely to be any major immigration legislation enacted until 2017 at the earliest.

---

[1] UN DESA reported that 28 percent of Australian and 22 percent of Canadian residents were born outside these countries in 2015.

Figure 1. Gallup: Should Immigration be Increased or Decreased, 1965-2014

In your view, should immigration be kept at its present level, increased, or decreased?

■ % Present level ■ % Increased % Decreased

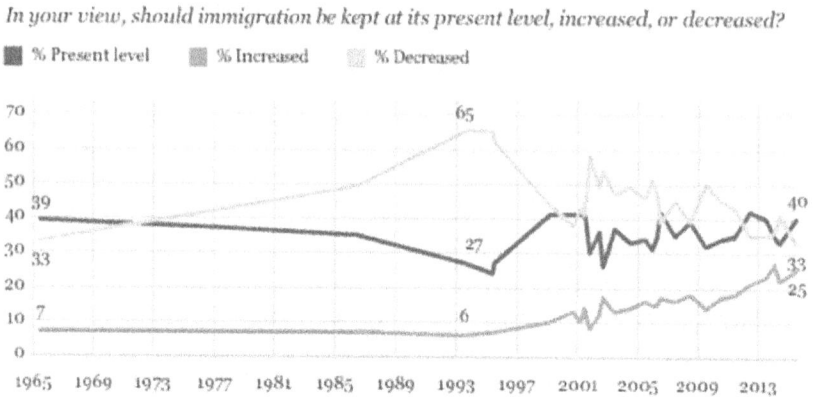

Source: http://www.gallup.com/poll/1660/immigration.aspx

Three entry doors

Foreigners enter the US through three major doors: front, side, and back. The US admitted 990,500 front-door settler immigrants in FY13, the most recent data available, an average of over 2,700 a day (DHS, 2014). For the past several decades, most immigrants have been from Latin America, but in 2013 the number of Asian immigrants, 400,500, slightly exceeded the number from Latin America, 390,000. Mexico was the birthplace of more front-door immigrants than any other country, about 135,000, as many as from China and India combined.

The US has a family-oriented immigration system, meaning that two-thirds of all immigrants invited as permanent residents are admitted because a relative in the US sponsored them, that is, the US-based relative asked the government to issue an immigrant visa to his or her relative. Two-thirds of family immigrants are spouses, children, and parents of US citizens who can immigrate without waiting. One-third are spouses and children of immigrants or more distant relatives, such as married and unmarried adult children of US citizens and their families, some of whom must wait years for immigrant visas. A sixth of immigrants are sponsored by US employers, and the remaining immigrants are refugees, diversity and other immigrants.[2]

Over half of all immigrants or green-card holders (immigrant visas used to be printed on green paper, and immigrants are still often called green-card holders) are already in the US when they receive immigrant visas, so that they adjust their status from temporary visitor, student, or from worker to immigrant. There were 173 million visitor admissions in FY13, but most involved Canadians and Mexicans entering the US for shopping or daily work. There were 61 million so-called I-94

---

[2] A 1990 law makes 50,000 immigrant visas available each year to citizens of countries that sent less than 50,000 immigrants to the US during the previous five years; winners of visas are selected by lottery from 10 million to 15 million entries. Until 2013, Bangladeshis submitted more 10 applications than any other country. Today, Ethiopians, Egyptians, and Iranians submit many of the 15 million applications.

admissions, meaning that a foreigner entered the US as a tourist, student, or worker and planned to stay from several weeks to several years, an average of 167,000 a day.

Unlike immigrants, side-door temporary visitors enter the US for a specific time and purpose. Most foreign visitors leave after a few weeks, months, or years, but some become immigrants by marrying US citizens or finding US employers to sponsor them. Many of the almost 900,000 foreign students enrolled in US colleges and universities stay in the US after graduation, sometimes as employees under Optional Practical Training programs that allow some foreign graduates of US universities to stay up to 36 months.[3] Others become temporary foreign workers with H-1B visas for up to six years.[4] A foreign student who begins as an undergraduate and earns a graduate degree before becoming an OPT intern and then an H-1B worker can be in a temporary status in the US for two decades, during which time many find US sponsors and become immigrants.

The third port of entry allows back-door foreigners to enter the US without inspection by eluding the Border Patrol or to enter legally but not abide by the terms of their visas, such as not departing as required or going to work without permission. About 55 percent of the 11.3 in 2014 million illegal, undocumented, or unauthorized foreigners entered without inspection and 45 percent arrived legally but violated the terms of their visas (Passel and Cohn, 2015a). The number of unauthorized foreigners peaked in 2007, and since the recovery from the 2008-09 recession has stabilized at about 11 million. The share of Mexicans among the unauthorized has fallen from almost 60 percent to just over half.

Almost three-fourths of unauthorized foreigners are in the US labor force, over eight million, making unauthorized workers over five percent of the 156 million-strong US workforce (Passel and Cohn, 2015b). Unauthorized workers are concentrated by geography, industry, and occupation, with especially heavy concentrations among farm workers employed in agriculture in California, laborers, drywallers, and roofers in construction in Nevada, and in low-wage service jobs in major cities, from lawn and gardening services to food preparation in restaurants. A quarter of US farm workers, a sixth of US janitors, a seventh of US construction workers, and a ninth of US food preparation workers are unauthorized (Passel and Cohn, 2015b).

One indicator of illegal immigration is how many foreigners are apprehended just inside the Mexico-US border, a number that has been falling. In FY2000, over 1.8 million foreigners were apprehended, an average of almost 5,000 a day. The

---

[3] In April 2008, USCIS extended from 12 to 29 months that foreign graduates of US universities with science, technology, engineering, or mathematics (STEM) degrees may remain in the US for study-related employment, and in March 2016 the maximum duration of OPT for STEM graduates was extended to 36 months. Many of the students in OPT jobs, whose number is not capped, are waiting for H-1B visas, whose number is capped. www.uscis.gov/eir/visa-guide/f-1-opt-optional-practical-training/f-1-optional-practical-training-opt

[4] The H-1B program makes it easy for most US employers to attest that they need foreigners with college degrees. It aims to protect US workers by limiting the number of visas to 65,000 a year, plus 20,000 for foreigners with advanced degrees from US universities, plus an unlimited number for nonprofits such as universities. Most US employers can obtain H-1B visas for foreign professionals without first trying to recruit US workers, and some have laid off US workers in order to hire H-1B workers. Most of the quota-limited H-1B visas go to outsourcers, often India-based firms that have some US employees and more abroad to do IT-work for US clients (Preston, 2015).

number of apprehensions fell to less than 2,000 a day in FY2011, and has continued to fall to less than 1,000 a day in recent years; there were 337,000 apprehensions in FY2015. The share of Mexicans among those apprehended, which was over 90 percent until 2008-09, is now 55 percent, reflecting less unauthorized Mexico-US migration and more unauthorized migration from Central America (Rural Migration News, 2016).

Figure 2. Unauthorized Migrants in the US, 1990-2014 (millions)

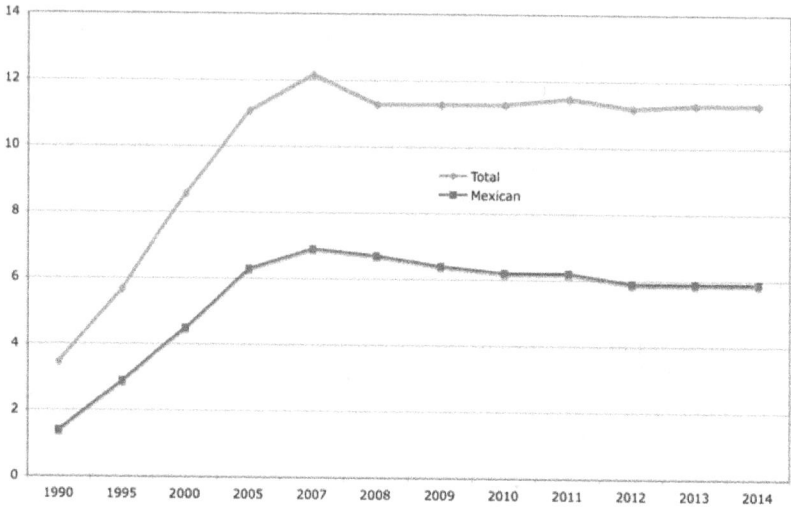

Source: Adapted from Passel and Cohn, 2015a

The unauthorized population in the US increased by an average of 1,000 a day between 2009 and 2014. However, the slowdown in newly arrived unauthorized foreigners, and the fact that more Mexicans in the US are returning to Mexico than are arriving from Mexico, means that many of the remaining unauthorized foreigners are settled in the US. Almost three-fourths of unauthorized adults have been in the US at least a decade, and 40 percent live with US-born children who are US citizens by birth (Passel and Cohn, 2015a).

Immigration debates

Each of the three major flows of foreigners to the US is controversial, raising questions about integration, labor market competition, and the rule of law. Immigrants sponsored by US relatives should have a relatively easy time integrating into the US, since their US-based relatives can help them to find housing and jobs and are legally responsible to support the immigrants they sponsor.[5] However, if the US relatives who sponsor immigrants have low levels of education and do not speak English, the relatives they sponsor may have difficulty finding jobs that pay

---

[5] Newly arrived settler immigrants are generally not eligible for federal welfare benefits until they work in the US for 10 years or become naturalized US citizens after five years. If an immigrant nonetheless receives federal welfare benefits, the US government can recoup any benefits paid from the immigrant's US-based sponsor.

enough to rise above poverty-level incomes.

Over half of US immigrants are from Latin America. Most have little education and are joining US relatives with little education. For this reason, many economists believe that the US should switch from a family-unification immigration selection system to an Australian- or Canadian-style point system and select immigrants whose personal characteristics make them likely to be successful in the US. Instead of giving 70 percent of immigrant visas to those with US relatives, they would give most immigrant visas to young foreigners with high levels of education, English, and US job offers (Orrenius, Zavodny, and LoPalo, 2014).

English is the key to upward mobility in the US labor market. Over 20 percent of US residents five or older speak a language other than English at home. Spanish is spoken at-home by two-thirds of those who do not speak English at home, followed by Chinese. Studies of immigrant integration find that today's immigrants are assimilating into American society as fast as previous immigrants, and learning English faster than those who arrived early in the 20th century (Waters and Gerstein, 2015). Half of immigrants report that they speak English "well," but the penalties for not knowing English are greater in today's service economy than they were a century ago in an agricultural and manufacturing economy.

Uncertainty about immigration selection and integration amidst employer pleas for foreign workers prompts calls for new and expanded temporary worker programs. Such programs have long been controversial in a nation of immigrants, raising fears that range from "unfair" competition for US workers to backdoor immigration. A series of Mexico-US programs that admitted so-called Braceros to work on US farms between 1942 and 1964 is widely blamed for depressing US farm wages and sowing the seeds of future illegal Mexico-US migration, largely by developing a mutual dependence between rural Mexico and rural America that defied efforts to stop Mexico-US migration when the program was ended during the 1960s Civil Rights era (Martin, 2003). Expanding current or creating new guest worker programs for low-skilled workers, some fear, could depress the wages of similar US workers and again sow the seeds for future illegal migration.

There are different concerns about side-door foreigners with college degrees. The US had almost a million foreign students in 2014-15, so that five percent of students at US universities were foreigners on temporary visas. About 20 percent were from China, followed by 15 percent from India (IIE, 2015). Among foreigners studying for US degrees, there were slightly more graduate than undergraduate students, with over half of the graduate students in master's degree programs.[6]

Many consider foreign graduates of US universities to be the ideal immigrants, since they have completed a US course of study, know English, and are attractive to US employers. With US universities the gatekeepers to the US, and US employers the gatekeepers to the US labor market, both Republicans and Democrats have decried US policies that force some foreign graduates of US universities who want settle in the US to leave when they fail to find a sponsor who will give them an

---

[6] See: www.iie.org/Research-and-Publications/Open-Doors/Data/International-Students/Academic -Level/2012-14

internship or a job.

The problem with the US system of student, guest worker, and immigrant is numbers. Imagine a funnel that begins with many foreign students, since there are no limits on how many can be admitted, and no limits on OPT employees after graduation. However, there are only 85,000 H-1B visas available for profit-seeking firms, and they and their families must compete for the 140,000 immigrant visas a year available to a wide range of foreigners seeking economic visas, from outstanding scientists to foreign investors. Foreigners who are in the US a decade or more can become very frustrated by the uncertainty and lengthy waits for an immigrant visa.

The H-1B program allows US employers to hire foreigners who have at least a bachelor's degree and who are filling US jobs that require such degrees (Martin, 2012). When the program was created in 1990, the assumption was that employers would request all available visas immediately to fill jobs in the expanding IT sector. Employer requests were expected to decline as more Americans earned computer-related degrees, but the opposite occurred. Employer requests climbed slowly until outsourcers appeared in the late 1990s, usually Indian-based firms that employ some H-1B workers in the US to understand the IT needs of a US firm, and then perform most of the firm's IT work in India.

Most US firms are not required to have their need for H-1B workers certified, meaning they do not have to try to find US workers before hiring H-1B foreigners. This allows them to lawfully lay off US workers and replace them with H-1B foreigners at lower wages, as Walt Disney and Southern California Edison did (Preston, 2015). Investigations of both firms found that they did not violate laws, since it is lawful for most US employers to lay off US workers and replace them with H-1B guest workers. Reforming the H-1B program is stalemated because those who want more protections for US workers have blocked proposals to simply increase the number of H-1B visas.

The US also has guest worker programs that admit low-skilled seasonal workers, called H-2A for farm workers and H-2B for nonfarm workers. There is no cap on the number of farm jobs that can be filled by H-2A foreigners, but there is a 66,000 a year cap on H-2B jobs. In recent years, about 140,000 farm jobs were certified to be filled by H-2A workers and 66,000 by H-2B workers (Martin, 2014). Both of these low-skilled guest worker programs are controversial, with employers calling for more "essential workers" to fill low-skilled US jobs and migrant advocates calling the conditions under which H-2A and H-2B workers are employed "close to slavery."[7]

The debate over guest workers mirrors broader debates over immigration. Employers say that foreigners fill the jobs US workers shun, and that the availability of guest workers helps to keep farms, restaurants, and ski resorts in business

---

[7] The Essential Worker Immigration Coalition wants "a workable guest worker program that properly accounts for America's current and future workforce needs." (http://ewic.org/). The Southern Poverty Law Center calls the current low-skilled guest worker programs "close to slavery." (www.splcenter.org/20130218/close-slavery-guestworker-programs-united-states)

(NFAP, 2005). Critics say that there is no shortage of US workers, only a shortage of jobs offering decent wages and working conditions, and that US workers rightly shun jobs that demand hard work for low wages (Costa, 2016). Immigration reform proposals that would create new guest worker programs must balance the competing interests of employer and worker advocates on issues that range from how many visas should be available to the minimum wages and working conditions that must be provided to US and guest workers; none has yet won majority support.

Reform proposals

The major immigration reform proposals considered in Congress over the past decade include three key elements: more enforcement to deter illegal migrants, legalization for at least some of the unauthorized in the US, and new or modified guest worker programs. Disagreements involve exactly what to do in each of the three areas, and how to phase in each element.

The most recent attempt to enact comprehensive immigration reform was the Border Security, Economic Opportunity, and Immigration Modernization Act (S 744), approved by the Senate in June 2013. The enforcement sections of S 744 included billions of dollars to "secure" the Mexico-US border so that at least 90 percent of foreigners attempting to cross illegally would be apprehended. The number of Border Patrol agents would have doubled to 40,000, and the amount of fencing on the Mexico-US border would have doubled to 700 miles (Migration News, 2013).

In order to deter unauthorized foreigners, including foreigners who enter the US legally but work or overstay, employers would have had to begin checking all newly hired workers with the internet-based E-Verify system. This involves newly hired workers presenting proof of their right to work in the US and employers verifying this information with the federal government, as with credit card purchases.

The US has over seven million employers who hire over 50 million workers a year (many workers are hired multiple times). The major issue is what to do about mistakes, as when the federal government says someone is not authorized to work when they in fact are authorized. In such cases, should the federal government have to pay lost wages to workers who were wrongly denied jobs?

S 744's main legalization program would have allowed unauthorized foreigners who had been in the US at least two years to become "registered provisional immigrants," with the right to live and work in the US for six years. After six years, and if the president deemed unauthorized migration to be "under control," registered provisional immigrants who could prove that they were working and paying taxes could apply for regular immigrant status and become naturalized US citizens. S 744 included a separate and easier legalization program for unauthorized farm workers, who would have to prove that they did farm work as unauthorized foreigners to qualify. They could become regular immigrants in as little as three years if they continued to do farm work.[8]

The US now has three major temporary worker programs that admit over 200,000 guest workers a year. S 744 would have almost doubled the number of H-1B visas, and could have increased the number even more if employers requested all available visas. There would have been a new guest worker program for low-skilled workers, with the number admitted determined by a new Bureau of Immigration and Labor Market Research that studied labor market indicators, including unemployment rates and employer labor shortage complaints. Admissions which have begun at 200,000 a year, and could have doubled or tripled if employers requested all available visas and unemployment was low.

S 744 also included two new farm guest worker programs. One would have allowed farm employers to offer contracts to guest workers that tied them to their farms, while the other would have admitted foreign guest workers who "floated" from farm to farm. Farm employers would not have had to provide housing for floating guest workers, who could remain legally in the US as long as they were not unemployed more than 60 days. Instead of being administered by the US Department of Labor, the new programs would be administered by the US Department of Agriculture, which is perceived as friendlier to farm employers (Rural Migration News, 2013).

S 744 was controversial and not enacted into law. Restrictionists who believe that the first priority is to reduce illegal immigration decried legalization, calling it "rewarding lawbreakers." On the other hand, admissionists who believe that a nation of immigrants should integrate foreigners who have settled regardless of their legal status worried that the path to regular immigrant status and US citizenship was too arduous. Many employers worried that the new guest worker programs were not sufficiently large to fill vacant jobs, while unions charged that more guest workers would increase exploitation and hold down wages.

Immigration and politics

The trade-offs embodied in the Senate's S 744 proposal were satisfactory to most Democrats, whose main goal was a path to US citizenship for unauthorized foreigners. However, many Senate Republicans objected to "amnesty," and they persuaded the House to embrace a step-by-step or piece meal approach to immigration reform that begins with making enforcement more effective. The House dealt with several immigration enforcement bills, but none was enacted.

President Obama, who made comprehensive immigration reform a top domestic priority during his 2008 campaign, repeatedly told migration advocates that he did not have the power to change immigration law on his own. However, Obama in November 2014 used his executive authority to announce several

---

[8] Unauthorized farm workers who did at least 100 days or 575 hours of US farm work in the 24 months ending December 31, 2012 could have received cards that allowed them to live and work in the US after providing "just and reasonable" evidence of their qualifying farm work. Their spouses and children could have also become probationary immigrants.

To become immigrants, unauthorized farm workers who registered would have had to do at least 150 days of farm work a year for three years. When farm workers qualify for immigrant visas, so would their family members, so that the agricultural provisions of S 744 could have legalized up to 1.5 million farm workers and family members.

immigration changes, including the Deferred Action for Parents of Americans and Lawful Permanent Residents (DAPA) program, which would have allowed an estimated four million unauthorized foreigners with legal US children to receive three-year renewable work permits. Obama also expanded the 2012 Deferred Action for Childhood Arrivals (DACA) program, which has given a temporary legal status to almost 700,000 unauthorized youth who were brought to the US before the age of 16 and who graduated from high school.

If DAPA had gone into effect and DACA were expanded, at least half of the unauthorized foreigners in the US could have received a temporary legal status. However, Texas and 25 other states sued, alleging that that DAPA and expanded DACA would impose costs on states, and thus the US constitution prohibited Obama from implementing them by executive order. Federal courts agreed with the states, and DAPA has not gone into effect and DACA has not been expanded. The US Supreme Court is expected to rule on the lawfulness of Obama's DAPA and expanded DACA by mid-2016.

There has also been activity in the states. Beginning with Arizona's SB 1070 in 2010, many states enacted laws that require employers to use the federal E-Verify system to check the legal status of newly hired workers. SB 1070 and some other state laws went further, requiring state and local police to determine the legal status of potentially unauthorized persons encountered during traffic and other investigations, and making illegal presence in the state a crime. Initial reports suggested that unauthorized workers left states with such laws, but many of the provisions of state laws were later found unconstitutional and suspended, limiting their long-term effects.

Meanwhile, California and a dozen other states began to issue driver's licenses and to offer in-state reduced tuition to unauthorized foreigners, taking the opposite approach to protect and to integrate unauthorized foreigners. These states welcomed DAPA, and some began to offer English and other classes to unauthorized foreigners to speed their integration.

Unauthorized migration became a major issue in the Republican presidential campaign in summer 2015 when Donald Trump accused some illegal Mexicans of "bringing drugs. They are bringing crime. They're rapists. But some, I assume, are good people." Trump called for a wall on the Mexico-US border financed by fees paid by border crossers and an end to birthright citizenship, so that babies born to unauthorized parents in the US would no longer be automatic US citizens. Trump continued to take tough line on unauthorized migration, calling on the US government to halt the entry of Muslims after the terror attacks in Paris in November 2015, and is the frontrunner for the Republican presidential nomination in spring 2016.

Republicans are divided into three major camps. Trump represents the enforcement-only camp that wants to remove unauthorized foreigners from the US and build fences and walls on US borders. Senator Marco Rubio (R-FL), Jeb Bush, and more centrist Republicans support the additional enforcement and guest workers included in S 744's comprehensive immigration reform, but they would allow unauthorized foreigners to earn only a legal status in the US that might not result in US citizenship. A third camp, exemplified by House Speaker Paul Ryan (R-WI), is more libertarian, urging Republicans to move away from barriers on the border and instead wall off welfare benefits, that is, admit migrants and let them work, but make it hard for them to receive welfare benefits.

Democratic presidential contender Hillary Clinton supported the enforcement, legalization, and guest worker package approved by the Senate in 2013, albeit with some changes. Clinton said that she would expand DAPA and DACA further if elected president, while Senator Bernie Sanders (D-VT) has expressed support for legalization but opposition to expanded guest worker programs.

What's next for US immigration?

Legal immigration seems likely to continue at a million a year, all signs point to a rising number of temporary visitors, especially those whose numbers are not capped such as students, and the unauthorized population is stabilizing in number and integrating into the US. The presidential campaign has kept the focus on illegal immigration, even though the number of unauthorized foreigners has stabilized. Some employers complain of too few workers, but most are adjusting to fewer newcomers eager for jobs.

There are unlikely to be any major immigration policy changes until 2017. When the immigration policy debate resumes, the major question is whether the emphasis will be on enforcement to prevent illegal migration or legalization of unauthorized foreigners in the US. The answer depends on the results of elections in November 2016.

References

Costa, D. (2016). *The H-2B temporary foreign worker program.* Economic Policy Institute. January. Available: http://www.epi.org/publication/h2b-temporary-foreign-worker-program-for-labor-shortages-or-cheap-temporary-labor/?utm_ source =Economic+Policy+Institute&utm_campaign=e37935904f-EPI_News_01_22 _161_21_2016&utm_medium=email&utm_term=0_e7c5826c50-e37935904f-55915029

DHS. (2014). *Yearbook of Immigration Statistics: FY2013.* DHS. http://www.dhs.gov /sites/default/files/publications /ois_yb_2013_0.pdf

IIE. 2015. Open Doors. http://www.iie.org/en/Research-and-Publications/Open-Doors/Data/International-Students/Leading-Places-of-Origin/2012-14

Martin, P. L. (2014). The H-2A Program; Evolution, Impacts, and Outlook. Pp 33-62. Chapter 2 in David Griffith, Ed. *(Mis)managing Migration. Guestworkers' Experiences with North American Labor Market.* SAR Press. http://sarweb.org/index. php?sar_press_mismanaging_migration

Martin, P.L. (2012). High-Skilled Migrants: S&E Workers in the United States. *American Behavioral Scientist.* August. Vol 56, pp 1058-1079 http://abs.sagepub.com/ content/56/8/1058.full.pdf+html

Martin, P.L. (2003). Does the US Need a new Bracero Program? *UC-Davis Journal of International Law and Policy.* Vol 9, No 2, Spring. 127-141. http://nationalaglaw center.org/publication/martin-does-the-u-s-need-a-new-bracero-program-9-univ-california-davis-j-international-l-policy-127-141-2003/

Migration News (2013). Senate Approves S 744. Vol 20. No 3. July. http://migration.ucdavis.edu/ mn/ more.php?id=3838

NFAP (2005). H-2B Visas: providing a legal regime for US employers. http://www.nfap.com/researchactivities/ studies/H2BVISAS2005.pdf

Orrenius P., M. Zavodny, and M. LoPalo (2014). The Economics of US Immigration Reform. *Capitalism and Society.* Vol 9. No 2. http://papers.ssrn.com/sol3/papers.cfm?abstract_id=2523494

Passel, J. and D'Vera Cohn. (2015a). Unauthorized immigrant population stable for half a decade. *Pew Hispanic.* July 22. www.pewresearch.org/fact-tank/2015/07/22/unauthorized-immigrant-population-stable-for-half-a-decade/

Passel, Jeffrey and D'Vera Cohn (2015b). Share of Unauthorized Immigrant Workers in Production, Construction Jobs Falls Since 2007. March 26. www.pewhispanic.org/2015/03/26/share-of-unauthorized-immigrant-workers-in-production-construction-jobs-falls-since-2007/

Preston, J. (2015). Large Companies Game H-1B Visa Program, Costing the U.S. Jobs. *New York Times.* November 10. www.nytimes.com/2015/11/11/us/large-companies-game-h-1b-visa-program-leaving-smaller-ones-in-the-cold.html

Rural Migration News (2016). DHS: Border, Visas. Vol 22. No 1. January. http://migration.ucdavis.edu/rmn/more.php?id=1944

Rural Migration News (2013). Immigration Reform: Agriculture. Vol 19. No 3. July. http://migration.ucdavis.edu/rmn/more.php?id=1769

UN DESA (2015). *Trends in International Migration*. Available: ww.un.org/en/development/desa/ population/migration/index.shtml [retrieved 12/3/16]

Waters, M. and M. Gerstein. Eds. (2015). *The Integration of Immigrants into American Society*. National Academies Press. www.nap.edu/catalog/21746/the-integration-of-immigrants-into-american-society

CHAPTER 4

Fleeing from the Global Compact for Migration: A Missed Opportunity for Italy

Chiara Scissa

Introduction

This article[1] explores a recent attempt to bridge the gap between migration governance[2] and migration policy[3] by means of a hoped-for 'universal' system of international cooperation – the Global Compact for Safe, Orderly, and Regular Migration (hereinafter GCM or Global Compact). In particular, this contribution examines the reasons that in December 2018 led both the Italian Parliament and Government to refrain from the Global Compact, which Italy first had promoted as a way to revitalise the European Union's solidarity and coordination, while lessening the uneven burden of migratory inflows into the country.

Although it has been argued that '*the opposition to the Compact has propagandistic objectives, that cannot be negotiated away*' (Gatti, p. 1), this paper aims to demonstrate the wide benefits that the GCM will bring to Italy if adopted, in other terms, the gains that an instrument of international migration governance will bring to national migration policy. This is believed to be the first thorough analysis of the political debate around the Global Compact in the case of Italy from a political and legal perspective. The first section draws up a list of major concerns expressed by right-wing parties during Parliamentary debates, prompting them to vote against the Global Compact, ranging from the '*annihilation of national borders, sovereignty and cultures*[4] to the perceived obligation to guarantee free and unconditional entry. The second section challenges these allegations, echoed also by other majority groups, by directly recalling not only principles of customary law and human rights law that Italy must comply with, but also the relevant law enforcement promoted by the European Court of Human Rights (ECtHR) and national tribunals, thus demonstrating the legal groundlessness of most of the arguments used to discredit the Global Compact. By deeply analysing institutional statistics and data as well as by relying on the existing literature on the matter, the second section also produces

---

[1] My deepest gratitude to Professor Marco Borraccetti for his constant support and wise advice, and to PhD Susanna Villani for her bibliographical suggestions

[2] Betts defines global migration governance as 'a range of norms, rules, principles, decision-making procedures that exists over and above the level of a single nation-state' (Betts, 2010). See also IOM 2019 Glossary on Migration, available at https://publications.iom.int/system/files/pdf/iml_34_glossary.pdf

[3] Bjerre et al. define migration policy as 'a government's statements of what it intends to do or not do (including laws, regulations, decisions or orders) in regards to the selection, admission, settlement and deportation of foreign citizens residing in the country' (Bjerre, Helbling, Römer, & Zobel, 2014)

[4] Quotation taken from the speech of Giorgia Meloni (Italian Deputy and leader of the right-wing party Fratelli d'Italia). See Italian Chamber of Deputies, 102nd Session – Debate on the adoption of the Global Compact for Migration, 18 December 2018, 9.30 AM

evidence of adequate migration governance solutions enshrined in the GCM. The specific socio-economic, fiscal, and demographic opportunities that the Global Compact offers to Italy and its whole community will be at the core of the third and last section.

This paper also finds that the Global Compact would add value to the EU migration governance with significantly positive national impacts. Among others, the collective effort to achieve Objective 4[5] would indeed allow the first two hierarchical criteria[6] of the Dublin III Regulation to take place, with a double immediate effect: 1) when these criteria apply to the case, designated EU countries other than the first entered should thus take on their responsibilities for the evaluation of the international protection request; 2) a subsequent, initial redistribution of migrants first arriving in Italy would finally start. Similarly, if Objective 5[7] is seriously implemented, EU institutions and Member States should then adopt and promote the use of humanitarian visas to regularly and safely travel to Europe for international protection purposes. Here again, the Italian burden would be relieved and thousands of lives would be spared.

On the Global Compact: merits and weaknesses of a soft law instrument

The Global Compact for Safe, Orderly and Regular Migration is the first-ever UN global arrangement that recognises that solid international cooperation is needed to maximise the overall benefits of migration (Rita, 2019), while minimising its risks for individuals and communities in vulnerability. This two-year negotiated agreement relies upon principles of State sovereignty, responsibility-sharing, the rule of law, and human rights and sets out 23 Objectives to make migration work for all.

Scholars' opinions on the merits of the Global Compact widely differ. Frequently, the reason for supporting its adoption or its rejection[8] lies in its non-binding nature. Accordingly, giving human rights-related arrangements some legal force may be, understandably, preferable to giving them no legal status (Roberts, 2001, p. 790).

Nevertheless, soft law instruments are progressively characterising contemporary international lawmaking, in preference to the conclusion of new treaties[9]. A. Boyle and C. Chinkin define soft law instruments as '*a variety of non-legally binding instruments [...], which encompasses inter-state conference declarations, interpretive guidance adopted by human rights treaty bodies, non-treaty inter-state agreements, and common international standards adopted by transnational networks of regulatory bodies*' (Boyle &

---

[5] Objective 4: Ensure that all migrants have proof of legal identity and adequate documentation, Global Compact for Safe, Orderly, and Regular Migration final draft

[6] Chapter III, Criteria for determining the Member State responsible, Articles 9-10 (Family members) and Article 12 (Issue of residence documents or visas). See Regulation (EU) No 604/2013 of the European Parliament and of the Council of 26 June 2013 establishing the criteria and mechanisms for determining the Member State responsible for examining an application for international protection lodged in one of the Member States by a third-country national or a stateless person (recast)

[7] Objective 5: Enhance availability and flexibility of pathways for regular migration, Global Compact for Safe, Orderly, and Regular Migration final draft

[8] (Nyers, 2019); (Chimni, 2018); (Carling, 2019); (Newland, 2018)

[9] (Helfer & Wuerth, 2016, p. 563). See also, (Helfer & Wuerth, Working paper: Custom in the Age of Soft Law)

Chinkin, 2007). I. Wuerth's analysis on customs and soft law showed that, despite the fact that the former is binding and the latter is not, they have several features in common. According to the author, akin to soft law, customs do not need to be entirely in line with States' consent or to be nationally ratified, they may have lower contracting costs, and they are flexible in content (Helfer & Wuerth, p. 2). In light of these similarities, Wuerth's study concluded that '*custom can be understood as existing on a continuum between treaties and soft law*' (Helfer & Wuerth, p. 4)

Moreover, soft law instruments might promote the development of customary laws, despite their lack of binding force, therefore generating new obligations for States. As recalled by M. Villegas Ergueta, Article 38 of the Statute of the International Court of Justice (ICJ) indicates two grounding elements for the establishment of customary laws: 1) a general, constant, and uniform practice; and 2) a recognition that such practice amounts to law, commonly known as *opinio iuris* (Villegas Ergueta, 2015, p. 189). Remarkably, L. Hannikainen noted that soft law instruments too can reflect general consensus (Hannikainen, 2006) and, according to the author, the affirmative voting of resolutions of international organs, typical examples of soft law, constitute not only relevant State practice but also *opinio iuris* of States as well as of the international organisations involved. Villegas Ergueta's study on soft law indicates that the ICJ interpreted several resolutions of the UN General Assembly as having a normative value that, according to her, may confirm the emerging existence or the establishment of *opinio iuris* (Villegas Ergueta, 2015, p. 195). The author stressed the particular case of human rights law, assessing that '*These fields share as a particular feature: strong opinio iuris, enshrinement in international conventions, and they are characterised by inconsistent state practice. In that sense, for instance, customary law that prohibits genocide remains intact, notwithstanding the multitude of examples of non-compliance, because opinio iuris regarding the duty of compliance continues to exist*'. Therefore, she concluded that '*Although, one may say that if a State consistently votes for such resolutions, it cannot rely on the assumption that this affirmative expression has no legal consequences*' (Villegas Ergueta, 2015, p. 196).

In evaluating the innovative content of the GCM, D. Vitiello considered both Global Compacts as '*reinforced*'[10] soft law instruments, given their formal adoption respectively by means of an intergovernmental conference and the General Assembly. Her study proceeded with an analysis of the 2016 New York Declaration that, pursuant to its preambular paragraph no. 2[11], could be seen as the international community's common response to large movements of refugees and migrants and, in her view, could thus amount to a tangible manifestation of *opinion iuris* of States in promoting a global governance of migration and refugee flows (Vitiello, p. 3).

The very fact that States came together to discuss such a broad range of migration issues demonstrates that States have recognised that they need to cooperate to adequately address both drivers and the effects of a global, long-lasting phenomenon. Given that these issues are likely to remain high on the agenda as

---

[10] (Vitiello, 2018, p. 3). Personal translation.
[11] New York Declaration on Refugees and Migrants, 19th September 2016, PP. 2: 'We have considered today how the international community should best respond to the growing global phenomenon of large movements of refugees and migrants'.

well as in public opinion's debates, not least with the impacts of climate change exacerbating people's vulnerability, States may agree to adopt soft law instruments on such complicated issues, which are frequently not consistent with national interests. Dealing with migration through non-binding arrangements still leads to monitoring and follow-up process through periodic reviews and maintains a strong focus on these themes (Solomon & Sheldon, 2018, p. 588).

Criticisms have been advanced not only on the nature of the Global Compact, but also on its content. Contrary to J. Carling's views, the Global Compact for Migration does not refer to 'any kind' of migration (Carling, 2019, p. 2). First of all, it does trace a difference between refugees and migrants to that extent that two separate documents have been drafted, discussed, and adopted. It, however, recognises that frequently the well-founded fear or harm suffered by refugees and migrants are similar, especially during their journey, where no legal status has been yet provided. It is therefore evident that some parts of the Global Compact for Migration and of the Global Compact for Refugees (GCR) address the same issue of vulnerability or crimes committed along the route, such as trafficking in human beings. Second of all, a relevant objective of the GCM is that of addressing the factors that compel people to leave, therefore clarifying the forced nature of the movement.

Nonetheless, as an agreement stemmed from intergovernmental negotiations, the GCM also embeds some weaknesses and gaps. Emblematically, it has been rightly noted that it does not succeed in gathering together the fragmented set of human rights provisions which apply to international migrants (Vitiello, 2018, p. 4), which leads to their different treatment, given the possibility for States to differentiate protection guarantees according to the position of the alien in their territory. However, common implementation of the Global Compact will lead to upholding the human rights of migrants and their assistance, as well as to enriching forms of protection to adequately address their vulnerability and needs.

Furthermore, although the GCM fails in addressing specific aspects concerning the successful integration of migrants - as rightly pointed out by Carling in the case of promoting leadership among female migrants (Carling, 2019, p. 2) - it is nonetheless an instrument of utmost importance that represents a breakthrough in States' approach to migration management, as demonstrated by the Italian position.

Indeed, Italy has been one of the initial promoters of this global attempt since the 2016 UN New York Declaration on Refugees and Migrants[12], given the overwhelming migratory pressure on its frontiers, especially at sea, and weak compliance by EU member states with the Dublin III Regulation. In June 2017, during the intergovernmental negotiations on migration governance, the former Prime Minister Paolo Gentiloni delivered a speech where he affirmed that Italy *'[...] promotes a common responsibility approach in managing the flows to ensure a safe and orderly migration, in protecting people on the move, in enforcing border control, and in tackling*

---

[12] New York Declaration on Refugees and Migrants, United Nations General Assembly A/71/L.1, 13 September 2016, Seventy-first session

issues relating to transnational organised crime, terrorism and illicit trade [13]. In October of the same year, the Institute for Research on Innovation and Services for Development – National Research Council of Italy was one of the academic institutions admitted to attend the preparatory process of the Global Compact, showing that regular pathways to Italy would significantly increase the successful integration of migrants (Institute for Research on Innovation and Services for Development – National Research Council of Italy, 12-12 October 2017).

In September 2018, after the change in government, the new Italian Prime Minister Giuseppe Conte confirmed his predecessor's belief, affirming that '*The migratory phenomenon we are facing requires a structured, multilevel, and short-medium-, and long-term response from the international community as a whole. It is on this basis that we support the Global Compact for Migration and refugees*' [14].

The Semblance

Alas, at the Intergovernmental Conference in Marrakesh on 10-11 December 2018, Italy abandoned the GCM. UN High Commissioner for Refugees Filippo Grandi considered this withdrawal as '*contradictory for a country directly exposed to unplanned migration flows and which has in the past lobbied for more cooperative approaches at both the European and international levels*' [15]. The primary aim of this paper is to gather the reasons which led Italy to flee from the Global Compact, and assess whether they were substantiated or led by political propaganda.

The semblance is that there were some ground reasons that made the GCM unacceptable to leading Italian forces. To begin with, the Governments that initially supported the Global Compact were of a different political colour than the one in charge at the moment of its adoption. In December 2018, the two parties in power were the League, represented by the former Deputy Prime Minister and Interior Minister Matteo Salvini, and the 5 Star Movement, whose spokesman and ex-Deputy Prime Minister was Luigi Di Maio. Together formed a centre-right populist executive, whose priorities were to eradicate poverty, stop irregular migration, and reverse the relationship with the EU. Though, the conception of the means of implementation required to reach those aims, the values behind those scopes, and the alliance at the national and EU level to foster their views completely diverged. This permanent and rooted opposition between the two main forces stuck the country several times and, in the case of the Global Compact, firstly resulted in uncertainty and then in Italy's withdrawal, as decided by the Italian Parliament and communicated by the Prime Minister Giuseppe Conte.

Additionally, the Italian Parliament alleges numerous substantial risks in terms of State's sovereignty. The aim of this first section is precisely to report the semblance, i.e. the misleading perception, fuelled by the leading forces of the

---

[13] International cooperation and governance of migration in all its dimensions, including at borders, on transit, entry, return, readmission, integration and reintegration, Panel 2, Speech of Italy, Palais des Nations, Room XIX, Geneva, 19-20 June 2017 https://refugeesmigrants.un.org/sites/ default/files/otaly_ts3_p2.pdf
[14] (Gatti, 2018). The video is available in Italian at https://www.youtube.com/watch?v= PtfwI1LmPgc&feature=youtu.be&t=262
[15] La Voce di New York, 17 December 2018, https://www.lavocedinewyork.com/?p=121200 in (Pastore, 2019)

Government and some associations[16], that made the GCM appear as an overall peril for Italy's public security and economic wealth.

The Global Compact for Migration: An attempt to annihilate Italian sovereignty?

F. Ferri correctly argued that the origins of both Compacts trace back to the 2016 New York Declaration on Refugees and Migrants, nonbinding itself, as well as to the 2015 UN Resolution on sustainable development[17], again, nonbinding (Ferri, 28 October 2019). The 2030 Agenda at the core of the UN Resolution recognised the opportunities of migration and migrants as agents of sustainable development and the need to reach a well-managed migration policy. Explicit and implicit cross-cutting linkages between the 17 Sustainable Development Goals (SDGs) and migration have been meticulously highlighted by UN Agencies. For instance, empowering migrants was an aim set not only in the Global Compact but already in the 2016 New York Declaration and previously in the 2030 Agenda. Similarly, the need to shift migration management from an emergency and temporary model to a more structured governance had been previously addressed. Therefore, it is not immediately clear why some EU Member States, including Italy, have withdrawn from a nonbinding document in line with the contents of formally adopted instruments.

Even more doubts arise if we compare the critics advanced by the political world with the substantial contents of this instrument, whose aim is to promote 'safe, orderly and regular migration', an expression already used in the 2030 Agenda and relaunched in the 2016 New York Declaration. The International Organization for Migration (IOM)[18] reflected on the existing principles surrounding this notion, and provided useful guidelines to gather the specific features of migration to be promoted through the Global Compact. In the absence of a commonly agreed definition, the UN Migration Agency defines 'orderly migration'[19] as the regular, legal movement of a person from their usual place of residence to a new one as well as the right of a State to regulate the entry. While the concept of 'orderly migration' focuses on the lawfulness of the movement, it is the (un) authorised channel used to migrate that determines its (ir)regularity.

Whereas these two features share a normative character, the concept of 'safe migration' has more to do with the well-being of migrants and, according to IOM, is not static in nature. In fact, *'the situation of migrants can change from safety, to unsafety throughout the various phases of their migratory process*[20]. On this behalf, M. Collyer found that *'to some extent the development of fragmented migration may be seen as a response to increasingly effective immigration controls in the most attractive destinations [...]'* (Collyer, 2010, p. 4) that, together with misinformation about the extreme dangers on the

---

[16] (Centro Studi Macchiavelli, 2018). See below for an in-depth analysis of the declarations made by Italian right-wing parties when discussing the adoption of, or withdrawal from, the Global Compact during Parliamentary sessions

[17] United Nations General Assembly Resolution A/RES/70/1, 25 September 2015, Seventieth session

[18] IOM, Facilitation of Safe, Regular and Orderly Migration, Global Compact Thematic Paper, available at https://www.iom.int/sites/default/files/our_work/ODG/GCM/IOM-Thematic-Paper-Facilitation-of-Safe-Orderly-and-Regular-Migration.pdf

[19] Idem. Please, see also IOM, Glossary on Migration, 2nd ed., IML No 25, 2011.

[20] Idem, p. 1

journey to Europe, do not allow for a safe access to the EU asylum system.

All being said, both the target and the aim of the Global Compact seem far from encouraging any kind of irregular cross-border movement, something that can be grasped even by a simple cursory reading of the text. Jean-Claude Juncker argued that a preliminary reading of the Compact would have led to another end[21].

Additionally, F. Pastore shaped a specific reason of withdrawal, namely a little tangible '*convergence of interests between high and low-income countries in the field of migration*' (Pastore, 2019, p. 4) at the basis of some States' hampering attitude. In his view, the grounding aspect that convinced States to undertake the GCR was its keener willingness to establish stronger cooperation between the North and the South to sustain low-income countries in preventing secondary movements, something that is less visible in the GCM. In the case of Italy, the most sceptic voices, which arose in the Chamber of Deputies as well as in the Senate, belonged to the exponents of the League and Fratelli d'Italia (FdI).

For instance, during the discussions upon the Global Compact within the Chamber of Deputies, FdI proposed a motion[22], whose contents were, in order, the following:

'It [the Global Compact, A/N] originates from the will to promote continuous flows, using both demographic and economic reasons.

[...] the Global Compact creates increasing obligations to States as regards to providing services to migrants, also regardless of their refugee status, and impeding to prosecute who provides illegal assistance to migration. It seems evident, therefore, that the Global Compact is nothing but the umpteenth dowel of a project aimed at annihilating borders, cultures, and, in particular, national sovereignty in the field of migration.

It is unacceptable that migrations are managed by supranational organisms with no democratic control by citizens of single States.

The purely demagogic configuration of the Global Compact, which de facto establishes a sort of <right to migrate> cannot be supported'.

Some of these assumptions were also sustained by the League and Forza Italia[23], confirming their concerns towards this global instrument. Conversely, left-wing parties highlighted solidarity and coordinated responses to migration as the key merits of this instrument that would have supported the country in building stronger and human rights-based partnerships with EU and extra-EU Member States[24].

---

[21] Jean-Claude Juncker argued that '*those countries that decided they are leaving the UN migration compact, had they read it, they would not have done it*', in Gotev G., Six EU countries – and counting – back out from the global migration pact, EURACTIV, 12 November 2018, https://www.euractiv.com/section/justice -home-affairs/news/six-eu-countries-and-counting-back-out-from-the-global-migration-pact/

[22] Italian Chamber of Deputies, 102nd meeting, Motion No. 1-00080 concerning the signature of the Global Compact for Migration by exponents of Fratelli d'Italia, 18 December 2018, personal translation from Italian

[23] For instance, Forza Italia endorsed assumption no. 1 and 4. See, Italian Chamber of Deputies, Motion No. 1-00099 Motion concerning the signature of the Global Compact for Migration by Forza Italia

[24] Italian Chamber of Deputies, 102nd meeting, Motion No. 1-00089 'Scalfarotto e altri' concerning the signature of

Another Perspective: Turning allegations into opportunities

These allegations, on the one hand, and the lack of a consensual position on this complicated theme among the 5 Star Movement, on the other, led firstly to postpone the decision and then to '*the most spectacular U-turn*' (Gatti, p. 3), where the Government decided not to participate in the Marrakesh Conference in late 2018. This second section challenges the aforementioned list of allegations, by directly recalling not only principles of customary law, human rights law, and international refugee law that Italy must comply with, but also the relevant law enforcement promoted by the ECtHR and national Tribunals, therefore showing the groundlessness of most of the arguments used to discredit the Global Compact. It also assesses whether these allegations are consistent with the provisions and aims of the GCM, by means of a meticulous point-by-point analysis. After having verified the legal and practical inconsistency of the major claims not to sign the GCM, the following paragraphs will also unveil both general and specific socio-economic, demographic and political benefits that Italy and the EU would gain through the implementation of adequate migration governance as set out in the Global Compact.

Law and jurisprudence

International human rights law and *jus-cogens* principles apply to all migrants, regardless of their status. These encompass the rights to life, liberty, and security; prohibition of torture and inhuman treatment; right to asylum; the principle of *non-refoulement*, among many others. These human rights are endorsed in treaties as well as in non-binding instruments, included but not limited to, the Universal Declaration of Human Rights (UDHR), the International Covenant on Civil and Political Rights, and the International Covenant on Economic, Social and Cultural Rights, the Geneva Convention relating to the Status of Refugees, the ECHR, the EU Charter and, finally, the Global Compact for Migration.

Calling on States to save lives at sea or condemning all forms of discrimination and racism are not admissions of a 'pro-immigrant manifesto', but a mere recognition of the rights that all migrants are entitled to, on the one hand, and of the obligations States must respect, on the other. Similarly, ensuring their access to basic services as stated in Objective 15 of the GCM responds to human rights provisions, something that States should already provide under binding treaties, notwithstanding the more favourable, non-discriminatory, measures that national authorities might grant to nationals and regular migrants.

The low observance of these basic human rights has frequently brought the Italian Republic in front of the judges in Strasburg. Italy has been, in fact, condemned for violation of Article 3[25] (prohibition of torture), Article 5 (right to

---

the Global Compact for Migration by exponents of centre-left wing party Partito Democratico, 18 December 2018; Italian Chamber of Deputies, 102nd meeting, Motion No. 1-00095 'Fornaro e altri' concerning the signature of the Global Compact for Migration by exponents of the left-wing party Sinistra Italiana, 18 December 2018

[25] European Court of Human Rights, Case of Khlaifia and others v. Italy, Grand Chamber, Application no. 16483/12, 15 December 2016, Strasbourg, https://hudoc.echr.coe.int/eng# {%22tabview %22:[%22document %22],% 22itemid %22:[%22001-170054%22]}, where Italy was held responsible also for breaches of Articles 5 and 13

liberty and security), Article 6 [26] (fair trial), Article 9[27] (freedom of expression), Article 13 (effective remedy), and Article 14[28] ECHR (non-discrimination), among others.

Likewise, it is worth mentioning that various national judgments[29] restored the right to all individuals to civil registration, put in jeopardy by Decree-Law 113/2018, well before the definitive judgment of the Constitutional Court. Italian Tribunals held that denying to asylum seekers the right to registration and the right to residence, the enjoyment of which is conditional upon registration at the registry office, violated the principle of equality enshrined by Article 3 of the Italian Constitution as well as the prohibition of discrimination under Article 14 ECHR. Endorsing the Global Compact would therefore remind and support Italy and the other Member States to observe their responsibilities, avoiding further breaches.

General benefits of the Global Compact for the EU

The EU is living a long and complex phase of revision of the Common European Asylum System (CEAS). As recently reiterated by the European Commission[30], a thorough set of norms is needed to fully comply with Article 78 TFEU, which gives competence to the EU to establish a common EU asylum policy for third-country nationals in need of international protection. The first reason why it has failed to provide adequate responses to protect and promote the human rights of people in vulnerability is the negligence of the Member States, which indeed have persistently refrained from correctly applying its provisions. The

---

[26] European Court of Human Rights, Case of Markovic and others v. Italy, Application no. 1398/03, Grand Chamber, 14 December 2006, Strasbourg, https://hudoc.echr.coe.int/eng#{%22tabview%22: [%22document%22] ,% 22itemid%22:[%22001-78623%22]}

[27] European Court of Human Rights, Case of Saadi v. Italy, Application no. 37201/06, Grand Chamber, 28 February 2008, Strasbourg https://hudoc.echr.coe.int/eng#{%22tabview% 22:[%22document%22] ,%22itemid %22:[%22001-85276%22]}

[28] European Court of Human Rights, Case of Dhahbi v. Italy, Application no. 17120/09, Grand Chamber, 8 July 2014, Strasbourg, https://hudoc.echr.coe.int/eng#{%22tabview%22 :[%22document %22],%22itemid%22 :[%22001-142504%22]}

[29] Civil Court of Florence, Order 361/2019, 18 March 2019, https://bit.ly/2TZ9DTG; Ordinary Tribunal of Bari, Order 16814/2019, 28 February 2019, https://www.asgi.it/wp-content/uploads/2020/03/ordinanza-Tribunale-di-Bari-16814-2019.pdf; Ordinary Tribunal of Bologna, Order 5022/2019, 2 May 2019, https://www.asgi.it/wp-content/uploads/2019/05/ Tribunale-di-Bologna-ordinanza-del-2-maggio-2019-est.-Betti-xxx-avv.-Zorzella-c.-Comune-di-Bologna-avv.-Montuoro.pdf; Ordinary Tribunal of Genova, Order 2365/2019, 22 May 2019, https://www.asgi.it/wp-content/uploads/2019/05/700-cpc-iscrizione-anagrafica-1.pdf; Ordinary Tribunal of Prato, Order 1183/2019, 28 May 2019, https://www.asgi.it/wp-content/uploads/2019/ 07/Tribunale-di-Prato-28-maggio-2019-est.-Bruno-xxx-c.-Comune-di-Prato.pdf; Ordinary Tribunal of Lecce, Order 5330/2019, 4 July 2019, https://www.asgi.it/wp-content/uploads/2019/07/Tribunale-di-Lecce-ordinanza-4-luglio-2019-est.-Barbetta-xxx-avv.-Leuzzi-c.-Comune-di-Lecce.pdf; Ordinary Tribunal of Cagliari, Order 4521/2019, 31 July 2019, https://www.asgi.it/wp-content/uploads/2019/ 08/Trib.-Cagliari-iscrizione-anagrafica.pdf; Ordinary Tribunal of Parma, Order 2379/2019, 2 August 2019, https://www.asgi.it/wp-content/uploads/2019/08/2019_8_2_Tribunale-Parma-ordinanza-2379-iscrizione-anagrafica-richiedenti-asilo.pdf; Ordinary Tribunal of Catania, Order 12686/2019, 1st November 2019, https://www.asgi.it/wp-content/uploads/2019/11/Tribunale-di-Catania-ordinanza-1-novembre-2019-est.-Cosentino-xxx-avv.-Campochiaro-c.-Comune-di-Catania-avv.-Santa-Anna.pdf; Ordinary Tribunal of Rome, Order 62244/2019, 19 November 2019, https://www.asgi.it/wp-content/uploads/2019/11/Tribunale-di-Roma-ordinanza-25-novembre-2019-est.-Di-Tullio-xxx-c.-Comune-di-Pomezia-e-Ministero-dellInterno.pdf; Ordinary Tribunal of Bergamo, Order 8772/2019, 14 January 2020, https://www.asgi.it/wp-content/uploads/2020/02/Tribunale-di-Bergamo-ordinanza-del-14-gennaio-2020-est.-De-Magistris-xxx-c.-Comune-di-Boltiere.pdf; Ordinary Tribunal of Palermo, Order 16945/2019, 23 January 2020, https://www.asgi.it/wp-content/uploads/2020/01/ 2020_1_23_Tribunale_Palermo_anagrafe_asilo.pdf

[30] COM(2020) 609 final, Communication from the Commission to the European Parliament, the Council, the European Economic and Social Committee and the Committee of the Regions On a New Pact on Migration and Asylum, Brussels, 23.9.2020

most emblematic example is the Dublin III Regulation, which clearly considers three hierarchical criteria to be applied in the order in which they are set out, to determine which State is responsible for the evaluation of an asylum request.

The first of the aforementioned criteria concerns the presence of family members who are already beneficiaries of international protection (Article 9) or who have applied for it and are waiting for a first-instance decision (Article 10) in a Member State. Where the applicant falls in the situation pursuant to Article 9 or 10, the Member State responsible for the evaluation of their family members is also responsible for theirs. If this is not the case, the second criterion as set out in Article 12 may apply. Accordingly, where the applicant is in possession of a valid residence document or visa, the Member State which issued the document is responsible for examining the application for international protection. This provision also provides hierarchical guidelines to be followed if the applicant owns more than one valid residence document or visa issued by different Member States, or if the required documents have expired. Lastly, only after having assessed that neither the provisions concerning family members nor those relating to valid travel documents pertain to the case, the third criterion concerning the first country of arrival or stay established in Article 13 applies. For its geographical position in the middle of the Mediterranean Sea, Italy and other Southern members have been more exposed than others to sea arrivals, yet the correct application of the hierarchical criteria established in the Dublin III Regulation could have lessened their migratory burden, sharing quotas with other competent EU States.

Objective 4 of the GCM aims at providing all migrants with a proof of legal identity *'upon entry, during the stay and for return as well as to ensure effective migration procedures, efficient service provision, and improved public safety'*. Fostering at all levels, civil registry systems and communication technology will help the compliance of the CEAS and bound all Member States to act accordingly.

Another relevant benefit, which the whole EU would gain from comprehensively applying the GCM, concerns the sponsorship of flexible pathways for humanitarian admission as well as for labour mobility and education opportunities, as indicated in Objective 5. Matching skills and facilitating labour mobility in accordance with national and EU market demands on the one hand, and building a common, sound system for humanitarian admission on the other will promote the required shift from a temporary, emergency, highly discretional reception system to a more structured and homogenised mechanism.

Whereas the Commission stated[31] in 2018 that *'the Union has built a comprehensive long-term strategy on migration covering all aspects of this phenomenon, from saving lives, offering protection to those in need, addressing the root causes of irregular migration'*, scholars tend to disagree with that. So far, as confirmed by M. Borraccetti, the EU system has focused more on return and removal measures rather than those facilitating common regular migration[32]. Similar investigations have concluded that EU

---

[31] European Commission, Proposal for a Council Decision authorising the Commission to approve, on behalf of the Union, the Global Compact for Safe, Orderly and Regular Migration in the field of development cooperation, COM(2018) 167, 21 March 2018. http://data.consilium.europa.eu/ doc/document/ST-7400-2018-INIT/EN/pdf

[32] (Carletti & Borraccetti, 2018, p. 44). See also Allinson, K., P. Erdunast, E. Guild, T. Basaran, GCM Commentary:

migration policies are 'European-centred' and based mainly on strategies of migration control. In Pascouau's view, '*There has been no consideration of the relevance of, or opportunity to, develop an alternative migratory flow management model on a European level*' (Pascouau, 2016, p. 3). Scholars also spotlight the lack of political will in dealing with the phenomenon of migration - whether regular or irregular, high-skilled or low-skilled - as demonstrated by recent tragic events[33]. This is particularly true in the realm of labour migration, where the EU still needs to coordinate and harmonise national standards on the admission of migrant workers (Pascouau, 2015, p. 3). However, the recently released European Commission's New Pact on Migration and Asylum seems to replicate the approach already endorsed by its predecessors[34]. If the intention is that of achieving the '*comprehensive long-term strategy on migration*' overstated by the Commission, the EU should take the GCM as a general guideline on which more efficient and exhaustive arrangements need to be based (Carrera, Lannoo, Stefan, & Vosyliūtė, 2018, p. 3).

Looking at the EU external dimension, several Objectives help revitalise the image of the EU as defender of human rights and democratic freedoms. For instance, sustaining middle- and low-income countries in addressing adverse drivers of forced migration through financial investments, entrepreneurship, education training, employment programmes and partnerships will give people the choice to stay in their own country while respecting human rights and fundamental freedoms. The GCM promotes this approach devoted to common solidarity and comprehensive partnership in opposition to the easier, yet human rights-breaching, praxis of externalisation of borders.

General benefits of the Global Compact for Italy

All the advantages outlined for the EU accordingly apply to Italy. Overall, the collective effort to achieve Objective 4 on legal identity would allow the first two hierarchical criteria of the Dublin III Regulation to take place, with a double immediate effect: 1) when these criteria apply to the case, designated EU countries other than the first entered should thus take on their responsibilities for the evaluation of the international protection request; 2) a subsequent, initial redistribution of migrants first arriving in Italy would finally start.

Similarly, if Objective 5 on pathways for regular migration is seriously implemented, EU institutions and Member States should then adopt and promote the use of humanitarian visas to regularly and safely travel to Europe for international protection purposes. Here again, the Italian burden would be relieved and thousands of lives would be spared. Besides, the GCM represents the first-ever concerted international network for migration management. This would give Italy

---

The Legal Status of the UN's Global Compact for Safe, Orderly and Regular Migration in International and UK Law, Refugee Law Initiative Blog, 31 January 2019; Carrera, S. and R. Cortinovis, EU's role in implementing Global Compact on Refugees: Contained mobility vs. International Protection, ReSOMA Discussion Brief/ CEPS Paper in Liberty and Security in Europe, April 2019, CEPS, https://www.ceps.eu/ceps-publications/eus-roleimplementing-un-global-compact-refugees/; Crépeau, F., Towards a Mobile and Diverse World: 'Facilitating Mobility' as a Central Objective of the Global Compact for Migration, 2018, International Journal of Refugee Law, 30(4), 650-656

[33] European Commission Press release: A European taskforce to resolve emergency situation on Lesvo, 23 September 2020, Brussels, available at https://ec.europa.eu/commission/presscorner/ detail/en/ip_20_1728

[34] COM(2020) 609 final

the unique opportunity to raise its voice to focus the international attention on national issues on migration, and calling for even greater solidarity and cooperation, making both the EU and its Member States responsible in front of the whole international community for their lack of commitment. Beyond these general positive outputs that pour out of the national level, the aim of this last section is to turn the former allegations used to discredit the Global Compact into actual benefits for Italy.

Specific benefits for Italy

The following section gives a specific overview of the main benefits that the Global Compact would bring to Italy, transforming the allegations advanced by FdI into factual opportunities to enhance the country's socio-economic growth and cultural development, while promoting a human rights-based migration governance.

Demographic and economic resources

Presumably, the demographic and economic reasons behind the promotion of continuous migration flows FdI referred to, concerned the inexorable decline in EU's fertility and mortality rate that is leading the EU to be the world's most rapidly ageing region after Japan[35].

Indeed, EUROSTAT future projections regarding the population expansion in the EU Member States confirm a demographic slowdown, such that within four decades the total number of inhabitants in the EU is projected to stagnate (EUROSTAT, 2015). The UN Development Programme confirmed this estimation, arguing that, in a zero-migration scenario, as late as 2025, only New Zealand and Ireland would still have growth in their working-age population (Apap, 2019, p. 2). The demographic decline we are living in has self-evident repercussions in the labour market. The share of the working-age population in the former EU-28's total population is, in fact, expected to decrease, with an overall reduction during the examined period of 44.5 million persons. Conversely, the share of the elderly is projected to increase from 97.7 million to 151.0 million by 2080 (EUROSTAT, 2015, p. 138). In other words, by 2080, there will be less than two persons of working-age for each elderly person.

The Italian demographic landscape does not draw a happier scenario. The case of the Basilicata region[36] in Southern Italy illustrates the slowdown in terms of population growth and the converse trend in population ageing that characterises the whole peninsula: it is estimated that by 2050, there will be 53 twenty-year-olds out of 100 over-seventy-year-old Lucanians. The Italian demographic gap cannot be fully explained solely by mentioning the decrease in the fertility rate and the increase in life span, but also taking into account the national emigration rate that, according to IOM[37], in the period 2007-2016 has increased and is currently higher

---

[35] (EUROSTAT, 2015, p. 22). It should be noted that these projections embrace all former 28 EU Member States, Great Britain included

[36] (Coniglio & Prota, 2003). See also, Coniglio N.D., 2019, Aiutateci a casa nostra. Perché l'Italia ha bisogno degli immigrati

[37] IOM, Migrants' contributions to Italy's welfare, IOM Italy Briefing, Issue No. 2, October 2017

than the number of citizens who return from abroad. According to the 2018 report on foreigners in the Italian labour market realised by the Italian Ministry of Labour, *'over the last few years, the foreign component in the labour market has become key in the Italian economy, not only because of the importance that foreign workers have had and continue to have in the performance of specific tasks, but also by virtue of the compensatory effect they have determined [...]'* (Ministero del Lavoro e delle Politiche Sociali, 2018, p. 3).

In this critical scenario, migration could contribute to filling both the demographic and labour gap that EU citizens alone cannot manage. For instance, migration can raise tax revenues and social contributions, which can then be spent on ageing populations (OECD, 2014). However, the Global Compact's acknowledgment of this state of affairs does not entail opening the gate to uncontrolled inflows of irregular migrants into the territory of EU Member States or Italy.

Concerning the role that migration is playing in the Italian labour market, it is relevant to note that the total working-age foreign population is about of 4milion people, half of which are employed. As portrayed by IOM, migrant and native workforce tends to both concentrate in complementary labour sectors, thus avoiding competition with nationals. Most foreign workers are employed in very specific sectors, such as the service sector (57% of the total), agriculture (16,6%), cleaning, and care. Frequently, hence, both male and female migrant workers are overrepresented in low-skilled occupations (37% versus 8% Italians)[38]. Conversely, less than 10% of migrants are employed in high-skilled occupations. An emblematic example of economic opportunities of migrant entrepreneurship is the emerging Chinese migrant enterprises in the Italian textile sector, which in Prato and Carpi have led to the revitalisation of the market[39].

On the other hand, IOM found that irregular migrants in Italy tend to concentrate in sectors in which labour law enforcement is weak and control is almost absent. It is not a coincidence that the highest percentage of irregular employees concerns agriculture, where 41% is estimated to be irregularly employed, followed by 27% in retail and trade[40].

The more migrants are active in the labour market, the better for national economic demand and supply. For instance, F. Furlanetto and O. Robstad found that a positive immigration shock lowers unemployment rates even among native workers, and has a measurable positive effect on public finances in the short-run (Furlanetto & Robstad, 2016). These results fit with the predominant thesis in literature, according to which there are significant long-term benefits in terms of a higher GDP per capita for countries of destination (Jaumotte, Koloskova, & Saxena, 2016).

---

[38] Idem, p.3
[39] (Barberis, Bigarelli, & Dei Ottati, 2011). For a deep analysis of immigrant entrepreneurship in the Italian city of Prato, see Dei Ottati G. (2013), "Imprese di immigrati e distretto industriale: un'interpretazione dello sviluppo delle imprese cinesi di Prato", Stato e Mercato, n. 98, agosto. Pp. 171-203. For a general overview of the role of migrants in shaping the Italian sector of small industries, see Chiesi A.M. (2011), "Il ruolo degli imprenditori immigrati nello sviluppo della piccola impresa in Italia", in CNEL, Il profilo nazionale degli immigrati imprenditori, Cnel, Roma, pp. 6-22.
[40] Idem, p. 5

This positive correlation has remained unchanged despite the wide quantitative and qualitative transformation of migration inflows over the decades. For instance, back in 2004, immigrants were estimated to spend around 30 euros/month on phone cards, and they also had a positive impact on the use of public transportation (Ricci, 2004). Italian wealth is shaped by migrants as well, producing 8.9% of the total GDP (around 130 billion euros) only in 2016 (Fondazione Moressa, 2017). In addition, migrants actively contribute to the production of Italian welfare, as demonstrated by numerous institutional sources. In 2016, foreign workers deposited €8 billion to the Italian social security system and received around 5 billion euros in social security benefits, according to the National Institute for Social Security[41]. Migrants' net contribution to the Italian social security system is therefore of 3 billion euros. Between 1960 and 2016, foreign workers have contributed €241.2 billion to the Italian social security system in social security benefits accrued, net of the pension benefits they will receive over their entire life cycle[42]. Moreover, up to now, there has been little evidence to the concern that immigrants depress wages of native workers (Peri, 2014), rather the prevailing opinion in the literature on average salaries is that, given the wage growth stagnation and worsening of working conditions in Western countries over last thirty years, the immigrant workforce in the Italian job market slightly increases the native wages.

Integrated border management

Another widely shared presumption among Italian parties and voters is that this non-legally binding document of global migration governance, agreed by national sovereign entities, would boycott national sovereignty in the field of migration, also leading to other catastrophic scenarios, such as the eradication of borders and native cultures.

Conversely, one of the guiding principles of the Global Compact explicitly concerns the acknowledgment of the sovereign right of States to determine their national migration policy and their prerogative to govern migration within their jurisdiction. Its statements also recognise that within their sovereign jurisdiction, States may distinguish between regular and irregular migration statuses.

Equally, Objective 11 directly deals with border management, thus emphasising their enhanced security rather than anticipating their dissolution. Furthermore, the allegation's attempt to demolish national sovereignty by impeding national authorities to prosecute illegal assistance to migrants does not find any reference in the GCM in general, and in Objective 8 in particular, which rather calls for a shared commitment to save lives and prevent migrant losses by means of individual or joint SAR operations, ensuring that the provision of *pure* humanitarian assistance, primarily provided by NGOs, is not considered unlawful.

As far as it concerns the assumption that the Global Compact would annihilate

---

[41] INPS, XVI Rapporto Annuale, Istituto Nazionale Previdenza Sociale, July 2017, available in Italian at https://www.inps.it/docallegatiNP/Mig/Dati_analisi_bilanci/Rapporti_annuali/ INPS_ XVI_Rapporto_ annuale_intero_030717%20.pdf
[42] Idem, p. 135

cultures, besides sovereignty and borders, FdI's motion clarifies this aspect in the following terms:

'Italy is one of the Southern borders of the European Union and, broadly speaking, of the Western world; hence, Italy can be considered as the <entrance door> to Western civilisation, to its lifestyle, rights and duties. Affirming the principle that everyone could freely have access to our nation, and therefore to Europe, would entail a truly genetic mutation of the functional dimension of the border [...], meant not only as a line of territorial demarcation [...], but also as a line of demarcation between two different civilisations, with respectively different characteristics, and the necessary differences'[43].

This passage seems to recall two well-known historical and political distinctions. The first one relies upon the dichotomy between the autonomous movements of people in search of safety or of a better life perceived as illegitimate in contrast with the only acceptable form of mobilities, namely those organised and authorised by States[44]. The second pertains to the difference between the wealthy, powerful, developed Europe (or the North) and the poor, powerless, developing Africa[45] (or the South). In the aforementioned declaration, borders are depicted as both symbolic and concrete demarcation between the *'familiar of here and the unfamiliar of there'* (Musarò, 2013, p. 42), or in other words, between *us* and *them*, performing the role of ordering society (Popescu, 2011). In light of this division, it has been affirmed that borders are socially constructed to serve the political purpose of creating and reinforcing national identity as well as national sovereignty and territory. In reflecting on the linkages between national sovereignty and national identity, C. Cantat straightforwardly affirmed that *'It is precisely the capacity to make these distinctions, to separate what qualifies as 'normal' and acceptable political identities, spaces and practices from what constitutes the exception, the abnormal, which provides the foundation of sovereignty'* (Cantat, 2016, p. 14). Similarly, P. Musarò interpreted borders as fabrications that political institutions make to legitimate distinctions between civilisations that they could not otherwise sustain (Musarò, p. 57).

The concept of national identity is dynamic, as it is affected by changes in space and time. The dimension of *us* in terms of Italian belonging could be still put into question, owing to a persistent economic, social, infrastructural, welfare gap between the Centre-North and South of the country, since 1861. Vast differences also endure in the public health and care systems, as the Covid-19 pandemic openly showed. Besides, for at least two decades, the League party, with also a young Matteo Salvini, based its political consensus on the call for separatism from the South. Covering State's inherent political and identity issues with external variables is at the core of De Genova's study of the 'border spectacle' (De Genova, 2015). Accordingly, spectacular mediatic scenes of enforcement at the border, where

---

[43] Italian Chamber of Deputies, 102nd meeting, Motion No. 1-00080 concerning the signature of the Global Compact for Migration by exponents of Fratelli d'Italia, 18 December 2018, personal translation. Senate exponents of Fratelli d'Italia presented the same text during the 65th meeting, 29 November 2018

[44] (Rajaram, 2015). See also (Cantat, 2016)

[45] Musarò P., 'Africans' vs. 'Europeans': Humanitarian narratives and the moral geography of the world, in (Musarò & Parmigiani, Beyond Humanitarian Narratives, 2013, p. 38)

irregular migrants are stopped and returned, serve the purpose of naturalising the exclusion of 'the others' justified by the need to protect national integrity.

In Crépeau's analysis on human mobility, he found that in spite of the propagandistic discourses of political leaders, States already know that the facilitation of regular migration is a much better solution than its prohibition (Crépeau, 2018, p. 651), and that the GCM facilitates the making of regular migration pathways in various ways. Most importantly for States, the GCM encourages the development of an effective border management that could support States in achieving national security in compliance with international law, while also protecting the rights of migrants and reducing their vulnerability. In 2015, IOM launched a multidimensional Migration Governance Framework[46] to help States in developing a well-managed migration policy, responding to Target 10.7 of the 2030 Agenda on Sustainable Development. To meet this goal, restated also in the GCM, migration management in terms of border control was deeply analysed and four main areas of interventions were found[47]:

Identity management. To enhance the flows of information of those crossing borders, Objective 4 of the Global Compact suggests enforcing the global efforts to register all citizens at birth, and to facilitate the issuance of reliable identity documents. To ensure the systematic identification of false or fraudulent travel documents, States may also rely on international organisations' expertise on travel document inspection. Moreover, Objective 11 envisages the use of communication technology, pre-screening and border crossing procedures, bearing in mind the full respect of the principle of non-discrimination as well as the right to privacy.

Border Management Information Systems. States parties of the Schengen Agreement can rely on the large flows of information and technical support provided by the Visa Information System on visa application, the Schengen Information System II on immigration purposes, and EURODAC on asylum. The significant contribution provided by this kind of regional border management cooperation at disposal of Member States, especially those at the external frontiers of the EU, is acknowledged by Objective 11 of the GCM.

Integrated Border Management (IBM). The European Commission[48] launched the concept of IBM to achieve the goal of having open, but controlled and secure borders, by enhancing the coordination and cooperation among all relevant border authorities at national and international levels. To meet this aim, IBM strengthens closer cooperation between Governments and their own immigration services and those of other countries to maximise the efficient and effective use of resources at borders.

Humanitarian Border Management (HBM). IOM's Migration Crisis

---

[46] IOM Council, Migration Governance Framework: The essential elements for facilitating orderly, safe, regular and responsible migration and mobility of people through planned and well-managed migration policies, C/106/40, 4 November 2015

[47] IOM, Border Management, Global Compact Thematic Paper, https://www.iom.int/sites/ default/ files/our_work/ODG/ GCM/IOM-Thematic-Paper-Border-Management.pdf

[48] European Commission, Guidelines for Integrated Border Management in European Commission External Cooperation, November 2010

Operational Framework emphases the role of HBM as a way to protect vulnerable groups in case of cross-border movement and to ensure the respect of their right to *non-refoulement*. Objective 11 embodies the need to provide timely assistance and protection of migrants in situation of vulnerability, while guaranteeing the respect of the best interest of the child in case of detected migrant minors. HBM includes, inter alia, assistance and preparedness to sudden mass inflows and emergencies, and creating inter-agency cooperation mechanisms for a coherent response during crisis.

Italy, and the EU Member States alike, could benefit from these international guidelines to both enhance national security and respect their international commitments.

Democratic control over migration

The Global Compact for Migration[49], akin to the GCR, espouses a whole-of-society approach, meaning the active and meaningful participation of refugees, migrants, host community members and organisations in the implementation of GCM's guidelines as well as in its follow-up and review at all policy levels, from the international to the local one. For this reason, a whole-of-society approach also envisages a whole-of-government approach, which includes both horizontal and vertical policy coordination (Domicelj & Gottardo, March 2019). These stem from the 2030 Agenda and the 2016 New York Declaration, where the need for a more integrated, cross-cutting, participatory approach to migration was first expressed to respond to the multidimensional, multilevel, and cross-sectorial reality of the phenomenon.

For the wide, broad, multilevel, and multi-stakeholder engagement in all phases of the GCM, it can be argued that the Global Compact rather enhances the democratic control over migration. Correlated benefits include an international prominence of national migration-related issues as well as multilevel, multi-stakeholder participatory engagement. In fact, the inclusion of civil society organisations in the implementation of the GCM is essential, not only for the process to be inclusive and holistic, but also for the crucial roles these actors play as agents of accountability, advocacy, service and data delivery.

For this reason, presuming that the United Nations, by means of a non-binding document, are attempting to limit the democratic debate on migration seems inconsistent. Conversely, Italy will benefit from committing to the GCM also in terms of democratic participation and control over migration.

The establishment of regular pathways

Article 13.2 UDHR establishes a right to *leave* a country[50] in the following terms: '*Everyone has the right to leave any country, including his own, and to return to his country*'. Article 12.2 of the 1966 International Covenant on Civil and Political Rights and Article 2.2 of the Protocol n°4 ECHR equally recognise this right. The right to leave a country, be it one's country of citizenship or current residence, is essential to the

---

[49] Preambular Paragraph No. 15, Global Compact for Migration
[50] For an in-depth overview of *ius migrandi* and *ius emigrandi*, see (Mazzarese, 2020)

fulfilment of other rights and principles, most notably the right to asylum that begins with the flight from their country of origin or residence and continues with the hosting State's duty to individually evaluate the correspondent international protection claim.

However, it does not entail a so-called 'right to migrate' (Carrera, Lannoo, Stefan, & Vosyliūtė, p. 6), meant by FdI and other right-wing parties as an unconditional, uncontrolled, unauthorised free entry of whoever accidentally crosses the Italian territory. Louise Arbour, UN Special Representative for International Migration, straightforwardly sustained that '*It is not correct to suggest that this Compact imposes obligations on Member States and infringes on their sovereignty. It does nothing of the sort, and it is not binding, as a treaty would be. It does not create a right to migrate. Under international human rights law citizens of a country have the right to enter, stay and leave their country but they don't have a right to go anywhere else unless they seek asylum, or are authorised by another country to enter its territory.*'[51]

Accordingly, the Global Compact seeks to prevent irregular migration[52], and rather aims at opening flexible pathways for regular migration to facilitate labour mobility in accordance with national labour market's needs, and to improve education opportunities through bi/multilateral labour agreements, cooperation arrangements, and academic exchanges just to name a few. These serve a double purpose: helping to fill the evident demographic, labour, and educational gap in most EU countries, Italy included, while meeting the needs of migrants, addressing their major vulnerabilities.

Facilitating mutual recognition of skills, qualification, and competences (Objective 18), promoting labour mobility cooperation and education opportunities (Objective 5) on the one hand, and establishing common rules and programmes for humanitarian admission, on the other, will promote regular migration in the first place, while enhancing national control over migration inflows in the second place. Migrants will be able to significantly contribute to Italian socio-cultural and economic development and welfare for the benefit of the entire community. Consequently, Italy will come a step closer to the achievement of sustainable development enclosed in the 2030 Agenda (Crépeau, p. 4). Similarly, ensuring humanitarian admission for people at risk and providing migrants with internationally required standards of basic services will foster Italian sustainable development, while sparing thousands of lives.

Conclusion

Gatti argues that 'European populists do not seem to have a problem with the Global Compact for Migration, they have a problem with migration as such [...]. The exit from the Global Compact is not a policy choice related to the content of this document. It is nothing more than populist propaganda, that can hardly be negotiated away' (Gatti, 2018, p. 1).

---

[51] Louise Arbour, Statement at Press Briefing Marrakesh, 11 December 2018, p. 2, http://www.un.org/en/conf/migration/assets/ pdf/Press-Briefing-11.12.2018-SRSG-Arbour.pdf.
[52] Objective 7, paragraph 23(h), Objective 9, paragraph 25(c, Objective 11, paragraph 27 of the Global Compact for Migration

Exactly for this reason, this paper demonstrated the multiple political and legal shortcomings of such propagandistic attitude in the case of Italy. The first section illustrated the economic, demographic, and political reasons that led Italy to abandon the Global Compact, which has been shared by the leading forces during Parliamentary discussions in late 2018. By depicting the GCM as a threat to the overall Italian sovereignty in the realm of migration, the country in fact refrained from an international instrument, which it initially supported to alleviate the migratory burden through a stronger partnership with third countries of origin and enhanced dialogue with the other EU Member States. The second section showed the merits and the weaknesses of this soft law instrument, underlining the GCM's potential contribution to customary law. Moreover, the second part assessed the inconsistency of the advanced allegations, which have been first contested with objective facts and data provided by reliable literature and institutional sources, as well as by national and supranational jurisprudence. These misleading claims were then turned into general benefits for a more comprehensive and human rights-based migration governance at the EU and domestic level. The last section shed light on the specific benefits that Italy would gain through the adoption of the Global Compact in terms of demographic and economic resources, enhanced border management, stronger democratic control over migration, and the creation of regular migration pathways, including for labour mobility and educational opportunities.

References

Allinson, K., Erdunast, P., Guild, E., & T., B. (2019, January 31). also Allinson, K., P. Erdunast, E. Guild, T. Basaran, GCM The Legal Status of the UN's Global Compact for Safe, Orderly and Regular Migration in International and UK Law. *Refugee Law Initiative Blog*.

Amnesty International. (12 December 2017). *Libya: European governments complicit in horrific abuse of refugees and migrants.*

Amnesty International. (2018). *Report: Libya 2017/2018.*

Amnesty International. (2020, January 30). *Libya: Renewal of migration deal confirms Italy's complicity in torture of migrants and refugees.* Retrieved from https://www.amnesty.org/en/latest/news/2020/01/libya-renewal-of-migration-deal-confirms-italys-complicity-in-torture-o

ANSA. ANSA, Migranti: Di Maio, ONG hanno trasportato criminali, 23 April 2017, https://www.ansa.it/sito/notizie/ politica/2017/04/23/migranti-di-maio-ong-hanno-trasportato-criminali-_48c4044a-7c54-42a0-ae81-99464536f076.html 2017, April 23). *ANSA Notizie*. Retrieved from https://www.ansa.it/sito/notizie/politica/ 2017/04/23/ migranti-di-maio-ong-hanno-trasportato-criminali-_48c4044a-7c54-42a0-ae81-99464536f076.html

Apap, J. (2019, January). *Apap J., A global compact on migration: Placing human rights at the heart of migration management, European Parliamentary ReEuropean Parliament Briefing.* Retrieved from https://www.europarl. europa. eu/RegData/etudes/BRIE/2017/614638/EPRS_BRI(

Arbour, L. (2018, December 11). Statement at Press Briefing Marrakesh.

Barberis, E., Bigarelli, D., & Dei Ottati, G. (2011). Distretti industriali e imprese di immigrati cinesi : rischi e opportunità con particolare riferimento a Carpi e Prato. In M. Bellandi, & A. Caloffi, *Innovazione e trasformazione industriale, la prospettiva dei sistemi di produzione locale italiani* (pp. 43-62). Bologna: Il Mulino.

Betts, A. (2010). *Global Migration Governance – the Emergence of a New Debate.* Oxford University Press.

Bjerre, L., Helbling, M., Römer, F., & Zobel, M. (2014). Conceptualising and Measuring Immigration Policies: A Comparative Perspective. *International Migration Review*.

Boyle, A., & Chinkin, C. (2007). The making of international law. *Oxford University Press.*

Cantat, C. (2016, 2). Rethinking Mobilities: Solidarity and Migrant Struggles Beyond Narratives of Crisis. *Intersections. East European Journal of Society and Politics*, pp. 11-32.

Carletti, C., & Borraccetti, M. (2018). Il Global Compact sulla migrazione tra scenari internazionali e realtà europea. *Freedom, Security & Justice: European Legal Studies*(2).

Carling, J. (2019). *Three reasons for rejecting a 'Global Compact for Most Migration'.*

Carrera, S., & Cortinovis, R. (2019, April). EU's role in implementing Global Compact on Refugees: Contained mobility vs. International Protection. *ReSOMA Discussion Brief/ CEPS Paper in Liberty and Security in Europe.*

Carrera, S., Lannoo, K., Stefan, M., & Vosyliūtė, L. (2018). Some EU governments leaving the UN Global Compact on Migration: A contradiction in terms? *CEPS Policy Insights*(2018-15).

Centro Studi Macchiavelli. (2018). *Dossier No. 9: I global compact su migrazioni e rifugiati.*

Chimni, B. S. (2018). Global Compact on Refugees: One Step Forward, Two Steps Back. *International Journal of Refugee*

Law, 630–634.

Collyer, M. (2010). Stranded Migrants and the Fragmented Journey. *Journal of Refugee Studies*.

Coniglio, N., & Prota, F. (2003). *Human Capital Accumulation and Migration in a Peripheral EU Region: the Case of Basilicata*.

Crépeau, F. (2018). Towards a Mobile and Diverse World: 'Facilitating Mobility' as a Central Objective of the Global Compact on Migration. *International Journal of Refugee Law, 30*(4), 650–656.

Crépeau, F. (2018). Towards a Mobile and Diverse World: 'Facilitating Mobility' as a Central Objective of the Global Compact on Migration, 2018. *International Journal of Refugee Law, 30*(4), 650-656.

Cusumano, E., & Villa, M. (22 November 2019). *Sea Rescue NGOs: a Pull Factor of Irregular Migration?* Migration Policy Centre, Robert Schuman Centre for Advanced Studies, European University Institute.

De Genova, N. (2015). The 'order spectacle of migrant "victimisation". *Open Democracy*.

De Genova, N. (2018). Migration and the Mobility of Labor. In M. Vidal, T. Smith, T. Rotta, & P. Prew, *The Oxford Handbook of Karl Marx*.

Del Guercio, A. (2018). Dal decreto Minniti-Orlando al decreto Salvini: decretazione d'urgenza, securitizzazione della politica d'asilo e compressione dei diritti fondamentali. Quando la legge genera vulnerabilità. In d. &. Visconti (Ed.), *Persone fragili: La vita psichica dei migranti forzati tra cura ed esclusione*.

Domicelj, T., & Gottardo, C. (March 2019). Implementing the Global Compacts: the importance of a whole-of-society approach. *Forced Migration Review online*.

European Commission. (1 February 2019). *European Commission, Opinion of the LegaThe legal effects of the adoption of Global Compact for Safe, Orderly and Regular Migration*. Brussels.

European Commission. (4 April 2016). *Press Release, Fact Sheet, Implementing the EU-Turkey Agreement - Questions and Answers*. Brussels.

European Parliamentary Research Service. (2019). A global compact on migration: Placing human rights at the heart of migration management. *European Parliament Briefing*.

EUROSTAT *Eurostat, Statistic Explained: Asylum Statistics*. Retrieved from http://ec.europa.eu/eurostat/statistics-explained/index.php?title=Asylum_statistics

EUROSTAT. (2015). *People in the EU: who are we and how do we live?*

Ferri, F. (28 October 2019). I patti globali su migrazioni e rifugiati tra vecchie e nuove dinamiche multilivello: alcune considerazioni di natura giuridica. *Questione Giustizia*.

Fondazione Moressa. (2017). *Rapporto annuale sull'economia dell'immigrazione – La dimensione internazionale delle migrazioni*.

Frelick, B. K. (2016). The Impact of Externalisation of Migration Controls on the Rights of Asylum Seekers and Other Migrants. *Journal on Migration and Human Security, 4*(4), 190-220.

Furlanetto, F., & Robstad, O. (2016). *Immigration and the Macroeconomy: Some New Empirical Evidence*.

Gatti, M. (2018, December 14). *EU Migration Law Blog*.

Global Detention Centre. (30 August 2018). *Immigration Detention in Libya: "A Human Rights Crisis"*.

Gotev, G. (2018, November 12). *Euractiv*. Retrieved from Gotev G., Six EU countries – and counting – back out from the global migration pact, Ehttps://www.euractiv.com/section/justice-home-affairs/news/six-eu-countries-and-counting-back-out-from-the-global-migration-pact/

Hannikainen, L. (2006). Customary Law: Are Rumours of Its Death Exaggerated? . *Baltic Yearbook of International Law*, 125-141.

Helfer, L., & Wuerth, I. (2016). Customary International Law: An Instrument Choice Perspective. *Michigan Journal of International Law*, 563-608.

Helfer, L., & Wuerth, I. (n.d.). *Working paper: Custom in the Age of Soft Law* .

Heller, C., & Pezzani, L. (2018). Blaming the Rescuers. Criminalising Solidarity, reinforcing Deterrence. *Forensic Architecture Agency - Goldsmith University*.

Human Rights Watch. (25 July 2018). *EU/Italy/Libya: Disputes Over Rescues Put Lives at Risk*.

Institute for Research on Innovation and Services for Development – National Research Council of Italy. (12-12 October 2017). *Regular and Undocumented Migrants, Fundamental Rights, Decent Work, and Integration in Italy: The Case of the Campania Region*. Geneva.

IOM. (2011). *Glossary on Migration* (2nd Edition ed.).

IOM. (4 November 2017). *IOM Learns of 'Slave Market' Conditions Endangering Migrants in North Africa*.

IOM. Facilitation of Safe, Regular and Orderly Migration, Global Compact Thematic Paper.

Italian Chamber of Deputies, 102nd Session. (18 December 2018). Debate on the adoption of the Global Compact for Migration. Rome.

Jaumotte, F., Koloskova, K., & Saxena, S. (2016). *Impact of Migration on Income Levels in Advanced Economies*.

Mazzarese, T. (2020). Diritto di migrare e diritti dei migranti. Una sfida al costituzionalismo (inter)nazionale ancora da superare. *Diritto, Immigrazione, Cittadinanza*.

Ministero del Lavoro e delle Politiche Sociali. (2018). *VIIIRapporto annuale. Gli stranieri nel mercato del lavoro*.

Musarò, P. (2013). 'Africans' vs. 'Europeans': Humanitarian narratives and the moral geography of the world. (M. &. Parmigiani, Ed.) *Sociologia della Comunicazione, Beyond Humanitarian Narratives*(45).

Musarò, P., & Parmigiani, E. (2013, 45). Beyond Humanitarian Narratives. *Sociologia della Comunicazione*.

New York Declaration for Refugees and Migrants (19 September 2016).

Newland, K. (2018). The Migration Compact: An Unlikely Achievement. *International Journal of Refugee Law, 30*(4), 657–660.

Nyers, P. (2019). Humanitarian hubris in the global compacts on refugees and migration. *Global Affairs*, 171-178.

OECD. (2014). *Migration Policy Debates*.

OHCHR. (2019, July 18). *OHCHR Press Release*. Retrieved from https://www.ohchr.org/en/NewsEvents/Pages/DisplayNews.aspx?NewsID=24833&LangID=E

OHCHR. (25 February 2016). *UN report documents litany of violations and abuses amid chaos in Libya.*

Pascouau, Y. (2015). EU Labour migration policy by other means? *Fieri working papers.*

Pascouau, Y. (2016). *A Jobseeker's visa: Towards a new mobility policy for third-country nationals.* Jacques Delors Institute.

Pastore, F. (2019). Not So Global, Not So Compact. Reflections on the Shitstorm Surrounding the Global Compact for Migration. *Istituto Affari Internazionali.*

Peri, G. (2014). Do immigrant workers depress the wages of native workers? *IZA World of Labor.*

Popescu, G. (2011). *Bordering and Ordering the Twenty-first Century: Understanding Borders.* Rowman & Littlefield Publishers.

Rajaram, P. (2015). Beyond crisis: Rethinking the population movements at Europe's border. *FocaalBlog.*

Refugees Deeply. (October 2017). *European Priorities, Libyan Realities.*

Ricci, A. (2004). *The impact of immigration on Italy's society: Technical Report.*

Rita, A. (2019). Guiding Principles of the Global Compact on Migration. *The Relevance of migration for the 2030 Agenda for Sustainable Development.*

Roberts, A. (2001). Traditional and Modern Approaches to Customary International Law: A reconciliation. *American Journal of International Law*, pp. 757-791.

Solidar. (2019, August 6). *Solidar.* Retrieved from https://www.solidar.org/en/news/italy-is-now-formally-criminalizing-solidarity

Solomon, M. K., & Sheldon, S. (2018). The Global Compact for Migration: From the Sustainable Development Goals to a Comprehensive Agreement on Safe, Orderly and Regular Migration. *International Journal of Refugee Law, 30*(4), 584–590.

Speech of Italy. (19-20 June 2017). *International cooperation and governance of migration in all its dimensions, including at borders, on transit, entry, return, readmission, integration and reintegration.* Geneva.

Stefanoni, F. (2018, August 14). *Corriere della Sera.* Retrieved from https://www.corriere.it/politica/18_agosto_14/di-maio-l-accusa-patto-ong-scafisti-magistrati-archiviano-605bfd50-9fa3-11e8-9437-bcf7bb

UN Press Release. (28 November 2017). *High Commissioner for Refugees Calls Slavery, Other Abuses in Libya 'Abomination' That Can No Longer Be Ignored.*

UNHCR. (17 October 2017). *Libya: Refugees and migrants held captive by smugglers in deplorable conditions.*

Villa, M., Corradi, E., & Villafranca, A. (2018). Fact Checking: migrazioni 2018. *ISPI.*

Villegas Ergueta, M. (2015, December). The multifaceted and dynamic interplay between hard law and soft law in the field of human rights. *Ciencia y Cultura*, pp. 185-202.

Vitiello, D. (2018, 3). Il contributo dell'Unione Europea alla governance internazionale dei flussi di massa di rifugiati e migranti: Spunti per una rilettura critica dei Global Compacts. *Diritto, Immigrazione e Cittadinanza.*

Vosyliūtė, L. (December 2019). What is the EU's role in implementation of the Global Compact for Migration? *CEPS Papers in Liberty and Security in Europe*(12).

PART 2: CONCEPTS AND THEORIES IN MIGRATION STUDIES

Essential Reading:

Massey, D. S. (2015). A missing element in migration theories. *Migration Letters*, 12(3), 279-299.

Sirkeci, I. (2009). Transnational mobility and conflict. *Migration Letters,* 6(1), 3-14.

Heim, D. (2016). "Old" natives and "new" immigrants: beyond territory and history in Kymlicka's account of group-rights. *Migration Letters*, 13(2), 214-227.

Further Reading:

Massey, D. S., Arango, J., Hugo, G., Kouaouci, A., Pellegrino, A., & Taylor, J. E. (1993). Theories of international migration: A review and appraisal. *Population and Development Review*, 431-466.

Sirkeci, İ., Eroglu Utku, Deniz & Yüceşahin, M. M. (2019). Göç çatışma modelinin katılım, kalkınma ve kitle açıkları üzerinden bir değerlendirmesi. *Journal of Economy Culture and Society*, 59(1), 157-184.

Amelina, A., & Vasilache, A. (2014). The shadows of enlargement: Theorising mobility and inequality in a changing Europe. *Migration Letters*, 11(2), 109-124.

Bilgili, Ö., & Siegel, M. (2014). Policy perspectives of Turkey towards return migration: From permissive indifference to selective difference. *Migration Letters*, 11(2), 218.

Eren, E. Y. (2019). Is Temporary Protection Eternal? The Future of Temporary Protection Status of Syrians in Turkey. *Border Crossing*, 9(2), 125-134.

Gezgin, E. (2016). On Anthony Giddens and the Theory of Structuration. *Border Crossing*, 6(1), 79-93.

Heim, D. (2016). "Old" natives and "new" immigrants: beyond territory and history in Kymlicka's account of group-rights. *Migration Letters*, 13(2), 214-227.

Kahn, Y., & Billfeld, N. (2015) Incentive to migrate and to return to home country: A comparison of Turkish, Moroccan and Egyptian cases in *Turkish Migration, Identity and Integration* edited by Ibrahim Sirkeci, Betül Dilara Şeker and Ali Çağlar.

Korpi, M., & Clark, W. A. (2017). Human capital theory and internal migration: do average outcomes distort our view of migrant motives?. *Migration Letters*, 14(2), 237.

Pinheiro, G. M. (2020). Climate Change Migration as an Adaptation Strategy:

The Adaptation Approach Theory And The Paris Agreement. In *Current Challenges in Migration Policy and Law* (pp. 65-73). Transnational Press London.

Rauhut, D. (2010). "VIEWPOINT: Adam Smith on migration," *Migration Letters*, vol. 7(1), 105-113

Sener, M. Y. (2020). Adaptation and identity shifts after migration and return migration: Turkish qualified returnees from Germany and the US. *Border Crossing*, 10(1), 3-28.

Verwiebe, R., Wiesböck, L., & Teitzer, R. (2014). New forms of intra-European migration, labour market dynamics and social inequality in Europe. *Migration Letters*, *11*(2), 125.

CHAPTER 5

A Missing Element in Migration Theories

Douglas S. Massey

In the 1990s, at the behest of Massimo Livi-Bacci, then President of the International Union for the Scientific Study of Population, I agreed to chair an interdisciplinary, international committee of migration scholars for the IUSSP. The committee's charge was to develop a unified theoretical framework for the study of international migration by identifying the key propositions derived from prevailing migration theories and then to assess them against empirical evidence from international migration systems around the world. The ultimate goal was to encourage researchers from different nations and disciplines to speak a common theoretical language, thereby enabling them to test hypotheses of mutual interest using comparable data and methods. The committee consisted of Joaquin Arango, a sociologist from Spain who was familiar with migration in Europe; Graeme Hugo, a geographer from Australia with knowledge of Asia and the Pacific; Ali Kouaouci, a social demographer from Algeria who covered Africa and the Middle East; Adela Pellegrino, a historical demographer from Uruguay with expertise in Latin America; and J. Edward Taylor an economist from the United States who, like me, did field research in Mexico and knew the North American migration system well, but also had published widely on issues of migration and development around the world.

As professional committees go, the IUSSP Committee on South-North Migration was rather productive. During 1991 and 1992 we met twice each year in Liege, Belgium (where the IUSSP was then headquartered). Each committee member presented the theoretical models he or she thought merited serious consideration and identified an empirical literature fir the committee to review. We then assigned tasks of reading, reviewing, and writing to committee members and began to publish our findings in 1993, when we offered an initial survey of the panorama of theories prevailing across disciplines circa 1990 (Massey et al., 1993). This article was followed a year later by an assessment of how the theories performed when applied to explain patterns and processes of international migration within North America, the region where empirical research was then most abundant (Massey et al., 1994).

While other committee members worked to assemble citations and sources and write chapters for the final book, Edward Taylor took the lead in putting together two additional articles reviewing theory and research on international migration and economic development, one focused on work at the community level (Taylor et al., 1996a) and the other focused at the national level (Taylor et al., 1996b), both of which later became book chapters. Writing on the book was completed in late 1997 and it was published in 1998 as *Worlds in Motion: Understanding International Migration at the End of the Millennium* (Massey et al., 1998).

In those days, no self-respecting IUSSP committee could fail to organize an international workshop of some sort, so the final act of the committee was to issue a call for papers and organize a small conference to present research findings relevant to the committee's integrated theoretical vision. The workshop convened in May of 1997 in Barcelona, Spain, and ultimately produced the edited volume *International Migration: Prospects and Policies in a Global Market* (Massey and Taylor, 2004). In this book, a diverse set of authors explored the contours of migration patterns and policies in the globalizing economy of the late 20th century.

In retrospect, I think the committee substantially met its goals and fulfilled its charge quite well. The original theoretical review article (Massey et al., 1993), as well as the more comprehensive book (Massey et al., 1998) have found their way into syllabi and curricula throughout the world. As a result, migration researchers today generally appear to be familiar with the leading theoretical frameworks coming from different disciplines and are increasingly addressing questions of common interest using similar methodologies. As the book was in production, however, I personally came to believe that the committee had overlooked a key actor in the process of international migration: namely, the state—the organ responsible for the formulation and implementation of immigration policy.

A key difference between the first round of globalization (between 1820 and 1920) and the second round (1970-present) was the degree of involvement of national governments in managing international population flows (Williamson, 2004). Prior to the First World War, a system of passports and visas did not exist and no country imposed quantitative limits on the entry of immigrants. Today, of course, passports are required for all international travel outside of migration unions such as the Schengen Zone, visas are required for most passports around the world, and all countries impose both quantitative and qualitative limitations on entry for permanent settlement. Thus nation states today necessarily play a role in determining the number and characteristics of immigrants flowing from country to country, apart from the social and economic factors covered in the theories reviewed by the IUSSP Committee.

Given this realization, I took it upon myself to undertake a review of theories and research on the role of states in formulating immigration policies and the likely effects of their attempts at implementation. The review, which I viewed as a compliment to the committee's book and papers, was published as an article in the *Population and Development Review* (Massey, 1999). It identified three broad sets of variables as key determinants of immigration policy formulation: macroeconomic conditions such as employment and wages, the relative size of the immigrant flow, and the ideological context of the time, with the actual effect of these policies being contingent on the capacity and efficacy of the state seeking to implement them (Massey, 1999).

Theorizing international migration

The end result of all of the foregoing work was a comprehensive framework that theorized five features of international migration (Massey, 2013): (1) the structural forces in sending nations that create a mobile population prone to migration; (2) the structural forces in receiving nations that generate a persistent demand for migrant workers; (3) the motivations of the people who respond to these structural forces by moving across borders; (4) the social structures and organizations that arise in the course of globalization to perpetuate flows of people over time and across space; (5) and the policies that governments implement in response to these forces and how they function in practice to shape the numbers and characteristics of the migrants who enter and exit a country.

The principal frameworks theorizing the creation of migrant-prone populations in sending countries are *world systems theory* in sociology (Portes & Walton, 1981; Sassen, 1988) and *institutional theory* in economics (North, 1990). Both perspectives posit that migrants originate in the structural transformation of societies brought about by the creation and expansion of markets in the course of economic development (Massey 1988). The transition from a command or subsistence economy to a market system typically entails a massive restructuring of social institutions and cultural practices, and in the course of these transformations people are displaced from traditional livelihoods in subsistence farming (as peasant agriculture gives way to commercialized farming) and state enterprises (as state-dominated sectors are privatized in former command economies).

The generation of a persistent demand for low-wage immigrant workers in post-industrial societies is theorized under the rubric of *segmented labour market theory*. Originally developed by Piore (1979) as dual labour market theory, this perspective traces the persistent demand for immigrant workers to the duality between labour (a variable factor of production) and capital (a fixed factor of production), which yields a capital-intensive sector to satisfy constant demand and a labour-intensive sector to accommodate variable demand associated with economic cycles that fluctuate over time. The resulting segmented labour market structure is reinforced by hierarchically-structured occupational structures, which create motivational problems at the bottom of the pyramid (where people are unwilling to work hard or remain long in low status jobs they can't escape) and structural inflation (where raising wages at the bottom generates upward pressures on wages throughout the job hierarchy). Under these circumstances, employers have a hard time recruiting and keeping native workers at profitable wages and seek foreign labourers instead, either prevailing upon governments to establish formal guest worker programs or engaging in private recruitment efforts. Portes and Bach (1985) later augmented Piore's dual labour market theory by pointing out that ethnic communities under certain circumstances can generate their own demand for immigrants and may, if the right conditions prevail, become vertically integrated in ways that generate a long-term demand for additional immigrant workers, thereby creating ethnic enclaves as a third potential labour market sector.

The motives of those who respond to the foregoing structural forces are theorized both by *neoclassical economics* and the *new economics of labour migration*. The former holds that people move to maximize lifetime earnings. Individuals assess the money they can expect to earn by working locally and compare it to what they anticipate earning at various destinations, both domestic and international. Then they project future income streams at different locations over their working lives (subject to a time-varying discount factor typically modelled as a negative exponential) and subtract out the expected costs of migration, yielding an estimate of expected net lifetime earnings at different destinations. In theory, people migrate to the location offers the highest lifetime returns for their labour so that in the aggregate labour flows from low- to high-wage areas until an equilibrium is reached (Todaro & Maruszko, 1986).

Rather than maximizing income, the new economics of labour migration argues that people use international labour migration to manage economic risk and overcome missing, failed, or inefficient markets for capital, credit, and insurance at places of origin (Stark 1991). In contrast to the permanent migration hypothesized by neoclassical economics, the new economic paradigm predicts circular movement and the repatriation of earnings in the form of remittances or savings. It also recognizes that people are embedded with households and therefore may engage in collective rather than individual decision-making. Rather than moving abroad permanently, people move abroad temporarily to diversify household incomes and accumulate cash they cannot save or borrow at home, and then return home with the means to solve specific household economic problems originally prompted them to move.

Although neoclassical theory is generally thought to predict permanent migration, Dustmann and Görlach (2015) have recently shown that the neoclassical model of Todaro and Maruszko (1987) is but a special case of a 267 more general model of migrant decision-making. In their theoretical formulation, wage differentials constitute the primary determinant of migration only under certain restrictive conditions, such as when preferences for consumption in both countries are identical; when national currencies do not differ in purchasing power; and when there is no skill accumulation abroad. They demonstrate that departures from these conditions lead to a variety of theoretically expected rationales for workers to prefer temporary over permanent international migration even under neoclassical assumptions.

Globalization inevitably entails the movement of people across international borders, either as bearers of labour or human capital, and the principal model articulated to describe the formation and elaboration of social structures during the course of migration itself is *social capital theory* (Massey et al., 1998). The first migrants to move abroad have no social ties to draw upon for assistance, and for them migration is costly, risky, and daunting, especially if it involves entering another country without documents. As out-migration progresses, however, a social infrastructure arises and often develops a powerful momentum to yield a self-perpetuating process known as cumulative causation (Massey, 1990; Massey & Zenteno, 1999).

Pioneer migrants are inevitably linked to non-migrants in their home communities through networks of reciprocal obligation based on shared understandings of kinship and friendship and non-migrants draw upon network ties to facilitate departure, migration, entry, employment, housing, and mobility at points of foreign destination, substantially reducing the costs and risks of international movement. Once the number of network connections in an origin area reaches a critical level, migration becomes self-perpetuating because migration itself creates the social structure necessary to sustain it, especially in rural areas where interpersonal networks are dense and social ties strong (Flores-Yeffal, 2012). The cumulative causation of migration through network expansion tends to be much weaker or inoperative in urban settings (Fussell & Massey, 2004).

According to the *theory of the state* outlined in my review, policies affecting immigration grow out of a political process in which competing interests interact within bureaucratic, legislative, judicial, and public arenas to influence the flow and characteristics of immigrants (Massey, 1999). In general, this competition of interests is posited to generate permissive immigration policies during periods of economic expansion and restrictive policies during periods of contraction. In most theoretical renderings, the critical actors are workers and employers, with politicians and government actors playing a mediating role in balancing the competing interests. During boom times unemployment rates fall and wages rise and employers lobby the government for more migrant workers, whereas during times of bust workers press demands through their legislators to restrict immigration; and public officials are basically hypothesized to alternate back and forth to satisfy the most vocal and demanding constituency at any point in time.

In addition to economic conditions, immigration policy is sensitive to the relative number of immigrants involved, with the politics of immigration becoming more conflictive and tending toward restriction as the volume of immigration rises (Massey, 1999). Immigration policies are also associated with broader ideological currents in society, tending toward restriction during periods of social conformity and conservatism and tilting toward expansion during periods of openness and liberalism. Policies are also shaped necessarily by geopolitical considerations, especially those dealing with refugees and asylum seekers.

Finally, whatever the direction specific national policies ultimately take— restrictive or permissive—an additional consideration is the ability of the state to enforce them. In my paper, I argued that state capacity varies along a continuum from low to high depending on the efficiency of the nation's bureaucracy, the strength of constitutionally embedded rights, the degree of judicial independence in enforcing those rates, and the relative demand for entry the country and the strength of its tradition of immigration. Thus the ability to enforce policy is strong in Gulf countries such as Saudi Arabia and Kuwait, which do not have a tradition of immigration and are dominated by absolute monarchies that offer no constitutional rights that are administered by rigid, citizen-run bureaucracies that answer to no independent judicial authority. In contrast the ability to enforce policy is more limited in liberal democracies which have constitutional rights, independent judiciaries, competitive elections, and diffuse and inefficient bureaucracies, especially in nations such as the United States which have a strong historical tradition of immigration and immigrant rights, as we shall see.

The missing element and Mexico-US migration

Since 1982, I have worked with my colleague Jorge Durand of the University of Guadalajara to build the Mexican Migration Project (MMP), which annually gathers data on international migration from representative samples of communities located throughout Mexico, along with network samples of branch communities in the United States (see Durand & Massey, 2004). Although small migration streams to Canada have recently emerged (Massey & Brown, 2011), the overwhelming majority Mexican migrants go to the United States as part of a tradition that dates back to the turn of the 20th Century (Cardoso, 1980; Massey et al., 1987; Durand & Massey, 1995).

Over the years, we have analysed these data drawing heavily on the composite framework described above to study the dynamics of Mexico-U.S. migration, seeking to connect variation in migration probabilities to variations over time in wage rates, labour demand, interest rates, and structural economic changes, changing stocks of human and social capital on both sides of the border, and policy-relevant variables such as U.S. enforcement efforts and access to legal visas (Massey and Espinosa, 1997; Massey, Durand, & Pren, 2014). The accumulated research literature based on MMP data suggests that all of the theoretical perspectives contribute something to the understanding of Mexico-U.S. migration, though the relative importance of different theoretical perspectives appears to vary across time (Garip, 2012) and from place to place (Durand & Massey, 2003).

From 1942 to 1965 Mexican migration generally behaved as expected under prevailing theories of international migration, being initiated by a government sponsored labour recruitment program (segmented labour market theory), growing as lawmakers increased access to temporary workers at the behest of employers (state theory), expanding also because of the elaboration of migrant networks (social capital theory), and fluctuating with respect to changing conditions of labour supply and demand on both sides of the border (neoclassical economics) as well geographic and temporal variation in access to markets for capital, credit and insurance (the new economics of labour migration) and the structural transformation of the Mexican economy under neoliberalism (world systems theory). During this time, migration was overwhelmingly circular, with male migrants moving back and forth to solve economic problems at home (in keeping with predictions derived from the new economics of labour migration and the recent reformulation of neoclassical economics).

In 1965, however, U.S. immigration law was reformed and the guest worker program was eliminated, in both cases for ideological reasons (consistent with state theory). In the context of a burgeoning civil rights movement the guest worker program came to be seen as racially discriminatory and exploitive while immigration quotas imposed in the 1920s were perceived as intolerably racist. The net effect of both actions was to reduce opportunities for legal entry from Mexico quite dramatically. As a result, after 1965 migration occurred under undocumented auspices given the existence of well-developed networks connecting migrants to employers (social capital theory), the continuation of strong demand in North American labour markets (segmented labour market theory), the persistence of a large binational wage gap (neoclassical economics), and the growing integration of the Mexican and U.S. economies (world systems theory).

From 1965 through 1985, migration nonetheless remained overwhelming circular, with male migrants moving back and forth to employers in traditional destination areas in tandem with fluctuating economic circumstances north and south of the border, repatriating earnings to family members at home, and participating well-developed migrant networks. Beginning in 1986 and accelerating through the 1990s, however, this stable pattern of migration shifted markedly. Circulation turned to settlement as rates of return migration plummeted, migrants began flowing to new rather than traditional destination areas, and as men stayed away longer women and children increasingly joined them north of the border. In short, between 1986 and 2006 Mexican migration shifted from a circular flow of male workers going to a few states into a rapidly growing settled population of families in 50 states.

However, this shift did not occur because of changes in labour demand, relative wages, cross-border integration, migrant networks, or because of a changed ideology or a new political balance between employers and works. Rather the driving force was the behaviour of self- interested bureaucrats, politicians, and pundits who sought to mobilize political and material resources for their own benefit irrespective of what effects their actions had on immigration itself. The end result was the creation of self-perpetuating cycle of rising enforcement and increased border apprehensions that resulted in the militarization of the border in a way that was largely disconnected from the processes hypothesized by prevailing theories of international migration.

The actions taken by actors in the federal bureaucracy did not emerge in response to the competing demands of workers, employers, and ordinary citizens, so much as the desire to accumulate power and resources. Although the self-interested actions of politicians and bureaucrats have been described and documented historically (see Calavita, 1992), heretofore they have not been properly theorized. The key to understanding opportunistic actions taken by actors in and outside of government lies in the transformed context of decision-making before and after 1965. Although little had changed in practical terms before and after this date (roughly the same number of migrants were migrating from the same regions of Mexico to the same places in the United States), the situation had changed dramatically in symbolic terms for after 1965 the vast majority of Mexican migrants were "illegal" and thus by definition "criminals" and "lawbreakers."

The rise of illegal migration created an opening for political entrepreneurs to cultivate a new politics of fear, framing Latino immigration as a grave threat to the nation (Santa Anna, 2002; Abrajano & Hajnal, 2015), creating a new meme in American public discourse that Chavez (2008) has called the "Latino Threat Narrative" in the U.S. media. His coding of cover stories in leading weekly news magazines showed that negative depictions of immigrants and immigration increased over time (Chavez, 2001); and Massey and Pren (2012a) likewise found that newspaper mentions of Mexican immigration as a crisis, flood, or invasion rose in tandem with border apprehensions from 1965 to 1979, pushing public opinion in a more conservative and anti-immigrant direction and creating pressure for ever more restrictive immigration and border policies (Massey & Pren, 2012b; Valentino et al., 2012).

By framing them as aliens, lawbreakers, and criminals, the Latino Threat Narrative distinguished undocumented migrants from mainstream Americans by a well-defined social boundary. Fear, of course, is a well-established tool for political mobilization and resource acquisition (Robin, 2006; Gardner, 2008) and across history it has proved difficult for humans to resist the temptation to cultivate fear and loathing of outsiders in order to achieve self-serving goals. In the United States, three prominent categories of social actors succumbed to the temptation for "othering" in response to rising illegal migration after 1965: bureaucrats, politicians, and pundits.

The bureaucratic charge was led in 1976 by the Commissioner of the U.S. Immigration and Naturalization Service, Leonard F. Chapman, who published an article in Reader's Digest entitled "Illegal Aliens: Time to Call a Halt!", warning Americans that a new "silent invasion" was threatening the nation:

> "When I became commissioner of the Immigration and Naturalization Service (INS) in 1973, we were out-manned, under-budgeted, and confronted by a growing, silent invasion of illegal aliens. Despite our best efforts, the problem---critical then---now threatens to become a national disaster. Last year, an independent study commissioned by the INS estimated that there are 8 million illegal aliens in the United States. At least 250,000 to 500,000 more arrive each year. Together they are milking the U.S. taxpayer of $13 billion annually by taking away jobs from legal residents and forcing them into unemployment; by illegally acquiring welfare benefits and public services; by avoiding taxes" (Chapman, 1976: 188-189).

Chapman went on to argue for the passage of restrictive immigration legislation in Congress that was "desperately needed to help us bring the illegal alien threat under control" because "the understaffed [Immigration] Service vitally needs some budget increases." Although the numbers were never justified and no "independent study" was ever released, they were useful in defining illegal migrants as a concrete threat ("taking away jobs and milking the taxpayer") and morally suspect (welfare abusers and tax cheats), following the classic logic of intergroup threat theory (Stephan & Renfro, 2002; Stephan, Ybarra, & Morrison, 2015).

The most prominent politician contributing to the Latino Threat Narrative was President Ronald Reagan, who in 1985 declared undocumented migration to be "a threat to national security" and warned that "terrorists and subversives [are] just two days driving time from [the border crossing at] Harlingen, Texas" and that Communist agents were ready "to feed on the anger and frustration of recent Central and South American immigrants who will not realize their own version of the American dream" (Massey, Durand, & Malone, 2002:87). More recently, Sheriff Joe Arpaio of Maricopa County, Arizona became his state's most popular politician by taking forceful action "on illegal immigration, drugs and everything else that threatens America" (Arpaio & Sherman, 2008).

Pundits made their contributions to the Latino Threat Narrative in order to sell books and boost media ratings. On his television program, Lou Dobbs (2006) nightly told Americans that the "invasion of illegal aliens" was part of a broader "war on the middle class" hatched by liberal elites. Political commentator Patrick Buchanan (2007), meanwhile, alleged that illegal migration was part of an "Aztlan Plot" hatched by Mexicans to recapture lands lost in 1848 while academic pundit and policy advisor Samuel Huntington (2004) portrayed Latino immigrants as a threat to America's national identity, warning that "the persistent inflow of Hispanic immigrants threatens to divide the United States into two peoples, two cultures, and two languages.... The United States ignores this challenge at its peril."

None of the foregoing pronouncements was based on any substantive understanding of the realities of undocumented migration. At best they were distortions designed to cultivate fear among native born white Americans for self-interested purposes of boosting ratings, selling air-time, and hawking books. As a result, even though the actual flow of undocumented migrants had stabilized by the late 1970s and was no longer rising (Massey & Pren, 2012b), the Latino Threat Narrative kept gaining traction to generate a rising moral panic about illegal aliens that produced a self-perpetuating increase in resources dedicated to border enforcement (Flores-Yeffal, Vidales, & Plemons, 2011). Over time, as more Border Patrol Officers were hired and given more equipment and resources, they naturally apprehended more migrants and the rising number of border apprehensions was then taken as self-evident proof of the ongoing "alien invasion," justifying agency requests for still more enforcement resources and ultimately yielding a self-feeding cycle of enforcement, apprehensions, more enforcement, more apprehensions, and still more enforcement.

Consequences of the Latino threat narrative

While not grounded in reality, the social construction of the Latino Threat Narrative had profound consequences for the Mexico-U.S. migration system. Figure 1 draws on official data to show the annual budget of U.S. Border Patrol from 1970 to 2010 in constant, inflation-adjusted U.S. dollars. From 1970 through 1985 in real terms the budget fluctuated around a value of $300 million with no trend upward or downward. With the Passage of the Immigration Reform and Control Act (IRCA) in 1986, however, the budget began to increase, accelerating during the 1990s with the launching two intensive border enforcement efforts at the two busiest crossing points—Operation Blockade in El Paso, Texas in 1993 and Operation Gatekeeper in San Diego, California in 1994 (Massey, Durand, and Malone, 2002). Border enforcement accelerated again after the passage of the 2001 USA PATRIOT Act and in 2010 the budget stood at $3.8 billion, nearly 13 times its pre-1986 level.

The massive increase in border enforcement and the early concentration of Border Patrol resources in two particular sectors had far-reaching consequences on the behaviour of undocumented migrants and the migratory outcomes they could expect at the border, which I document here using data from the Mexican Migration Project (Durand and Massey, 2004). Since 1982 the MMP has conducted random household surveys in selected communities throughout Mexico and compiled network samples of households from those same communities in the United States. The accuracy and representativeness of the MMP data have been validated by systematic comparisons with data from nationally representative samples (Massey

& Zenteno, 2000; Massey & Capoferro, 2004) and are publicly available from the project website (http://mmp.opr.princeton.edu/), which contains complete documentation on sample design, questionnaires, and data files. Here I make use of the MMP143 database, which includes surveys of undocumented migrants originating in 143 Mexican communities.

Figure 1. Border Patrol budget in millions of 2013 Dollars

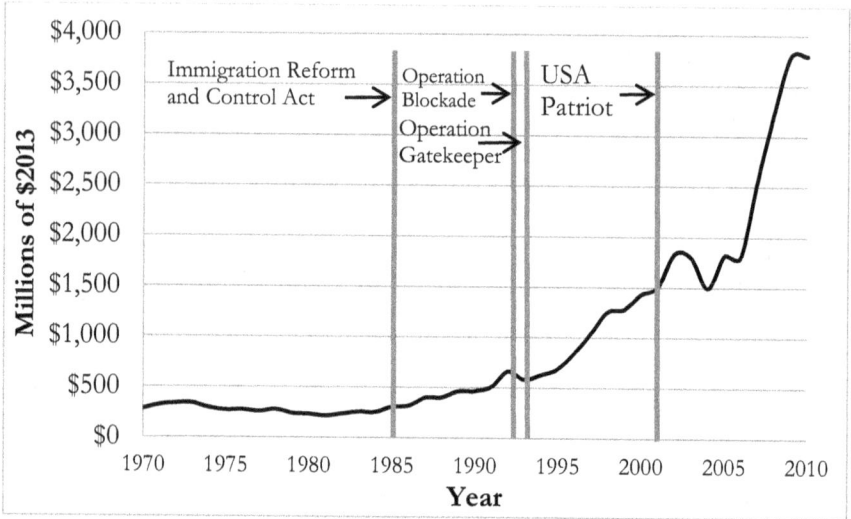

Figure 2. Probability of border crossing at a traditional location 1970-2010

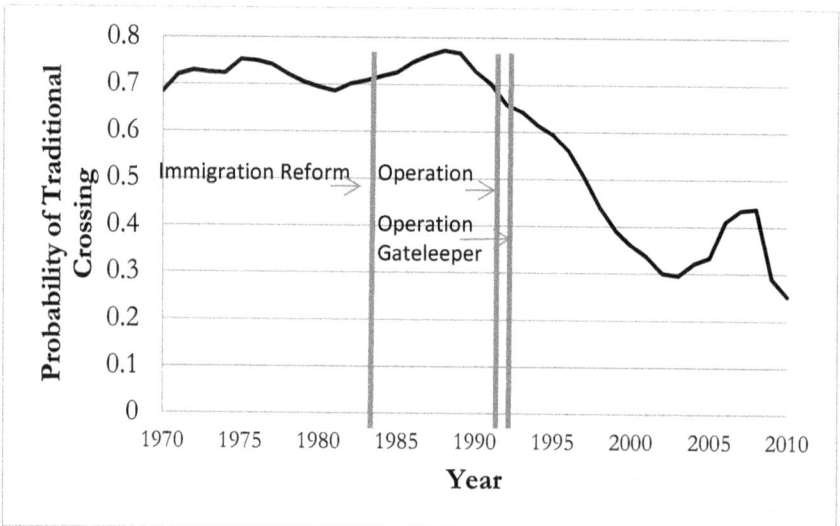

The militarization of the border beginning in 1986 with the passage of IRCA, and especially the launching of Operation Blockade and Operation Gatekeeper in

1993 and 1994, diverted flows of undocumented migrants away from well-travelled routes in the urbanized areas of San Diego and El Paso into unpopulated desert territory between these two sectors. Figure 2 illustrates the geographic diversion that occurred by graphing the probability that undocumented migrants crossed the border at a traditional location (El Paso or San Diego) from 1970 to 2010. While the likelihood fluctuated between 0.69 and 0.77 from 1970 through 1989, thereafter it fell dramatically to reach just 0.25 in 2010. Once diverted away from traditional destinations in states such as California, migrants continued on to new destinations throughout the United States. Thus, whereas 63% of Mexicans who arrived in the United States 1985-1990 went to California, by 1995-2000 the figure had dropped to 28% and new destination areas in the south and midwest came to house the most rapidly growing Mexican populations (Massey and Capoferro, 2008).

Figure 3 documents the rising costs of border crossing associated with this shift by plotting the average fee paid (in 2010 U.S. dollars) to a "coyote" to be smuggled across the border from 1970 to 2010. Whereas the cost fluctuated between $500 and $700 between 1970 and 1989, thereafter it underwent a sustained increase that culminated in an average cost of $2,700 in 2010, a 450% increase over the average before 1989. Figure 4 documents the increased risks faced by undocumented migrants crossings shifted into more hostile terrain at isolated segments of the border by showing the number of border deaths from 1985 (when estimates first become available) to 2010. From 1985 to 1993, the number of deaths actually fell, going from 147 in the former year to 67 in the latter. Thereafter, deaths along the border proliferated, steadily climbing to peak at almost 500 in 2005.

Figure 3. Coyote costs paid for undocumented border crossing 1970-2010

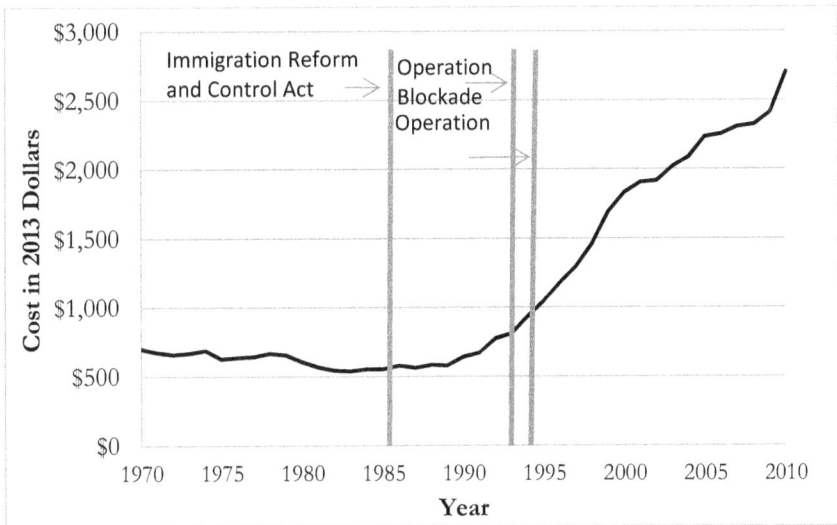

Although rising border enforcement may have had strong effects on the costs, risks, and locations of undocumented border crossing, Figure 5 reveals that it had little effect on the likelihood of being caught while attempting an unauthorized entry. The solid line shows the probability of being apprehended on a first undocumented trip to the United States from 1970 to 2010. As can be seen, the likelihood of getting caught has remained relatively constant despite the massive increase in border enforcement over the past three decades. During the early 1970s the probability of apprehension on any given attempt varied around 0.40 before declining to around 0.21 in 1989 and then rising back up to around 0.40 in 2010. Whatever the likelihood of apprehension on any single attempt, the dotted line at the top of the figure shows the probability of ultimately achieving entry over a series of attempts is and has always been extremely high, being 0.95 or greater from 1970 through 2008.

Figure 4. Migrant deaths along the Mexico-U.S. Border 1985-2010

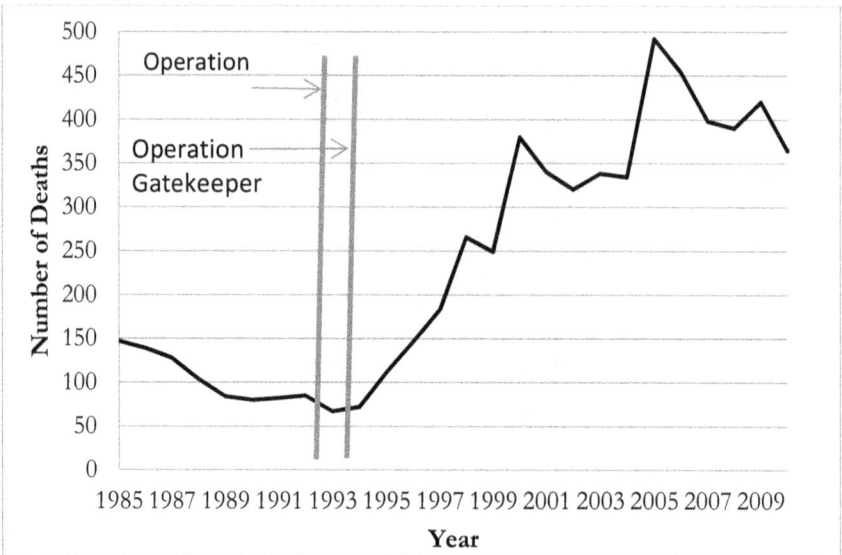

To this point, I have shown that the build-up in border enforcement after 1986 (depicted in Figure 1) was associated with a sharp drop in the likelihood of crossing the border at traditional, relatively safe urban locations (Figure 2) producing sharp increases in the costs (Figure 3) and risks (Figure 4) of unauthorized entry but had no effect on the likelihood of apprehension or the odds of ultimately achieving entry (Figure 5). These enforcement-induced shifts in outcomes along the border shifted the context of migrant decision-making, however. Whereas before 1986 undocumented migrants knew they could reliably gain entry to the United States at modest cost and low risk, afterward they could still reliably be assured of successful entry but at much greater cost and higher risk to life and limb. As a result, conditions at the border still favoured departing for the United States without documents to gain access to high-paying U.S. jobs, but they no longer favoured regularly circulating back and forth. Under these circumstances, once a successful entry had been achieved migrants increasingly tended to hunker down and remain north of the border rather than returning to face even greater costs and risks next time.

Figure 5. Probabilities of apprehension on first attempt and likelihood of eventual entry 1970-2010

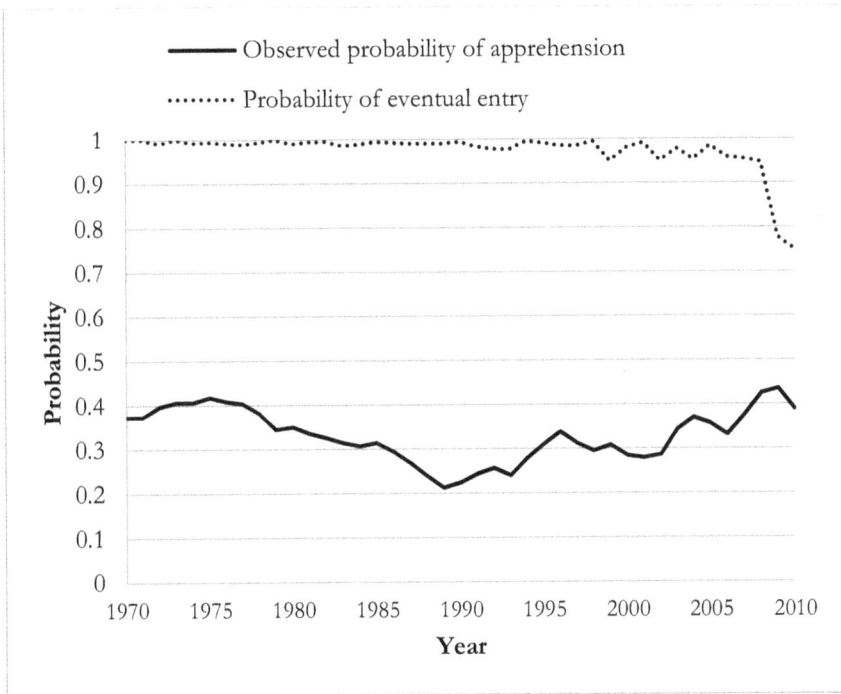

Figures 6 and 7 show the effect that these shifting incentives had on migrant decision-making by plotting, respectively, the likelihood of leaving and returning from a first undocumented trip to the United States between 1970 and 2010. Despite considerable year-to-year volatility there is no discernible trend in the probability of leaving Mexico without documents from 1970 to 2000, despite the exponential increase in enforcement. In contrast, the likelihood of a return trip fell steadily after1986 when it stood at 0.46 to reach 0.29 in 2000 before dropping to zero in 2010.

With undocumented departures continuing at historical rates but returns to Mexico falling rapidly from 1986 to 2000, the net rate of undocumented migration rose and undocumented population growth accelerated. According to the best demographic estimates, the size of the undocumented population increased from 1.9 million in 1988 to 8.5 million in 2000, rising by an average of around 550,000 persons per year (Wasem, 2011) After 2000, the rate of growth decelerated and the population peaked at 12 million in 2008. This deceleration corresponds to the steady decline in the likelihood of taking a first undocumented trip from 0.011 to 0.002 between 1999 and 2008. Then with the onset of the Great Recession the undocumented population fell to 11 million in 2009, where it has roughly remained ever since, reflecting the fact that probabilities of undocumented departure and return had both fallen to around zero by 2010, as shown in Figures 6 and 7.

Figure 6. Probability of first undocumented migration 1970-2010

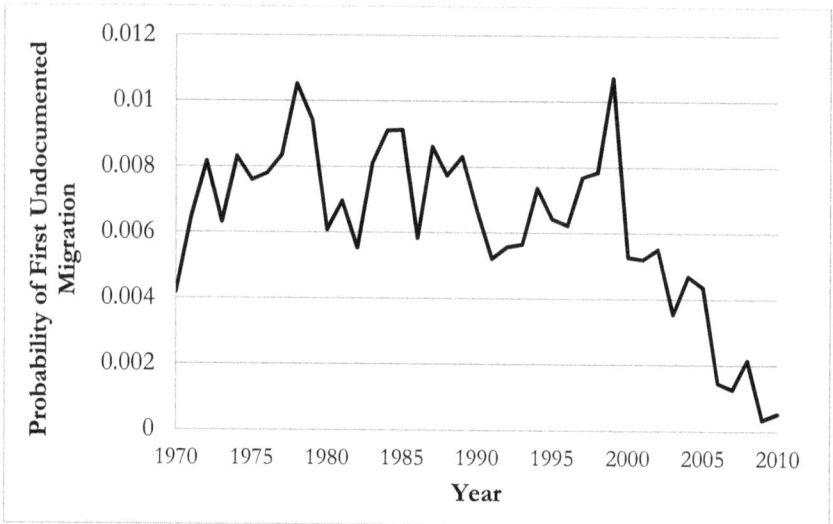

Figure 7. Probability of return within 12 months of first undocumented trip

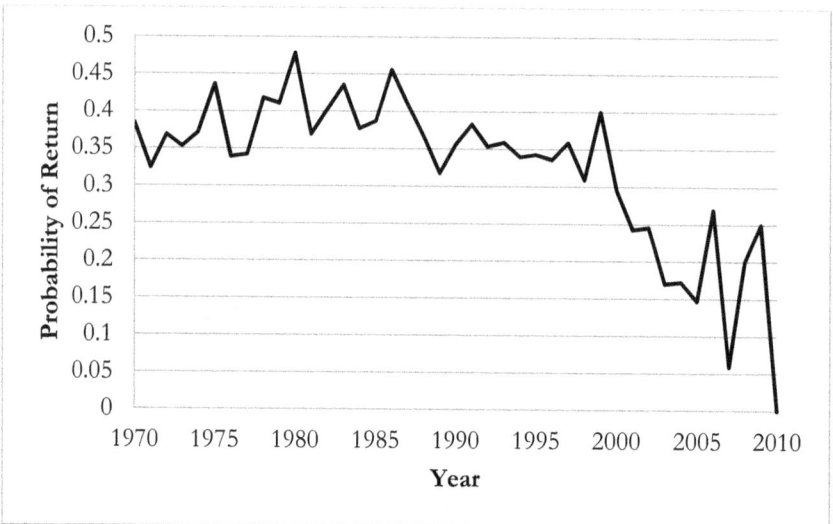

Conclusion

In the end, changes in U.S. immigration and border policies enacted beginning in 1986 transformed what had been a circular flow of male workers going to three states (California, Texas, and Illinois) into a settled population of families living in 50 states while doubling the net rate of undocumented migration and markedly accelerating undocumented population growth. This transformation occurred not because of shifts in the social and economic variables specified in the theories reviewed by Massey et al. (1998) or because of state actions hypothesized by the theories considered in Massey (1999), but because of actions taken by self-serving bureaucrats, politicians, and pundits who gained power and resources by manufacturing an immigration crisis where none existed.

Although in practical terms little had changed in the Mexico-U.S. migration system after 1965, by curtailing opportunities for legal entry Congress in that year brought about the rise of illegal migration and created a golden opportunity for entrepreneurial agents to create a Latino Threat Narrative centred on the fact that Mexican migrants were "illegal" and thus by definition "criminals" and "lawbreakers" who constituted a grave threat to American society. The propagation of this threat narrative, in turn, drove forward a self-perpetuating cycle of increased border enforcement and rising apprehensions. Even though the volume of undocumented migration had levelled off and stabilized by the late 1970s, additional border enforcement efforts produced more apprehensions, which were taken as self-evident proof of the continuing illegal invasion and the need for more enforcement resources, which produced even more apprehensions to justify the still more resources for enforcement.

The end result of this dynamic cycle was a moral panic centred on the trope of illegality and the border as a barrier between American society and the threats this illegality supposedly carried. In the process, pundits sold books, garnered higher media ratings, and increased earnings while politicians mobilized voters to gain power and officials within the immigration bureaucracy accumulated a treasure trove of resources. The massive expansion of the immigration enforcement system, in turn, created a multitude of jobs that made public sector unions happy and increased the profits of firms such as the Corrections Corporation of American and the Geo Group, which built and operated immigration detention facilities. Local law enforcement agencies jumped on the bandwagon when congress created a special program to provide them with new resources to assist in immigration enforcement.

In short, the Latino Threat Narrative was manufactured and sustained by an expanding set of self-interested actors who benefitted from the perpetuation of an immigration crisis, which drove an unprecedented militarization of the border that radically transformed a long-standing migration system from a circularity to settlement. Although the graphs presented here only represent associations, recent work by Massey, Durand, and Pren (2016) using instrumental variable regressions confirm that rising border enforcement was indeed the causal factor driving the geographic diversification of immigrant destinations and the shift from sojourning to settlement among Mexican migrants.

These same regressions also indicate that undocumented migration came to an end in 2008 and is unlikely to return, not because of border enforcement or to changed economic circumstances but as a result of Mexico's demographic transition from a fertility rate from 7.2 children per woman in 1965 to just 2.3 children per woman today, above replacement level. As a result, over the past two decades the rate of labour force growth has fallen and Mexico has become an aging society, with the age of those exposed to the risk of U.S. migration rising rapidly beyond the upper end of the migrant-prone age range. If international migration is not initiated between the ages of 15 and 30, it is unlikely to begin later, and in their study Massey, Durand, & Pren (2016) found that the average age of Mexicans in the labour force but lacking prior migratory experience steadily rose steadily from 23.4 in 1972 to 45.9 in 2010. As a result, net migration from Mexico–not just undocumented migration but migration in general–now hovers around zero (Passel, Cohn, & Gonzalez-Barrera, 2012).

The transformation of Mexican immigration from circularity to settlement and its geographic spread throughout the United States between 1986 and 2008 has transformed the social demography of the United States, increasing the percentage of Latinos to 17.3% and making them by far the largest minority group in the United States. Moreover, no matter what the future of Mexican migration might be, this transformation is already built into the demographic structure of the United States for in 2012 less than half of all U.S. births were to non-Hispanic whites while a quarter were Latino (Passel, Livingston, and Cohn, 2012). This remarkable transformation arose from a dynamic socio-political process that was completely untheorized by prevailing models of international migration but which in two decades will nonetheless turn the United States into a "minority-majority" nation in which European origin whites no longer predominate.

References

Abrajano, Marisa, & Zoltan L. Hajnal (2015). *White Backlash: Immigration, Race, and American Politics*. Princeton, NJ: Princeton University Press.

Arpaio, Joe, & Len Sherman (2008). *Joe's Law: America's Toughest Sheriff Takes on Illegal Immigration, Drugs and Everything Else That Threatens America*. New York: AMACOM Books.

Buchanan, Patrick J. (2006). *State of Emergency: The Third World Invasion and Conquest of America*. New York: Thomas Dunne Books.

Calavita, Kitty. (1992). *Inside the State: The Bracero Program, Immigration, and the I.N.S.* New York: Routledge.

Chapman, Leonard F. (1976). "Illegal Aliens: Time to Call a Halt!" *Reader's Digest*, October, pp. 188-192.

Cardoso, Lawrence (1980). *Mexican Emigration to the United States 1897-1931*. Tucson: University of Arizona Press.

Chavez, Leo R. (2001). *Covering Immigration: Population Images and the Politics of the Nation*. Berkeley: University of California Press.

_____ (2008). *The Latino Threat: Constructing Immigrants, Citizens, and the Nation*. Stanford, CA: Stanford University Press.

Dobbs, Lou (2006). *War on the Middle Class: How the Government, Big Business, and Special Interest Groups Are Waging War on the American Dream and How to Fight Back*. New York: Viking.

Durand, Jorge, & Douglas S. Massey (1995). *Miracles on the Border: Retablos of Mexican Migrants to the United States*. Tucson: University of Arizona Press.

_____ (2003). *Clandestinos: Migración México-Estados Unidos en los Albores del Siglo XXI*. México, D.F.: Editorial Porrua.

Durand, Jorge, & Douglas S. Massey (2004). *Crossing the Border: Research from the Mexican Migration Project*. New York: Russell Sage Foundation.

Dustmann, Christian, & Joseph-Simon Görlach (2015). "The Economics of Temporary Migrations." *Journal of Economic Literature*, forthcoming. Pre-publication version available at: http://www.cream-migration.org/publ_uploads/CDP_03_15.pdf.

Flores-Yeffal, Nadia Y. (2012). *Migration-Trust Networks: Social Cohesion in Mexican US-Bound Emigration*. College Station: Texas A&M University.

Flores-Yeffal, Nadia Y., Guadalupe Vidales, & April Plemons (2011). "The Latino Cyber-Moral Panic Process in the United States." *Information, Communication, and Society* 14:568-489.

Fussell, Elizabeth, & Douglas S. Massey (2004). "The Limits to Cumulative Causation: International Migration from Mexican Urban Areas." *Demography* 41:151-71.

Gardner, Daniel (2008). *The Science of Fear: Why We Fear the Things We Shouldn't--and Put Ourselves in Greater Danger*. New York: Dutton.

Garip Filiz (2012). "Discovering Diverse Mechanisms of Migration: The Mexico-U.S. Stream from 1970 to 2000." Population and Development Review 38(3):393-433.

Huntington, Samuel P. (2004). "The Hispanic challenge," Foreign Policy, March/April, pp. 1-12. Accessed 6/15/11 at http://www.foreignpolicy.com/ story/ cms.php?story_id=2495.

Massey, Douglas S. (1988). "International Migration and Economic Development in Comparative Perspective." *Population and Development Review* 14:383-414

_____ (1990). "Social Structure, Household Strategies, and the Cumulative Causation of Migration." *Population Index* 56:3-26.

_____ (1999). "International Migration at the Dawn of the Twenty-First Century: The Role of the State." *Population and Development Review* 25:303-23.

_____ (2013). "Building a Comprehensive Model of International Migration." *Eastern Journal of European Studies* 3(2):9-35.

Massey, Douglas S., Rafael Alarcón, Jorge Durand, & Humberto González (1987). *Return to Aztlan: The Social Process of International Migration from Western Mexico.* Berkeley: University of California Press.

Massey, Douglas S., Joaquín Arango, Graeme Hugo, Ali Kouaouci, Adela Pellegrino, & J. Edward Taylor (1993). "Theories of International Migration: A Review and Appraisal." *Population and Development Review* 19:431-66.

_____ (1994). "An Evaluation of International Migration Theory: The North American Case." *Population and Development Review* 20:699-752.

_____ (1998). *Worlds in Motion: International Migration at the End of the Millennium.* Oxford: Oxford University Press.

Massey, Douglas S., & Amelia E. Brown (2011). "New Migration Streams between Mexico and Canada." *Migraciones Internacionales* 6(1):119-144.

Massey, Douglas S., & Chiarra Capoferro (2004). "Measuring Undocumented Migration." *International Migration Review* 38:1075-1102.

_____ (2008). "The Geographic Diversification of U.S. Immigration." In Douglas S. Massey, ed., *New Faces in New Places: The Changing Geography of American Immigration.* New York: Russell Sage, pp. 25-50.

Massey, Douglas S., Jorge Durand, & Nolan J. Malone (2002). *Beyond Smoke and Mirrors: Mexican Immigration in an Age of Economic Integration.* New York: Russell Sage Foundation.

Massey, Douglas S., Jorge Durand, & Karen A. Pren (2014). "Explaining Undocumented Migration." *International Migration Review* 48:1028-1061.

_____ (2016). "Why Border Enforcement Backfired." *American Journal of Sociology*, forthcoming.

Massey, Douglas S. & Kristin E. Espinosa (1997). "What's Driving Mexico-U.S. Migration? A Theoretical, Empirical and Policy Analysis." *American Journal of Sociology* 102:939-999.

Massey, Douglas S., & Karen A. Pren (2012a). "Origins of the New Latino Underclass." *Race and Social Problems* 4(1):5-17.

_____ (2012b). "Unintended Consequences of US Immigration Policy: Explaining the Post-1965 Surge from Latin America." *Population and Development Review* 38:1-29.

Massey, Douglas S., & J. Edward Taylor (2004). *International Migration: Prospects and Policies in a Global Market.* Oxford: Oxford University Press.

Massey, Douglas S., and René Zenteno (1999). "The Dynamics of Mass Migration." *Proceedings of the National Academy of Sciences* 96(8):5328-335.

_____ (2000). "A Validation of the Ethnosurvey: The Case of Mexico-U.S. Migration." *International Migration Review* 34:765-92.

North, Douglass S. (1990). *Institutions, Institutional Change and Economic Performance.* Cambridge, UK: Cambridge University Press.

Passel, Jeffrey S., D'Vera Cohn, & Ana Gonzalez-Barrera (2012). *Net Migration from Mexico Falls to Zero-and Perhaps Less.* Washington, DC: Pew Research Center. http://www.pewhispanic.org/2012/04/23/net-migration-from-mexico-falls-to-zero-and-perhaps-less/.

Passel, Jeffrey S., Gretchen M. Livingston, & D'Vera Cohn (2012). *Explaining Why Minority Births Now Outnumber White Births.* Washington, DC: Pew Research Center. http://www.pewsocialtrends.org/2012/05/17/explaining-why-minority-births-now-outnumber-white-births/.

Piore, Michael J. (1979). *Birds of Passage: Migrant Labor in Industrial Societies.* New York: Cambridge University Press.

Portes, Alejandro, & Robert L. Bach (1985). *Latin Journey: Cuban and Mexican Immigrants in the United States.* Berkeley: University of California Press.

Portes, Alejandro, and John Walton. (1981). *Labor, Class, and the International System.* New York: Academic Press.

Robin, Corey (2006). *Fear: The History of a Political Idea.* Oxford, UK: Oxford University Press.

Santa Ana, Otto (2002). *Brown Tide Rising: Metaphors of Latinos in Contemporary American Public Discourse.* Austin: University of Texas Press.

Sassen, Saskia (1988). *The Mobility of Labor and Capital: A Study in International Investment and Labor Flow.* Cambridge: Cambridge University Press.

Stark, Oded (1991). *The Migration of Labor.* Cambridge: Basil Blackwell.

Stephan, Walter G., & Lausane Renfro (2002). "The Role of Threat in Intergroup Relations." In D. M. Mackie & E. R. Smith (eds.), *From Prejudice to Intergroup Emotions: Differentiated Reactions to Social Groups.* New York: Psychology Press, pp. 191-207.

Stephan, Walter G., Oscar Ybarra, & Kimberly Rios Morrison (2015). "Intergroup Threat Theory." In T. Nelson (Ed.), *Handbook of Prejudice.* Mahwah, NJ: Lawrence Erlbaum Associates.

Taylor, J. Edward, Joaquin Arango, Douglas S. Massey, Graeme Hugo, Ali Kouaouci, & Adela Pellegrino (1995). "International Migration and National Development." *Population Index* 62-181-212.

_____ (1996). "International Migration and Community Development." *Population Index* 63:397-418.

Todaro, Michael P. & L. Maruszko (1986). "Illegal Migration and U.S. Immigration Reform: A Conceptual

Framework." *Population and Development Review* 13:101-14.
Valentino, Nicholas A., Ted Brader, & Ashley E. Jardina (2013). "Immigration Opposition among U.S. Whites: General Ethnocentrism or Media Priming of Attitudes about Latinos?" *Political Psychology* 34:149-166.
Wasem, Ruth E. (2011). Unauthorized Aliens Residing in the United States: Estimates since 1986. Washington, DC: Congressional Research Service.
Williamson, Jeffrey G. (2004). *The Political Economy of World Mass Migration: Comparing Two Global Centuries.* Washington, DC: AEI Press.

CHAPTER 6
Transnational mobility and conflict

Ibrahim Sirkeci

Introduction

Transnationalism opened up the discussion in international migration studies by abandoning the unidirectional and static understanding of the phenomenon. In Faist's three generations typology, transnationalism corresponds to the third generation of migration theories recognising migration practices connecting both sending and receiving worlds (2000:12). This may sound quite motionless, but yet he argues "migrations are not singular journeys but tend to become integral part of migrants' lives" blurring the distinction between countries of origin and destination (2000:13). The focus here is onto the transnational geography or transnational social space where migrations occur. Thus, we may avoid a) the dullness and simplicity of pull-push models which tend to see migration as a move from A to B determined by the relative attractiveness of both ends; b) self-fulfilling prophecy (Merton, 1959:423) of network models; c) bureaucratic definition of international migration (i.e. changing place of residence for 12 months or more); d) providing a space to abandon the separation e.g. migrants and non-migrants; e) theoretically useless migration typologies (e.g. voluntary vs. forced, economic vs. political etc.) which does not help in understanding migration behaviour.

Based on these premises, the paper develops a conceptualisation based on conflict as a core dynamic force determining and shaping transnational human movements. As opposed to what Düvell (2007) proposes in a recent article, it is not the 'conflict over migration' but migration as a function of conflict what matters. After elaborating briefly on the theoretical added value of transnationalism in the next section, I will delineate the concept of human insecurity and its link to conflict. The scope of conflict and transnational movement as a cost incurred by conflicts will be the focus in section four. Finally, I will discuss the building blocks of a possible conflict model of transnational migration.

Transnationalist intervention in migration theory

Transnationalism has created a rich space for social scientists. On the one hand, it shifted the focus to the continual links across borders and proved to be useful in "decentering the gaze of the analyst from the singular nation-state" (Harney and Baldassar, 2007: 190). Many of us refer to the concept of transnationalism to describe and analyse processes and patterns connecting people, businesses and other entities in different places of the world. While this approach widens the understanding of human movement some would still argue that such "macroscalar associations do have their interpretive limits, obscuring and eliding different scales, networks and manifestations of connections, which, as a result, diminish its clarity as a conceptual tool" (Harney and Baldassar, 2007:190).

A bourgeoning literature provides a wealth of applications of the transnationalism concept for understanding international migration (Basch et al. 1994; Ferguson, 1999; Glick-Schiller et al. 1992; Kivisto, 2001; Levitt et al. 2003; Smith, 2001; Smith and Guarnizo, 1998; Vertovec, 1999). Transnational literature helps us to move away from linear migration models to circular, fluctuating and dynamic ties built by human movements across borders making conceptualisations of multiple 'heres' and 'theres' possible as opposed to origin and destination. While emphasising the process and movement, transnationalism also decentralises the nation and refer to trans-local belongings and identities (Werbner, 1999; Wimmer and Glick-Schiller, 2003), which is argued to be the main form of migrant belonging in the future (Castles, 2002:1158).

However, the gap in the literature is evident regarding the conflict element of transnational mobility. For example, Koser (2007) underlines the absence of asylum-seekers and refugees in transnationalism studies. He argues that this is because these groups offer very limited potential for the development of transnational identities and activities in this regard as they are thought to maintain very few links to the origin (Koser, 2007:237). However, for me, refugees and asylum seekers are the prime examples for development of a conflict-oriented model of transnational migration because these two groups exemplify few of the various conflict situations. For instance, asylum seekers and refugees (perhaps all displaced populations) are often the main target of restrictive admission policies of states as well as being subject to a variety of threats paving way to strong human insecurity perceptions. The basis of this conflict also lies in the fact that transnational movement of these groups along with undocumented migrants undermines the power of nation states, "challenging the ability of states to control their borders, their identities and their residents" (Koser, 2007: 242).

Human insecurity

According to Bilgin, the concept of human security recognises that the security of individuals and communities do not necessarily match that of the state (2003:213). Thus, the security of migrants and non-migrants often differs from the security of states, at origin, in transit or in destination. A clear formulation of the concept of human security appeared in the United Nations Development Program' 1994 Human Development Report, where the emphasis shifted towards 'people's security'[1] (UNDP, 1994 in Bilgin, 2003:214). Amartya Sen, a pioneer in conceptualizing human security, linked human security to threats to "the survival, daily life, and dignity of human beings and to strengthening the efforts to confront these threats" (2000:1).

Abraham Maslow's five stage hierarchy of needs model, often depicted in a

---

[1] Aradau (2008) criticises those claiming a switch from state to individual security pointing out that primary role of the state according to "the fiction of social contract" is ensuring individual security. Perhaps one could elaborate on this and say the exclusion of others in the social contract fiction and inclusivity of all vulnerable people in today's human security concept may mark the line between.

pyramid showing needs or motivational drives in order of importance, places security and safety on the second level following the basic needs such as air, food, shelter, and sex (1943). He argued such lower level needs must be satisfied before higher needs can be attended. This prioritisation can be debatable but the importance of such needs is not. Hence, one would need the security of a home and family, community, neighbourhood and country -also recognising the fact that satisfaction is relative and personal.

Formulations of human security often emphasize the welfare of ordinary people (Paris, 2001). Thomas argues "that material sufficiency lies at the core of human security" and "the problems of poverty and deepening inequality are central concerns" (2001:159). In their elaboration of the Index of Human Insecurity, Lonergan et al. underline that "human security has been endangered not only by military threats, but also of resource scarcity, rapid population growth, human rights abuses, and outbreaks of infectious diseases, environmental degradation, pollution, and loss of biodiversity" (2000: 1; also see Homer-Dixon, 1994).

Human insecurity can be seen as a concept defining various situations where conflicts lead to perception of deprivation of some kind, among certain people, in a given context. It can be civil strife for Sudanese minorities or environmental hazards for Indonesian islanders. It is perceived subjectively by individuals (and/or households, communities and so on). Thereby human insecurity is relative, subjective and may arise from civil conflicts, wars, latent tensions, environmental catastrophes, etc.

Perception of human insecurity can be based on material or non-material environments. For example, members of a minority group may feel insecure because they are not allowed to practice their own cultural traditions and develop their mother language. The non-material environment of human insecurity can also be pinned down in another context by mere feeling of oppression (or resentment) by minorities. Yet, there are examples of the material environment of human insecurity triggered by not only political and ethno-political conflicts (e.g. ethnocentric governance) but also by lack of economic opportunities (e.g. high unemployment, low GDP), high risk of natural environmental disasters (e.g. tsunami, drought) or man-made ones (e.g. building dams). We need to bear in mind that one or more of these may affect any given population at any given time, and that material and non-material underpinnings interact with each other. This interaction may increase or decrease the feeling/perception of human insecurity. Confrontation between different groups is also likely: those who are advantaged by (or in) the situation against those who are disadvantaged.

Thus, I argue that main motive in international migration can be formulated as seeking (human) security; or avoiding (perceived) human insecurity as the root cause. Thereby we override the existing typologies (e.g. labour, family, asylum, irregular migrations etc.) which have been so far unhelpful in the endeavour of conceptualising the phenomenon. These categories are often reflections of legislation that do not provide clues to help understand migration behaviour. The threats to human security appearing in many forms may channel populations towards the exit option (i.e. emigration).

Human security and insecurity should be constructed on a continuous scale where flows are expected to occur from insecurity end towards security end (Figure 1). In a sense, we can see human insecurity aligned with push factors whereas human security with pull factors referring to the so-called push-pull models of international migration (van der Erf and Heering, 1995).

Figure 1: Environment of Human Insecurity and Conflict

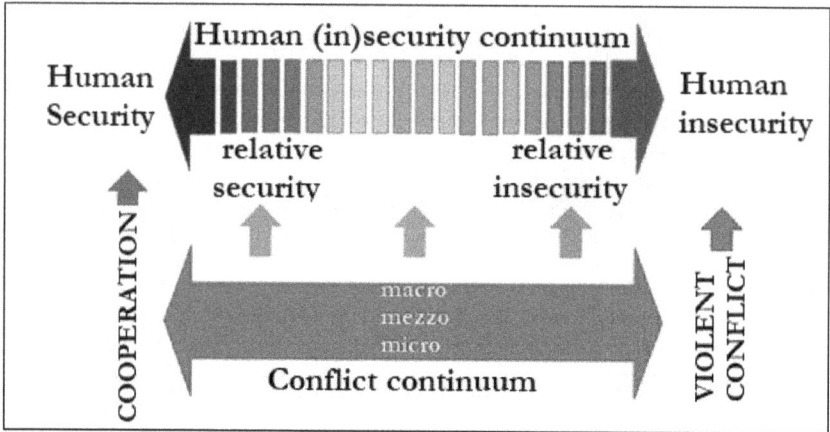

Conflict

In developing an understanding of international migration revolving around the concept of conflict, I have adopted the definition by Ralf Dahrendorf (1959). His definition of conflict does not necessarily equate to violence. It embraces a range of conflict situations from latent tensions to violent conflicts, which does not necessarily to be ethnic or religious oriented. According to him, conflict is not only about manifest clashes (e.g. revolts, wars, armed conflict) but also contests, competitions, disputes, and tensions (Dahrendorf, 1959). These may be explicit (overt) or latent (covert) (Parsons, 1954:329). It covers all relations that involve incompatible differences in objectives (Dahrendorf, 1959:135). Thus, I conceptualise conflict on a continuum: from cooperation, where differences are cleared to violent conflicts where consensus is either not possible or not preferred (Figure 1). Applied to the international migration, for instance, bilateral labour migration agreements between countries can be seen as examples of cooperation while refugee crises seen in war zones would fall towards the other end of the continuum.

Therefore, we can identify conflict situations at various levels and stages of international migration process. Accordingly, transnational space is such *a conflict-space characterised by conflict-potentials*. According to Rummell (1976) it is a space within which conflict can occur, although at any moment there may be no ongoing conflict. The transnational space is constantly transformed by conflicts and migrations. There the dynamic nature of conflict and migration influences the structures, actors and processes. In due course, different channels of migration become available while some others disappear. Thus we see changing admission rules, visa policies, border control policies as well as new migration routes, migration mechanisms and new migration types while these movements may also change the conflicts they are originated from or linked to.

Conflict is important within the international migration context as it leads to the perception of human insecurity. However, this perception does not always lead to migration, which is just one of the strategic options available to those subject to an *environment of* -human- *insecurity (EOI)*[2] (Sirkeci, 2006). Emphasising the shift towards human security, I revise this concept to call it an "environment of *human* insecurity" (EOHI) (Sirkeci, 2007). It is characterised by *material* (e.g. armed conflict, deprivation, lack of employment, poor infrastructure) and *non-material* (e.g. discrimination, oppression, human rights violations, fear of persecution, language barriers) insecurities (Sirkeci, 2006, 2005a) and often induced by conflict. People exposed to the EOHI have two options: a) status quo and b) exit. The status quo option primarily refers to those who stay and align with the dominant ethnic group, and/or the government forces; whilst the exit option may involve joining the rebels, or leaving the conflict zone, which is where migration occurs (Sirkeci, 2006). There can also be mixed strategies locating and moving individuals, families and groups along the lines set in the insecurity continuum in Figure 1.

Sources, levels and streams of conflict and transnational migration

In 'transnational migration space', there are conflicts among individuals, ethnic or religious groups, social classes, countries, supranational agencies, and so on. Transnational migration may incur as a cost of such conflicts. The conflict continuums illustrated in Figure 1 are also reflective of various (economic, political, cultural) indicators commonly used in migration literature because all these environmental influences shape the perception of human insecurity. Thus, people may not respond to the conflict stimulus in the same way in different contexts; which can explain some of the non-migration. It is important to admit the complexity of making migration decision. Therefore, the continuums in Figure 1 should be read carefully bearing in mind the contextual influences.

One obvious source to promote migration is violent and armed conflicts. In a rare study Naude (2008) showed that an additional year of conflict will raise the net migration 1.35 per thousand while an additional natural disaster will increase it further 0.6 per thousand in Sub-Saharan Africa underlining the key role of conflict (p.17). There are also other studies pointing at similar causality between migration and conflict in Africa and Middle East (Hatton and Williamson, 2002, Sirkeci, 2006, 2005a and 2005b, Stansfield, 2004, Lubkemann, 2005, Hourani & Sensenig-Dabbous, 2007). Forced migration studies, in general, can also be inspected for such cases.

Another source of conflict revolves around gender security. Gender inequalities and traditional gender roles as well as unwanted female children are areas with

---

[2] The 'environment of insecurity' (EOI) concept was applied to the Kurdish rivalry in Turkey (Icduygu et al. 1999). I have expanded it to analyse the Turkish Kurdish emigration from Turkey to Germany (Sirkeci, 2003, 2006). EOI as a background contexts was later used to explain Iraqi and Turkmen migration (Sirkeci, 2005a, 2005b), Lebanese migration (Hourani & Sensenig-Dabbous, 2007), and Alevi migration (Zirh and Erdemir, 2008).

conflict potential. One related area is the homosexuality and attitudes towards it in some origin countries (e.g. Iran) and asylum seeking gays escaping from such places (Spring, 2008; Manalansan, 2006). These conflicts can be expressed at cross levels (i.e. individual versus state) and/or mezzo (e.g. households) or individual levels.

Koser's (2007:243-50) three case studies on refugees, asylum seekers and smuggling provide evidence to the conflicts arising between immigrants and host societies. The tensions between immigrants and the locals or natives are real. For example, he refers to tensions between Bosnians and Eritreans in the UK and the government as well as tensions with their respective host countries. These tensions involving refuges, asylum seekers, and smuggling (i.e. conflicts) have an impact upon states. Attempts to build –inevitably- 'transnational governance' regarding international migration should be seen as a result of the conflicts between various actors including states, individuals and groups. At a similar level, asylum-seekers, rejected refugees, and those undocumented who are likely to be forced into the cheap labour experience another source of conflict in the 'destination'.

A further source of conflict and insecurity is environmental disasters. Many people are displaced within their countries while some cross borders because they "can no longer gain a secure livelihood" in their homeland due to environmental problems (Myers, 1993:752 cited in Renaud et al. 2007). This may cause conflict between communities and individuals over scarce resources such as water; once these sufferers cross an international border, it may also lead to conflict between states. Border crossing is a crucial issue as borders are increasingly militarised and tightened – often at the expense of human lives (for examples, see Yaghmaian, 2005, Cornelius, 2001, Esbach et al. 1999), and despite the fact that migration control is a myth (Cornelius et al. 1994 and 2004).

Factors such as lack of job opportunities, socio-economic deprivation, and wage differentials can be conceptualised as sources of conflict, albeit non-violent one. Similarly, dual labour markets and ethnic discrimination in destination countries would also reflect a conflict between immigrant labourers and natives.

In Figure 1, three levels of conflict are defined: *macro* (e.g. conflicting policy preferences in sending, receiving and transit countries), *mezzo* (e.g. tensions among migrant and non-migrant households and communities; also regarding gender roles within households), *micro* (e.g. conflicts between individuals; non-migrants versus migrants), and *across* levels (e.g. conflict between regulating agencies –border patrols, visa officers, etc.- and migrating individuals).

At macro level, conflicts appear between the sending and receiving countries because they often have incompatible interests (e.g. need for IT professionals in Germany versus high unemployment in Turkey).

Across level conflict occur when actors at different levels have incompatible interests. For example, at the country of origin, certain interests of minority members may diverge from national interests, which can be expressed in various forms of forced migration. The continuous conflict between the regulating and migrating human agency forces changes in migration regulations (e.g. tightening admission rules) and in response to these changes, migrating human agency changes

70

his or her strategies, mechanisms, routes, and pathways of international migration. For example, we can consider discrimination against or suppression of minorities in across level conflicts (e.g. Berbers vs. Morocco, Kurds vs. Iraq).

International migration's influence on gender roles within families left behind are to look for mezzo level and micro level conflicts. For example, when husbands move abroad as "guest workers" or else, women often take control of households left behind as lengthy absences of men are inevitable. These can cause tensions within the household and may even lead to violent conflicts (i.e. domestic violence); also upon the return of immigrant men who often want to be household head again.

Concluding remarks: Towards a conflict-based understanding

Based on the continuums of (human) security and of conflict, the main assumptions of such a model would be as follows:

1. Migration is initiated by conflict situations where incompatible interests are expressed by the parties involved.

2. The level and intensity of conflict and potential and actual perceived damages or hurt determine the pace and type of migration.

3. Admission rules are closely affected by the repercussions of conflict situations but often chase the movement. Thus, it is also source of conflict influencing migration.

4. Conflict creates an insecurity perception which shapes the migration process as a whole.

5. This human insecurity perception may weaken or strengthen throughout the migration process; sometimes leading to onward migration or return migration or re-migration.

6. The environment of human insecurity may arise from conflicts over material or non-material sources.

7. Macro (state, nation; e.g. countries limiting foreign labour versus those with excess labour), mezzo (household, community; e.g. empowered wife left behind versus returnee husband over heading the household), and micro (individual; e.g. achieving better careers, working in a secure environment, lack of jobs) levels can be identified as levels of conflict where cross level tensions are also possible (e.g. border crossing migrants versus border patrols or passport control officers; ethnic minority members versus oppressing government forces).

These premises of course are not denying the contributions of network theory, economic theories, and cultural theories regarding their explanations on the causes, direction and composition of transnational migration but rather reorganises them with the lenses of conflict.

A conflict-oriented conceptualisation of international migration can help us to better understand process and acknowledge its dynamic nature. Typologies of international migration may follow once this conflict model is established as different conflicts, or different aspects of different conflicts may determine different migration patterns which are responsive to regulations within a broader environmental context. Defining the conflict on a continuum, on the other hand, help us to accommodate the overlaps between different migration categories, which have been used so far in the literature and policy making. This model is informed by past scholarship on international migration but attempts to go beyond it by borrowing from the concepts of human security and environment of human insecurity. In short, the approach proposed here argues that migration is a search for (human) security.

References

Aradau, C. (2008). Rethinking Trafficking in Women. Politics out of Security. Basingstoke: Palgrave Macmillan.

Basch, L., Glick Schiller, N. and Szanton-Blanc, C. (1994). Nations Unbound: Transnational Projects, Postcolonial Predicaments, and Deterritorialized Nation-States. New York: Gordon and Breach.

Bilgin, Pinar (2003). Individual and societal dimensions of security. International Studies Review, 5, pp. 203-222.

Castles, S. (2002). Migration and community formation under conditions of globalization. International Migration Review, 36(4):1143-1168.

Cornelius, W. A. (2001). "Death at the border: Efficacy and unintended consequences of US immigration control policy", Population and Development Review. 27(4):661-685.

Cornelius, W. A., Martin, P.L. and Hollifield, J. F. (1994). Controlling Immigration: A global perspective. Stanford, Calif., US: Stanford University Press.

_____ (2004). Controlling Immigration: A global perspective. 2nd ed., London: Europan.

Dahrendorf, R. (1959). Class and Class Conflict in Industrial Society. Stanford, California: Stanford University Press.

Düvell, F. (2007). "Towards sustainable migration policies", in Innovative Concepts for Alternative Migration Policies, edited by M. Jandl. Amsterdam: Amsterdam, University Press.

Eschbach, K., J. Hagan, N. Rodriguez, R. Hernandez-Leon, S. Bailey (1999). "Death at the border", International Migration Review, 33(2):430-454.

Faist, T. (2000). The Volume and Dynamics of International Migration and Transnational Social Spaces. Oxford: Oxford University Press.

Ferguson, J. (1999). Expectations of Modernity: Myths and Meaning of Urban Life on the Zambian Copperbelt. Berkeley: University of California Press.

Glick Schiller, N., Basch, L. and Blanc-Szanton, C. (eds) (1992). Towards a Transnational Perspective on Migration: Race, Class, Ethnicity and Nationalism Reconsidered. New York: New York Academy of Science.

Harney, N. D. and Baldassar, L. (2007). "Tracking transnationalism: Migrancy and its futures", Journal of Ethnic and Migration Studies, 33(2): 189-198.

Hatton, T.J. and Williamson, J.G. (2002). "Demographic and economic pressure on emigration out of Africa", IZA Discussion Paper 250, Bonn: IZA.

Homer-Dixon, T. F. (1994). "Environmental scarcities and violent conflict: Evidence from cases", International Security, 19(1):5-40.

Hooglund, E. (1991). "The other face of war", Middle East Report, No.171, pp.3-7 and 10-12.

Hourani, G. and Sensenig-Dabbous, E. (2007). "Insecurity, migration and return: The case of Lebanon following the Summer 2006 War". CARIM Research Reports, No. 2007-01, RSCAS, European University Institute.

Icduygu, A., Romano, D. & Sirkeci, I. (1999). "The ethnic question in an environment of insecurity: the Kurds in Turkey", Ethnic and Racial Studies, 22(6):991-1010.

Kivisto, P. (2001). "Theorising transnational immigration: a critical review of current efforts", Ethnic and Racial Studies, 24(3): 549-77.

Koser, K. (2007). "Refugees, Transnationalism and the State", Journal of Ethnic and Migration Studies, 33(2): 233-254.

Levitt, P., DeWind, J. and Vertovec, S. (2003). "International perspectives on transnational migration: an introduction", International Migration Review, 37(3): 565-75.

Lonergan, S., Gustavson, K. & Carter, B. (2000). "Index of human insecurity", AVISO: news of the Canadian Palliative Care Association, 6: 1-7.

Lubkemann, S. (2005). "Migratory Coping in Wartime Mozambique: An Anthropology of Violence and Displacement in 'Fragmented Wars," Journal of Peace Research 42(4): 493-508.

Manalansan IV, M.F. (2006). "Queer intersections: Sexuality and gender in migration studies", International Migration Review, 40(1):224-249.

Maslow, A. H. (1943). "A theory of human motivation", Psychological Review, 50(4):370-396.

Merton, R. K. (1959). Social Theory and Social Structure. New York: Free Press.

Naude, W. (2008). "Conflict Disasters, and No Jobs", UNU-WIDER, Research Paper No.2008/85.

O'Hanlon, M. E. & Campbell, J.H. (2008): Iraq Index, Tracking Variables of Reconstruction & Security in Post-Saddam Iraq. Brookings Institute. [online] Available from http://www.brookings.edu /fp/saban /iraq/index.pdf. [Accessed 20 Feb. 08].

Paris, R. (2001). "Human security: Paradigm shift or hot air?" International Security, 26(2):87-102.

Parsons, T. (1954). Essays in Sociological Theory. The Free Press, Glencoe, Illinois.

Renaud, F., Bogardi, J.J, Dun, O. and Warner, K. (2007). "Control, adapt or flee: How to face environmental migration?"InterSecTions, No.5/2007, Bonn: Publication Series of UNU-EHS.

Rummel, R.J. (1976). Understanding Conflict and War: Vol. 2 The Conflict Helix. Beverly Hills, California, Sage Publications

Sen, A. (2000). "Why human security?" In International Symposium on Human Security. Commission on Human Security, Tokyo, Japan.

Sirkeci, I. (2003). "Migration from Turkey to Germany: an ethnic analysis," New Perspectives on Turkey, 28-29, 198-208.

_____ (2005a). "War in Iraq: Environment of insecurity and international migration", International Migration, 43(4):197-214.

_____ (2005b). Turkmen in Iraq and International Migration of Turkmen. Ankara, Turkey: Global Strategy Institute.

_____ (2006). The Environment of Insecurity in Turkey and the Emigration of Turkish Kurds to Germany. New York, US: Edwin Mellen Press.

_____ (2007). "Human insecurity and streams of conflict for a re-conceptualisation of international migration", Population Review, 46(2):32-50.

Smith, M.P. (2001). Transnational Urbanism: Locating Globalization. Oxford: Blackwell.

Smith, M.P. and Guarnizo, L.E. (eds) (1998). Transnationalism from Below. New Brunswick: Transaction Publishers.

Spring, U.O. (2008). "Gender and disasters, human, gender and environmental security: A huge challenge", SOURCE, No.8/2008, Bonn: Publication Series of UNU-EHS.

Stansfield, J. (2004). Ethiopian / Eritrean Migration and Identity. Unpublished PhD thesis, University of Sheffield, UK.

Thomas, C. (2001). Global governance, development and human security: exploring the links. In: Third World Quarterly. vol. 22, no. 1, pp. 159-175.

Van der Erf, R and L. Heering (eds.) (1995). Causes of International Migration. Luxembourg: Eurostat.

Vertovec, S. (1999). "Conceiving and researching transnationalism", Ethnic and Racial Studies, 22(2):447-62.

Werbner, P. (1999). "Global pathways. Working-class cosmopolitans and the creation of transnational ethnic worlds", Social Anthropology, 7(1): 17-35.

Wimmer, A. and Glick Schiller, N. (2003). "Methodological nationalism, the social sciences and the study of migration: an essay in historical epistemology", International Migration Review, 37(3): 576-610.

Yaghmaian, B. (2005). Embracing the Infidel. New York: Delacorte Press.

Zirh, B. C. and Erdemir, A. (2008). "From raindrops to hailstones: Environments of insecurity in the case of immigration from Turkey to London", in Rittersberger-Tilic, H. et al. (eds.) Rethinking Global Migration: Practices, Policies and Discourses in the European Neighbourhood, Ankara, Turkey: KORA - Center for Black Sea and Central Asia and Middle East Technical University, pp. 177-185.

CHAPTER 7

"Old" natives and "new" immigrants: beyond territory and history in Kymlicka's account of group-rights

Darian Heim

Introduction

Imagine that the Chinese in Canada claimed the same rights as the Québécois. This would involve among other things a public administration and schools run in Chinese or a regional Chinese parliament with wide-ranging autonomies. However, some might reply, none of the institutions needed to sustain Chinese culture in Canada have been created so far. Such scepticism notwithstanding, this example can be revealing for discussing the underlying normative question: on what grounds are the rights of "old" minorities, as the Québécois, different from "new" immigrant groups, such as the Chinese? The answer, for some, lies in the fact that the Québécois – and not the Chinese – have a history on their territory.

Will Kymlicka holds such a view in this thought-experiment (Kymlicka, 2001: 160). In his theory, only "historical" national groups[1] have a right to political self-determination and can engage in a process of "nation-building". Immigrant groups have waived this right upon leaving their homeland. Indeed, Kymlicka argues, they have neither been able nor willing to take up such a process.[2] Barring the Chinese in Canada from this right is a *normative* argument which hinges on *empirical* premises as the following: immigrants' preferences and which group has arrived first on a territory – e.g. the Québécois in Canada.

This paper analyses Kymlicka's conclusion of this thought-experiment. To do so is both necessary and fruitful. His typology of groups – national, indigenous, and immigrant – in diverse societies has, on the one hand, served as a benchmark for the moral or normative[3] entitlements of minorities since the appearance of *Multicultural Citizenship* in 1995. On the other hand, Kymlicka's empirical facts of history and territory serve as explicit criteria for the differentiation between old and new groups. Nevertheless, in this paper I will be disapproving of these criteria and argue that they are inconclusive for the analysis of group-rights – history and territory are morally contingent factors beyond the control of individuals that privilege national groups unfairly over immigrants. And even if Kymlicka claims that immigrants have had no interest in being granted more rights, this preference cannot be based on an artefact of the social, cultural and political conditions

---

[1] I take them to include the majority, national minorities as well as indigenous peoples on a given territory.
[2] "The historical evidence is that the capacity and motivation to undertake such an ambitious nation-building project is only found in national minorities, rather than immigrant groups" (Kymlicka, 2001: 159).
[3] For the purpose of this paper I will use the terms "moral" and "normative" interchangeably as attributes about how the world *should* be according to our best ideals – which are not the same as existing laws.

determined by the national group. Given that Kymlicka's goal is an inclusive and fair coexistence between groups immigrants are justified in claiming more rights, even for projects as ambitious as "nation-building".

In the following section, I will critically assess Kymlicka's account and focus on three aspects: (i) how history and territory prioritises "old" national over "new" foreign minorities; (ii) what this implies for immigrants in national substate minorities; and (iii) why recognition of all minorities matters. In the last section, I will be discussing the potential of criteria for collective rights other than history and territory: merit, participation, and need. While none replaces history and territory altogether, a sharper focus on need in particular is a better warrant for Kymlicka's own goal: inclusion.

Kymlicka's multicultural agenda

History, territory, and minorities enjoying priority

Kymlicka has traditionally focussed on the status of "old", i.e. settled "homeland" minorities rather than "new" groups who have immigrated recently.[4] Issues involving immigrants are, as a consequence, discussed mostly in contrast to "national" minorities. And this focus is due to the fact that most conflicts in the world coincide with the presence of national minorities. Immigrants, in turn, are not as violent and organised as national minorities:

> "[T]he presence of migrant workers is rarely a source of civil war or ethnic insurgencies. Even when migrant workers are mistreated and exploited, as they are in much of the world, they rarely take up arms, or seek to overthrow the state" (Kymlicka, 2007: 175).

Does this passage imply that immigrants would need to take up arms to achieve similar rights as "homeland" minorities? Kymlicka provides two observations: first, no recent immigrant group has voiced demands of self-determination, and second, the international community has pursued only "half-hearted" attempts in this direction.[5] His response turns thus around how things *are*. But why *should* immigrant minorities have less rights?

According to Kymlicka, it is because they have not been on their host society's territory for long enough.[6] National groups, in turn, have an independent and continued history which has given rise to their distinct cultural traits.[7] And this historical "societal culture" provides the members of groups "with meaningful ways of life across the full range of human activities, including social, educational,

---

[4] Cf. Kymlicka (2007, 2011a, 2011b). As to the limitations of this approach, cf. Parekh (1997: 62): "[Kymlicka's] theory is unduly heavily mortgaged to his moral preferences. It would also seem that it is deeply embedded in and in part an articulation of the Canadian political reality. While this political context and the concomitant historical experiences give it a focus and vitality, they also limit its wider application."

[5] Cf. Kymlicka (2007: 175). Such attempts are, e.g., the 1990 UN Convention for the Rights of Migrant Workers. More generally, there is a consensus in normative and legal theory that *a* set of rights for migrants exists – only few question, e.g., the right to family unification. But the concrete scope of these rights tends to be controversial, i.e. whether it extends to the core or wider family (Carens, 2013: 179ff.).

[6] Kymlicka (2007: 226): "...liberal multiculturalism does attach importance to facts of history and territory."

[7] Kymlicka (1995: 19): "I am using 'a culture' as synonymous with 'a nation' or 'a people'—that is, as an intergenerational community, more or less institutionally complete, occupying a given territory or homeland, sharing a distinct language and history."

religious, recreational, and economic life, encompassing both public and private spheres" (Kymlicka, 1995: 76). Having a culture is thus essential to lead an autonomous life. Without the background of a "territorially concentrated" (ibid.) historical culture, individuals would make their choices from "nowhere" – a logical and empirical impossibility. And since immigrants cannot re-create their societal culture in the hosting country, they are better off adapting to the "mainstream" culture, at least in public life (Kymlicka, 1995: 96).

This account of a societal culture shaped by history aims thus at protecting territorially bound national minorities from the pressure of more dominant groups.[8] Immigrants, however, experience the same pressure even if they are not in "their" territory, regardless of whether they live in a region of the national majority or minority. However, Kymlicka's priority of national groups due to their territorial history clashes with his general concern of protecting weaker groups. If the aim of his theory is to protect minorities from the discretion of majorities, then the history of those groups should play no role. To wit, the majority could theoretically also be an immigrant group which does not pressure other groups.

In practise – and in contrast to the theoretical *normative* conclusion –, national minorities appear to better defend their culture than immigrants. And this brings us back to the starting point which is the blurred distinction between reality and morality. It is not clear where Kymlicka's statements are to be placed:

> "The assumption that national minorities are the potential cause of, or pretext for, geo-political conflict has been omnipresent in all of the international deliberations (...) As a result, discussions of national minority rights are heavily 'securitised', in a way that precludes recognition of, or even discussion of, the 'common normative considerations' that connect indigenous peoples and national minorities" Kymlicka (2011a: 202).

If Kymlicka is concerned about the spill-over effects of national minorities' reputation on the "normative" claims of other groups, why does he stop short of immigrants? It is not clear why they are categorically less vulnerable than indigenous groups. But more generally, even if national minorities involve more violence, this fact cannot justify the priority of their rights over those of other groups. Under ideal conditions of mutual fairness – and this is the playing field Kymlicka (1995: 99) seems to have chosen – violence is not legitimate. The priority of the rights of national groups, justified in this manner, thus falls. But is there no other way to accommodate immigrants within host societies – if they so wish at all?

Minorities within minorities: artefacts and limited identities

According to Kymlicka, immigrants are entitled to "polyethnic rights". These encompass, e.g., public funding for cultural practises, exemptions from laws which disadvantage certain religions (e.g. wearing helmets for Sikhs), or the right to

---

[8] Torbisco Casals (2006: 8) points out that the principle of territory was introduced after the French Revolution: as the new basis for granting citizenship, it has replaced feudal privileges of inherited social rank (clergy, nobility, and "serving" estate). My motivation is similar in spirit. If territory and history justify group-rights then certain groups are favoured analogous to the feudal nobility: the right kind of citizenship, so justified, is "an inherited status that greatly enhances one's life chances" (Carens, 1987: 252).

bilingual education. These rights serve "to promote [fairer] integration into larger society, not self-government" (Kymlicka, 1995: 31). Moreover, immigrants should take part in "negotiating" (or rejecting) the aspirations of some national minorities to become independent if they live in their territory (Kymlicka 2011b). For the Scottish independence project, for instance, to be successful and legitimate, Pakistani immigrants should voice their conditions for joining this project (ibid.). In fact, any citizenship idea, be it in favour or against the independence of substate national minorities, has to be more inclusive of immigrants, Kymlicka argues.

However, this inclusiveness is limited. Immigrants can adopt the discourses of two mutually exclusive groups: either the substate minority or the majority nation-state.[9] Beyond their "polyethnic" rights, immigrants thus have to adapt their own identity to fit either discourse of recognised "nations" and eventually integrate into the dominant national minority or majority.[10] And the space for multiple identities is restricted due to Kymlicka's "monolithic" and homogenous vision of intra-group identity:

"By making the concept of a societal culture (with monolingual speakers on a mononational territory) as the empirical and normative starting point, Kymlicka tends to homogenize cultures through a rather dubious and biased bottle-neck" (De Schutter, 2005: 30).

The bottle-neck being that the importance of a societal culture resides in the membership in *a* locally dominant group, and not one's own culture. But if this is true, then "it is unclear how he can stop at polyethnic rights, and not proceed to self-government [for ethnic immigrants]" (Choudhry, 2002: 62). If polyethnic rights protect *immigrants'* distinct culture, why should they still integrate into *a* mainstream culture, be it majority's or national minority's?

Now, in practical terms, a certain convergence and a common cultural basis to guarantee everyday interaction among the members of a society seem necessary. But this argument is compatible with immigrants having no less rights than national minorities – having *a* common language is what matters. And to decide this question on the basis of history and territory systematically and unfairly handicaps immigrants. But polyethnic rights do not make things easier: they have to remain "consistent" and serve the integration to the mainstream, i.e. limited to "the private sphere—at home and in voluntary association" without involving "the establishment of distinct and institutionally complete societal cultures" (Kymlicka, 1995: 78).

Alternatively, implementing a right to national self-determination for immigrants might be too costly as it would imply a change in the institutional

---

[9] Kymlicka (2011a) works with the same implicit assumption. However, there might be no alternative because groups compete with each other. That is, in order to sustain its cultural practises over time, a group needs a high degree of "institutional completeness", i.e. its own media, charities, commerce, churches, schools, etc. (Breton 1964; for the nature and completeness of immigrants' institutions: Choudhry, 2002; for an overview of the recent general literature: Léger, 2014: 424-425). But even if there is such competition, no group should unfairly be privileged at the cost of another. And my argument is that considerations of history and territory unfairly favour national groups over immigrants.

[10] Cf. Young (1997). According to her, "ethnic" migrants have no choice than to assimilate to the national territorial culture – the sovereignty over which is under dispute in the regions under discussion here.

language, the adaptation of curricula, and require nationals to learn a new language, etc. Cost of transition, however, is a poor normative benchmark – it perpetuates deeply entrenched injustices (Carens 2000). This is why I use the term "normative" throughout this paper as transcending these costs.[11] History and territory describe best how certain groups have achieved their status, but they are not decisive for the question as to which group *should* enjoy how many rights.[12] Otherwise, individuals turn into slaves of past actions of their ancestors – factors beyond control and hence beyond their liability, blame or praise. This arbitrariness of history and territory is problematic.

One argument, however, might trump all previous considerations. What if immigrants genuinely preferred to integrate into the national group where they emigrated to? In the UK, for instance, immigrants generally feel quite "British" (Kymlicka, 2011b: 284). Indeed, immigrants themselves might, upon leaving their homeland, *voluntarily* accept to integrate into the society of arrival.[13] However, this assumption is controversial[14] and it is critically addressed more in detail elsewhere (Choudhry, 2002). For now, consider the following counter-argument: Kymlicka's argument is based on an artefact.

An example of such an artefact is when immigrants identify with the dominant group to achieve another goal, e.g. overcome their relative socio-economic disadvantage. But feeling "British" does not make one less disadvantaged. Their expressed preferences to integrate might thus not be "manifestations of the natural phenomenon under investigation" (Hilpinen, 2011). And the phenomenon under investigation here is their *genuine* will to integrate. The declared self-perception as "British" is an artefact of the dominant social arrangement just as "a path through a forest (…) can be an unintended product of people's habit of following the same route when they walk through the forest" (ibid.). But there might be paths to overcome disadvantage other than identifying with the majority. Alternatives which are not considered due to an unjustified fixation with existing national groups.

How to get to the bottom of their preferences then? Individuals need to be able to make decisions free of constraints and limitations.[15] And the options Kymlicka's theory offers are unnecessarily limited. His account does not guarantee immigrants'

---

[11] Kymlicka himself seems to understand "normative" in such a manner when he suggests that his argument applies only "in a just world [of ideal theory]" (Kymlicka, 1995: 99). My present account stands thus in line with Kymlicka's own "left-wing liberal egalitarianism" where "[morally arbitrary] inequalities which are not chosen or deserved—are unjust and should be rectified" (Kymlicka, 1998: 132).

[12] History and territory are inadequate normative factors even for justifying individual aspirations or the viability of institutional change because "they unduly limit our sense of the possible" (Choudhry, 2002: 67).

[13] "[Immigrants] voluntarily relinquished their national membership, and the national rights which go with it" (Kymlicka, 1995: 62). Voluntariness is central to distinguish immigrant from national minorities. According to Kymlicka, only the latter "are involuntarily incorporated members" (Kukathas, 2003: 580). This characterisation of immigrants as *voluntary* is crucial because it does not demand for any rectification or any recognition within "luck egalitarianism" – the philosophical tradition of his theory.

[14] "[M]any immigrants do not come voluntarily: children, refugees, displaced persons fleeing war or famine, all move less because they want to than because they are forced to by others or circumstances. Equally, some national minorities have every opportunity to choose voluntarily between living as adherents of a minority culture or as cosmopolitans. (…) [I]t is not the voluntariness of their choices that (…) provides the basis for their differential treatment in a multicultural society" (Kukathas, 2003: 580).

[15] Asking why other immigrant groups have not managed to re-create their culture to the same degree as the Cubans in Miami, Rubio-Marín (2003: 172) concludes: "From this it does not follow that they would not do so, were they given the option and were they to find the right environment."

genuine consent to integration. Surely, life is full of constraints and not all are illegitimate. But my account describes an ideal which we should aim to implement in our everyday practises. And conceiving immigrants' rights in dependence of those of national minorities – but not on their own – is no step in this direction. This does not mean that Kymlicka's categorisation is useless. New and old minorities are treated differently in public administration on grounds he has laid out. However, these practises do not have to inform our *normative* demands.

Recognition, fairness, and integration

In Kymlicka's reasoning, individuals have special rights through their belonging to a collective. And this membership needs to be defined by objective criteria such as history and territory. Such an account calls thus for a contextual, case-specific, and "targeted" analysis of each group. This contrasts with universal and "generic" rights and duties attributed to members of all groups (Kymlicka, 2007: 199ff.).

This distinction is useful when we attempt to mediate between individual and collective rights. A woman, for instance, might have to choose between following the traditions of her religious community and her right to gender-equality. But she might consent to the specific gender role her religion prescribes as a matter of her autonomy.[16] This line of reasoning stands in the tradition of a debate on the "politics of recognition" (Taylor 1995). A central premise is that individuals can and do identify as members of a group. And this identity deserves to be recognised and protected. Depending on this specific background, issues of fairness or distribution should be dealt with differently (cf. Eisenberg; 2005, 2009).

Kymlicka's account is similar. Any minority right is one of "external protection" from possible interventions – even if the majority considers it tricky, the woman from our example could not be forbidden to abide by the traditional rules of her group. But this conception excludes anti-liberal "internal restrictions", i.e. the oppression or unequal treatment of an individual member in the name of the culture of her group.[17] This is why in Kymlicka's liberal theory, individuals can choose the culture they belong to, demand change within or, as a last resort, actively opt out of it (Kymlicka, 1995: 33-45).[18]

This is an argument about the internal functioning of groups and not about its relative position compared to other groups. It would thus be possible – and indeed more coherent and liberal – to leave it to immigrants to choose between integration

---

[16] Cf. Eisenberg (2005: 52ff.). One could argue that this sort of assumption is equally prone to the artefact objection I made earlier-on: how to guarantee that a woman's choice, for instance, to wear a niqab is not the result of her being socialised by her community into endorsing this oppressed role? The presence of safe and achievable exit options is indeed primordial for a *real* choice – and there is no *real* alternative for immigrants to either feel "British" or "Scottish" in Kymlicka's theory.

[17] "[A] liberal view requires *freedom within* the minority group, and *equality between* the minority and majority groups" (Kymlicka, 1995: 152). The subordination of women, e.g., does thus not stem from group rights. Note that "[e]xternal protections are legitimate only in so far as they promote equality between groups, by rectifying disadvantages or vulnerabilities suffered by the members of a particular group" (ibid.). In principle, immigrants hence qualify for external protection from national groups.

[18] However, if an immigrant in Canada decides not be, e.g., Chinese anymore, she does not automatically become Canadian. Group-belonging is not only an individual choice but also a matter of collective recognition – merely deciding to be Canadian does not make one hold a Canadian passport with all its rights and duties.

and political self-determination and to weigh their costs and benefits.[19] However, Kymlicka is unequivocal on this possibility: "immigrant groups are not 'nations', and do not occupy homelands" (Kymlicka, 1995: 14).[20] "And they never will…" I am tempted to add in line with his reasoning. The problem is that even if immigrants have left their homeland, even if they prefer to integrate, and even if they do not voice a clear demand for self-determination as national minorities – even then, they should not, explicitly or through unintentional institutional design, be hindered from pursuing a national project peacefully. Not doing so is to mistake an "is" for an "ought" – which is an inverted normative logic (Choudhry, 2002: 67ff.).

Therefore, Kymlicka's contextual analysis grounded on facts of history and territory favours national groups over immigrants. This does not match, however, his overall goal of empowering minorities and ensuring a "fairer integration" of immigrants in the receiving society (Kymlicka, 2001: 162ff.). Yet, one might reply, this is still better than a Hobbesian state of nature and no objective criteria at all for judging competing claims between groups. If this is true, are there better alternatives then?

Beyond history and territory: alternative criteria for minority rights

Before discussing a list of such alternative candidates, note that criteria of group identification do not have to be of ethnic nature to be objective.[21] Instead they can be based on institutional or cultural facts, e.g. religion, language, or collective history. Assuming that objective criteria are feasible and desirable, I shall not argue that history and territory are no grounds to differentiate groups and their rights but rather that they *alone* are not. Combined with criteria of merit, participation, and need, a fairer account of group rights can be achieved. The goal of this section is thus mainly to highlight the intuitive possibility and rough limits of such a plurality of considerations.

Merit: recognition needs to be deserved

Several Western States naturalise foreigners who serve in their armed forces.[22] The idea is that an individual can *deserve* to become a national.[23] Although this case is about individuals entering a collective – and not about the rights of collectives themselves – its underlying logic can be useful for the current discussion:

---

[19] It is another question of whether engaging in a "nation-building" process would be in the interest of immigrants or how many would eventually take it up. One of the cornerstones of liberal theory, however, is that nothing is said about what a *good* decision involves. Liberalism guarantees the right conditions for autonomous choices – being barred from certain choices on arbitrary grounds does not enhance that goal.

[20] More generally, this possibility would clash with Kymlicka's distinction between "contextual" and "generic" analysis: "Any attempt to articulate liberal multiculturalism as if it were purely a matter of generic minority rights is doomed to failure. The logic of multiculturalism cannot be captured in the form (…) 'all persons belonging to minorities have a right to X'" (Kymlicka, 2007: 79).

[21] Theoretically, choosing a group identity can be based on non-objective criteria. In a perfectly liberal society they might be totally subjective to the point that there was no group identity anymore. In Marx' (1845) Communist utopia, "to hunt in the morning, fish in the afternoon, rear cattle in the evening, criticise after dinner [is possible] … without ever becoming hunter, fisherman, herdsman or critic."

[22] The French Foreign Legion is well known. Eligibility to French citizenship follows after three years of service or after being wounded in combat. But other states, e.g. the US or Spain, know similar rules.

[23] In political philosophy, it is more common to speak of considerations of "desert" rather than merit, but for the purpose of simplicity I will not delve into this technicality.

recognition is conditional of contributions also in fields other than national defence – improving the balance of the social security system, excelling in construction or engineering, mediating of conflicts or filling gaps of the internal labour market, e.g. nursing or elderly care. These are all potential considerations on the basis of which individuals of certain groups could deserve (more) rights.

Such an account is clearly less prone to the arbitrariness of considerations of history and territory – immigrants can actively improve their situation. However, not all immigrants might qualify as soldiers, nurses, engineers, or mediators. Not all will have the necessary talent. And considerations based on talent are ultimately as unchosen and arbitrary as reference to history and territory. Arguably, considerations of merit are *less* exclusive as some immigrants will have the necessary talents. What is sure is that contributions to public goods other than national security deserve rewards similar to those granted when serving in the armed forces. Take the Chinese workers who have worked, often under critical conditions, in the construction of Canadian railways throughout the last two centuries (the "coolies"). They, and their descendants, would have deserved to be naturalised, granted cultural or even political self-determination depending on the sacrifice or risk of their contribution. The list could be supplemented with more contemporary examples (e.g. health care).

Participation: interaction as a sign of genuine interest

In legal theory, there are two well-known principles about how citizenship can be acquired: *ius sanguinis* and *ius soli*. Whereas the first is historical (citizenship is inherited from one's parents) and the second is territorial (citizenship comes from the State where one is born), a third principle is discussed in the literature: the "genuine, effective link" of integration[24] – candidates for naturalisation need to prove a link with the local society and culture based on participation and integration.[25] This way of acquiring a new nationality allows individuals to express their preferences beyond historic and territorial considerations. This legal concept is thus instructive as an alternative criterion for granting rights.

In this spirit, members of an immigrant group could serve the public good by getting involved in community councils, civil rights movements, sports or cultural associations, NGOs or the like. Such a criterion is less prone to the arbitrariness of history and territory or even talent. That is, such participation depends on sacrificing personal time in a common project where different tasks are available, e.g. administration, public relations, education. Individuals of a certain group can take responsibilities according to their capabilities.

These are the advantages. The major drawback, however, is that immigrants have to bring an *additional* effort to achieve the rights of locals. Whereas non-participative nationals still enjoy the privileged rights of their group, immigrants have to bring themselves in to achieve a better status. Moreover, group-

---

[24] Cf. Adjami & Harrington (2008). The origin of this way of conceiving nationality, as well as the specific wording quoted here, are found in the so-called "Nottebohm-case" from 1955: Lichtenstein vs. Guatemala (ICJ), according to: http://www.icj-cij.org/docket/files/ 18/2674.pdf, last retrieved: 31/08/2015.

[25] In practical terms, this clause is usually combined with the requirement of legal residence of a minimum duration within the hosting State. It is thus not a perfectly independent alternative to history and territory.

participation is a double-edged sword: in its negative form, all immigrants can be lumped together and in the positive, only the individual effort is rewarded with more rights or naturalisation. That is, those members of the immigrant group who do participate are reduced to those who do not.[26] This might tear a group apart into the participative ones and those who are not, and lead to a dilemma: either one's people are left behind or one renounces to a better status. Nationals do not impose such a choice on their own members. If the definition of participation is too easily manipulated and too sensitive to the mentioned problems, then we are well-advised to look for a better criterion.

Need: the most inclusive and just option

Next to positive contributions which can lead to greater recognition, there are also criteria which arise from negative considerations, e.g. incurred harm or socio-economic disadvantage. Those in need should be granted greater recognition since they belong to a group whose members require assistance.[27] Surely, there will be poor and rich – the more and less needy – among immigrants as well as within national minorities. But if members of a certain group have a significant and systematic need then this group has to be protected and their situation improved. And I take it that poverty is still one of the main motivations for many to migrate in the first place. This makes them vulnerable and in need of assistance at different levels: economically as they take low-paying jobs, socially as they tend to cluster in tough neighbourhoods, health-wise as they engage in risky professions, psychologically as they experience acculturation and alienation, etc.

Now, why would a right to political self-determination improve their situation? If at all, it would seem in the interest of the privileged to get rid of the needy. The point of this paper, however, is not its *actual* implementation but rather the claim that immigrants' categorical exclusion from such rights is untenable as we have seen in the prior sections of this paper. Recognising that – in principle – immigrants are entitled to the same rights as national groups might tackle some causes which lead to immigrants being in need in the first place: e.g. discrimination, exploitation, and exclusion. And for this purpose it is essential that members of national groups *see* the arbitrariness of their privilege and *act* to minimise its impact – which is the goal of this paper.

Need has furthermore a cross-cultural character which goes beyond national boundaries. It inclusiveness has a major intuitive appeal: few question that, e.g. disabled people need assistance or that both a local professor and settled foreign fruit-picker are entitled to unemployment benefits. Need can also account for the claims of national minorities towards the majority. If they can prove to have been discriminated and marginalised due to their origin, they can appeal to the need of self-government as a remedy for the wrong-doing. Referring to history and

---

[26] This account is deliberately simplified in order to provide an outline of the alternatives discussed above. Notably, it makes abstraction from national advocacy movements in favour of immigrants.

[27] The normative issue is more complex. The non-needy who pay the assistance cannot always be held responsible for their need. However, such net contributors are not entitled to any privilege that accrues from their not being in need – or, only to the extent that it benefits the worst off (Rawls 1971). Despite being a historical criterion, need is the most promising candidate for granting rights because it addresses *negative* arbitrary outcomes, rather than being based on *positive* arbitrary privileges.

territoriality (alone) does not help in this context. Need is a better alternative.

Taking stock: a Chinese "national" minority in Northern America?

Recall the initial thought-experiment of this paper. Kymlicka states that it is possible for "an immigrant group within the United States or Canada — say, the Chinese — (…) *in theory* (…) to become a national minority, if they settle together and acquire self-governing powers" (Kymlicka, 2001: 160).[28] But as none of Chinese public institutions have been created so far, Kymlicka concludes, they are entitled merely to polyethnic rights and not to political self-determination as *actual* and established national minorities.

However, the state of affairs should result from our normative ideals and not vice-versa. Even beyond strictly normative considerations, I have argued here, Kymlicka's priority of national minorities has several drawbacks: (i) it implies that violence is a promising strategy for groups to obtain more rights, (ii) it assumes rather than proves that immigrants genuinely prefer to integrate into the hosting culture, and (iii) it fosters the exclusion rather than the "fair" integration of immigrants by unduly limiting their identities to locally dominant and historical "nations" – they can either be "British" or "Scottish".

I have discussed three alternative objective criteria to history and territory: the Chinese in Canada should be granted more rights if they a) *deserve* it based on their substantial contributions to a public good, e.g. serving national armed forces; b) have *participated* in democratic or social processes of the host society, e.g. by fostering trade relations with the Chinese homeland; or c) share characteristics of *need*, e.g. socio-economic disadvantage and marginalisation. It is true that these considerations are historical on their own: whether one has the right talent to contribute or a recognised need are both arbitrary results. This is why I advocate a fair plurality of different considerations without prioritising history and territory, where agents have more control over the outcomes. Arbitrariness is central only in its negative form – those who have suffered harm are prioritised over those who already benefit from belonging to a privileged group.

Acknowledgements

I thank the participants and organizers of the EURAC workshop on "Old and New Minorities" held in February 2015 in Bozen (Italy) for valuable comments on an earlier version of this paper. My argument has improved substantially thanks to the feedback provided by Paula Casal, Enric Bea Seguí, Marcos Andrade Moreno, and the referees of this journal. I would also acknowledge funding provided by the Swiss National Science Foundation – SNF.

References

Adjami, M. and Harrington, J. (2008). "The Scope and Content of Article 15 of The Universal Declaration of Human Rights", *Refugee Survey Quarterly*, 27 (3): 93-109.

Breton, R. (1964). "Institutional Completeness of Ethnic Communities and the Personal Relations of Immigrants", *The*

---

[28] In fact, he expands that immigrants would need to behave just as the English, Spanish, or French colonisers did in the New World to achieve this goal. This analogy of his is unfortunate as it endorses my earlier point on incentivising violence. It also illustrates the arbitrariness of drawing a line of *whose* history guarantees more rights on *what* territory and *when* it does not.

American Journal of Sociology, 70 (2): 193-205.

Carens, J. H. (1987). "Aliens and Citizens: The Case for Open Borders", *Review of Politics,* 49: 251–273.

Carens, J. H. (2000). *Culture, Citizenship, and Community: A Contextual Exploration of Justice as Evenhandedness.* New York: Oxford University Press.

Carens, J. H. (2013). *The Ethics of Immigration.* New York: Oxford University Press.

Choudhry, S. (2002). "National Minorities and Ethnic Immigrants: Liberalism's Political Sociology", *The Journal of Political Philosophy*, 10 (1): 54-78.

De Schutter, H. (2005). "Nations, Boundaries and Justice: on Will Kymlicka's Theory of Multinationalism", *Ethical Perspectives: Journal of the European Ethics Network*, 11 (1): 17-40.

Eisenberg, A. (2005). "Identity and Liberal Politics: The Problem of Minorities Within Minorities." In: A. Eisenberg and J. Spinner-Halev (eds.) *Minorities Within Minorities. Equality, Rights, and Diversity*, New York: Cambridge University Press.

Eisenberg, A. (2009). *Reasons of Identity.* New York: Oxford University Press.

Hilpinen, R. (2011): "Artifact". In: *Stanford Encyclopedia of Philosophy.* Retrieved from http://plato.stanford.edu/entries/artifact/, last access: 18/02/2014.

Kukathas, C. (2003). "Immigration". In: LaFollette, H. (ed.). *The Oxford Handbook of Practical Ethics.* New York: Oxford University Press.

Kymlicka, W. (1995). *Multicultural Citizenship. A Liberal Theory of Minority Rights.* New York: Oxford University Press.

Kymlicka, W. (1998). "Liberal Egalitarianism and Civic Republicanism: Friends or Enemies?". In: A. L. Allen and M. C. Regan (eds.) *Debating Democracy's Discontent. Essays on American Politics, Law, and Public Philosophy*, New York: Oxford University Press.

Kymlicka, W. (2001). *Politics in the Vernacular: Nationalism, Multiculturalism and Citizenship.* New York: Oxford University Press.

Kymlicka, W. (2007). *Multicultural Odysseys. Navigating the New International Politics of Diversity.* New York: Oxford University Press.

Kymlicka, W. (2011a). "Beyond the Indigenous/Minority Dichotomy?" In: S. Allen and A. Xanthaki (eds.) *Reflections on the UN Declaration on the Rights of Indigenous Peoples.* Oxford: Hart Publishing.

Kymlicka, W. (2011b): "Multicultural Citizenship Within Multination States", *Ethnicities*, 11 (3): 281-302.

Léger, R. (2014). "Non-territorial Autonomy: Reply to Chouinard", *Ethnopolitics: Formerly Global Review of Ethnopolitics*, 13 (4): 418-427.

Marx, K. (1845). *German Ideology.* Retrieved from http://www.marxists.org/ archive/marx/works/1845/german-ideology/ch01a.htm#a4, last access: 10/02/2014.

Parekh, B. (1997): "Dilemmas of Multicultural Theory of Citizenship", *Constellations*, 4 (1): 54-62.

Rawls, J. (1971). *Theory of Justice.* Revised edition 1999. Cambridge MA: Harvard University Press.

Rubio-Marín, R. (2003). "Exploring the Boundaries of Language Rights: Insiders, Newcomers, and Natives." In: S. Macedo and A. Buchanan (eds.) *NOMOS XLV: Secession and Self-Determination.* New York: New York University Press.

Taylor, C. (1994). "The Politics of Recognition." In: A. Gutman (ed.) *Multiculturalism. Examining the Politics of Recognition.* Princeton NJ: Princeton University Press.

Torbisco Casals, N. (2006). *Group Rights as Human Rights: A Liberal Approach to Multiculturalism.* Amsterdam: Springer.

Young, I. M. (1997). "A Multicultural Continuum: A Critique of Will Kymlicka's Ethnic-Nation Dichotomy", *Constellations*, 4 (1): 48-53.

PART 3: DATA AND METHODS IN MIGRATION STUDIES

Essential Reading:

Ullah, A. A., Hossain, M. A., Azizuddin, M., & Nawaz, F. (2020). Social Research Methods: Migration in Perspective. *Migration Letters*, 17(2), 357-368.

Iosifides, T., & Sporton, D. (2009). Biographical Methods in Migration Research. *Migration Letters*, 6(2), 101-108.

Mata-Codesal, D., Kloetzer, L., & Maiztegui-Oñate, C. (2020). Strengths, Risks and Limits of Doing Participatory Research in Migration Studies. *Migration Letters*, 17(2), 201-210.

Further Reading:

Berger, J., & Strohner, L. (2017). Economic Analysis of the Refugee Influx to Austria. *Border Crossing*, 7(1), 1-12.

Christou, A. (2009). Telling Diaspora Stories: theoretical and methodological reflections on narratives of migrancy and belongingness in the second generation. *Migration Letters*, 6(2), 143-153.

Czaika, M. (2005). A Refugee Burden Index: methodology and its application. *Migration Letters*, 2(2), 101-125.

Fleming, J. H., Esipova, N., Pugliese, A., Ray, J., & Srinivasan, R. (2018). DATA-SURVEY: Migrant Acceptance Index: A Global Examination of the Relationship Between Interpersonal Contact and Attitudes toward Migrants. *Border Crossing*, 8(1), 103-132.

Kanitkar, K. (2012). The European migrant experience. *Migration Letters*, 9(2), 177-191.

Ozkul, D. (2020). Participatory Research: Still a One-Sided Research Agenda?. *Migration Letters*, 17(2), 229-237.

Rother, N. (2010). The German Integration Panel: how to measure the influence of integration courses on migrants integration?. *Migration Letters*, 7(1), 43-55.

CHAPTER 8

Social Research Methods: Migration in Perspective

AKM Ahsan Ullah, Md. Akram Hossain, Mohammad Azizuddin, and Faraha Nawaz

Introduction

Migration research is newer than the phenomenon itself owing to the fact that the phenomenon per se received delayed attention from researchers, academia, policymakers and international communities. This resulted in deficiencies in unified-but-suitable migration research methods for various socioeconomic settings and geopolitical locales. As migration connects both developed and developing worlds and the recent proliferation of migrants all over the world suggests the importance of migration research at multidisciplinary level (Vargas-Silva, 2012). The striking fact is that scholarly interest in migration studies unprecedentedly increased over the last two decades. Two decades ago, migration research had a negligible presence in social scientific inquiry. Today, however, growing scholarly interest in migration is undisputable (Yalaz & Zapata-Barrero, 2017). 'While half a century ago, migration research was a peripheral area of study within traditional academic disciplines, today it has become a firmly established interdisciplinary field (Yalaz & Zapata-Barrero, 2017:3).'

Quantitative oriented researchers tend to place boundary from those who are qualitatively oriented and vice-versa. Quantitative method was leading in social science research until the 1980s when qualitative research approach arrived resulting in the emergence of mixed method approach (Creswell, 2014; Grove & Zwi, 2006) with an argument that the blend of the both yields a better outcome. Quantitatively garnered information is painlessly analyzable statistically and fairly reliable but it goes with criticism for not providing an in-depth description. Qualitative methods, however, provide a more in-depth and rich description of a phenomenon. Middle range theorist Robert Merton (1949) considers quantitative data as precise and systematic while qualitative data is less scientific, too imprecise, flexible and open-ended. Most studies had positivist approach than post-positivist. Anselm L. Strauss (1967) criticizes quantitative data that are typically forced to fit into the pre-formulated categories and concepts. They emphasize on rapport building and empathetic relationship with the subjects to better understand the social reality, which is possible in qualitative data (Layder, 2011; Ullah, 2016). Quantitative approaches—numerical measurements, which are the preferred methodologies of empirical, hypothetico-deductive and experimental migration research with aims to test hypotheses, and identifies numerical differences between the groups under study. Qualitative approaches, by contrast, associate with a broader theoretical critique of quantitative models.

We argue that no way is researching in normal condition similar to the precarious conditions [forced] migrants go through. The expansions of migration, demographic transformations, and its significant impact on social, political and economic life have brought unprecedented methodological challenges. Similarly, upholding an ethical standard at every stage of migration research is more relevant than other social research fields.

The obvious gap in migration research knowledge invites us to address the fact how differently migration research should be designed depending on geopolitical and socioeconomic settings. This paper deals with the ethical issues in any scientific research process and argues for special attention in migration research due to its complex nature of investigation with comparatively vulnerable group of people. This paper brings in knowledge garnered experientially from a number of researches conducted on migration in the South, South-East Asia, East Asia, North America, Europe and the MENA region.

What is special about migration research?

Methodologies for conducting migration research are never static as opposed to subject to modification with pattern of migration. Research methods that are generally applied in migration studies include quantitative such as inferential statistics, and qualitative methods such as ethnography and case study. Hoerder (2012) explains migration research as a translocal, transregional, and transcultural and transnational that requires an interdisciplinary approach. Due to the multidisciplinary and cross-country nature of migration research, it places extra demands on research methods, analysis, and rigorous attention to maintain ethical standard (Schweitzer, Melville, Steel, & Lacherez, 2006).

What makes migration a subject of investigation are processes like Europeanization, globalization, and economic polarization often problematizing the free movement of people (Tholen, 2005). Researchers attempt to address the challenges in migration research through employing multidisciplinary approaches, collecting data at cross-country level with the help of appropriate tools and techniques in order to have clear understanding about the processes, directions, volumes and patterns of migration (Phillips & Burbules, 2000).

Any research can be categorized into three groups: first, quantitative that adopts objective surveys and statistical analyses; second, qualitative that emphasizes on contextual analysis of human behaviour; and finally, mixed-method that combines the both. Experiences, however, bear out that each approach has affirmative attributes as well as limitations. This paper, therefore, emphasizes that depending on objectives of the research, types of migration, research questions and contexts and the logistical convenience researcher may go for either quantitative or qualitative or for both. It is a widely accepted fact that migrants cannot be moulded into a single category. While European migration research had its origin in studying guest workers in the 1950s and the 60s (Castles & Kosack, 1973), today, the category of the class has been largely in shadow. This is probably one of the first consequences of migration-related analytical frameworks such as transnationalism

(Levitt & Jaworsky, 2007) and super-diversity (Vertovec, 2007; 2015). Feminization of migration was documented a long time ago (Castles & Miller, 1993). As female migration is increasing, scholars expected to see gender becoming a prominent category in migration studies (Lee et al. 2014). We have not, however, observed an increase in the number of research that categorized migrants with respect to gender categories.

As the migration research requires ensuring objectivity, generalizability and reliability, researchers need to select the subjects through an unbiased manner. This paradigm produces quantifiable and reliable data that is usually generalizable to some larger population (Phillips & Burbules, 2000). However, Massey (1987; 2014) offered another approach to migration research, which is the Ethnosurvey. This is, however, explicitly designed to provide quantitative data for multi-level analysis by compiling data at the individual, household, and community levels (Massey, 1987). But, in this case, a representative sample survey is not required. The ethnosurvey, because of its costs and professional demands, is hard to implement within a representative sampling framework. Promising results obtained in applying the ethnosurvey to study immigration suggest that it may profitably be applied to investigate other longitudinal social processes as well, such as status attainment, occupational mobility, and residential mobility (Massey, 2014). We often use ethnographic studies but usually are time intensive. However, using Phenomenology to gain descriptions of the experiences would take less time if that is what the research is interested in describing.

When a particular research requires deeper perspectives about the subjects through immersion, researchers have to choose a qualitative approach. Here, the presence of researchers in data collection is crucial, and the results are highly contingent upon who conducts the research (Creswell, 2014; Leech, 2008).

With the continuous changes in the dynamics of migration, diverse methodological challenges are defining the landscape of migration research. Migrants could be irregular and undocumented and psychologically disturbed. They may be mourning the bereavement of their family members. They might be in search of their close ones who got lost at point of the transits; they might be looking for any opportunity for their mere survival. They might have escaped wars, persecution or gross human rights violations. All the migrant populations have a cultural context in whatever society is researchers need to be appreciative of the cultural context they come from. Wimmer and Schiller (2003) examine the 'problem' of methodological nationalism. Methodological nationalism is the naturalization of the nation-state by the social sciences.

Research methodology

Scholars identify elements of research in different ways, as Creswell (2014) defines it as the intersection or combination of three elements- philosophical ideas, strategies of inquiry, and specific methods to be used for data collection, analysis and interpretation. Yin (2009) terms it as logic of sequence that makes a bridge of the initial research questions to the best possible answers (p. 26). King et al. (1994) focus on four components of research design: research question, theory, data collection and analysis. Similarly, Yin (2009) mentions about five components of research design. The first three components; research questions, propositions and units of analysis, indicate what data to be collected whereas the rest two components are data linked with the propositions and the data analysis.

Researchers make a number of decisions during the research design process. The implementation strategies of those decisions are quite different across the methodological approaches- qualitative, quantitative or mixed-method. Depending on the research design, a researcher employs pertinent techniques for data collection and analysis. For example, quantitative design includes survey and experiment methods; ethnographies and case studies under qualitative approach; while mixed-method brings both together in different forms, e.g. explanatory (starts with quantitative then qualitative), exploratory (qualitative to quantitative), and convergent (both at the same time) etc.

When researchers get to do research in an unconventional situation, some non-traditional methods are recommended to apply for example, rapid research assessment (RRA). This is a combination of RRA and Qualitative Research (QLR). This may make these methodologies more cost-effective and closer to local conditions, but they produced complementary and systematic outputs, and not holistic ones (Schonhuth & Kielvelitz, 1994:51-71).

Debates on methods: The most common notion about the difference is that qualitative method uses words, meanings, narratives, open-ended questions in interviews while quantitative method deals with numbers, uses closed-ended questions in surveys and experiments. Cresswell (2014) explains the gradations of differences between the two approaches from three perspectives: philosophical assumptions, research strategies, methods employed for data collection and analysis. Here, researchers study things in their natural settings, attempting to make sense of, or interpret, phenomena in terms of the meanings people bring to them (Denzin & Lincoln, 2018). It involves a variety of empirical case study, personal experience, introspective, life story, interview, observational, historical, interactions, and visual texts the described routine and problematic moments and meanings in individuals' lives (Strauss, 2007; Kerlinger, 1964; Cresswell, 2014).

The common argument is that in quantitative research generalization is widely accepted where inferences are made from sample to population, but is more difficult and challenging for the results derived from qualitative research (Polit & Beck, 2010). Therefore, qualitative research findings, however, are not aimed at generalizing a wider population.

The debates on generalizability revolve around different sampling techniques and the representativeness. Quantitative method follows the principle of probability (e.g. random, stratified, cluster techniques etc.) whereas qualitative research uses non-probability techniques (convenience, quota, purposive, snowball etc.). Probability sample ensures that everyone in the population has an equal chance to be selected in the sample hence it is unbiased (Daniel, 2012). The representativeness of samples is the main issue of contention among the research methodologists. Scholars arrived at a consensus that representative samples could hardly be achieved due to constraints like complex nature of society and culture, non-availability of sample frame and the possibility of non-responses (Gobo, 2004). However, if inferences are not a precondition for the research, representativeness is not obligatory (Gomm, Hammersley & Foster, 2000; Bailey, 1978; Sandelowski, 1997; Ullah, 2015).

If the objectives of the particular research are to go deep into the phenomenon then there is no point to take a large sample. Large samples do not necessarily provide in-depth information, and a qualitative study concerns with the quality of information rather than quantity of data. Therefore, the number of cases is not relevant in qualitative study. Nevertheless, scholars from qualitative research challenge this particular debate and provide strong arguments in favour of generalizability of findings from few cases (even a single case), even though the samples are non-representative (Flyvbjerg, 2006; Yin, 2009; Layder, 2011; Weis & Willems, 2017).

Mixed method approach: The above demonstrates evidences of dichotomous relationship between qualitative and quantitative research methods. Researchers in both domains are found quite 'antagonistic' to each other where one group of researchers presents arguments to relegate others. We think the necessity should determine the kind of approach to be adopted. Cresswell (2014), in this context, argues that instead of being polar opposites or dichotomies, qualitative and quantitative researchers should work together representing different ends on a continuum. In the mixed method, qualitative methods are often treated as starting points or foundational strategies that are followed by quantitative methodologies (Newman & Benz, 1998). Similarly, Creswell (2014) states that the qualitative phase may contribute to building an appropriate instrument or specify variables to be used in the follow-up quantitative phase. Qualitative researchers think that this support undermines the role of qualitative research. Supportive role, however, can be performed by both methods to improve the quality of research through an integrated effort (Bazeley, 2003). In fact, we noticed from numerous major researches conducted on migration and refugees, qualitative and quantitative approaches play a complementary role to each other and thus strengthen research findings. A researcher needs to make a decision about particular method to be employed depending on the research questions, arguments and objectives to be addressed. Newman and Benz (1998) state that research question guides the research methods not vice versa. Similarly, Mcmahon (1999) suggests that the method should not dictate whether the research is qualitative or quantitative.

Therefore, a fundamental question arises that what approach best fits in migration research given the fact that migration takes place under a range of circumstances such as a sample frame might be notoriously difficulty to locate, and a migrant under stress (for a range of reasons) may not be in a position to talk to a researcher. Does this imply that quantitative research is not possible to conduct on migrants? We believe in such circumstance, the mixed-method is a good approach to go about. Mixed method research resides in the middle of the qualitative-quantitative continuum that incorporates the elements of both qualitative and quantitative approaches (Newman & Benz, 1998). There are rooms for flexibilities.

Migration researchers need to be reflexive about their own positions in social settings, our own thought categories, beliefs, emotions, points of view and conceptual schemes. Matters of relations between the researcher(s) and research participants, reflexivity and positionality are of great importance, as they are part of or influence significantly the theoretical and conceptual frameworks at hand, the ways that data are collected and produced and the approaches within which findings are interpreted and presented (Denzin & Lincoln, 2018; Iosifides, 2008). Mystifying reality is vital in researching migration processes and phenomena. Racism, for example, of any form and type, either every day, institutional, collective or political, is one such set of interpretations and discourses, which tend to mystify reality and obscure real relations of domination and exploitation.

Methods in migration research

Migration research field might be notoriously complex due to the diverse cultural background of the subjects. They might be from multi-ethnic and vulnerable groups, and difficult to reach out. As a result, investigators undergo several challenges (i.e. locating data sources, access to data, analyzing the garnered evidences with appropriate contextual understanding). Scholars identify several challenges (lack of a clear sampling frame; constrained access to migrants due to their situation, hidden communities, security problems, issues of disclosure and lack of trust) that hinder adopting representative sampling in migration research (Birman, 2006; Jacobsen & Landau, 2003; Ullah, 2010; 2014; 2015). For example, it will be naïve to expect a sample frame from war-ravaged Syria or in Arakan in Myanmar due to lack of access to that area (Ullah, 2014; Ullah & Diotima, 2018). This implies that migration researchers in certain circumstance are left with no choice but to employ non-probability sampling techniques, like snowball or convenience sampling, though that increases the potential risk of bias and omission of large number of migrants (Jacobsen & Landau, 2003) who could provide different perspective to the findings. Due to the absence of adequate sampling frame respondent-driven sampling (RDS) and quota sampling are two common strategies in migration research (Gorny & Napierała, 2016). But, if a research is conducted on a refugee camp run under the UNHCR, there is highly likely that a sample frame is available. This means that quantitative approach could be applied and that a representative sample would be possible to draw.

If research is undertaken on the experiences of children and women, there are several approaches one can take. Then that is an interpretive question that would necessitate that researchers speak to directly and try to understand their individual experience of the of migration. The fact that the researcher is interested in vulnerable populations and women and children in particular might indicate that we are positioning ourselves within critical theories. The most appropriate methodologies are developed out of the specific theoretical understandings that undergird them. Without situation yourself theoretically and knowing what it is, exactly, it is impossible to determine which data collection method will help you achieve that aim.

Borkert et al. (2006) reiterate that research question in migration research should dictate what methodological approach to be adopted. This is not to ignore the fact that logistical convenience is something researchers have to take into account while designing the research. A researcher considers certain methods depending on some elements of philosophical reasoning. Ontological and epistemological positions have implications for the decision of a researcher about different methodological approaches.

A researcher considers certain methods depending on some elements of philosophical reasoning. Ontological and epistemological positions have implications for the decision of a researcher about different methodological approaches. The varying categorizations of such philosophical positions are anti-foundationalism/interpretivism/constructivism/ relativism (qualitative approach); foundationalism/positivism/objectivism (quantitative) and realism or pragmatism (mixed-method) (Cresswell, 2014; Iosifides, 2012). The mingling of the researcher's own orientation, philosophical worldview, consideration of potential risks, convenience and comfort with any particular approach can yield a better decision on which approach to apply. Hence, Vargas-Silva (2012) favours both qualitative, quantitative mixed-method approaches in migration research.

The research on migration can also accomplish in a sequential process following theoretical underpinnings. The concepts and their relationships are cumulative in nature that accumulates through the interplay of data collection and analysis. Employing theoretical sampling plan, the research can be conducted in a cumulative process until theoretical saturation is reached for the concepts and when no new data is available and the concepts are clearly explained (Strauss & Corbin, 1998). Gobo (2018) explains this process as 'the reflexive and spiralling nature of ethnographic research' where a concept requires re-specification or reconceptualization with new data, indicators and hypotheses until the researcher reaches conclusion. He presents (in Figure 1) the whole process in three stages (deconstruction, construction and confirmation), and each stage includes different sampling techniques and new data.

Without research, the world would not have seen so many advances in societies. Research has contributed to modifications in policies and plans made for human improvement. Therefore, the basis of research should be grounded by a sound and ethical standard (Resnik, 2015; American Psychological Association, 2002). Ethical issues have occupied significant space in the discourse of migration research primarily because migrants (forced or voluntary) are one of the most vulnerable groups in the world. Research studies conducted on this group require ensuring that their rights are protected and privacies are maintained. Evidently, conventional techniques in social sciences including migration research were not concerned much about ethical issues. Power relations often create insider-outsider dilemmas for the researcher, problems of representation and how 'race' of researcher affects trust in field research and other ethical considerations. The recent endeavour is the introduction of the approval from the ethics committee[1] (in organizations/institutions, if any) to protect the rights of the participants and

---

[1] Different countries introduce the research ethics committee with various names such as International Review Board – IRB; National Ethics Committee (NEC); Independent Ethics Committee (IEC), Research Ethics Board (REB), etc.

obstruct the researchers from playing dominance over the respondents.

Figure 1. Cumulative research design (Gobo 2018:76). (Permission obtained)

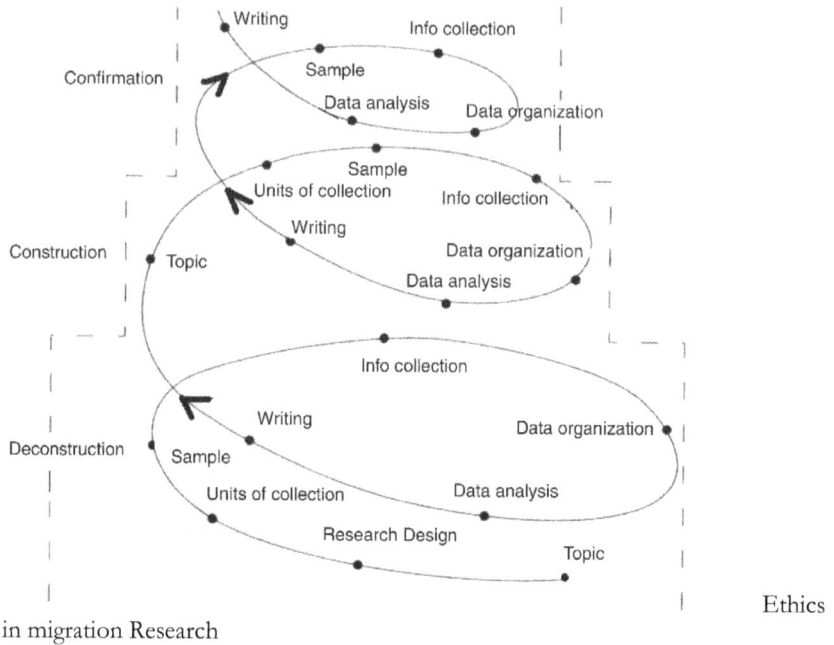

in migration Research Ethics

Historically, the context for ethical regulation was created for the first time during the Doctors Trial of 1946-1947, which was a part of the Nuremberg Trials for Nazi war criminals (University of Minnesota, 2003). There were serious allegations against Nazi physicians in the Doctors Trial that they conducted torturous experiments with concentration camp inmates as some of the experiments involved exposing victims to extreme temperatures and altitudes (University of Minnesota, 2003:1). Just a decade ago, in the 'researcher–researched' power hierarchy, researchers were considered more powerful than the researched. Researched were placed in a position that they felt obliged to provide information for research (Sales & Folkman, 2000; Angell et al., 2006). However, some changes happen over the last few years and scholars are discussing openly about ethical dilemmas in research (Ullah, 2010). We concur with Castles & Miller (1993) and contend that research ethics shift power from researchers to the researched.

The situation, as if, has been like whatever questions a researcher has could be asked of the respondents. Privacy, potential harm, vulnerability and related consequences were not taken into consideration. The researched invests time and energy, and provides information without any benefit. Yet, they have been considered as someone subjected to provide information no matter how harmful or risky was this for them. This is proven unethical.

Evidently that research ethics and methodologies are intertwined as the principle of ethics reinforces methodological soundness at different steps of research process because many methodological problems lead to ethical lapses (Jacobsen & Landau, 2003). This section is meant to expound the essence of research ethics and the processes involved in the ethical application process. Research challenge is primarily an issue related to the interest of researchers and research ethics are related to the interests of researched. Researchers tended to conflate research challenges with research ethics at the time when ethics were considered trivial.

Hammersley (2015:433) describes the formulation of ethical codes and frameworks that "principles are useful, so long as they are treated as reminders of what ought to be taken into account, rather than as premises from which specific ethical judgments can be derived. At the same time, any move towards formulating codes in terms of principles is likely to make little difference in practice for researchers under the present regime of ethical regulation."

Why research has to follow ethical standard? The primary objective of ethics in research is to protect human and animal participants from risks and vulnerabilities emanating from the research they are involved in. A researcher, for instance, who fabricates data, either deliberately or carelessly, may harm or even kill the subject, and similarly, if a researcher is not careful enough about some regulations (e.g. relating to radiation or biological safety), it may jeopardize the safety of the subjects (Resnik, 2015). This indicates that in any critical cases like migrant (forced or else) research subjects are even more vulnerable to harm if the safety is not protected. Therefore, the elements of research ethics such as risk management, confidentiality, informed consent, etc. are required to examine during the approval process of any research activities and projects.

Researches on migrants and refugees are conducted inevitably in complex and risky conditions. The precarious situation, along with the vulnerable and marginalized position of the participants, can cause violation of ethical principles (Hugman, Pittaway & Bartolomei, 2011). Unlike many other typical research setting, migration research, therefore, requires researchers to be more careful about methodological and ethical soundness in order to produce valid data without placing them at risks. Jacobsen and Landau (2003) identify some challenges related to both research methodology and ethics in refugee field which include: construct validity, objectivity and reactivity, bias, translation and the ethics of using local researchers, problems of confidentiality, missing control groups, and problems of representativeness (Nowak, 2006; Gajjar, 2013; Stair, 2001; Colt & Mulnard, 2006). In researching migration (forced or voluntary, regular or irregular), it is crucial that researchers internalize the notions of sensitivity and vulnerability to better address the ethical questions.

Conclusions

Researching hard-to-reach people is not easy. Migrants and refugees are, of course, not like the other research participants. They might be traumatized, wounded physically or mentally, suffering from separation anxiety, disturbed with future, and broke. If the participants are visible minority or women, they are more vulnerable than anyone (Martha et al., 2017). In such circumstances, being interviewed by a researcher is not something they hope for.

When it comes to individual interviewing, how sensitive an interviewer should be in different settings (cultural, religious, gender and geographical) is important to consider. Once the respondents open up and get to speak candidly, they may undergo a process of release. Although the best interview plans may go awry, it is essential to permit the commentary to unfold even though some of the 'information that emerge may be upsetting to the researcher, when graphic stories of abuse emerge concerning violence or brutality, in detailed descriptions of war atrocities, or in stories of abuse during flight to asylum' (Vargas, 1998:42).

Recently migration research has significantly developed with the advent of different academic programs integrated in many disciplines and with the emergence of migration-specific journals (Vargas-Silva, 2012). However, migration friendly and migration sensitive research techniques do not seem to appear until recently (Singleton, 1999; DeTona, Frisina, & Ganga, 2010). The precarious situation migrants, in general, live in is not conducive to bringing under research initiative. Given the importance of ethics for conducting research, it should come as no surprise that many different professional associations, government agencies, and universities have adopted specific codes, rules, and policies relating to research ethics (Resnik, 2015).

Methods to be applied in particular research should be region or country specific too because cultural and religious norms, political systems and socio-economic condition may vary widely across region. These conditions have got crucial bearing on the methods to be applied for migration research. For instance, the methods applied in traditional migration research derived from the Western countries have manifested challenges in applying them elsewhere. This implies that research setting often dictates the types of methods to be better fit in certain setting. Therefore, adopting a qualitative, quantitative or mixed method for a research on migrant population may depend on the context, volume, directions, political system and culture.

References

American Psychological Association (2002). Ethical principles of psychologists and code of conduct. American Psychologist, 57(12):1060-1073. https://doi.org/10.1037/0003-066X.57.12.1060

Angell, E., Sutton, A. J., Windridge, K., & Dixon-Woods, M. (2006). Consistency in decision making by research ethics committees: a controlled comparison. Journal of Medical Ethics, 32(11):662-664. https://doi.org/10.1136/jme.2005.014159

Bailey, K. D. (1978). Methods in Social Research. New York: Free Press.

Bazeley, P. (2003). Teaching mixed methods. Qualitative Research Journal, Vol. 3(SI):117-126.

Birman, D. (2006). Ethical Issues in Research With Immigrants and Refugees. In J. E. Trimble & C. B. Fisher (Eds.), The Handbook of Ethical Research with Ethnocultural Populations & Communities. https://doi.org/10.4135/9781412986168.n9

Borkert, M., Pérez, A. M., Scott, S., & De Tona, C. (2006, May). Introduction: Understanding migration research in Europe. In Forum Qualitative Sozialforschung/Forum: Qualitative Social Research, Vol. 7(3): 132

Castles, S., & Kosack, G. (1973). Immigrant workers and class structure in Western Europe. London: Oxford University Press.

Castles, S. & Miller, M. J. (1993). The age of migration. New York: Guilford Press.

Corbin, J., & Strauss, A. (2007). Basics of qualitative research: Techniques and procedures for developing grounded theory. London: Sage Publications. https://doi.org/10.4135/9781452230153

Colt, H. G., & Mulnard, R. A. (2006). Writing an application for a human subjects institutional review board. Chest, 130(5):1605-1607. https://doi.org/10.1378/chest.130.5.1605

Creswell, J. W. (2014). Research design: Qualitative, quantitative, and mixed methods approaches (fourth edition). Thousand Oaks, CA: SAGE Publications Ltd.

Daniel, J. (2012). Sampling essentials: Practical guidelines for making sampling choices. Sage Publications. https://doi.org/10.4135/9781452272047

Denzin, N., & Lincoln, Y. (2018). The SAGE handbook of qualitative research (Fifth ed.). Los Angeles: Sage.

DeTona, C., Frisina, A., & Ganga, D. (2010). Research Methods in Ethnic and Migration Studies. Migration Letters, 7(1):1-6. https://doi.org/10.33182/ml.v7i1.175

Flyvbjerg, B. (2006). Five misunderstandings about case-study research. Qualitative inquiry, 12(2):219-245. https://doi.org/10.1177/1077800405284363

Gajjar, D. (2013). Ethical consideration in research. Education, 2(7):8-15.

Glaser, B. G., & Strauss, A. L. (1967). The Discovery of Grounded Theory: Strategies for Qualitative Research. Chicago: Aldine Publishing Company.

Gobo, G. (2018). Upside down - reinventing research design. In U. Flick (Ed.), The sage handbook of qualitative data collection (pp. 65-83). London: SAGE Publications Ltd. https://doi.org/10.4135/9781526416070.n5

Gobo, G. (2004). Sampling, representativeness and generalizability. In C. Seale, G. Gobo, J. F. Gubrium, D. Silverman. (Eds.), Qualitative Research Practice (pp. 435-456). London: Sage.

Gomm, R. Hammersley, M., & Foster, P. (Eds.) (2000). Case Study Method. London: Sage Publications.

Gorny, A., & Napierała, J. (2016). Comparing the effectiveness of respondent-driven sampling and quota sampling in migration research. International Journal of Social Research Methodology, 19(6):645-661. https://doi.org/10.1080/13645579.2015.1077614

Grove, N. J., & Zwi, A. B. (2006). Our health and theirs: Forced migration, othering, and public health. Social science & medicine, 62(8), 1931-1942. https://doi.org/10.1016/j.socscimed.2005.08.061

Hammersley, M. (2015). On ethical principles for social research. International Journal of Social Research Methodology, 18(4):433-449. https://doi.org/10.1080/13645579.2014.924169

Hoerder, D. (2012). Transnational - transregional -translocal: transcultural. In C. Vargas-Silva (Ed.), Handbook of research methods in migration (69-91). London: Edward Elgar.

Hugman, R., Pittaway, E., & Bartolomei, L. (2011). When 'do no harm'is not enough: The ethics of research with refugees and other vulnerable groups. The British Journal of Social Work, 41(7):1271-1287. https://doi.org/10.1093/bjsw/bcr013

Iosifides, T. (2012). Migration research between positivistic scientism and relativism: A critical realist way out. In C. Vargas-Silva (Ed.), Handbook of Research Methods in Migration (pp. 26-49). London: Edward Elgar.

Jacobsen, K., & Landau, L. B. (2003). The dual imperative in refugee research: some methodological and ethical considerations in social science research on forced migration. Disasters, 27(3):185-206. https://doi.org/10.1111/1467-7717.00228

Kerlinger, F. (1964). Foundations of behavioral research. New York: Holt, Rinehart & Winston.

King, G., Keohane, R. O., & Verba, S. (1994). Designing social inquiry: Scientific inference in qualitative research. Princeton, New Jersey: Princeton University Press. https://doi.org/10.1515/9781400821211

Layder, D. (2011). Sociological practice: Linking theory and social research. London: Sage publications.

Lee, J., Carling, J., Orrenius, P. (2014). The international migration review at 50: Reflecting on half a century of international migration research and looking ahead. International Migration Review, 48, S3-S36. https://doi.org/10.1111/imre.12144

Leech, N. L., & Onwuegbuzie, A. J. (2009). A typology of mixed methods research designs. Quality & quantity, 43(2):265-275. https://doi.org/10.1007/s11135-007-9105-3

Levitt, P. & Jaworsky, B. N. (2007). Transnational migration studies: Past developments and future trends. Annual Review of Sociology, 33(1):129-156. https://doi.org/10.1146/annurev.soc.33.040406.131816

Massey, D. (2014). Challenges to surveying immigrants. In R. Tourangeau, B. Edwards, T. Johnson, K. Wolter, & N. Bates (Eds.), Hard-to-Survey Populations (pp. 270-292). Cambridge: Cambridge University Press. https://doi.org/10.1017/CBO9781139381635.017

Massey, Douglas S. 1987. The Ethnosurvey in Theory and Practice. International Migration Review, 21:1498-1522. https://doi.org/10.1177/019791838702100426

McMahon, T. (1999). Is reflective practice synonymous with action research? Educational action research, 7(1):163-169. https://doi.org/10.1080/09650799900200080

Merton R. K. (1949). On Sociological Theories of the Middle Range. In R. K. Merton (Ed.), Social Theory and Social Structure (pp. 39-53). New York: The Free Press.

Newman, I., & Benz, C. R. (1998). Qualitative-quantitative research methodology: Exploring the interactive continuum. Southern Illinois University Press.

Nowak, K. S., Bankert, E. A., & Nelson, R. M. (2006). Reforming the oversight of multi-site clinical research: a review of two possible solutions. Accountability in research, 13(1):11-24. https://doi.org/10.1080/08989620600588845

Nguyen Jacqueline, Harnandez Maria G, Saetermoe Carrie, Suarez-Orozco Carola. (2013). An Ethical Frame for Research with Immigrant Families, New Directions for Child and adolescent development. Fall (141):1-7. https://doi.org/10.1002/cad.20039

Phillips, D. C., & Burbules, N. C. (2000). Post-positivism and educational research. Lanham, US: Rowman & Littlefield.

Polit, D. F., & Beck, C. T. (2010). Generalization in quantitative and qualitative research: Myths and strategies. International Journal of Nursing Studies, 47(11):1451-1458. https://doi.org/10.1016/j.ijnurstu.2010.06.004

Resnik D. B. (December 1, 2015). What is ethics in research & why is it important? National Institute of Health. US.

Sales, B. D., & Folkman, S. (Eds.). (2000). Ethics in research with human participants. Washington, DC: American Psychological Association.

Sandelowski, M. (1997). To be of use: enhancing the utility of qualitative research. Nursing Outlook 45(3):125-132. https://doi.org/10.1016/S0029-6554(97)90043-9

Schweitzer, R., Melville, F., Steel, Z., & Lacherez, P. (2006). Trauma, post-migration living difficulties, and social support as predictors of psychological adjustment in resettled Sudanese refugees. Australian and New Zealand Journal of Psychiatry, 40(2), 179-187. https://doi.org/10.1080/j.1440-1614.2006.01766.x

Singleton, A. (1999). Combining quantitative and qualitative research methods in the study of international migration. International Journal of Social Research Methodology, 2(2):151-157. https://doi.org/10.1080/136455799295113

Stair, T. O., Reed, C. R., Radeos, M. S., Koski, G., Camargo, C. A., & The MARC. (2001). Variation in institutional review board responses to a standard protocol for a multicenter clinical trial. Academic emergency medicine, 8(6):636-641. https://doi.org/10.1111/j.1553-2712.2001.tb00177.x

Strauss, A., & Corbin, J. (1998). Basics of Qualitative Research: Techniques and Procedures for Developing Grounded Theory. London: Sage publications.

Tholen, B. (2005). The Europeanisation of migration policy-the normative issues. European Journal of Migration and Law, 6(4):323-35. https://doi.org/10.1163/1571816044088827

Ullah AKM Ahsan. (2010). Rationalizing Migration Decisions: Labour Migrants in South and South-East Asia. Aldershot: Ashgate.

Ullah AKM Ahsan. (2014). Refugee Politics in the Middle East and the Africa: Human Rights, Safety and Identity. London: Palgrave McMillan. https://doi.org/10.1057/9781137356536

Ullah AKM Ahsan. (2015). The independent migrants: Syrian separated children fleeing war. Migration Policy Practice Journal, Vol V(4):7-14.

Ullah AKM Ahsan. (2016). Refugee mobility: Causes and perspective in the Middle East. Orient, 1:1(61-69).

Ullah AKM Ahsan and Chattoraj D. (2018). Roots of discrimination against Rohingya minorities: Society, Ethnicity and International Relations, Intellectual Discourse, 26(2): 541-465.

University of Minnesota (2003). A guide to research ethics. Center for Bioethics, Minnesota: University of Minnesota.

Vargas-Silva, C. (Ed.) (2012). Handbook of research methods in migration. United Kingdom: Edward Elgar. https://doi.org/10.4337/9781781005231

Vargas C. M. (1998). Ethical challenges in refugee Research: Troublesome questions, difficult answer. Refuge, 17(3):33-46.

Vertovec, S. (Ed.) (2015). Routledge international handbook of diversity studies. London and New York: Routledge https://doi.org/10.4324/9781315747224

Vertovec, S. (2007). Super-diversity and its implications. Ethnic and Racial Studies, 30(6):1024-1054. https://doi.org/10.1080/01419870701599465

Weis, D., & Willems, H. (2017). Aggregation, validation, and generalization of qualitative data-methodological and practical research strategies illustrated by the research process of an empirically based typology. Integrative Psychological and Behavioral Science, 51(2):223-243. https://doi.org/10.1007/s12124-016-9372-4

Wimmer A & Schiller NK. (2003). Methodological Nationalism, the Social Sciences, and the Study of Migration: An Essay in Historical Epistemology, International Migration Review, 37(3):576-610. https://doi.org/10.1111/j.1747-7379.2003.tb00151.x

Yalaz Evren & Zapata-Barrero Ricard. (2017). Mapping the Qualitative Migration Research in Europe An Exploratory Analysis, GRiTim Working paper series, Vol. 32(Summer). https://www.upf.edu/web/gritim/wp-32

Yin, R. K. (2009). Case study research: Design and methods (fourth edition). California, USA: Sage publications.

CHAPTER 9
Biographical methods in migration research

Theodoros Iosifides and Deborah Sporton

Biographical methods and research practice

During the last decades, qualitative biographical/narrative methods gained a prominent position within the spectrum of social science methodology and research practice, mainly due to a reaction to the positivist-empiricist dominance and associated views of social reality. After an initial interest to biographical methods, which followed the edition of 'The Polish Peasant in Europe and America (1919-1921)' by Thomas and Znaniecki (1958), biographical and generally qualitative research methods gave way to empiricist-quantitative approaches and only since the end of 1960 the positivist domination begun to be unsettled (Halfacree and Boyle 1993; Findlay and Li 1997; Tsiolis 2006).

Empiricism reduces social reality to a series of observable and discrete, highly atomistic entities (events, behaviours etc.), which may be allegedly categorized and measured with the use of 'objective' quantitative methods by more or less 'neutral' social scientists (Iosifides 2008). The purpose of this, is the discovery of empirical, 'law like' regularities between variables, which are considered to exhaust both social processes and causal relations (Iosifides and Spyridakis 2006; Iosifides 2008). Against this a view of social reality as consisted by meaningful actions and social interaction gives great emphasis on individual meanings and interpretations and moves human subjectivity and social inter-subjectivity from the periphery to the center of social inquiry. Instead of variable-oriented law like explanations, such a view adopts an understanding (verstehen) approach to social phenomena, granting qualitative methods (including biographical/narrative approaches) an indispensable position in social research practice (Iosifides 2008). In-deed biographical approaches aim at the reconstruction of life trajectories of research participants and of the ways of making sense of the world, of their conceptualizations, meanings and representations of it. We would add to those, the investigation of their practices, actions, interactions, the influence of socio-economic and cultural context and the role of the personal, familial and social material conditions and circumstances (Iosifides 2008).

Biographical methods in the social sciences lead to an increased appreciation of the role of agency and subjectivity in producing and reproducing social reality, of the ways of mediation of broader social structures by an active human agency and of the efforts of constructing coherent biographies through different and diverse experiences, conceptualizations and events (Katrivesis, 2004; Tsiolis 2006; Apitzsch and Siouti 2007; Creswell 2007). As regards research practice, the biographical interview differs considerably from other types of interviewing, for example from the more focused in-depth qualitative interviewing. The main difference lies to the special role of the researcher as an 'active listener' of the life story/biographical narrative of participant which is the result of a well designed and carefully formulated 'generative question' (Tsiolis 2006). The main purpose of the biographical interview is the production of a detailed biographical narrative with the least possible interventions by the researcher. After the narration phase, a more active interaction between the participant and the researcher, in the form of classical qualitative interviewing, may follow (Iosifides 2008). Thus, biographical research, aims at the production of a reconstruction of the biography/life history of the participants, which may be simultaneously characterised by elements such as narratives of efforts for the realisation of personal plans, interactions with institutional and societal rules and demands, biographical experiences of powerlessness and weakness, phases of rapid and unforeseeable change and biographical ruptures and the multi-dimensional relations between events, societal influences, meanings, representations, decision making processes and the continuing struggle to formulate and maintain a sense of biographical coherence over time (Tsiolis 2006, 2007; Iosifides 2008). There is probably no other social phenomenon which marks personal biographies with almost all the above ways than migration. For this reason the next sections turn to a more analytic debate of some key issues in biographical migration research.

Biographical methods in migration research

The study of migration phenomenon was, for a long time, dominated by empiricist-positivist approaches, concerning mainly with the process of migration decision making and modeling aspects of the phenomenon as determined by a series of discrete, interrelated variables, either at the levels of the individual and small groups (i.e. family, household etc.) or at the macro level such as country or regional development performance, unemployment rate etc. The call to incorporate biographical/narrative methods in studying migration aims at overcoming the limitations of empiricist approaches in a series of ways (Halfacree & Boyle 1993; Findlay & Li 1997). The first is related to placing agential intentionality and meaning making processes at the centre of migration research practice and thus moving away from deterministic and law-like causal explanations. The second is related to paying attention to the importance of 'practical consciousness' along with the unconscious and the discursive, that is paying attention to the ways which agents act in everyday life without reflecting thoroughly or plan upon their actions. Finally, other ways include the detailed investigation of the multiplicity and multi-dimensionality of subjective migration experiences and the attention on the cultural dimension of processes related to migration phenomena.

Nevertheless, in many instances, reaction to empiricism in migration studies took, the form of exaggerations as regards the role of agency and subjectivity in producing and reproducing social reality, leading to neglect of broader structural factors, voluntarism and an almost total replacement of efforts to discover and analyze social causation processes with 'interpretative understanding' through lay discourses. In this paper, we adopt a more balanced position as regards the role of biographical methods in migration studies. We view those methods as extremely useful devises for understanding and causally explain the complex interplay between meaningful action and structural/cultural context (Laoire 2000; Iosifides 2004).

Key issues in biographical migration research

The quality-quantity debate

Qualitative methods and in particular biographical methods can enrich our understanding of the complex and multidimensional phenomenon of migration as compared mainly to the traditional positivist employment of quantitative techniques to migration studies. This employment entails methodological individualism, a utilitarian ontology of the self and uniform concept of rationality (Boswell 2008: 552). On the contrary, biographical and qualitative methods in general, may help to take into account the social and cultural context of any 'rational' decision making and the meanings and interpretations that actors ascribe to their actions and to the actions of others. Some of the most well-known strengths of biographical, and to some extent of almost all qualitative methods, are the in-depth and holistic understanding of phenomena and processes, the avoidance of imposing commonsensical or the researcher's categories to actors, subtlety, detail and the avoidance of the limitation of the discourses of actors to some (usually pre-selected) quantitative variables (Rubin and Rubin 2005). One example, showing the potentially valuable role of biographical and qualitative methods in general, in researching various aspects and dimensions of migration phenomenon, is related to the different meanings, that some migrants within certain contexts, attach to 'friendship' and in particular to 'friendship with natives'. For them, 'friendship with natives' means 'superficial friendly contact' and not 'more or less stable relations of reciprocity and solidarity'. So the positive response to a question about whether migrants have native friends refers to the former concept of friendship and not to the latter (Iosifides et al. 2007). Thus, only the in-depth investigation of the life course of immigrants and their biographical experiences of social relations in the host country may highlight the reasons for the adoption of this particular meaning of 'friendship with natives' rather than other alternative meanings and interpretations.

Biographical methods in migration studies may be applied to a series of specific domains related to different aspects of biographical migratory experiences such as for example migration decision making and motivation, identity formation and change (see for example Kazmierska 2003), the role of social capital and social networks, processes of social integration and/or exclusion, political/social participation and mobilization etc. Biographical methods can lead to thorough investigation of the above aspects of migratory processes mainly because they place temporality, sequenciality, trajectory paths, and personal and/or collective memory at the center of social inquiry (Apitzsch and Siouti 2007). Furthermore, biographical methods may lead to detailed and comprehensive reconstructions of linking chains between events, meanings/interpretations, actions and practices. As regards practices, the examination of their genealogy and evolution may result in theoretical propositions of embeddedness within broader social structures which function quite independently of interpretations of actors. To give but one example, individual reasons and interpretations of migrants for the acceptance of specific kind of jobs need not have any direct relation to the functioning of 'ethnic specialization' systems in the labour market, which often result in channeling migrants of specific ethnic background or gender to certain economic and labour market niches, irrespective of educational and other skills (Iosifides et al., 2007). This last remark leads us to the examination, in the next section, of the relation between agency and structure, and how this relation can be incorporated in or highlighted from biographical migration research.

The relation between agency and structure

Generally, the relation between agency and structure is probably the most important issue of interest for sociological theorizing, addressed implicitly or explicitly in almost every theoretical and methodological strategy in the social sciences. There has been a quite powerful tendency in social theory either to reduce agency to structure (structuralism) or structure to individuals or interactions between individuals (methodological individualism and situationism) (Mouzelis 1991, 1995; Archer 1995). Efforts to resolve the 'paradox' of structure – agency relations include conceptualizations of structure and agency as mutually constitutive, granting to structure a 'virtual existence' coming into being through the social practices of actors (structuration theory) (Archer 1995). Finally, discursive analytic approaches to social theorizing tend to fall either in methodological individualism/situationism or macro-constructionism (Burr 2003).

A thorough critique of the above approaches exceeds the scope of the present paper. Nevertheless it has to be noted that biographical approaches are usually viewed and applied as part of the micro-sociological paradigm in the sense that the existence and influence of structural factors on individuals or social groups are undervalued and the powers (intentional and through discourse) of actors are exaggerated. Problems associated with those approaches may be resolved subject to a different conceptualisation of the relations between agency and structure. This conceptualisation entails a view both of agency and structure as existent in a separate way (analytic dualism), holding distinct characteristics and powers irreducible to one another and being in a constant interplay (Archer 1995). In this way biographical methods may contribute in a significant way not only to the investigation of the ways that individual or social interpretations and discourses produce results such as social action but also of the ways broader societal factors and structures condition meanings and interpretations (Sims-Schouten et al. 2007). Returning to the example of immigrant social networking and 'ethnic specialisation' (see previous section), a biographical approach may highlight in great detail the life trajectories of immigrants resulting in social networking along with the associated in depth examination of immigrant's meanings and interpretations related to crucial decisions and actions. But, equally importantly, biographical approaches may contribute to our understanding of how broader contextual and structural features of immigrant's social networks, condition (constrain or enable) actions and meaning making processes (see also Archer 2000, 2003).

The realism-relativism debate

The crucial question about the way of conceptualisation and interpretation of the biographical narrative, about its usefulness and its relation to broader social processes, introduces us inevitably to some form of the realism-relativism debate. Relativist positions, mainly those of the strong version of social constructionism, stress that biographical narratives are the mere product of the communicative interaction between the researcher and the research participant in the present (that is at the time of interaction), and cannot be used in order to highlight the impacts and role of any 'real' processes (see Tsiolis 2006). Thus, a narrative of an immigrant about her trajectory of spatial and social mobility in the host country, about passing different stages and phases resulted in modified social situation and relations, have value only as 'accounts' that is as interpretations or discourses. As those accounts or interpretations/discourses exhaust the domain of the social, they cannot inform us about any 'reality' behind the told story (Steensen n.d.a.).

The problems of strong versions of social constructionism and relativism in general, are manifold. Those versions cannot lead to satisfactory explanations of how discourses are produced and changed and on why some discourses are characterized by more durability and impact than others. This is because strong social constructionism does not acknowledge the dialectical interplay between discursive and extra-discursive elements and factors, falling to a form of 'discursive reductionism' (Sims-Schouten et al. 2007). Furthermore, those versions of constructionism tend to ignore social hierarchies and the positioning (or conditioning) of discourses within hierarchical social and organisational systems and sub-systems (Mouzelis 1991). Thus, the discourses of migration policy officials, employers, immigrant community leaders and immigrants with different social characteristics do not 'construct' social reality in the same way and to the same extend. Whose constructions matter, when and why, is not a feature of discourse alone but of extra-discursive factors as well (social hierarchies, systems of material recourse and power distribution, structured positions systems etc.).

Those points remind us the centrality of interpretative/action power of human agency along with the fact that those powers are always exercised within given circumstances and structures, are characterized by unintended consequences and influenced by the intentions and unintended outcomes of actions of others (Iosifides 2008). Especially in the field of migration studies, biographical narratives may lead to deeper understanding of social processes and inform policy making, subject to their conceptualisation not just as 'stories', but as reconstructions of the complex and dialectical interplay between agency action and meaning making with certain structural and systemic conditions, constrains and enablements (Archer 1995, Iosifides 2008).

References

Apitzsch, U. and Siouti, I. (2007) Biographical Analysis as an Interdisciplinary Research Perspective in the Field of Migration Studies. Frankfurt am Main: Research Integration, Johann Wolfgang Goethe Universität, University of York.

Archer, M. (1995). Realist Social Theory: The Morphogenetic Approach. Cambridge: Cambridge University Press.

Archer, M. (2000). Being Human. The Problem of Agency. Cambridge: Cambridge University Press.

Archer, M. (2003). Structure, Agency and the Internal Conversation. Cambridge: Cambridge University Press.

Bauman, Z. (2001) The Individualized Society, Cambridge: Polity.

Beck, U., and Beck-Gernsheim, E. (2002) Individualization. London: Sage.

Boghossian, P. (2006) Fear of Knowledge. Against Relativism and Constructivism. Oxford: Oxford University Press.

Boswell, C. (2008) 'Combining economics and sociology in migration theory', in Journal of Ethnic and Migration Studies, 34 (4): 549-566.

Burr, V. (2003) Social Constructionism. Second Edition. London: Routledge.

Creswell, J.W. (2007) Qualitative Inquiry and Research Design, Choosing Among Five Approaches. Second Edition. Thousand Oaks, CA: Sage.

Findlay, A.M. & Li, F.L.N. (1997) 'An Auto-Biographical Approach to Understanding Migration: The Case of Hong Kong Emigrants' in, Area, 29(1): 34-44.

Halfacree, K.H. & Boyle, P.J. (1993) 'The challenge facing migration research: the case for a biographical approach', in Progress in Human Geography, 17 (3): 333-348.

Iosifides, T. (2004) "Relativist approaches in social sciences: impacts and critique", in Theseis, 86: 57-67 (in Greek).

Iosifides, T. (2009) Review of the book 'The Cultures of Economic Migration: International Perspectives' edited by Suman Gupta and Tope Omoniyi, Aldershot: Ashgate, 2007, 226 pp. Journal of Ethnic and Migration Studies, 35 (3): 510-511.

Iosifides, T. (2003) "Qualitative migration research: some new reflections six years later", in The Qualitative Report, 8 (3): 435-446. www.nova.edu/ssss/QR//QR8-3/iosifides.pdf.

Iosifides, T. (2008) Qualitative Research Methods in the Social Sciences (revised edition). Athens: Kritiki (in Greek).

Iosifides, T. and Spyridakis, M. (2006) (Eds.) Qualitative Social Research. Meth-odological Approaches and Data Analysis. Athens: Kritiki (in Greek).

Iosifides, T., Lavrentiadou, M., Petracou, E., Kontis, A. (2007) Forms of social capi-tal and the incorporation of Albanian immigrants in Greece, in Journal of Ethnic and Migration Studies, 33 (8): 1343-1361.

Katrivesis, N.S. (2004) Sociological Theory. Contemporary Currents of Sociological Thought. Athens: Gutenberg (in Greek).

Kazmierska, K. (2003) 'Migration experiences and changes of identity: an analysis of a narrative', in Forum: Qualitative Social Research, 4 (3), Article 21.

Laoire, C.N. (2000) 'Conceptualising Irish rural youth migration: a biographical approach', in International Journal of Population Geography, 6: 229-243.

Mouzelis, N.P. (1991) Back to Sociological Theory. The Construction of Social Orders. London: Macmillan.

Mouzelis, N.P. (1995) Sociological Theory – What Went Wrong? Diagnosis and Remedies. London: Routledge.

Rubin, H.J. and Rubin, I.S. (2005) Qualitative Interviewing. The Art of Hearing Data. Second Edition. Thousand Oaks: Sage.

Sayer, A. (2004) Realism and Social Science. London: Sage.

Sims-Schouten, W., Riley, S. C. E. & Willig, C. (2007) Critical Realism and Dis-course Analysis. A Presentation of a Systematic Method of Analysis Using Women's Talk of Motherhood, Childcare and Female Employment as an Example. Theory and Psychology, 17 (1), 101-124.

Steensen, J. (no date available) Biographical Interviews in a Critical Realist Perspective. Department of Education, Learning and Philosophy, Aalborg Uni-versity, Denmark (uit.no/getfile.php?PageId=8315&FileId=31, accessed 28.05.2009)

Thomas, W. and Znaniecki, F. (1958) The Polish Peasant in Europe and America (1919-1921). New York: Dover.

Tsiolis, G. (2006) Life Histories and Biographical Narratives. The Biographical Ap-proach in Sociological Qualitative Research. Athens: Kritiki (in Greek).

CHAPTER 10

Strengths, Risks and Limits of Doing Participatory Research in Migration Studies

Diana Mata-Codesal, Laure Kloetzer and Concha Maiztegi

Participatory Research in Migration Studies

50 years on, Sherry R. Arnstein's critical words on participation in policy and social planning remain very relevant: "The idea of citizen participation is a little like eating spinach: no one is against it in principle because it is good for you. Participation of the governed in their government is, in theory, the cornerstone of democracy-a revered idea that is vigorously applauded by virtually everyone. The applause is reduced to polite handclaps, however, when this principle is advocated by the have-not blacks, Mexican Americans, Puerto Ricans, Indians, Eskimos, and whites. And when the have-nots define participation as redistribution of power, the American consensus on the fundamental principle explodes into many shades of outright racial, ethnic, ideological, and political opposition" (Arnstein, 1969, p.216). According to her, what participation should be, however, is very different: "citizen participation is a categorical term for citizen power. It is the redistribution of power that enables the have-not citizens, presently excluded from the political and economic processes, to be deliberately included in the future. It is the strategy by which the have-nots join in determining how information is shared, goals and policies are set, tax resources are allocated, programs are operated, and benefits like contracts and patronage are parcelled out. In short, it is the means by which they can induce significant social reform which enables them to share in the benefits of the affluent society" (ibidem, p. 216). Whereas her critical call was related to participation of citizens in State and local policies, it is fully relevant to the current analysis of the (non) participation of (non) citizens in supranational, national or local policies governing international migrations.

This special issue presents a range of participatory research approaches in the field of migration studies. More precisely, we could argue that most authors of this Special Issue would not spontaneously self-identify with the field of migration studies, although they have all been working, some of them for decades, on topics which are directly and undoubtedly relevant to it. They might instead self-identify as coming from the field of feminism, action-research or being "activist-scholars" (as Valerie Francisco-Menchavez and Ethel Tungohan and Elsa Oliveira and Jo Varey explicitly do in their articles). The focus on the methodology of participatory research, which is not only a set of creative methods, as we will see below, but also an epistemology and an ethics of research, implies a different way of relating to our research objects, participants, and colleagues, superseding academic divisions among specialisation and expertise. Following the steep increase in the number of papers linked to Migration Studies in the last 20 years, there has been a paralleled increase in the number of papers published drawing on qualitative methodology (Sirkeci et al., 2019). Although the study of migration was initially dominated by empiricist-positivist and quantitative approaches, by now there is an established and growing tradition of qualitative studies. However, in leading journals of the field, participatory research, action research, and the use of creative participatory methodologies remain uncommon. Most of the time, creative methodologies like photo-elicitation are used as support to traditional ways of conducting research without further social engagement with the communities or participatory ethos (see for example Long et al., 2014).

An interesting paradox is that other fields, not principally labelled as Migration Studies, have been developing a very strong qualitative and participatory tradition dealing with migrant populations. For example, researchers within the field of feminist studies, research aiming at decolonizing psychology and anthropology, culturally-sensitive research, social work, critical psychology or education, have frequently conducted innovative research with alternative, often culturally-relevant or arts-based methods, to engage mobile people in collective explorations of issues linked to migration (see for example Iosifides and Sporton, 2009; Kontopodis, 2012; O'Neill, 2008; Lenette, 2019). We could even argue that outside Migration Studies, there has been a surge of explorative, innovative creative participatory research involving migrant populations. However, these highly creative and socially responsible research trends seem disconnected from the strongly emerging and recently structured field of Migration Studies. This Special Issue aims at bridging this gap by making a set of participatory research papers highly visible in the field of Migration Studies. We believe that participatory research, with all its intrinsic methodological creativity but also research ethics, practice and interest for social action, has a lot to bring to the field of Migration Studies when it comes to both understanding and transforming the life experience of mobile populations.

Participatory research (PR from here onwards) questions well-established dichotomies such as those existing between researcher and research participants, or between academia, activism and social work (Pereira et al., 2016). So far, though, these studies have not received systematized attention and to a large extend remain as isolated small case studies. Trying to redress this situation, this special issue aims to showcase overall connections and developments by providing an updated account of participatory approaches in migration studies, and to provide a forum to reflect on the possibilities, limits and challenges of making use of participatory methods in migration research.

Defining Participatory Research

Participatory research is an umbrella term under which nests, more or less comfortable, a wide-ranging variety of research projects using different methodological approaches and research techniques, whose main aim is to achieve an equal distribution of power among all those involved in the research process. Reciprocity between community participants and researchers, sharing and valuing various forms of knowledge, are essential elements of PR. PR is not only a methodological approach, it is also an organizing strategy (Fox et al., 2010), an orientation to inquiry (Bradbury and Reason, 2006), a research tactic (see Valerie Francisco-Menchavez and Ethel Tungohan in this special issue), an ethical stance, an epistemological questioning, and a human encounter (Marit Aure et al. in this special issue). The ten articles in this special issue well exemplify this breadth of scope, each of them operationalizing PR in specific ways and by drawing on specific technical strategies related to PR.

PR projects are termed with a variety of names including action research, collaborative research, community-based research, co-creation, and even arts-based research. This terminology span reflects disciplinary differences and technique preferences but despite differences, PR "share a common set of core principles and characteristics" (Letiecq and Schmalzbauer, 2012, p.247). PR implies an understanding of the research process in which all parties involved (researchers, other research participants and even audiences) are conceived as co-creators in what is often an explorative process of knowledge production (Bradbury and Reason, 2006). Through participatory methodologies researchers contribute to create spaces for the co-creation of knowledge, in partnership with research subjects and institutions. Dialogic engagement is a key element for truly participatory projects to achieve less-hierarchical, non-extractive and more decolonized methodologies (Hennink et al., 2011, p.51). However, these spaces are not always conflict-free and the conditions for true dialogue are not always easy to achieve.

For the sake of clarity, we can arrange the diversity of terminologies and definitions of PR according to which steps of the research process are open to the participants for co-design and exploitation. This continuum would go from narrow conceptualizations of collaboratively problem-detection projects to critical emancipatory approaches which question the very basic foundations of what is considered as proper knowledge and who the experts producing such knowledge are. In this sense, PR is closely linked to decolonial and feminist understandings of doing research. A basic conceptualization of PR would conceive it as a problem-solving technique which often involves researchers and research participants working together to examine a problematic situation, action or issue (Milne, 2016). As it is, PR creates projects of social relevance for the communities involved. More complex and critical understandings of PR would emphasize the importance of the research process itself, as a dynamic educational process that enables and legitimizes social research and often leads to action. Thus, PR represents a way of overcoming prevailing extractivist logics of doing research. This latter approach is closely related to the work of Paulo Freire, with some of his developments concerning voice and participation being key for participatory research. In particular, the need to recognize the most vulnerable participants' voice, as well as their awareness processes, is a true challenge for researchers who need to develop what Martha Montero-Sieburth calls in her article in this special issue "cultural humility". These elements are all related to some of the postulates of Slow Academia and feminist approaches to academic life and purpose which go beyond finalist logics and focus more on the processes involved (Caretta and Riaño, 2016; Mountz et al., 2015).

Technique creativity is often an intrinsic feature of participatory research projects, which are frequently labelled after the selected research technique.

Published research shows that PR pairs well with a broad range of research techniques, and in particular with arts-based ones such as video and other visual techniques, as well as embodied techniques like theatre and other performative methods. An important number of participatory projects has used photography, under for instance the form of photovoice (Wang and Burris, 1997; see also Magdalena Arias Cubas in this special issue), participatory photography or photowalks. Through this creative technique, PR projects offer a way of gaining new insights, reflections and narratives, through working with artistic methods and involving artists in the process. Non-academic participants themselves come to realize, reflect on, and express their experiences and views in a novel way that may not be captured in verbal and more conventional research methods. Similarly, reaching out and engaging with wider audiences through these newly acquired narratives is made possible, namely when artistic and creative practices are involved. Recognizing the potential of PR creatively to develop and engage with different research techniques does not have to mean falling into the negative consequences of what Derya Ozkul in her article in this special issue calls the "glorification of methods". The emphasis on "innovative and creative" methods (Wiles et al., 2011) can sometimes conceal the absence of meaningful participation and in some cases even disguise the one-sided nature in which so called participatory projects are implemented.

What is Participatory Research good for?

Compared to classical research strategies, participatory research is a more complex research process, as it involves simultaneous strategies for knowledge production and for social transformation. The ultimate objective of PR is social justice (Letiecq and Schmalzbauer, 2012) for which its core activities include not only research but also education and other actions (Balcazar, 2003).

Regarding knowledge production, participatory research improves research thanks to four main dimensions: 1) a sounder research question; 2) attention to complexity, social dynamics, power dynamics, and dynamics of change through long-term personal engagement with social situations and people; 3) social validation by research participants thanks to relationships of trust and the habitus forged by critical collaboration; and 4) explicit conceptualization of research as a learning process involving reflexivity, subjectivity, and emotions.

Firstly, participatory research requires a delicate interplay between the choice of a scientific question by the researchers, which is usually an epistemic runway object already grounded in a disciplinary literature and way of asking research questions, and openness to the redefinition of the goal of the research with the research participants, individually and collectively. True engagement of the research participants requires that the researchers do their best to pursue the research questions set by the research participants and local communities, usually linked to everyday life and challenges, as well as their own research questions, usually linked to a disciplinary tradition as well as personal life experience. Achieving a good balance between multiple interests regarding the goal of the research is essential and has consequences for the design of the research. The research question is stronger in participatory research because it has two related and complementary faces: a socially relevant face, and a scientific face. It is also evolving through the course of the research and the changing modes of participation involved. This epistemic flexibility is a strength of participatory research, which closely and dynamically follows the lessons learnt from the fieldwork, the concerns of the participants and the theoretical interests of the researchers. However, it can be a drawback to secure funding for the research, as all research questions cannot be defined in advance: only one thing is sure - they will evolve through the research process itself.

Secondly, building trust with research participants, who are also research partners, is a key dimension of participatory research. Among its main advantages, we can argue that the long-term engagement of researchers with local communities and specific people makes the researchers less naïve regarding the overgeneralisation of conclusions that could be drawn in comparison to shorter engagement with the field from a "single-point, static snapshot" of the situation. The complexity of social situations, the power dynamics at all levels, and the dynamics of change at the individual and collective levels better appear with long and informal conversations with research partners as well as with repeated research events and discussions. Working together (professional researchers and research participants, sometimes also with artists or activists) allows all to better understand their different points of view, life experiences, life concerns, life trajectories and past, present and future interests.

Thirdly, truly participatory research requires validation by research participants at all steps of the research process: definition of the research object and goal of the research, choice of methods, discussion of first empirical findings, construction and discussion of analyses, construction and discussion of conclusions and presentations, oral and written communication strategies. This engagement of the research participants places the researchers under the control of their social partners. If the mutual trust relations are correctly established, a true, critical, open and constructive dialogue is possible and makes the data collection, data analyses and conclusions of the research stronger. This way, social validation increases the validity of qualitative research (Cho and Trent, 2016).

Finally, participatory research posits research as an open-ended, partly unpredictable, learning process, for all participants including the researchers. It therefore encourages a reflexive and critical analysis of the researchers' positioning, interests and agenda in the research process. From an epistemological point of view, Balcazar (2003) states that the first proposal of PR is an experience that allows participants to "learn how to learn". This is a position also influenced by Freire, which implies understanding participants' role in the process of transformation of their social reality, not as victims or passive spectators, but as central actors in the process of change. During the PR process, participants are involved in deliberative projects that require them to assume leadership in their local communities. This involvement relates to the concept of empowerment in the sense that it develops the necessary capacities to enhance the possibilities for a person to decide and act consistently on all that affects their own life (Soler Masó et al., 2017). In such processes, participation constitutes a methodological principle for achieving the mentioned goal. As the same time, the participation process involves critical and creative reflection. It is considered a right and an opportunity for learning and for raising awareness. From this perspective, participation generates a first level of group empowerment that presupposes the creation of a collective subject capable of reflecting with critical awareness (Mata-Codesal et al., 2018).

Regarding the second constituent element of PR, action, participatory research is from the outset much better positioned as traditional qualitative or quantitative research, as it puts action first. Participatory researchers try and engage the participants who can themselves make the situation evolve, and not only help us understand, describe, analyse, and report it. The outreach of research beyond academia and its higher societal impacts are not by-products of research process but its core motivation. Although the process of social transformation might be very difficult and unsuccessful, the reflection on action and social transformation is present from the beginning of the research project and informs its design. Furthermore, this reflection on intended social transformations is shared with the research participants, making it more probable that the final outreach of the research meets true social expectations.

Finally, we can pose the question of participatory research as being considered more ethical than traditional research. This question has been much debated in some of the workshops on participatory research in migration studies that we have organized in recent years. The answer mostly depends on what is considered "good research" from an ethical perspective. Ethics is extremely challenging in the case of qualitative research regarding delicate, sensitive social topics with vulnerable populations, especially considering the recent requests for open data. In participatory research, ethics is not limited to extracting consent from the participants in oral and written form, signing participation agreement, as well as anonymization of the data for publication. All of these things can be impossible sometimes precisely for ethical reasons. The core of the ethics of participatory research is on building and honouring mutual relations of trust, which rely on the recognition of participants and professional researchers as equal human beings who want to enter into relation to collaborate on a specific topic, with specific methods and a structured process. It also requires conscientization of the structural power relations within and beyond the research process.

Power Issues in Participatory Research

Following an extensive literature review on the involvement of migrants in health-related participatory research, Vaughn and colleagues concluded that partnering with immigrants have numerous benefits for immigrants and their communities: "it has the potential to positively influence immigrants through the development of practical skills, community awareness, community action and change, and possible health outcomes" (Vaughn et al., 2017, p. 1465). However, the ways in which migrants are involved in PR do not always reach the highest participation levels identified by Sherry Arnstein (1969). Returning to Arnstein's words at the beginning of this article, we cannot emphasize enough that participation is all about power distribution: in order for PR to become really such, researchers must share power. Conflict in the form of tensions among differing schedules of the academic and non-academics participants, different objectives or unlike ways of doing is often mentioned in accounts of participatory research projects. As redistribution attempts are regularly met with conflict, we could even argue that if there is no conflict, then it may not be true participation. Hence, instead of taking conflict as an undesirable outcome of PR, we need to find ways to incorporate it into research in a way that accounts for it and feeds back into the research.

Power constitutes an optimal lens through which to understand specific elements in the application of PR in migration studies. In particular, power asymmetries explain the presence and absence of specific groups and topics in PR, as well as the consideration and level of implementation of PR regarding geographies and disciplines.

PR has been frequently applied when working along/with vulnerable groups. Although some authors have noted the advantages of using PR working with specific vulnerable populations (Aldridge, 2014), there is no practical reason why PR cannot be used for other types of non-marginalized (or not totally marginal) groups (Riaño, 2016). This is not exclusively of PR but a general trend in research where groups previously marked as problematic become research topics (Delgado, 1999, p.10), while elites and other powerful groups remain as unmarked categories of research. This tendency can create participation biases that need to be dealt with.

The gendered nature of this SI authorship (all but one being female scholars) is not random. It reflects a propensity of PR to be applied by female academics. This gendered nature of PR was one of the elements often discussed in the different meetings we have set up over the years, since we suspect that this intriguing element was hiding more far-reaching consequences of PR in particular, and the way research and knowledge-production is conceived in general. The feminization of the politics and practices of care in our society was put forward in some of those meetings as an explanation for this gender imbalance, as PR can be conceived as a more caring way of pursuing research. However, this care hypothesis does not explain why, in parts of the world, this gender unbalance is not present. Participatory methods are used in Latin America indistinctly by both male and female scholars, but in the European and Anglo-Saxon world mostly by female academics. A more satisfying explanation would relate to the power hierarchies that structure current Academia. In Latin America, PR has a long and respectable tradition, with key figures like the already mentioned Brazilian Paulo Freire, or Colombian Fals Borda[1]. Given that participatory methods are established, using them is considered as "proper" research. Meanwhile in Europe and the US, and more so in the field migration studies, PR does not account for the level of peer prestige it has in Latin America. We could argue then that only when a methodology becomes established and recognized, established and recognized scholars start using it. That would explain why in European and the Anglo-Saxon Academia, it is mostly women (who are often early career researchers or in precarious job

---

[1] Also, two early world meetings about participatory research were held in the region (in Colombia in 1977 and Nicaragua in 1989).

situations) apply PR.

Power hierarchies would also explain the uneven application of PR among traditional disciplines. The so-called "participatory turn" has remained almost unnoticed in disciplines like economics, law or even political science. Within social sciences, these are considered as "powerful" or hard disciplines. Flora Di Donato's article in this special issue provides a good perspective of the limited application of PR in law where even basic collaboration is considered as PR. On the opposite side of the hierarchy, PR is more common in disciplines and subfields like development studies, gender studies, education or social anthropology where a growing number of research projects present some sort of participatory elements.

Acknowledging the Limits of Participatory Research

Several of the articles in the ML Special Issue caution about the limits and risks of working with participatory research in the context of a productivity-driven neoliberal academia in a time where outreach beyond academia is becoming a must. Aaron Malone analyses the risks of implementing lite or faux forms of PR in a context where academia has been prone to accept watered-down versions of participation where no actual re-distribution of power takes place. Furthermore, Valerie Francisco-Menchavez and Ethel Tungohan, who self-define as women of colour and scholar activists, explore the tensions between the requirements on scholars of that same neoliberal academia and the purposes of participatory research for non-academic partners. In a context of strong pressure to produce research in the form of publications, the timings and tempos of PR are difficult to accommodate, and the risks of implementing projects which look like PR, but which do not involve meaningful forms of participation, are very real. Carrying PR in the current academic context requires a careful and continuous consideration of every step taken, so not to let down the core principles of PR that are mostly related to redressing power imbalances, in society and academia in general, and between researchers and companions in PR projects. Thus, PR urges us to explore the politics of knowledge production.

Researchers using PR should avoid conflating the (political and ethical) need to struggle and advocate for social change with an entrepreneurial understanding of the self as able to overcome obstacles to social justice which are beyond one's own reach. Placing the burden of social change on marginalized individuals not only blames them for their situation, it also misunderstands the role that neoliberalism, racism, patriarchy, and colonialism play in sustaining systemic structural violence (Walsh 2016, p.407). There are still structural elements which heavily shape social relations. Hence PR must be honest and humble enough not to create high expectations, as research can lead to nowhere reinforcing the sense of marginalization and powerlessness by some groups (as showed by Elsa Oliveira and Jo Vearey in their article in *Migration Letters* special issue).

References

Aldridge, J. (2014). Working with vulnerable groups in social research: dilemmas by default and design. *Qualitative Research*, 14(1), 112-130.

Arnstein, S. R. (1969). A ladder of citizen participation. *Journal of the American Institute of planners*, 35(4), 216-224.

Balcarzar, F. E. (2003). Investigación acción participativa (IAP): Aspectos conceptuales y dificultades de implementación. *Fundamentos en Humanidades*, 7(8), 59-77

Bradbury, H., and Reason, P. (2006). Conclusion: Broadening the bandwidth of validity: Issues and choice-points for improving the quality of action research. *Handbook of action research*, pp.343-351.

Caretta, M. A. and Riaño, Y. (2016). Feminist participatory methodologies in geography: creating spaces of inclusion. *Qualitative Research*, *16*(3), 258–266

Cho, J. and Trent, A. (2006). Validity in qualitative research revisited. *Qualitative Research*, *6*(3), 319–340.

Delgado, M. (1999). *El Animal Público*. Barcelona: Anagrama.

Fox, M., Mediratta, K., Ruglis, J., Stoudt, B., Shah, S., and Fine, M. (2010). Critical youth engagement: Participatory action research and organizing. *Handbook of Research on Civic Engagement in Youth*, pp.621-649.

Hennink, M.; Hutter, I. and Bailey, A. (2011). *Qualitative Research Methods*. London: Sage.

Iosifides, T. and Sporton, D. (2009). Biographical methods in migration research. *Migration Letters*, 6(2), 101-108.

Kontopodis, M. (2012). *Neoliberalism, Pedagogy and Human Development: Exploring Time, Mediation and Collectivity in Contemporary Schools*. London and New York: Routledge

Lenette, C. (2019). Mental health and critical multicultural practice: An arts-based approach. In Nipperess, S. and Williams, C. (eds.) *Critical Multicultural Practice: New Perspectives in Australian Social Work*, pp.101-115.

Letiecq, B. and Schmalzbauer, L. (2012). Community-based participatory research with Mexican migrants in a new rural destination: A good fit? *Action Research*, *10*(3), 244–259.

Long, J.; Hylton, K. and Spracklen, K. (2014). Whiteness, blackness and settlement: Leisure and the integration of new migrants. *Journal of Ethnic and Migration Studies*, 40(11), 1779–1797. https://doi.org/10.1080/1369183X.2014.893189.

Mata-Codesal, D.; Pereira, S.; Maiztegui-Oñate, C.; Ulloa, E., Esesumaga, E. and López del Molino. A. (2018). Con la Cámara a Cuestas: Aportaciones de la fotografía en procesos participativos de investigación-intervención. *Forum: Qualitative Social Research*. 19(1), Art. 14.

Milne, E.J. (2016). Critiquing participatory video: experiences from around the world, *Area*, 48(4), 401-404.

Mountz, A.; Bonds, A.; Mansfield, B.; Loyd, J.; Hyndman, J., Walton-Roberts, M., Basu, R.; Whitson, R.; Hawkins, R.; Hamilton, T. and Curran, W. (2015). For slow scholarship: A feminist politics of resistance through collective action in the neoliberal university. *ACME: An International E-Journal for Critical Geographies*, 14(4), 1235-1259.

Pereira, S.; Maiztegi, C. and Mata-Codesal, D. (2016). Transformative Looks. Practicing citizenship through photography, *Journal of Social Science Education*, 15(4), 14-21.

O'Neill, M. (2008). Transnational refugees: The transformative role of Art? *Forum: Qualitative Social Research* 9(2), Art. 59.

Riaño, Y. (2016). Minga biographic workshops with highly skilled migrant women: enhancing spaces of inclusion. *Qualitative Research*, *16*(3), 267–279.

Sirkeci, I.; DeTona, C.; Iosifides, T. and Frisina, A. (2019). *Reader in Qualitative Methods in Migration Research*. London: Transnational Press London

Soler Masó, P.; Trilla, J.; Jiménez, M. and Ucar Martínez, X. (2017). The construction of a pedagogical model of youth empowerment: spaces, moments and processes. *SIPS - Pedagogía Socia. Revista Interuniversitaria, 30*, 19-34

Vaughn, L., Jacquez, F. Lindquist-Grantz, R., Parsons, A. and Melink, K. (2017). Immigrants as Research Partners: A Review of Immigrants in Community-Based Participatory Research (CBPR). *Immigrant Minority Health*, 19, 1457–1468. Doi: 10.1007/s10903-016-0474-3

Walsh, S. (2016). Critiquing the politics of participatory video and the dangerous romance of liberalism, *Area*, 48(4), 405–411.

Wang, C. and Burris, M. A. (1997). Photovoice: Concept, methodology, and use for participatory needs assessment. *Health Education and Behavior*, *24*(3), 369-387.

Wiles, R., Crow, G., and Pain, H. (2011). Innovation in qualitative research methods: a narrative review. *Qualitative Research*, 11(5), 587-604.

PART 4: MIGRATION, SECURITY, AND RIGHTS

Essential Reading:

Bauhn, P. (2019). Universalist Rights and Particularist Duties: The Case of Refugees. *Migration Letters*, *16*(2), 145-153.

Koca, B. T. (2019). Bordering Practices Across Europe: The Rise of "Walls" and "Fences". *Migration Letters*, 16(2), 183-194.

Sirkeci, I. (2017). Turkey's refugees, Syrians and refugees from Turkey: a country of insecurity. *Migration Letters*, 14(1), 127-144.

Further Reading:

Ahmed, I. (2017). Migration and security: in search of reconciliation. *Migration Letters*, *14*(3), 371-383.

Civelek, Y. (2017). Biopolitical problematic: Syrian refugees in Turkey. In *Turkey's Syrians: Today and Tomorrow* (pp. 23-44). Transnational Press London.

Çilingir, S. (2020). The Securitisation-Integration Dilemma: The Case of British Muslims. *Migration Letters*, *17*(1), 165-177.

Gülsoy, L. Ş. (2018). Global Security and International Migration: Intolarable Weight of the Other in the Global Village. *Border Crossing*, *8*(2SI), 557-570.

Horvath, K. (2014). Securitisation, economisation and the political constitution of temporary migration: The making of the Austrian seasonal workers scheme. *Migration letters*, *11*(2), 154-170.

Hyökki, L. (2019). The EU and human rights as institutional facts in the Finnish political discourse on family reunification. *Migration Letters*, *16*(2), 317-328.

Lego, J. (2020). Criminalized and Vulnerable: Refugees and Asylum Seekers in Thailand and Malaysia. In *Agency and Immigration Policy* (pp. 7-28). Transnational Press London.

Markova, E., Paraskevopoulou, A., & McKay, S. (2019). Treading lightly: regularised migrant workers in Europe. *Migration Letters*, *16*(3), 451-461.

Medda-Windischer, R. (2016). New minorities, old instruments? Diversity governance from the perspective of minority rights. *Migration Letters*, *13*(2), 178-192.Cundal, K., & Seaman, B. (2012). Canada's temporary foreign worker programme: A discussion of human rights issues. *Migration Letters*, *9*(3), 201.

Mustasaari, S. (2017). Ruling on belonging: transnational marriages in Nordic immigration laws. *Migration Letters*, *14*(1), 25-37.

Papadopoulos, A. G. (2007). Migration and human security in the

Balkans. *Migration Letters*, *4*(2), 95-100.

Sert, D. Ş. (2019). Property rights in the Syrian conflict: remedy for the displaced. *Migration Letters*, *16*(2), 195-206.

Stępka, M. (2018). Humanitarian Securitization of the 2015 "Migration Crisis": Investigating Humanitarianism and Security in the EU Policy frames on operational Involvement in the Mediterranean. In *Migration Policy in Crisis* (pp. 9-30). Transnational Press London.

Suárez-Krabbe, J. (2013). Democratising democracy, humanising human rights: European decolonial social movements and the "alternative thinking of alternatives". *Migration Letters*, *10*(3), 333-341.

Tragaki, A. (2007). Demography and migration as human security factors: The case of South Eastern Europe. *Migration Letters*, *4*(2), 103-118.

CHAPTER 11

Universalist Rights and Particularist Duties: The Case of Refugees

Per Bauhn

Introduction

Human rights seem to co-exist uneasily with the idea of sovereign territorial nation-states. At least at a first glance, as a doctrine of normative ethics, human rights would seem to imply a moral cosmopolitanism, according to which all human beings, regardless of their nationality and citizenship, have equal rights to certain basic goods generally needed for human agency and a decent human life, such as life, health, and freedom. And if human rights apply to all human beings, so do the corresponding duties and responsibilities. In the words of Kwame Anthony Appiah, "the one thought that cosmopolitans share is that no local loyalty can ever justify forgetting that each human being has responsibilities to every other" (Appiah, 2006: xvi). This would make state borders appear morally irrelevant. Whether you live in South Sudan or South Dakota, your rights should be the same.

However, as is well known from the history of refugees, this is not the reality of the world in which we find ourselves. Refugees may not only be denied protection of their human rights by the state of which they are citizens but may also find themselves denied such protection by any other state of which they are not citizens – even by states that recognise a moral duty to uphold human rights for their own citizens.

We can think of the conflict between the human right of refugees to be admitted to a safe country and the right of states to deny refugees entry on their territory as a conflict between two normative systems. According to *ethical universalism*, all humans are equal in their human rights regardless of their citizenship and hence states are not justified in ignoring the basic rights of non-citizen refugees for the sake of protecting less important rights of their own citizens: "There are few strong grounds for giving preference to the interests of one's fellow citizens, at least when subjected to the test of impartial assessment, and none that can override the obligation that arises whenever we can, at little cost to ourselves, make an absolutely crucial difference to the well-being of another person in real need" (Singer, 2016: 206). Likewise, ethical universalists would deny that fellow citizens could be justified in prioritizing each other's rights and interests over those of non-citizens:

> People who are committed to standing in morally acceptable relations with other people would affirm the equal moral status and claims of persons generally, regardless of national identity and physical location. Associative obligations to our fellow citizens cannot override the more fundamental

moral requirement that the impact of our conduct on other people be compatible with their most basic interests (Kelly, 2004: 178).

According to *ethical particularism*, on the other hand, although humans may be equal in their human rights, the primary duty of states is to uphold these rights for their own citizens, not for mankind in general. Now, ethical particularists may very well recognize that non-citizens have human rights and that one should not interfere with these rights. Hence, ethical particularists might accept a *negative* moral duty *not to harm* innocent human beings, whether or not they are fellow citizens. Such a negative duty figures in just war theory in the form of a prohibition against targeting noncombatants. For instance, the ethical particularist Michael Walzer, who holds that "[s]tates exist to defend the rights of their members" (Walzer, 2000: 136), also defends the idea that states at war must accept moral constraints of a non-particularist kind: "A legitimate act of war is one that does not violate the rights of the people against whom it is directed" (Walzer, 2000: 135).

However, when it comes to the *positive* moral duty of *actively assisting* people in need, ethical particularists are less likely to accept that their government should treat the rights of fellow citizens and the rights of non-citizens on an equal footing, not even when it is a matter of sacrificing less important rights of fellow nationals for the sake of securing more important rights of strangers. For ethical particularists, positive moral duties require a background of special relationships. According to Thomas Nagel, the very existence of sovereign states "is precisely what gives the value of justice its application, by putting the fellow citizens of a sovereign state into a relation that they do not have with the rest of humanity" (Nagel, 2005: 120). Moreover, "[j]ustice is something we owe through our shared institutions only to those with whom we stand in a strong political relation. It is ... an *associative* obligation" (Nagel, 2005: 121; emphasis in the original). According to Nagel, obligations concerning positive rights to democracy, equality, and welfare are "fully associative"; hence, we have such obligations only in relation to fellow citizens (Nagel, 2005: 127). As taxpayers, we may have a particular and civic duty to finance education and health care for our fellow citizens, but we have no similar duty regarding non-citizens.

The Positive Duties of States

In this paper, I intend to show that it is possible to combine universalist and particularist perspectives in a rational argument about the duty of states to assist non-citizen refugees. It is important to note that this argument is one of *normative ethics*, not a descriptive one about the contents of international law, the UN Declaration of Human Rights, the Geneva Convention, or any other similar political or legal document. This is an argument about what the international law *could* and *should* be, not about what it actually happens to be. Hence, my argument relies on certain philosophical assumptions about morally justified human rights and what they imply rather than on account of what this or that convention actually says. Conventions and declarations of human rights are political documents, reflecting what states and governments at a certain point in time accept and recognise. However, as James Griffin has pointed out, "[i]t is a feature of the international declarations in general that they pay little attention to reasons or justifications" (Griffin, 2008: 192). This very lack of justificatory arguments in the existing declarations and conventions about human rights invite scepticism and criticism as to their validity and bindingness. As Amartya Sen has noted, "the basic idea of human rights, which people are supposed to have simply because they are human, is seen by many critics as entirely without any kind of a reasoned foundation. The questions that are recurrently asked are: do these rights exist? Where do they come from?" (Sen, 2010: 355).

The philosophically and intellectually more challenging task is to go beyond the mere exposition of existing human rights declarations and conventions, addressing more fundamental questions concerning what rights we *should* recognise. The kinds of questions asked about human rights by a philosopher are hence different from those asked by an international law scholar or a political scientist. Amy Gutmann has listed some of the philosophical questions:

> What is the purpose of human rights? What should their content be? When do violations of human rights warrant intervention across national boundaries? Is there a single moral foundation for human rights that spans many cultures, or are there many culturally specific moral foundations, or none? In what sense, if any, are human rights universal? (Gutmann, 2001: viii)

Here I intend to develop a normative ethical argument that combines universalist human rights, applying to all human beings, with the particularist duties of nation states regarding their own citizens. As a first step, we should note that states themselves can be given a universalist moral justification as being instrumentally necessary to the local protection of the human rights of their citizens. According to this kind of justification, the state is "a means to protect the rights of individuals rather than an end or good in itself"; consequently, "the preservation of the state or of the nation is valuable and worthy only insofar as this is of benefit to its individual members" (Gewirth, 1982: 235). Even liberals who stress the importance of individual freedom find reasons to embrace the idea of states since "justice requires states; there is no way equal freedom could be attained without them" (Stilz, 2009: 103). Hence, although actually existing states do not always conform to the requirements of human rights, this should be considered as a reason to modify the ways in which these particular states function rather than to try to abolish states as such.

The next step involves outlining what duty states may have to assist non-citizen refugees. Now, in the words of George Kennan, a government's "primary obligation is to the *interests* of the national society it represents", namely, "those of its military security, the integrity of its political life and the well-being of its people" (Kennan, 1985: 206; emphasis in the original). However, even if a state's *primary* obligation is to protect its own citizens' rights, this is not necessarily the state's *only* obligation. Even Thomas Nagel, who argues that we have obligations of justice only to fellow citizens, admits that we may have an additional duty to assist non-citizens whose negative rights have been violated in their home country: "In extreme circumstances, denial of the right of immigration may constitute a failure to respect human rights or the universal duty of rescue" (Nagel, 2005: 130).

One way of illuminating and justifying the existence of certain positive duties to non-citizens is to point to the fact that we may harm others not only by what we do to them but also by our inaction. Hence, what might, at first sight, appear as a positive duty to assist might at least sometimes actually be a case of the negative duty not to harm. Inaction, as Alan Gewirth has pointed out, is not the same as non-action (Gewirth, 1978: 219). While non-action is simply the absence of any action (as when we are asleep), inaction is the deliberate and purposive refraining from action, which itself is a kind of action. If I choose to remain passive when a person in danger calls out for my help and when I could have intervened at little cost to myself, then I perform an action, namely, the action of refusing to help that person. And if the person in need of help, as a consequence of my inaction, dies or suffers an injury, I have at least some responsibility for this, as my inaction is causally related to her death or injury.

That the passivity of wealthy societies in the face of global inequality can be tantamount to harming the global poor has been argued by Thomas Pogge: "[T]he better-off – we – are *harming* the worse-off insofar as we are upholding a shared institutional order that is *unjust* by foreseeably and avoidably (re)producing radical inequality" (Pogge, 2005: 42). My argument, however, is not about whether or not wealthy political communities have a general duty to transfer resources to poor political communities (this, I believe, would depend on many other considerations, including previous exploitation of the poorer societies by the wealthier ones, the role played by undemocratic and corrupt leaders in the poorer societies, and so on). Instead, I will limit myself to the issue of what duties states and political communities have regarding non-citizen refugees.

To the extent that states have a negative duty not to inflict harm on non-citizens (which we have already assumed), and given that inaction can cause unjustified harm, it would follow logically that states have a positive duty to assist non-citizens, at least when not doing so would cause these non-citizens to suffer an unjustified harm and when assisting them would not inflict any comparable cost or harm on the assisting state and its citizens. The latter condition, about comparable cost, recognizes that states have a prior and permanent duty to protect their own citizens' rights. The condition would permit states to refuse to help refugees who can be expected to inflict harm on their citizens, such as terrorists and other militant extremists.

At one extreme, the positive duty to assist non-citizens could justify military intervention against a dictatorship that oppresses its own citizens, at least when there is no other way of relieving these people of their oppressors. This is, for instance, the line taken by Erin Kelly, when she argues that "it is hard to understand how states that form a global society through their complex interrelations could together affirm a conception of global justice that does not treat the systematic violation of human rights as morally urgent enough to warrant intervention" (Kelly, 2003: 133). However, for such an intervention to be morally justified, it must itself be carried out in a manner consistent with the human rights of the persons involved, including both the citizens and soldiers of the intervening state and the innocent citizens of the state that is the target of the intervention. Here I do not intend to deal with the complexities relating to the justification of humanitarian interventions but will instead focus on the more general topic about how the human rights of refugees can be reconciled with the particularism of individual states and their duties to their own citizens.

The argument developed so far lends some support to ethical universalism by recognising that states do indeed have a duty to assist refugees. But what is involved in this duty? Here we can expect that ethical universalists and ethical particularists will come to different conclusions, depending on their different outlooks. While ethical universalists are likely to hold that human rights override the rights of states and their citizens, ethical particularists are equally likely to defend the right of states to give priority to the protection of their own citizens.

Ethical Universalism

Ethical universalism, when applied to migrants and refugees and as outlined by Joseph Carens, claims that the international system of independent states is unjust, since it arbitrarily leaves some people – namely, those who are ruled by oppressive governments – deprived of their human rights and without any assurance that they will have their rights protected by any other government. This moral failure of the state system can, according to Carens, only be rectified by an open borders principle, making it a duty for all states to admit refugees who are escaping the oppressive politics of their own government: "Because the state system assigns people to states, states collectively have a responsibility to help those for whom this assignment is disastrous" (Carens, 2013: 196). According to Carens, the duty to admit refugees involves much more than just allowing them to cross the border to a safe country:

> A rich democratic state cannot create camps where refugees are prevented from having contact with the rest of the population and are provided only with basic levels of food, clothing, and shelter, even if the provision of such basic levels of support would be equal to what the refugees could have expected if their membership rights had been respected in their country of origin. If a democratic state admits refugees, it must provide the refugees with most of the rights that others living in the society enjoy. Over time, it must accept them as members (Carens, 2013: 204).

According to Carens, given the urgent and basic needs of refugees, wealthy democratic states will in many cases be morally obligated to give priority to the interests of refugees over the interests of their own citizens: "When are we justified in turning away genuine refugees? ... My own answer is 'almost never.' ... If one takes the moral claims of refugees seriously, ... it is not clear why their claims to an admission which is necessary to protect their most basic rights should be subordinated to much less vital interests of members of the receiving state" (Carens, 2013: 218–219). This is the *comparable cost argument*, briefly referred to above in our account of why states may have positive duties regarding non-citizens. According to this argument, if the refugees' cost of not being admitted is higher than the receiving political community's cost of admitting them, then the right of the refugees to be admitted overrides the right of the receiving political community to deny them entry and subsequent protection of their well-being.

Now, this argument assumes that states should not discriminate between citizens and non-citizens when it comes to responding to people's need for protection of their human rights; only the importance of the need itself should guide their decisions. Of course, much depends here on what is meant by terms such as "most basic rights" and "much less vital interests". Even an ethical particularist might accept that saving refugees from being massacred is morally more important than spending resources on building a new motorway or a new airport (which might be bad for the environment anyway). But should a state also be morally obligated to forgo a reform that would provide free university education for all its citizens for the sake of spending these resources on sheltering non-citizen refugees instead? Granted, even if we accept that there is a human right to education, this right would seem to be less fundamental to human well-being than being alive and physically safe – but is this all that matters here? Does a state have a duty to sacrifice free higher education for its own citizens for the sake of rescuing refugees regardless of whether or not such a sacrifice is *necessary*, given the capacity of *other* states to admit refugees? This question points to the need for combining the comparable cost argument with a fair share argument. We will return to comparable costs and fair shares below.

Ethical Particularism

Ethical particularism questions the assumption that a state is morally obligated to open its borders to all refugees who want to enter its territory and to provide them with the same rights as its own citizens have. According to an argument developed by Christopher Heath Wellman and based on the principle of freedom of association, a state should be free *not* to associate with people who want to be admitted to its territory. In Wellman's words, "legitimate political states are morally entitled to unilaterally design and enforce their own immigration policies, even if these policies exclude potential immigrants who desperately want to enter" (Wellman & Cole, 2011: 13). Now, Wellman recognises that the needs of refugees might call for urgent acts of assistance and he does not exclude that a state might be morally obligated to assist refugees in *other* ways than by admitting them on its territory, for instance by helping them in their home country. He also accepts that it might be at least temporarily necessary for a state to host refugees "until their protection against persecution can be guaranteed" (Wellman & Cole, 2011: 122). However, unlike Carens, he believes that the host state does not have the same kind of extensive duties to the refugees as it has to its own citizens. This is what Wellman calls the case of the baby on the doorstep: "Suppose ... that I open my front door in the dead of winter and find a new-born baby wrapped in blankets. Clearly, I must bring the infant in from the cold, but it does not follow that I must then adopt the child and raise her as my own" (Wellman & Cole, 2011: 122).

However, when it comes to the rights of refugees, things are not so straightforward. True, the receiving state might not be under any obligation to offer citizenship to newly arrived refugees (the equivalent of adopting the child on the doorstep). But this does not mean that the receiving state has no supportive responsibilities at all. Once the refugees are admitted, they will need shelter, food, and sometimes also medical care; likewise, their children will need at least some basic education. And the refugees will depend on the receiving state for these goods. Moreover, they might depend on the receiving state for quite a while, given that it will take some time before they have acquired sufficient linguistic and other skills to be able to support themselves by means of productive and remunerative employment.

Comparable Costs and Fair Shares

Now, an ethical particularist might accept that a state has indeed a duty to open its borders to refugees but instead qualify this duty by a *fair share argument*, briefly referred to above. The intuition behind the fair share argument has been captured by Liam Murphy: "We should do our fair share, which can amount to a great sacrifice in certain circumstances; what we cannot be required to do is other people's shares as well as our own" (Murphy, 1993: 278). This argument also forms a part of the assumptions underlying Appiah's ideal of cosmopolitanism: "[O]ur obligation is not to carry the whole burden alone. Each of us should do our fair share; but we cannot be required to do more" (Appiah, 2006: 164).

Applied to the case of refugees, the fair share argument suggests that the duty to admit refugees and to protect their rights should be fairly distributed among all states in proportion to their capacity to contribute and not only be assigned to the state that happens to be the nearest or most attractive for refugees to enter; moreover, no state would have a duty to contribute more than its fair share. Hence, David Miller argues that "the obligation to protect human rights extends only to doing what a fair distribution of responsibility demands; or at least that is all that a state can be required to do as a matter of justice" (Miller, 2016: 36). One practical implication of the fair share argument is that refugees could be distributed among different host states in accordance with the capabilities of these states to protect the refugees' rights rather than in accordance with the wishes of the refugees themselves: "the refugee's claim is to reside somewhere where her human rights are secure, and this need not be the place that she most prefers" (Miller, 2016: 86). Interestingly enough, the ethical universalist Joseph Carens agrees: "Refugees have a moral right to a safe place to live, but they do not have a moral entitlement to choose where that will be" (Carens, 2013: 216). In what follows, I intend to show that the fair share argument associated with ethical particularism can be combined with the comparable cost argument associated with ethical universalism into a moral principle regulating states' duties regarding refugees.

To begin with, we need to clarify the meaning of "fair shares". Fair shares in relation to what? Wealth, size of the population, previous capacity to absorb refugees, the degree of democracy? Here I intend to suggest one way of calculating fair shares (but without claiming that it is the only possible one), namely, by relating the share of refugees that a state has a duty to assume responsibility for to that state's share of the global gross domestic product (GDP). Now, the UNHCR estimates the global number of refugees (including asylum-seekers) to 28.5 million (UNHCR, 2018). According to the IMF, the value of the global GDP in 2017 was US \$79.87 trillion (IMF, 2018). At the same time, the GDP of the US was US \$19.39 trillion, or 24.28 per cent of the global GDP. According to the UNHCR, the US has admitted 929,850 refugees or 3.26 per cent of the world's refugees. Likewise, China with a GDP of US $12.01 trillion or 15.04 per cent of the global GDP has admitted 322,439 refugees, which is equivalent to 1.13 per cent of the total number of refugees in the world. In absolute numbers, it is slightly less than the number of refugees admitted by Sweden (327,709 or 1.15 per cent of the global refugee population) with a GDP of US $0.54 trillion or 0.68 per cent of the global GDP. Turkey, on the other hand, with a GDP of US $0.85 trillion (1.06 per cent of the global GDP), has admitted 3,789,320 refugees (13.3 per cent of the global refugee population). Relying on figures like these, we have reason to assume that some states do more and other states do much less than their fair share as regards protecting the human rights of refugees.

Of course, a state could assist refugees in other ways than by admitting them on its territory, for instance, by contributing to other states that receive refugees or to organisations like the UNHCR or by trying to improve conditions in the refugees' home country so that they might be able to return. Hence, it would be misleading to accuse a state of not doing its fair share based only on how many refugees it admits on its territory. However, given that we include both direct and indirect forms of protection, relating the share of refugees that a state assists in one way or another to its share of the global GDP would still work as a way of assessing how well it fulfils its moral duties regarding refugees. A state with x per cent of the global GDP should assist x per cent of the world's refugees, either directly, by admitting them on its territory, or indirectly, by helping other states or organisations to protect them, or by enabling them to return to their home country.

From a fair share point of view, we should expect every state to accept responsibility for a share of the global refugee population that is at least equivalent to its share of the global GDP. However, if a state is capable of accepting a larger share of refugees *without* having to sacrifice any of its own citizens' rights, then it has a moral duty to do so. Here we depart from ethical particularism and its fair share argument, which holds that no state has a duty to do more than its fair share. On the other hand, we depart from ethical universalism and its comparable cost argument by assuming that no state would have a duty to sacrifice *any* rights of its own citizens (including rights that are of less importance than the rights of the refugees) for the sake of assisting a larger share of refugees than is equivalent to its share of the global GDP. Hence, our argument can best be described as a *combined comparable cost and fair share argument*.

The outcome of the reasoning presented here is a morally legitimate and workable policy for states concerning their duties regarding refugees. We should retain the universalist idea that the justification of the duty of states to admit and protect refugees is to be found in human rights and in the fact that refugees stand to lose much more in terms of rights if they are not admitted than do the receiving states if they are admitted – that is, the comparable cost argument. We should also recognize that the particularist fair share argument sets limits to this duty, by stating that no state is morally obligated to do more than its fair share if doing so would impair its capacity to uphold the rights of its own citizens, regardless of whether or not these rights are more important than the rights of the refugees. (Hence, a state would *not* be morally obligated to forgo its own citizens' right to free university education for the sake of admitting more than its fair share of refugees.) However, if it turns out that a particular state can indeed do more than its fair share to protect refugees *without* risking any rights of its own citizens, then it would indeed have a duty to do so. In this way, the comparable cost principle remains in force, admitting of exceptions only when it is true *both* that a state has done its fair share *and* that further contributions would endanger the rights of its own citizens.

Now, if only some states fulfil their positive duties to non-citizen refugees in accordance with the combined comparable cost and fair share argument while other states do not, this would leave a certain number of refugees without any protection of their human rights. In such a case, it is not the states that have done their fair share that should be blamed for the fate of the refugees who are left without sufficient protection, but rather the states that have *not* done their fair share.

Here we should note the complication that some states both receive and produce refugees (Sirkeci, 2017). That is, while they fulfil the positive duty of assisting non-citizen refugees, they also violate the negative duty of not forcing their own citizens to become refugees. Obviously such states, in spite of what they do for non-citizen refugees, are morally deficient, as they fail in their primary duty to maintain and protect their own citizens' human rights.

To sum up, the solution to the problem of how to accommodate the duties of states and the human rights of refugees lies not in choosing either ethical universalism or ethical particularism, but rather in combining these two strands of ethical reasoning. By combining the universalist comparable cost argument and the particularist fair share argument, we can provide ourselves with a normative instrument for the ethical assessment of states and their duties regarding non-citizen refugees.

References

Appiah, K. A. (2006). Cosmopolitanism: Ethics in a World of Strangers. London: Allen Lane.

Carens, J. (2013). The Ethics of Immigration. New York: Oxford University Press.

Gewirth, A. (1978). Reason and Morality. Chicago: The University of Chicago Press.

Gewirth, A. (1982). Human Rights. Chicago: The University of Chicago Press.

Griffin, J. (2008). On Human Rights. Oxford: Oxford University Press. https://doi.org/10.1093/acprof:oso/9780199238781.001.0001

Gutmann, A. (2001). "Introduction". In: A. Gutmann (ed.), Human Rights as Politics and Idolatry (pp. vii–xxviii). Princeton, NJ: Princeton University Press.

IMF. (2018). World Economic Outlook Database, April 2018. Retrieved September 27, 2018, from https://www.imf.org/external/pubs/ft/weo/2018/01/weodata/index.aspx

Kelly, E. (2003). "The Burdens of Collective Liability". In: D. K. Chatterjee and D. E. Schied (eds.), Ethics and Foreign Intervention (pp. 118–139). Cambridge: Cambridge University Press.

Kelly, E. (2004). "Human Rights as Foreign Policy Imperatives". In: D. K. Chatterjee (ed.), The Ethics of Assistance (pp. 177–192). Cambridge: Cambridge University Press. https://doi.org/10.1017/ CBO9780511817663.010

Kennan, G. F. (1985). "Morality and Foreign Policy". Foreign Affairs, 64 (2): 205–218. https://doi.org/10.2307/20042569

Miller, D. (2016). Strangers in Our Midst. Cambridge, MA: Harvard University Press. https://doi.org/10.4159/9780674969827

Murphy, L. (1993). "The Demands of Beneficence". Philosophy and Public Affairs, 22 (4): 267–292.

Nagel, T. (2005). "The Problem of Global Justice". Philosophy and Public Affairs, 33 (2): 113–147. https://doi.org/10.1111/j.1088-4963.2005.00027.x

Pogge, T. (2005). "Real World Justice". The Journal of Ethics, 9 (1–2): 29–53. https://doi.org/10.1007/ s10892-004-3313-z

Sen, A. (2010). The Idea of Justice. London: Penguin Books.

Singer, P. (2016). One World Now. New Haven: Yale University Press.

Sirkeci, I. (2017). "Turkey's Refugees, Syrians, and Refugees from Turkey: A Country of Insecurity". Migration Letters,

14 (1): 127–144. https://doi.org/10.33182/ml.v14i1.32

Stilz, A. (2009). Liberal Loyalty. Princeton, NJ: Princeton University Press. https://doi.org/10.1515/ 9781400830701

UNHCR. (2018). Figures at a Glance. Retrieved September 25, 2018, from http://www.unhcr.org/figures-at-a-glance.html

Walzer, M. (2000). Just and Unjust Wars. New York: Basic Books.

Wellman, C. H. & Cole, P. (2011). Debating the Ethics of Immigration. New York: Oxford University Press. https://doi.org/10.1093/acprof:osobl/9780199731732.001.0001.

CHAPTER 12

Bordering Practices across Europe: The Rise of "Walls" and "Fences"

Burcu Toğral Koca

Introduction

In the wake of the geopolitical changes that have roiled the globe since the 1980s—notably the fall of the Berlin Wall–a "borderless and deterritorialised world" discourse rose to prominence (Newman 2006). Pioneered by the advocates of globalization, this discourse envisaged a new era in which the world would see the free movement of capital, goods and people. This discourse has also become a dominant theme in analysing the European integration process. The so-called "borderless" Europe debate emerged with the introduction of the Single Market and Schengen area which called for the free movement of capital, goods and people within the European Union (EU). Within the process of the EU enlargement, nationals of EU member states (and of some privileged non-member countries belonging to the Global North) enjoy this freedom without much interruption. However, at the same time, we have witnessed that same Europe has become characterised by a hardening of existing borders and the construction of new ones for certain groups of people, especially for those migrants coming from poor and Muslim countries, refugees, asylum seekers and undocumented immigrants. As widely discussed in the literature, this hardening of borders has become more evident following the September 11 and subsequent attacks, which provided a useful pretext to justify the introduction of more sophisticated and draconian measures for border policing (see Vallet and David 2012).

These claims have been ratified once more in the wake of the spike in refugee movements since 2010, which undoubtedly form the largest since World War II. Following the outbreak of the Syrian war in 2011, millions of people were forced to flee their homes, initially to neighbouring countries and from there to Europe. Using mainly Turkey and Libya as transit routes, these refugees have risked their lives in search of safety and better life opportunities in Europe. In the face of their suffering, European countries' restrictive policies have increasingly attracted a great deal of criticism from the international community. Even though in the beginning some countries, such as Germany and Sweden, did grant protection—especially to Syrian refugees—this support has remained limited in the face of ever-increasing numbers fleeing the region. In the name of the fight against uncontrolled migration and terrorism, European countries have adopted stringent measures which are likely to prevent people from seeking protection. Most notably, when Europe saw a rising number of arrivals, especially from Syria, from 2015—"the most deadly year of to date for would-be asylum seekers braving Europe's border" (De Genova, 2016: 135)—walls and fences returned as key instruments for the control of refugee movements. These instruments have been built to "separate EU nations from states outside the bloc, but some (have been erected) between EU states, including members of Europe's passport-free zone" (Baczynska and Ledwith, 2016).

In the light of these developments, this article discusses these recent bordering practices across and around Europe with a special focus on the construction of walls and fences. Drawing on critical border studies, the article engages first with the pre-existing theoretical and conceptual discussions on the bordering practices in general and walls/fences in particular for better comprehending the current debates. Shifting from a traditional understanding of "borders" to a broader notion of "bordering practices, critical border studies have shed much-needed light on the way "borders" are constructed, reproduced—as well as circumvented—by different players at multiple scales and the many and varied types of actors involved in this process, as well as the various kinds of "borders" thus produced. In line with these discussions, the article focuses on the material and discursive underpinnings of these practices and explores how they are justified as strategies to control, contain and filter unwanted mobility while being, at the same time, contested/challenged by various state and non-state actors. To do so—and to uncover the discursive and non-discursive interventions of both states and non-states actors in bordering practices—I have collected data through archival research of statements of state agencies and politicians, reports from Non-Governmental Organizations (NGOs), and newspapers. Concomitantly, the article also reflects on the detrimental impacts of these practices on the rights of refugees and problematizes the approaches of European states vis-à-vis current refugee movements.

Critical Border Studies: From "Borders" to "Bordering Practices"

As mentioned, in the aftermath of the fall of the Berlin Wall many theorists assumed that globalization would produce a "borderless" world and/or Europe "where walls and fences would become increasingly anachronistic" and "the free flow of capital, goods, and people around the world" would be the order of the day (Rosiere and Jones, 2012: 217). Contrary to these assumptions, what has been witnessed across the world is the introduction of new border control practices and the transformation of existing ones against the movement of people. As Andreas (2003: 79) has rightly noted, increasing investment in law enforcement and surveillance technologies, adoption of stricter visa and border control regimes, enhanced cooperation with third countries as well as the increasing resort to military personnel and devices prove this tendency. These developments have been clearly visible in Europe, which is now "characterized by a proliferation of borders (both in the territorial sense of borders between an increasing number of EU member states in addition to an array of new and shifting European borders, but also in the sense of diffuse institutional, legal, economic, social borders)" (Rumford, 2006a: 135). Hence, as Rumford says, "we are not living in a 'borderless Europe': we are living in a Europe made up of borders and borderlands" (2006a: 135).

Closely tracking these empirical realities, a bourgeoning literature on "borders" and "bordering practices" has emerged. Of those, critical border studies, which question and challenge the traditional state-centric understanding of borders, developed fundamental insights into the transformation of "borders" and "border controls" (see among others, Balibar 2004; Brown, 2010; Walker 2010; Jones, 2016; Paasi 1998; Rumford 2006a, 2006b; Walters 2004; Rosiere and Jones 2012; Vaughan-Williams 2012). With a specific focus on the EU as well as on the U.S.–Mexico border zone, they cast light on various aspects of bordering practices including the operation, technologization and militarisation of bordering practices as well as the role of multiple actors engaging in these practices. Their contribution can be summarized under three rubrics. The first is the transformation of the meaning of the border and the dynamics of bordering practices. The second is the proliferation of actors in bordering processes. The last is the selectivity and symbolic function/value of border controls.

Regarding the first point, rather than treating borders as fixed lines at the edges of states' territories, critical approaches analyse them as "processes, practices, discourses, symbols, institutions or networks through which power works" (Johnson et al., 2011: 62). As Rumford argues: "Borders are no longer seen only as lines on a map, but as spaces in their own right (as in the idea of 'borderlands') and as processes; in short, there has been a shift from borders to bordering (or rebordering, on some accounts)" (Johnson et al., 2011: 67). In this respect, contemporary walls and fences are interpreted as sites, spaces or borderlands signifying "the production of difference in space" (De Genova, 2016: 4) that seek to contain, control, and filter population movements. Those following a Foucauldian approach treat them as security barriers dividing "not land, but populations" (Buur et al., 2007: 6). Concomitantly, these studies also shed light on how these bordering practices are supplemented by the process of technologization and militarisation "for achieving the subjugating of bodies and the control of population" (Foucault, 1978:140).[1]

The second point underlines that border control issues should not be seen as fields under the exclusive authority of nation-states. Recent studies, especially those focusing on EU-level developments, illustrate that not only states and official agencies but private bodies –IT companies, citizens, migrants, smugglers as well as NGOs—are increasingly involved in the business of bordering, which Rumford has termed "borderwork" (Rumford, 2008:). According to Rumford, "borders can be created, shifted, and deconstructed by a range of actors (…) borderwork is no longer the exclusive preserve of the nation-state (…) Citizens as well states, have the ability to shape debordering and rebordering" (Rumford, 2006b: 164–165). This is an important break from the traditional state-centric thinking underestimating the role of the agency of other actors in shaping and challenging states' bordering practices. As the "conflict model of migration" developed by Sirkeci eloquently puts it, the bordering practices and the transnational space, in which these practices operate, are "constantly transformed by conflicts and migrations" (Sirkeci, 2009: 8). For Sirkeci, "the continuous conflict between the regulating and migrating human

---

[1] Different from the past, under the process of technologization, contemporary bordering practices are equipped with high-tech and costly equipment, including "fixed radars, ground sensors, remote control barriers and software linking border agents to control towers" (Rosiere and Jones, 2012: 226). Besides, as Lutterbeck notes, contemporary bordering practices also reflect a process of militarization characterized by an "increasing mobilization of both paramilitary police and military security forces, as well as a resort to a growing amount of military-style hardware in preventing irregular immigration and cross border crime" (Lutterbeck, 2006: 61).

agency forces changes in migration regulations (e.g. tightening admission rules) and in response to these changes, migrating human agency changes his or her strategies, mechanisms, routes, and pathways of international migration" (Sirkeci, 2009: 11).

Similarly, in her extensive field works on walls and fences, Pallister-Wilkins also draws the attention to the relationship between the agency of non-state actors and bordering practices by arguing that "walls work to govern populations through their relationship to mobility. Populations and their capacity for mobility are the logic that bind walls across spatio-temporal scales" (Pallister-Wilkins, 2015: 443). For example, rather than being only "victims" as portrayed by the public, migrants (together with smugglers) challenge states' bordering practices and force them to enact new measures and control techniques. In this context, it is widely argued that walls, fences and other border control practices can only divert the movements rather than eliminating and controlling them, as migrants and smugglers are continuously developing new strategies and finding new routes en route to the developed Global North. Hence, bordering practices are structured by multiple actors ranging from governmental authorities to the very people on the move (Jones and Johnson, 2016).

Under the third rubric, first, in terms of selectivity, bordering practices in general (and walls/fences in particular) must not be understood as lines seeking total closure of a certain space, but as "biopolitical architectures concerned with regulating circulation" (Pallister-Wilkins, 2016a: 156), filtering and categorizing wanted/desirable and unwanted/undesirable as well as worthy and unworthy of protection. In this respect, as security barriers, border control practices in general (and walls/fences in particular) aim at "stabilizing centres from undesired flows from the periphery (…) and creating an efficient system of selection that determines which types of mobility to allow" (Pallister-Wilkins, 2016a: 231–232). About this selectivity of borders, Rumford points out that "spaces and borders are not necessarily experienced in the same way by all (people). What forms a common space of freedom justice and security for some can constitute a threat to others" (Rumford, 2006a: 135). In short, as the securitization literature highlights, for certain group of migrants—including refugees, asylum seekers, undocumented migrants and those coming from poor and Muslim countries, who are being administered as a as a security threat and linked to various security problems ranging from criminality and cultural/religious threat to terrorism—borders are more real and selective in nature (Bigo, 2002).

In addition to the selective nature of borders, these scholars further point to the symbolic function/value of bordering practices. They argue that these instruments have a deterrence effect for those seeking to cross borders and send the message that "governments are doing something" (Vallet and David, 2012: 114–115). Hence, other than material functions, such as "protection, separation and even segregation", walls and fences offer a clear image of a fortified and controlled border (Vallet and David, 2012: 114–115) and have a "symbolic role (…) in reaffirming the power of state and its old, but still strong, territoriality" (Rosiere and Jones, 2012: 226).

Bordering Europe Through Walls and Fences

Bordering through walls and fences has a long history, dating back to the building of the Great Wall of China and the Roman Limes, which are the most prominent examples. These barriers were constructed against foreign invasion as well as unwanted migration. In the twentieth century, the tradition has remained alive and well. From the end of World War II to the end of the Cold War, nineteen walls and barriers were erected (Vallet and David, 2012: 113). Especially during the Cold War, "the borderlines dividing Western and Eastern Europe were intensively patrolled and marked by barbed wire fencing, watchtowers, land mines, and automatic weapons" (Andreas, 2003: 100). As mentioned, the end of the Cold War—especially the fall of the Berlin Wall—was perceived as "an end to the process of separation through fencing and walling" (Pallister-Wilkins, 2016b: 65). However, since then European countries have erected or started 1,200km (750 miles) of anti-immigrant walls and fences at the cost of at least €500 million ($570 million) (Baczynska and Ledwith, 2016). Especially those member states located on the geographical periphery of the EU have fortified their borders through walls and fences.[2]

This bordering process through walls and fences has reached its peak following the Syrian war in 2011 but especially in the face of the increasing attempts of refugees to reach Europe in the year 2015. Against these arrivals, growing tensions among European countries have emerged, and Europe has experienced rising support for anti-immigrant parties, and the weakening of "Europe's passport-free travel zone" (Tasch and Nudelman, 2016). To control refugees attempting to enter Europe through Greece, Italy, and Hungary, the European Commission proposed refugee quotas to distribute the burden between the member states. However, this proposal led to a contentious debate and many Balkan states refused to adopt this system (Dzenovska, 2016). After being approved by the European Parliament in September 2015, this system was initially supposed to resettle 120,000 refugees (Dzenovska, 2016). Yet, rather than follow this plan, both the EU and non-member European countries have reacted by hardening their bordering practices by constructing walls and fences.

First, Balkan countries fortified their borders from mid-October 2015, as around 180,000 migrants have entered Europe through the Balkans, from Turkey via Greece, Macedonia, Serbia and Croatia via Slovenia and into western Europe (Oliveira, 2015). Hungary has become the leading country closing and fencing its borders against the arrivals of refugees. It first sealed the border with Serbia in September 2015 with a 109-mile-long, barbed-wire border fence and then later in October 2015 the Croatian border with a 175-kilometre fence equipped with razor

---

[2] For example, the border fences constructed around Ceuta and Melilla, the two Spanish enclaves located in North Africa. After having become one of the main destinations for unauthorized migrants attempting to enter the EU, the Civil Guard—the Spanish national paramilitary police—upgraded its policing efforts in these two cities and constructed a double fence around them from the beginning of the 1990s (Pugh, 2000: 39) Similarly, becoming another major point of entry for unauthorized migration following the hardening of border controls along the Spanish coast, Greece also constructed a 10.5 km-long and 4 meter-high, barbed-wire fence that cost more than €3 million along its border with Turkey in 2012. As in the Spanish case, this border fence has been continuously upgraded and supplemented by watchtowers, thermal vision cameras and other night vision devices.

wire (Taylor, 2015). Prime Minister Orbán—known for his tough anti-immigrant stance—further announced that "his government is also ready to extend the fence to Romania" (Deutsche Welle 2016). Finally, in 2016, Hungary decided to upgrade border security with a new and even "more massive" fence (Dearden, 2016). Orbán stated: "Technical planning is under way to erect a more massive defence system next to the existing line of defence, which was built quickly last year" (Dearden, 2016). He defended the new plan as a response to a "greater need for security" and continued with his securitarian discourse framing migrants as a security threat by saying that:

> Immigration and migrants damage Europe's security, [they] are a threat to people and bring terrorism upon us [and] this was caused by allowing the uncontrolled entry of large numbers of people from areas where Europe and the Western world are seen as the enemy (Dearden, 2016).

He further securitized Muslim migrants by arguing that the door would be closed to them in order to defend "European Christianity against a Muslim influx" (Traynor, 2015). This statement not only signifies the selective approach justified by securitizing certain group of migrants through linking it with terrorism, but also what De Genova (2016: 137) says:

> people on the move across state borders are not in fact considered to be the genuine bearers of any presumptive (purportedly universal) 'human right' to asylum but rather are always under suspicion of deception and subterfuge, produced as the inherently dubious claimants to various forms of institutionalized international protection.

Recently the Greek border has attracted much of the attention, as the Greek islands emerged as the key entry point for majority of refugees from the beginning of 2015. After this time, Orbán called for a fence on the northern-border of Greece to block this route (Deutsche Welle, 2016). Another contentious step was taken in March 217, when the Hungarian Parliament passed a new law allowing the detention of all asylum seekers in camps built from shipping containers at the country's borders while their applications are being processed. This law will be applied to "all adult asylum-seekers regardless of gender, age and vulnerability, as well as children traveling with adults and unaccompanied minors above the age of 14" (Amnesty International, 2017). Gauri Van Gulik, Amnesty International's Deputy Director for Europe, commented that:

> Plans to automatically detain some of the world's most vulnerable people in shipping containers behind razor wire fences, sometimes for months on end, are beyond the pale. This new border detention package is just the latest in Hungary's aggressive crackdown on refugees and migrants (Amnesty International, 2017).

However, it should also be mentioned that despite the securitarian discourses and policies of the Hungarian government toward refugees, it has kept the door open for those migrants with enough money under the Hungarian residency bonds program introduced in 2012 (Korkut, 2017). According to this program, resident permits and a path to citizenship are granted to foreigners who invest at least

€300,000 in Hungarian government securities (Korkut, 2017). Initially, Chinese traders and later investors from the Middle East have purchased bonds (Korkut, 2017). This once again confirms the selective nature of bordering practices.

Hungary's move led other Balkan countries to take similar measures. For example, complaining about the mass entry of migrants trying to get through its territory into Austria and Germany after Hungary sealed its border with Croatia, Slovenia decided to harden border control measures in 2015. Militarisation of the bordering process sped up with new legislation passed in October 2015 that grants the army extensive power to support the police force in protecting borders following thousands of arrivals from Croatia after the closure of the Hungarian border (NBC News, 2015). In particular, the army can now "take part in patrols along the 670-kilometre border, detain people, hand them to police and issue orders to civilians" (Chadwick, 2015). Second, the government also decided to build some temporary technical obstacles on the border with Croatia. Prime Minister Miro Cerar explained that: "These obstacles, including fences if needed, will have the objective of directing migrants towards the border crossings. We are not closing our borders" (Telegraph 2015). In the end, metal fences were erected at its border crossing of Sredisce ob Dravi, "which forced refugees to wait for around 14 hours on the border, without food or shelter" (Webb and Squires, 2015). Besides, Slovenia has also adopted a selective approach in its bordering process as well by admitting only people from Syria, Iraq and Afghanistan and excluding other nationals seen not as worthy of protection (Deutsche Welle, 2015a).

In 2015, Macedonia also started to erect a border fence—similar to the one constructed by Hungary—along its southern border with Greece to control and contain entry of unauthorized migrants. Criticizing the Hungarian justifications of fences as a way to protect European wealth and Christian values against migrants, the government spokesman Aleksandar Gjorgjie said the fence was constructed only to "to direct the inflow of people toward the controlled points for their registration and humane treatment" and the border would remain open to refugees (Deutsche Welle, 2015b). However, this "humanitarian" justification was followed by a selective approach toward refugees. Similar to Slovenia, refugees from countries other than Syria, Afghanistan and Iraq have been denied entry into Macedonia (Deutsche Welle, 2015b). In response to this selective approach, Greek authorities stated that this selective policy "has led to some 800 migrants of other nationalities being stranded in Greece at the Macedonian border. Iranians, Pakistanis, Moroccans and others have held days of protests, and several migrants broke through a flimsy barrier into Macedonia" on November 2015 (Deutsche Welle, 2015b). It is further reported that:

> More than 10,000—a third of them children—are camped in flimsy tents near the fence. Many families have refused to leave the border, waiting instead for it to open, as respiratory infections spread and frustration mounts (Baczynska and Ledwith, 2016).

While having previously followed a liberal stance toward refugees and criticized the construction of the walls and fences, Austria also announced its plan of sealing off its borders at the Spielfeld border crossing with Slovenia and started constructing a 2.3-mile metal fence on November 2016 after Germany's announcement about reintroducing border checks Austrian border (Jamieson, 2016). The previous Austrian Chancellor Werner Faymann claimed that the fence would not close the border totally but would provide better control of movements of migrants on its border with Slovenia (BBC 2015, October 28). The government justified this plan with the following words: "Austria was being overwhelmed 'because Germany is taking too few' migrants" (Graham-Harrison, 2015). It was further stated that the fence was necessary for "crowd management" (Baczynska and Ledwith, 2016). Miki-Leitner, from the center-right Austrian People's Party, also stated that "This is about ensuring an orderly controlled entry into our country, not about shutting down the border" and further argued that:

> We know that in recent days and weeks individual groups of migrants have become more impatient, aggressive and emotional. If groups of people push from behind, with children and women stuck in between, you need stable, massive measures (Dallison, 2015).

On the other hand, it is claimed that such a short fence has only a symbolic effect rather than a material one by delivering "a clear message: the doors to Austria are closed and migrants are no longer welcome" (Granados et al., 2016). This move can also be regarded that "a fence had been built inside Europe's border-control-free Schengen Area" (Taylor, 2015).

Another contentious bordering process has been taking place around the port of Calais "home to a controversial makeshift camp known as 'the jungle' where thousands of displaced people live in squalid conditions" (Britton, 2016). Being a hot spot for the entry of unauthorised migrants from France to the UK, Calais has been continuously fortified through security barriers. In 2014, the UK devoted £ 12 million over three years to control and contain migrants from the port and "built a 15ft fence along the motorway leading to the port" which was supported by "detection technology such as the heartbeat and carbon dioxide detectors" and (dog searches)" (BBC, 2016a). The fence was justified not only with reference to controlling and containing unauthorised migration but also to blocking the entry of "foreign jihadists" into the UK by the former Minister of Integration James Bronkenshire (Ross et al., 2015). Concerning the stopping of jihadists, he said: "the public can be assured that it is the government's highest priority to protect Britain from attack" (Ross et al., 2015). This symbolic message was replicated in his further statements arguing that "erecting the fences is part of a bid to send a message that the UK is 'no soft touch' for migrants" (Perrin, 2014). The port has also come to be militarized by armed French and British forces following the August 2015 agreement between the two sides (BBC, 2016a) As the fences have not been able to stop migration through Calais, the UK (in cooperation with France) decided to build a wall—dubbed the "Great Wall of Calais" by some media—along both sides of the main road to the Calais port in 2016 (BBC, 2016b). Goodwill, the Immigration Minister, said that "People are still getting through. We have done the fences. Now we are doing the wall" (York, 2016). He further justified the wall to ensure security at the port and stated that:

> We are going to start building this big, new wall as part of the £17m package

we are doing with the French. There is still more to do. We have also invested in space for 200 lorries at Calais so that they have somewhere safe to wait (Britton, 2016).

He also criminalized migrants and framed them as a threat to the UK's own well-being, by adding that: "It would be a negotiating objective of the UK to remove people working and living there, making a contribution to our health service, to our agriculture, to all other areas that they do" (York, 2016). Some supported these measures and argued for their effectiveness. For example, Eurotunnel—one of the firms operating the tunnel between France and the UK— stated that "since a major security upgrade around its French terminal last October [2015], migrants have ceased to cause troubles (Baczynska and Ledwith, 2016). Eurotunnel spokesperson John Keefe further claimed, "There have been no disruptions to services since mid-October 2015, so we can say that the combination of the fence and additional police presence has been highly effective" (Baczynska and Ledwith, 2016). However, strong criticisms were also raised by different sections of society within the UK and France. For example, British truck drivers complaining about the jumping of migrants on trucks in their attempt to cross the French–UK border, interpreted the wall as a "poor use of taxpayers' money". The head of the Road Haulage Association Richard Burnett argued that "it is imperative that the money to pay for a wall would be much better spent on increasing security along approach roads" (Travis and Chrysalis, 2016). On the other hand, human rights organizations draw attention to the negative impacts of the walling practices on the rights of migrants. François Guennec of Auberge des Migrants—a French aid group in Calais—criticised the wall by arguing that:

> When you put walls up anywhere in the world, people find ways to go around them. It's a waste of money. It could make it more dangerous people, it will push up tariffs for people smugglers, and people will end up taking more risks (Travis and Chrysalis, 2016).

Furthermore, rights groups contend that these security barriers prevent people from seeking asylum, thereby infringing the very basic principles of European law (Baczynska and Ledwith, 2016).

As stated before, bordering practices are not likely to stop migration, but divert it to more dangerous routes as well as the so-called border work involves various actors including migrants, smugglers and citizens who can challenge and transform the states' bordering practices. This is well ratified by the fact that migrants living in the "Jungle" and not being able to pay for the smugglers have already attempted to "hide on trucks and other vehicles by using makeshifts barriers to block traffic and climb board" (Breeden, 2016).

Northern European countries including Norway and Sweden have also introduced new security measures on their borders. For example, Norway—part of the Schengen zone but not the EU—established border checks at popular land crossing points with Sweden as a response to the growing number of refugees entering the country from the latter (Tasch and Nudelman, 2016). Norwegian officials were also authorised to check all ferry arrivals from Sweden, Denmark, and

Germany (Tasch and Nudelman, 2016). Besides, in the face of the arrival of Syrian refugees starting from 2015, it was planned to erect a fence at its so-called Arctic border with Russia in August 2016. The fence is to be about 200m (650ft) long and four meters high and equipped with CCTV (Johnson, 2016). Deputy Justice Minister Ove Vanebo supported the fence as a "responsible measure" (Osborne, 2016).

Similarly, having previously stood with Germany in support of refugees, Sweden also announced it would introduce border controls with Denmark to prevent migrants from entering the country in early January 2016 (Tasch and Nudelman, 2016). The country fenced off the platforms at Copenhagen's Kastrup rail station to control the entry of migrants through Malmo from Denmark across the Oresund Bridge (Economist, 2016). Just after this decision, Denmark decided to adopt similar measures at its border with Germany (Tasch and Nudelman, 2016).

Concluding Remarks

This article demonstrates that contrary to the arguments pioneered by the supporters of globalisation about the emergence of "borderless and deterritorialised world" (Newman 2006), the European case tells another story signifying the hardening of bordering processes through the walls and fences. With the intensification of refugee movements especially since 2015, European countries have been building walls and fences to control, contain and filter the movements of people coming from the "underdeveloped" part of the world. Rather than as means of demarcating territorial borders or as strategies against military/foreign invasion, current walls and fences as a part of bordering processes have emerged as the means or institutional frameworks "for the production of space, or indeed, the production of difference in space" (De Genova, 2016: 4) that seek to eliminate the perceived dangers of uncontrolled mobility of certain group of migrants. In this respect, rather than being fixed material constructs, walls and fences imply "processes, practices, discourses, symbols, institutions or networks through which power works" (Johnson et al., 2011: 62).

However, refugees with their own political agency together with other non-state actors continue to challenge these state policies and force governmental authorities to implement new measures including more walls and fences. In other words, borders have been transformed, de- and re-constructed by various actors and have only been able to divert (rather than stop) population movements. To put it differently, the conflict between "regulating agencies—border patrols, visa officers, etc. and migrating individuals" has continuously forced European countries to implement new measures and erect walls and fences across and around Europe (Sirkeci, 2009: 12).

To conclude, instead of solving the structural problems, wars, and poverty that produce refugees in the first places, these border control mechanisms have only resulted in human rights violations and, paradoxically, legitimation of more barrier constructions. It is likely that states continue to dwell upon these border controls instruments, especially on their symbolic power to assert their sovereignty and send a message to the "undesirable" migrants and the public that they are securing their borders against mobile "risks" or security threats. Hence, more academic and public voices must be raised, and more empirical research has to be done about these bordering practices, which produce intensified suffering and death for migrants.

References

Amnesty International (2017). "Hungary: container camp bill is flagrant violation of international law", Amnesty International News. Retrieved from: https://www.amnesty.org/en/latest/news/2017/03/hungary-container-camp-bill-is-flagrant-violation-of-international-law/.

Andreas, P. (2003). "Redrawing the Line: Borders and Security in the Twenty-First Century", International Security, 28 (2): 78–111. https://doi.org/10.1162/016228803322761973

Baczynska G. and Ledwith, S. (2016). "How Europe built fences to keep people out", Reuters. April 4. Retrieved from: http://www.reuters.com/article/us-europe-migrants-fences-insight-idUSKCN0X10U7.

Balibar, E. (2004). We, the People of Europe? Reflections on transnational citizenship. Princeton, N.J.: Princeton University Press.

BBC (2015). "Migrant crisis: Austria plans Slovenia border fence", BBC. October 2015. Retrieved from: http://www.bbc.com/news/world-europe-34657187.

BBC (2016a). "Calais migrants: How is the UK-France border policed", BBC. March 3. Retrieved from: http://www.bbc.com/news/uk-33267137.

BBC (2016b). "Calais migrants: Work to start on UK-funded wall", BBC. September 7. Retrieved from: http://www.bbc.com/news/uk-politics-37294187.

Bigo, D. (2002). "Security and Immigration: toward a critique of the governmentally of un- ease", Alternatives, 27 (1): 63–92. https://doi.org/10.1177/03043754020270S105

Breeden, A. (2016). "Britain and France to Begin Work on Wall Near Calais to Keep Migrants from Channel Tunnel", New York Times. September 7. Retrieved from: https://www.nytimes.com/2016/09/08/world/ europe/calais-jungle-refugees.html?_r=0.

Britton, B. (2016). "Calais wall: UK to build wall to stop migrants", CNN. September 7. Retrieved from: http://edition.cnn.com/2016/09/07/europe/calais-wall-migrants/.

Brown, W. (2010). Walled States, Waning Sovereignty. New York: Zone Books.

Buur, L., Jensen, S. and Stepputat, F. (2007). "The Security-Development Nexus." In: L. Buur, S. Jensen, S. and F. Stepputat (eds.). The Security-Development Nexus: Expressions of Sovereignty and Securitization in Southern Africa. Uppsala: Nordiska Afrikainstitutet and Cape Town: Hsrc Press.

Chadwick, V. (2015). "Slovenian boosts army powers at Croatia border.", Politico. Retrieved from: https://iconline.microsoft.com/#ieslice.

Dallison, P. (2015). "Austria to build Slovenia border fence.", Politico. http://www.politico.eu/article/ migrant-refugee-crisis-austria-to-build-slovenia-border-fence-seehofer-merkel-migration-refugees-croatia-hungary/.

De Genova, N. (2016). "The 'Crisis' of the European Border Regime: Towards a Marxist Theory of Borders", International Socialism, 150: 31–54.

Dearden, L. (2016). "Hungary planning 'massive' new border fence to keep out refugees as PM vows to 'hold them back by force'", Independent. August 27. Retrieved from: http://www.independent.co.uk/news/world/europe/hungary-massive-new-border-fence-to-keep-out-refugees-prime-minister-orban-turkey-eu-hold-them-back-a7212696.html.

Deutsche Welle (2015a). "UNHCR: Balkan states turning away 'economic migrants'," Deutsche Welle. November 21. Retrieved from: http://www.dw.com/en/unhcr-balkan-states-turning-away-economic-migrants/a-18866765.

Deutsche Welle (2015b). "Macedonia reinforces fence at Greek border 'to control migrant inflow'", Deutsche Welle. November 28. Retrieved from: http://www.dw.com/en/macedonia-reinforces-fence-at-greek-border-to-control-migrant-inflow/a-18881634.

Deutsche Welle (2016). "Hungary to block passage for migrants calls for fences", Deutsche Welle. January 22. Retrieved from: http://www.dw.com/en/hungary-to-block-passage-for-migrants-calls-for-fences/a-18999604.

Dzenovska, D. (2016). "Eastern Europe, the Moral Subject of the Migration/Refugee Crisis, and Political Futures," Near Futures Online. Retrieved from: http://nearfuturesonline.org/eastern-europe-the-moral-subject-of-the-migration-refugee-crisis-and-political-futures/.

Foucault, M. (1978). A History of Sexuality: An Introduction. New York: Random House.

Graham-Harrison, E. (2015). "Still the refugees are coming, but in Europe the barriers are rising.", Guardian. October 31. https://www.theguardian.com/world/2015/oct/31/austria-frace-slovenia-wire-europe-refugees.

Granados, S., Murphy, Z., Schaul, K. and Faiola, A. (2016). "Fenced out", Washington Post. October 14. https://www.washingtonpost.com/graphics/world/border-barriers/europe-refugee-crisis-border-control/.

Jamieson, A. (2016). "Trump Wants Border Wall, but Britain Is Building One in France", NBC News. September 12. Retrieved from: http://www.nbcnews.com/storyline/europes-border-crisis/trump-wants-border-wall-britain-building-one-france-n645571.

Johnson, H. (2016). "Norwegians laugh at new fence on Russian border", BBC. October 7Retrieved from: http://www.bbc.com/news/world-europe-37577547.

Johnson, C., Jones, R., Paasi, A., Amoore, L., Mountz, A., Salter, M., and C. Rumford 2011. "Interventions on Rethinking 'the Border' in Border Studies", Political Geography, 30 (2), 61–69.

Jones, R. (2016). Violent Borders: Refugees and the Right to Move. London: Verso.

Jones, R. and Johnson, C. (eds.) (2016). Placing the Border in Everyday Life. London and New York: Routledge.

Korkut, U. (2017). "Open to those who can pay: the hypocrisy of how Hungary treats asylums seekers", Conversation.

Retrieved from: http://theconversation.com/open-to-those-who-can-pay-the-hypocrisy-of-how-hungary-treats-asylum-seekers-75333.

Lutterbeck, D. (2006). "Policing Migration in the Mediterranean", Mediterranean Politics, 11 (1): 59–82.

NBC News (2015). "Slovenia Gives Army More Power Amid Migration Crisis", NBC News. October 21. Retrieved from: http://www.nbcnews.com/storyline/europes-border-crisis/slovenia-gives-army-more-power-amid-migration-crisis-n448241.

Newman, D. (2006). "The lines that continue to separate us: borders in our borderless world", Progress in Human Geography, 30 (2): 143–161. https://doi.org/10.1191/0309132506ph599xx

Oliveria, I. (2015). "Slovenia erects fence on Croatian border", Politico. Retrieved from: http://www.politico.eu/article/slovenia-to-build-croatia-border-fence-miro-cerar-migrants-control/.

Osborne, S. (2016). "Norway to build border fence with Russia to keep out refugees", Independent. August 25. Retrieved from: http://www.independent.co.uk/news/world/europe/norway-border-fence-russia-refugees-refugee-crisis-schengen-syria-war-a7208806.html.

Pallister-Wilkins, P. (2015). "Bridging the Divide: Middle Eastern Walls and Fences and the Spatial Governance of Problem Populations", Geopolitics, 20:438–459. https://doi.org/10.1080/ 14650045.2015.1005287

Pallister-Wilkins, P. (2016a). "How Walls Do Work: Security Barriers as Devices of Interruption and Data Capture", Security Dialogue, 47(2): 151–164. https://doi.org/10.1177/0967010615615729

Pallister-Wilkens, P. (2016b). "The Tensions of the Ceuta and Melilla Border Fences." In: P. Gaibazzi, A. Bellagamba, and S. Dünnwald (eds.) EurAfrican Borders and Migration Management: Political Cultures, Contested Spaces, and Ordinary Lives. Basingstoke: Palgrave.

Paasi, A. (1998). "Boundaries As Social Processes: Territoriality in the World of Flows", Geopolitics, 3(1): 69–88.

Perrin, B. (2014). "Nato fencing sent to Calais to foil migrants", Sun. September 7. Retrieved from: https://www.thesun.co.uk/archives/news/291504/nato-fencing-sent-to-calais-to-foil-migrants/.

Pugh, M. (2000). "Europe's Boat People: Maritime Cooperation in the Mediterranean", EU-ISS Chaillot Paper 41.

Ross, T., Sawer, P. and Henry, S. (2015). "Calais migrants: Britain o build huge fence at Channel Tunnel port in France," Telegraph. June 27. Retrieved from: http://www.telegraph.co.uk/news/uknews/immigration/ 11703636/Calais-migrants-Britain-to-build-huge-fence-at-Channel-Tunnel-port-in-France.html.

Rosiere, S. and Jones, R. (2012). "Teichopolitics: Re-considering Globalisation Through the Role of Walls and Fences," Geopolitics, 17 (1): 217–234. https://doi.org/10.1080/14650045.2011.574653

Rumford, C. (2008). "Introduction: Citizens and Borderwork in Europe", Space and Polity, 12 (1): 1–12. https://doi.org/10.1080/13562570801969333

Rumford, C. (2006a). "Rethinking European Spaces: Territory, Borders, Governance", Comparative European Politics, 4:127–140. https://doi.org/10.1057/palgrave.cep.6110089

Rumford, C. (2006b). "Introduction: Theorizing Borders", European Journal of Social Theory, 9 (2): 155–169.

Sirkeci, I. (2009). "Transnational mobility and conflict", Migration Letters, 6 (1): 3–14.

Tasch B. and M. Nudelman (2016). "This map shows how much the refugee crisis is dividing Europe", Business Insider Deutschland. Retrieved from: https://www.businessinsider.com.au/map-refugees-europe-migrants-2016-2

Taylor, A. (2015). "Map: Europe is building more fences to keep people out", Washington Post. October 28. Retrieved from: https://www.washingtonpost.com/news/worldviews/wp/2015/08/28/map-the-walls-europe-is-building-to-keep-people-out/?utm_term=.0145f38b16f4.

Telegraph (2015). "Refugee crisis: Slovenia to build 'temporary obstacles' on its border with Croatia", Telegraph. November 10. Retrieved from: http://www.telegraph.co.uk/news/worldnews/europe/ slovenia/ 11987447/Refugee-crisis-Slovenia-to-build-temporary-obstacles-on-its-border-with-Croatia.html.

Travis A. and A. Chrisafis (2016). "UK immigration minister confirms work to start on £1.9m Calais wall", Guardian. September 7. Retrieved from: https://www.theguardian.com/world/2016/sep/06/uk-immigration-minister-confirms-work-will-begin-on-big-new-wall-in-calais.

Traynor, I. (2015). "Migration crisis: Hungary PM says Europe in grip of madness", Guardian. September 3. Retrieved from: https://www.theguardian.com/world/2015/sep/03/migration-crisis-hungary-pm-victor-orban-europe-response-madness.

Vallet, E. and C. P. David. (2014). "Walls of Money: Securitization of Border Discourse and Militarization of Markets." In: E. Vallet (ed.) Borders, Fences and Walls: State of Insecurity?, London: Routledge.

Vaughan-Williams, N. (2012). Border Politics: The Limits of Sovereign Power. Edinburgh: Edinburgh University Press.

Walker, R.B.J. (2010). After the globe, before the world. London: Routledge. https://doi.org/10.4324/9780203871249

Walters, W. (2004). "Secure borders, safe haven, domopolitics", Citizenship Studies, 8 (3): 237–260. https://doi.org/10.1080/1362102042000256989

Webb, O. and N. Squires (2015). "Refugees suffer in mud and rain as European countries bicker," Reuters. October 19. Retrieved from: http://www.telegraph.co.uk/news/worldnews/europe/slovenia/ 11941213/Refugees-suffer-in-mud-and-rain-as-European-countries-bicker.html.

York, C. (2016). "Great Wall of Calais' Refugee Migrant Barrier To Be Built In France, Robert Goodwill Confirms", Huffington Post. September 7.

CHAPTER 13

Turkey's Refugees, Syrians and Refugees from Turkey: A Country of Insecurity

Ibrahim Sirkeci

Introduction

On 18 November 2016, NATO's Secretary General, Jens Stoltenberg said "some Turkish officers working in NATO command structure… have requested asylum in the countries where they are working" months after the failed coup attempt in Turkey and the purges that followed.[1] This is simply adding fuel to the fire in Europe. The European Union (EU) has faced one of its biggest crises with the rise of population flows through its Eastern and Southern neighbours as well as movements within the EU. In 2016, the Brexit referendum and debates surrounding it in the UK were largely focused on restricting EU immigration to the UK whereas eastern and central European members were raising concerns about and reluctant to comply with the refugee quota proposals and the burden sharing they often included[2].

The Syrian crisis has displaced millions in the country (Yazgan et al., 2015). At least 4,810,710 Syrians (2,823,987 in Turkey alone) were registered as refugees[3] abroad by 26 September 2016 (UNHCR, 2016). While 494,411 of these refugees lived in camps the overwhelming majority remained outside camps and relied on their own means. According to the UNHCR, 1,177,914 Syrians filed asylum applications in Europe and about two thirds of these were lodged in Germany (449,770), Serbia and Kosovo (314,852), Sweden (109,664), and Hungary (76,116).

Turkey has been known as a source country (and therefore, I define it as a "country of insecurity") for international population movements until very recently. Currently, Turkey qualifies as a country of immigration (hence called a "country of security") with about 4 per cent of its inhabitants being refugees, and another 2 percent being non-refugee foreign borns by 2016. By the end of December 2016, 2,823,987 Syrian refugees registered in the country (DGMM, 2016) represent about 55 percent of the total displaced Syrian population. Turkey also accommodates

---

[1] https://www.theguardian.com/world/2016/nov/18/turkish-officers-seeking-asylum-after-failed-coup-nato-chief-jens-stoltenberg. Accessed:18/11/2016.
[2] For an overview of the EU level burden sharing issues from 2010 and 2015 see: Thielemann et al. (2010) and Carrera et al. (2015).
[3] We should note though that Turkey is one of very few countries that impose a geographical restriction on the 1951 Geneva convention by not accepting refugees from outside Europe. Therefore, Syrian refugees in Turkey are officially registered under temporary protection regime and often referred to as "guests". For details see Öner & Genç (2015), pp.254-255.

about 300,000 refugees from other countries.[4]

Despite these incoming movers registering under international temporary protection, Turkey has not ceased to be a *country of insecurity* (meaning source country). There are still strong outflows and increased mobility among Turkish citizens (as well as among others who arrived as refugees, see Genç & Öner, 2016) while large diaspora populations exist in countries such as Germany, France, the Netherlands, Austria, Switzerland (Sirkeci et al., 2015).

In this article, the impact of recently increased insecurity in Turkey on emigration pressures is discussed in terms of number of asylum applications lodged by Turkish citizens. These flows are directed to traditional destinations for movers from Turkey following migration networks as well as legal frameworks and political perceptions. Current statistics of Syrian arrivals in Turkey as a country of security are also presented. Hence, the article shows how a country like Turkey swings between 'insecurity' and 'security' over time and in relation to conflict. Based on current asylum flows, Turkey appear as a country of relative (in)security that both receives and produces significant number of refugees.

Growing refugee flows and Turkey

The total number of international movers according to the widely used definition of changing place of residence for 12 months or longer from one country to another is about 3.4 per cent (about 250 million) (Figure 1). Refugees comprised an even smaller segment of the total of 244 million migrants in 2016. Among over 65.3 million displaced people, only 21 million were refugees by the summer of 2016, representing an increase from 16 million in 2015 (Sirkeci & Martin, 2016:329; Martin, 2016:305). Despite the animosity over migration in the debates in the decade to 2016, international migration is still not a norm but exception (Martin & Sirkeci, 2017:573). This is more or less also true for Turkey where about 5% of the population is made up by immigrants, even in the face of a mass inflow of millions of Syrians in the past five years.

International migration is driven by three Ds: **development** (or economic) **deficit** (referring to adverse economic conditions marked by inequalities across society and geography), **democratic deficit** (referring to presence of representation issues, particularly for minorities), and **demographic deficit** (characterised by high fertility and growth rates), between and within countries at a time when revolutions in communications, transportation, and rights make it easier to learn about opportunities abroad, travel, and stay abroad. The recent failed military coup in Turkey highlighted the three Ds in the country and thus added to migration challenges in Europe because (a) Turkey may not be considered "safe" anymore and (b) there is an increasing number of Turkish citizens and others fleeing the country in response to the emergency rule since the failed coup attempt on 15 July 2016 and increasing number of terror attacks. Growing perception of insecurity among Turkish citizens and immigrants in Turkey means growing outflows. It may also result in a change of direction for flows in certain migration corridors such as

---

[4] http://data.unhcr.org/syrianrefugees/country.php?id=224 also http://www.goc.gov.tr/ icerik6/uluslararasi-koruma_363_378_4712_icerik. Accessed 4/10/2016.

between Germany and Turkey which has been reversed since about 2006 as more people moved from Germany to Turkey (Sirkeci & Zeyneloğlu, 2014).

Figure 1. Movers and non-movers in the world, 1960-2015 (in millions)

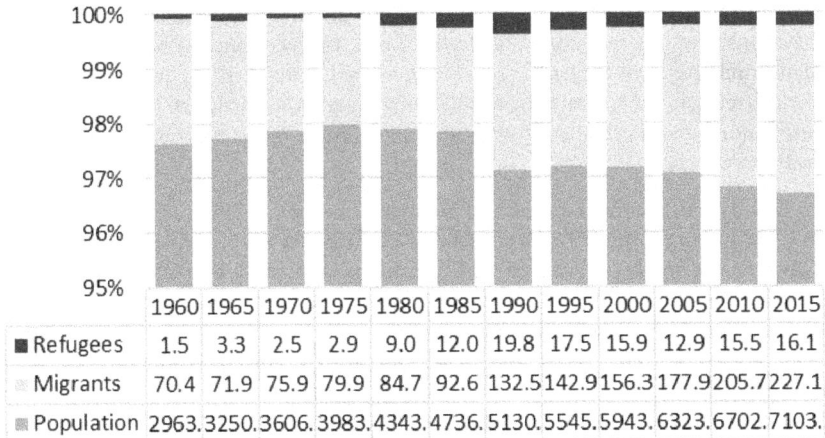

	1960	1965	1970	1975	1980	1985	1990	1995	2000	2005	2010	2015
■ Refugees	1.5	3.3	2.5	2.9	9.0	12.0	19.8	17.5	15.9	12.9	15.5	16.1
Migrants	70.4	71.9	75.9	79.9	84.7	92.6	132.5	142.9	156.3	177.9	205.7	227.1
■ Population	2963.	3250.	3606.	3983.	4343.	4736.	5130.	5545.	5943.	6323.	6702.	7103.

Source: United Nations, UNHCR, and World Bank.

Turkish citizens have become increasingly mobile as a result of established migration networks and existing migration culture as well as the relative prosperity and stability in the country since the turn of the 21st century. Turkey is currently officially the largest refugee hosting country in the world, which perhaps is not a coincidence given its geographical proximity to major conflict zones in the world as well as its location at the periphery of the EU.

Turkey has long been a country of immigration and emigration; a country with a diaspora population of over 5 million dispersed across the world and with a refugee population of over 3 million in the country along with another 1.5 million foreign born according to official reports (Pusch & Sirkeci, 2016). From 2011 onwards, the country saw substantial changes in its legislation and infrastructure to deal with migration. For example, a new migration management directorate was created alongside a set of new legislations drawing on the 2013 *Law of Foreigners and International Protection* (no. 6458) (Sağıroğlu, 2016). As debates and negotiations continue on readmission agreements, visa free travel in the EU for Turkish citizens and burden sharing schemes (Sözen, 2016; Genç & Öner, 2016), there are still ongoing processes that will affect migration policies as well as migration experiences in Turkey.

Historically, a combination of major conflicts, uneven development, and demographic pressures in Turkey has driven migration abroad. Turkish citizens, Turks, Kurds and others alike, have fled the country in large numbers to seek economic, cultural, and political security elsewhere (Sirkeci, 2003b). Depending on the admission policies and international "deals" of the time, varying across destinations, they were reported as guest workers, family migrants, refugees, asylum seekers, irregular migrants, imported brides, students, labour migrants, Ankara agreement movers, and adventurers. One may find several periodisations often based on these administrative categories (Sirkeci, 2005a). Population movements were in response to labour market dynamics (e.g. Martin, 1991; Reniers, 1999), or the Kurdish conflict (e.g. Sirkeci, 2006a; Başer, 2015), or marriage and family connections (e.g. Kulu-Glasgow & Leerkes, 2013; Lievens, 1999). Nevertheless, the common ground for all these movers were the discomforts, tensions and conflicts they considered as insecurity and found easier to overcome by *voting with the feet*. Many millions have returned, some *re*-migrated, but all these moves created a Turkish culture of migration consolidating migration corridors between several destinations and Turkey and over time diversifying the composition of flows in both directions.

Turkey has become increasingly prosperous since the 1980s with record levels of GDP growth in the 1990s and 2000s (World Bank, 2016), while suffering from a protracted armed conflict with the Kurdish minority predominant in the East and South of the country. Nevertheless, the conflict over the Kurdish minority (Sirkeci, 2000 and 2003a), increasing Islamisation (Kaya, 2015), political polarisation (Dalay, 2015) under the AKP (Justice and Development Party) rule, and adverse influences of the Syrian and Iraqi crises with coinciding ISIS attacks in Turkey (Milan, 2016), caused the country to swing towards *insecurity* again in the mid-2010s.

Turkey's Kurdish question is at least as old as the Republic dating back to the 1920s (Yeğen, 2007; Sirkeci, 2003b; McDowall, 1996), and it has characterised a significant portion of migration outflows from Turkey ever since (Sirkeci, 2006a). However, this became more apparent particularly from the 1980s through the 2000s, when 1,017,358 asylum applications were lodged by (mostly Kurdish origin) Turkish citizens in the industrialised countries (Sirkeci & Esipova, 2013:3). In the 1960s and the 1970s, many members of minority groups including the Kurds along with left wing activists moved abroad as guest workers, workers' families, and students. In the 1980s, when the insecurity in Turkey was intensified with the 1980 military coup and the armed conflict with the PKK (Kurdistan Workers Party), from 1984 onwards, seeking asylum became the only choice for many who could not satisfy the ever-tightening visa or work permit requirements of the destination countries.

Partly mixed with and certainly eclipsed by the Kurdish conflict, another major issue of insecurity in Turkey is that of the Alevis. Alevis are a heterodox Islamic population in Turkey with strong secularist characteristics, numbering around 20 million with a concentration in Central and Eastern provinces and some coastal areas in the south and west (Issa, 2017; Dressler, 2013; Massicard, 2013; Shankland, 2003; White & Jongerden, 2003). Similar to Kurds, Alevis are overrepresented in the Turkish diaspora (Sirkeci et al., 2016; Issa, 2017); and they were heavily targeted by right wing groups in Turkey during the 1970s and onwards (Kosnick, 2004).

The contemporary Turkish context is characterised by mass purges that followed the failed coup on 15 July 2016, Turkey's military incursions into Iraq and Syria, and intensified armed conflict with Kurdish guerrillas in the southeast Turkey. The lack of Kurdish and Alevi representation in politics and governance contributes to the growing frustration of the Kurds and secular people who are increasingly alienated. Since July 2016, there is an emergency rule, and by 12 presidential decrees, more than 80,000 people have been expelled, over 2,600 organisations including 15 universities shut down, 39,378 arrested out of 96,000 suspects investigated in relation to the failed coup attempt by 22 November 2016. These constitute key elements of the current democratic deficit in Turkey.

Democratic deficit, although, appears to be the key driver for most recent outflows from Turkey, development deficit and demographic deficit also play a part. For example, in 2015, Turkey ranked among the bottom four of the OECD in terms of its Gini coefficient; has nearly 20% of its population below the poverty line (which is 3 percentage points higher than the 1990s); and the richest 10% having about a 15 times higher income than the poorest 10% (Keeley, 2015). Regional socio-economic development disparities remain strong (Gül & Çevik, 2015) and they are known to increase migration propensities (Sirkeci et al., 2012). Demographic deficit in Turkey is characterised by disparities in fertility rate and in net migration across regions and between western and eastern provinces (Ediev & Yücesahin, 2016:382). Total fertility rate in Turkey stands at 2.17 whilst it is 1.57 in the EU countries (Scherbov et al., 2016). These three Ds combined with an existing Turkish culture of migration (Sirkeci & Cohen, 2016; Sirkeci et al., 2012; Sirkeci, 2006a; 2006b) is likely to direct Turks towards key European destinations such as Germany, France, Austria, UK, Sweden where strong diaspora communities exist.

Movers and refugees in Turkey

Turkey as a country of immigration and a "country of security" has attracted movers including refugees from around the world since its foundation in the 1920s. Officially, it is claimed that Turkey has received over 3 million applications for protection including Syrians and 2,442,159 regular movers with residence permits between 2002 and 2015.[5] Among regular movers, the returnees from countries like Germany or second and third generation Turks from these countries constituted the majority. German nationals constituted 32.5% of all foreigners in Turkey according to the 2000 census followed by Bulgarians with 13.4% for a total of 1,260,530 foreign born in the country, over 84% of whom were Turkish citizens born abroad (Sirkeci, Cohen, Can, 2012 and Sirkeci & Zeyneloğlu, 2014).

Table 1. Top 10 nationalities among resident permit holders in Turkey, 2015.

Nationality	N	Nationality	N	Nationality	N
Iraq	33,202	Russia	22,377	Libya	14,421
Syria	32,578	Georgia	19,242	Iran	14,276
Azerbaijan	32,476	Ukraine	16,951	Others	199,554
Turkmenistan	22,891	Uzbekistan	14,927	TOTAL	422,895

Source: DGMM (2016)

More recently reports indicate over 1.4 million foreign born but these numbers are often contested. An analysis of border statistics indicates that, for example, a surplus population of 7,011,745 between 1995 and 2015 (Sirkeci & Martin, 2014; GDMM, 2016). Nevertheless, it has to be noted that asylum and migration statistics in Turkey are overall unreliable and inaccurate. Yet, it is clear that a sizeable foreign born population is present, particularly concentrated in large cities and coastal areas.

---

[5] http://www.goc.gov.tr/icerik/goc-tarihi_363_380 Accessed 4/12/2016. Iraqis are unsurprisingly the largest group as a result of long term insecurity in Iraq (see Sirkeci, 2004; 2005b; 2006b)

Despite sizeable groups from Germany, Russia, and Britain are present among Turkey's immigrants, dominant nationalities in all immigration categories are Syrians, Iraqis, and Afghans. In 2015, the top ten nationalities among the resident permit holders were all from Middle Eastern and former Soviet Union countries (Table 1). Compared to large Turkish diaspora populations in Europe and elsewhere, these numbers are significantly small. However, in the decade to 2015, in main corridors such as Germany and Turkey, net migration flows were reversed as the numbers arriving in Turkey had surpassed those leaving. Number of resident permit holders in Turkey was 422,895 in 2015 which was about 11% higher than 2014 and 35% higher than the 2013 figures[6]. 202,403 of them were for short term residence, 73,705 belonged to families, 67,529 to students and 62,756 were work permits. This paper focuses on refugees who are dominantly from Syria (2.8 million), Iraq (125,879), Afghanistan (113,756), Iran (28,534), and other countries (12,195).[7] In the last ten years, the number of asylum applications lodged in Turkey totals 216,351 in a gradually growing fashion until 2015, when the numbers suddenly doubled to 64,232 (Table 2).[8]

Table 2. Applications for international protection in Turkey, 2005-2015.

Year	N	Year	N	Year	N	Year	N
2005	2,935	2008	12,002	2011	17,925	2014	34,112
2006	3,550	2009	6,792	2012	29,678	2015	64,232
2007	5,882	2010	8,932	2013	30,311	TOTAL	216,351

Source: DGMM (2016)

In 2015, Turkish authorities had apprehended 146,485 irregular migrants (including 73,422 Syrians). In 2016 (by 22 November), 67,358 more Syrians were apprehended along with 29,782 Afghans, 29,117 Iraqis, and 15,699 Pakistanis amounting to a total of 163,278. Hence the total number of apprehensions since 1998 reached 1,270,781.[9] In 2015 and 2016, number of human smugglers arrested has also sharply increased in Turkey from 1,506 in 2014 to 4,471 in 2015 (it was 3,052 in the 11 months, by 28 November 2016). Responding to the 2013 EU-Turkey readmission agreement, 468 individuals were readmitted from Greece to Turkey.

Syrians have become the largest immigrant group in Turkey and it is very likely that they will be the centre of attention in migration debates for the foreseeable future. Syrians have a young population with 38.7% younger than 15. This is significantly different than Turkey's age composition (in which the demographic group make up the 24% of the population). Among those younger than 55, the majority are males (53.3%) while among those 55 and over it is females (51.2%) (Figure 1 and Table A1 in Appendix). Syrian migration to Turkey needs to be considered in relation to Turkey's ethnic minorities. Kurdish and Arabic speaking minorities in Turkey's southern provinces have friendship and family ties to Syrians across the border. This is one of the reasons why Syrian refugees are concentrated

---

[6] http://www.goc.gov.tr/icerik3/ikamet-izinleri_363_378_4709 Accessed 4/10/2016.

[7] UNHCR (2016) Turkey Fact Sheet. http://data.unhcr.org/syrianrefugees/download.php?id=11928.

[8] http://www.goc.gov.tr/icerik6/uluslararasi-koruma_363_378_4712_icerik Accessed 4/12/2016. Relatively small number of applications is partly due to the geographical limitation on the Geneva Convention imposed by Turkey (see Sirkeci & Pusch, 2016; Kirişçi, 1996).

[9] http://www.goc.gov.tr/icerik3/duzensiz-goc_363_378_4710 Accessed 4/10/2016.

in this region although large metropoles, such as Istanbul, Izmir and Bursa are among the top receiving provinces. (Map 1).

Figure 2. Population Pyramid of Syrians in Turkey

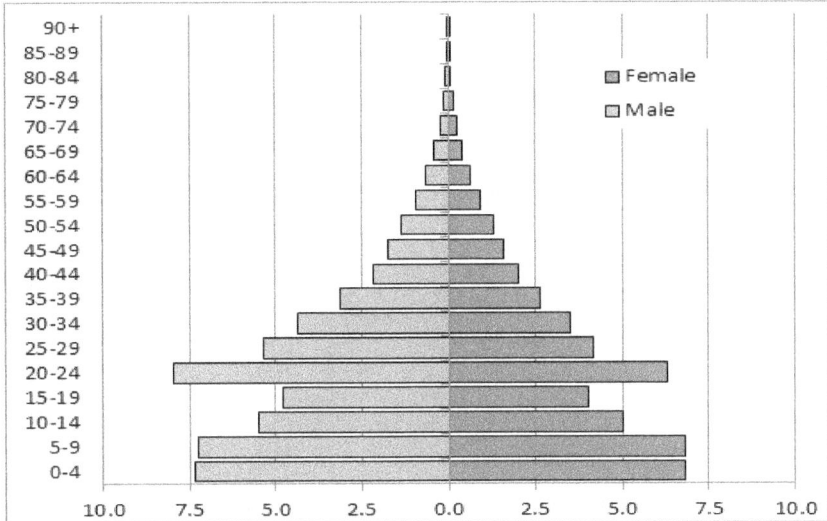

Source: GDMM, *http://www.goc.gov.tr/icerik3/gecici-koruma_363_378_4713*. Accessed 1/12/2016.

Concentration in the border provinces of Kilis, Hatay, Sanliurfa, and Gaziantep is at alarmingly high levels where the ratio of Syrians to the usual resident population rises up to 93% (Appendix Table A2). This has enormous implications on public service provision and resources especially regarding schooling, health and housing provisions at the local level. For example, although only about 15% of Syrian children at school age were enrolled by July 2016[10], to provide schooling for all of them at the same standards with Turkey's usual residents, it was estimated that government would need over 40,000 new classrooms and about 80,000 additional teachers. This strengthens the environment of insecurity and hence increases the out-migration pressures within the refugee population too. The impact of refugee arrivals on economy overall is yet inconclusive as there are both positive and negative influences observed in these provinces (see Lordoğlu & Aslan, 2015).

Table 3. Syrian refugees in camps in Turkey, 29 December 2016.

Location	Population	Location	Population	Location	Population
Sanliurfa	114,218	Kahramanmaras	17,968	Osmaniye	7,250
Gaziantep	39,082	Malatya	10,301	Mardin	4,113
Kilis	36,338	Adiyaman	9,589	Adana	341
Hatay	19,397			Total	258,597

Source: DGMM (2016)

---

[10] According to the Education Ministry in Turkey, only 170,000 of 625,000 school-aged Syrian children living in Turkey were receiving formal education http://www.hurriyetdailynews.com/less-than-one-third-of-syrian-children-in-turkey-in-formal-education.aspx?pageID=238&nID=101498&NewsCatID =341. Accessed 1/10/2016.

Map 1. Syrians distribution across provinces of Turkey, 2016.

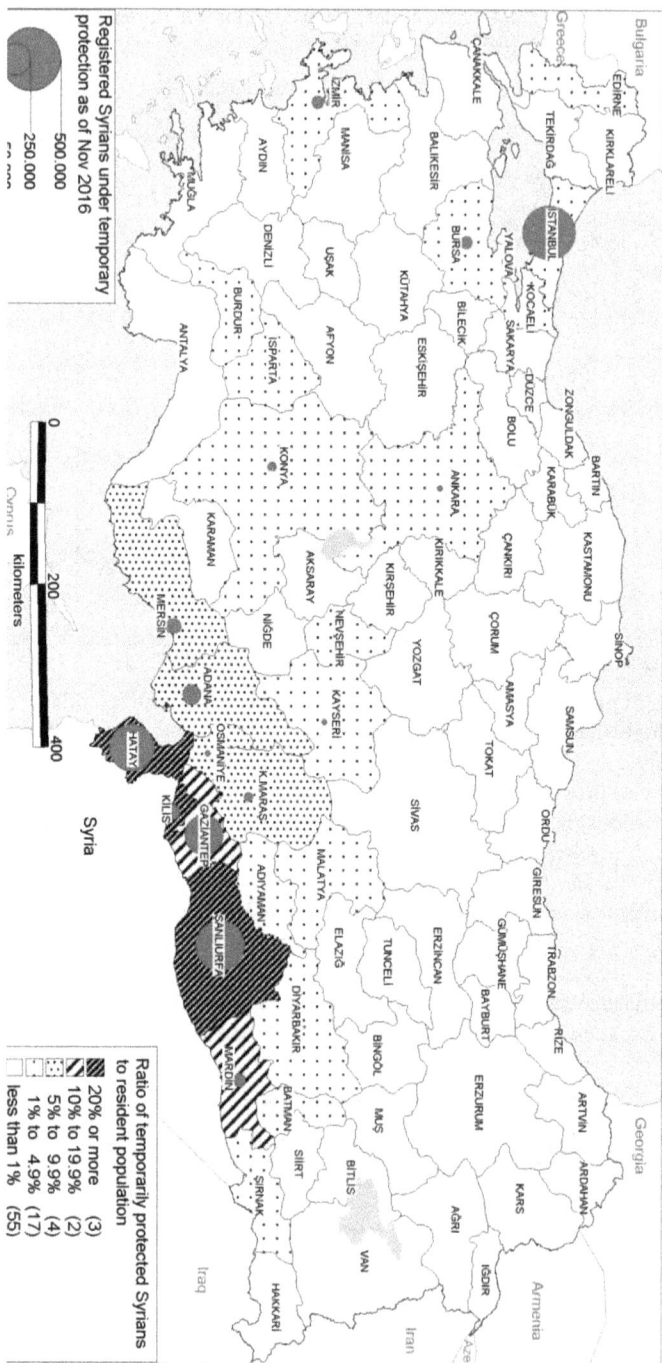

Registered Syrians under temporary protection as of Nov 2016

500,000
250,000

Source: http://www.goc.gov.tr/icerik3/gecici-koruma_363_378_4713

0   200   400
kilometers

Syria

Ratio of temporarily protected Syrians to resident population

20% or more   (3)
10% to 19.9%   (2)
5% to 9.9%   (4)
1% to 4.9%   (17)
less than 1%   (55)

About 9% (258,597) of Syrians were living in refugee camps set up in provinces within 200 kilometres to the Syrian border by December 2016 (Table 3).

Turkey's deal with the EU and the 2013 readmission agreement are probably one of the reasons of a sudden surge in unauthorised border crossings from Turkey to Greece and Bulgaria in the second half of 2015 and early 2016, since the agreement has a clause stating that the deal would come in force in three years. Thus to avoid being sent back, over one million of refugees risked their lives to leave Turkey before the agreement was implemented. So far only 2,655 Syrians have been resettled in the EU against the unauthorised migrants Turkey readmitted since April 2016 within rules of the EU-Turkey agreement. Half of these readmitted movers were from Pakistan and Afghanistan (DGMM, 2016). While understanding foreigners in need of humanitarian protection in Turkey trying to leave the country, we should also look into the number of Turkish citizens applying for international protection elsewhere and Turkey as a country of insecurity.

Refugees from Turkey, a country of (in)security

Citizens of wealthier countries, which we may call "countries of security", also seek refuge elsewhere, but the numbers are negligible. For example, the number of German citizens applied for asylum in other countries were about 40-50 per annum over the period from 1999 to 2016. One of these countries of security, Turkey is also a *country of insecurity* with a steady outflow of refugees (Table A4 in Appendix). The total number of asylum seekers with Turkish citizenship in industrialised countries exceeded one million between the 1980 military coup and 2011 (Sirkeci & Esipova, 2013) and the total number from January 1999 till October 2016 was 233,091 (Figure 3). Since the second half of 2015, there has been a sharp increase in the number of asylum applications by Turkish citizens abroad. For example, the volume of Turkish (first time) asylum applications in the EU countries had increased by 48% in the first quarter of 2016 and 100% in the second quarter (Eurostat, 2016); applications in the third quarter increased from 985 in 2015 to 3,779 in 2016. These trends show a possibly larger increase will follow in 2017 and onwards.

The striking feature that emerges in the trends shown in Figure 3 is the sudden but expected jump in asylum applications since July 2016, when the failed coup attempt was made. As seen in Table A3 in Appendix, between January and October 2016, the total number of asylum applications lodged by Turkish citizens was about 140% higher than the total in 2015. Applications between July and October in 2016 (5,161) quadrupled in comparison with the same period in 2015. The increase was even sharper in the case of Germany as the number of applications in 2016 was three and a half times higher than 2015 whilst the increase in the July-October period was 7 times (2,501) higher than that of the same period in 2015 (361).

This was expected within the conflict model of migration (Sirkeci, 2009) as the failed military coup in Turkey was followed by a mass purge by the government and hundreds of thousands of public workers including judges, police officers, and academics lost their jobs and many were arrested. This can be seen as the beginning of a period of increased asylum seeker flows from Turkey. Turkey has been one of the top source countries for asylum migration in the 1990s and early 2000s (Sirkeci, 2006; Sirkeci & Esipova, 2013). Germany as the host country for the largest segment of Turkish populations abroad has been historically the main destination for asylum seekers, too. This is simply because, asylum seeking migration is only slightly different from any other migration in terms of administration but when it comes to the support of migrant networks, there is virtually no difference. Earlier research shows, for example that in Germany, that there was fluidity between categories such as guest workers and asylum seekers over time (Sirkeci, 2006). Disproportionate numbers targeting Germany is likely to be partly due to the presence of a large Turkish diaspora in the country.

Figure 3. Asylum applications by Turkish citizens lodged in 38 European and 6 non-European countries (i.e. Australia, Canada, Japan, New Zealand, South Korea, United States), 1999 -2016

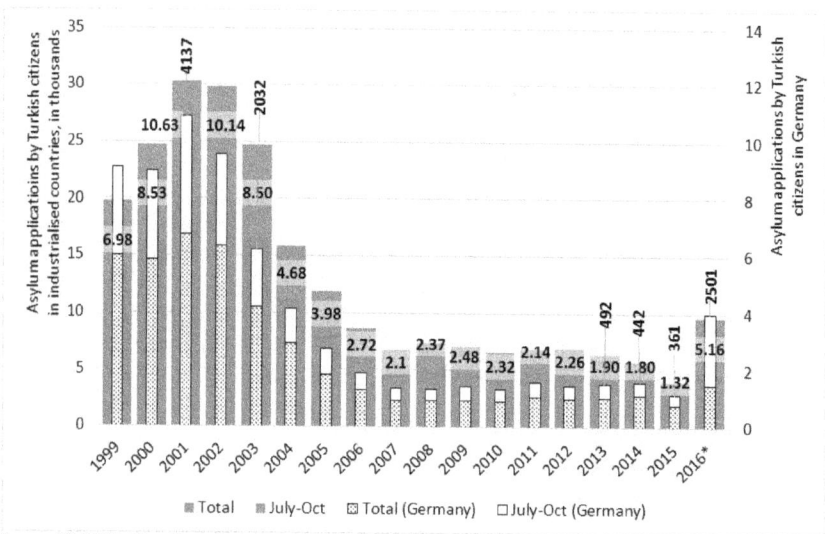

Source: UNHCR. * Jan-Oct only

If we project the numbers for the rest of the year, as the situation in Turkey has been deteriorating, given that the total number of asylum applications continued at similar levels until the end of 2016, the numbers in Germany is likely to exceed 5,000 which is close to the levels in the early 2000s. Corresponding projected figure for all 38 European countries and 6 non-European destinations would take the tally for 2016 to about 11,500 at the end of the year. This negates Turkey's profile as a 'country of security'.

This is alarming news since Turkey is increasingly unstable and highly polarised after the failed military coup, yet hosts over 3 million refugees. Given the selective nature of the purges (i.e. targeting professionals such as judges, academics, government officers) following the failed coup and emergency rule in place, these asylum seeker outflows from Turkey are likely to have involved high number of high skilled movers. These movers are capable and equipped with social and human capitals, hence are likely to overcome imposed barriers (e.g. costs, exit and entry restrictions). With the purges, government targeted high rank and high skilled groups such as 3,800 judges and prosecutors, and over 6,300 academics were among 115,000 people who lost their jobs and 82,000 who were detained. These are clear indicators of a brain drain risk for Turkey, but also an indication of a steady outflow of population in years to come. As suggested by the conflict model, the impact or repercussions (including emigration in response to it) of an environment of insecurity continues even after the original triggers of conflict disappears. It is also to be noted that this environment of insecurity affects not only Turkish citizens but immigrants including Syrian and other refugees in Turkey. Therefore, their flight will also continue despite all agreements between Turkey and the EU.

Conclusion

Turkey, once again, has become a country of origin for sizeable number of Turkish citizens filing asylum applications in industrialised countries and elsewhere. An environment of human insecurity has become more apparent in Turkey in 2016 after a relatively smooth period in the last decade. Yet, a country of (human) security, millions of Syrians and other refugees arrived and remained in Turkey, perhaps many hoping eventually to be resettled somewhere more stable and democratic. The Truce may stem further outflows from Syria but it would be naïve to expect significant numbers returning from Turkey or elsewhere back to Syria any time soon. Emerging Turkish-Syrian culture of migration would be just another driver to maintain flows from Syria to Turkey in the near future.

Coinciding with frequent terrorist attacks and occasional tensions with neighbouring countries, Turkey also faces an economic downturn marked by high inflation, high unemployment levels and slow (or negative) growth. Absence of competitive job markets and large regional disparities in development as well as high inequality levels highlight Turkey's Development Deficit. Situation in Syria was even worse and has deteriorated further during the civil war since 2011.

Development Deficit often goes along with Democratic and Demographic Deficits. Democratic Deficit is about political representation, or the lack of it. Countries such as Syria denied basic citizenship rights to segments of their residents. For example, the Kurds were denied passports by the Assad regime until 2011 when some were granted citizenship (CNN, 2011; HRW, 1996). Similar democratic disenfranchisement was evident in Iraq under Saddam and an armed conflict with Kurds is still ongoing in Turkey. However, this does not have to be as drastic as in Syria. Long term frustration in politics where one group is disadvantaged and have no prospect of being involved in governance can create a perception of (political) insecurity leading people to consider moving elsewhere. Current circumstances in Turkey and tensions arising from an increasingly oppressive and authoritarian conservative government with strong religious tones imposing a kind of polity over a secular minority. Secularists and many other opposition groups in Turkey have already been frustrated with almost zero prospect of becoming an influential part of the governance. The purges and wider adverse effects of mass sackings, detentions and polarisation make the country an insecure place.

Demographic Deficit is about high fertility and high population growth rates in contrast to limited job and opportunity creation for a growing population. Most source countries in the developing world have high fertility rates and growing populations, whereas most destination countries have stagnant or declining populations characterised by ageing populations with low fertility levels. This contributes to emigration pressures at countries of high fertility. Turkey's fertility levels are relatively higher than its European neighbours and lower than Middle Eastern neighbours Syria and Iraq. This means that migration pressures and hence, inflows from Middle East and outflows to Europe are likely to continue in the foreseeable future.

These three deficits are the root causes of most human mobility we observe around the world today. Therefore, any policy attempt to tackle migration must address these three deficits, root causes of environment of human insecurity and thus drivers of migration, internal and international alike. Otherwise, it will be simply indulging into costly adventures such as building walls, fences, Frontex and deals with Turkey and other countries.

References

Baser, B. (2015). Diasporas and homeland conflicts: A comparative perspective. Farnham: Ashgate.

Carrera, S., Blockmans, S., Gros, D., & Guild, E. (2015). The EU's Response to the Refugee Crisis: Taking Stock and Setting Policy Priorities. CEPS Essay, (20/16). Available at SSRN: http://ssrn.com/abstract=2715460 Accessed: 10/10/16.

CNN (2011, April 8). Stateless Kurds in Syria granted citizenship. http://edition.cnn.com /2011/WORLD/meast/04/07/syria.kurdish.citizenship/. Accessed 29/9/2016.

Dalay, G. (2015). Forming Turkey's Next Government: What are the Implications for Polarization and Policies? German Marshall Fund. http://www.gmfus.org/publications/ forming-turkeys-next-government. Accessed: 19/10/16.

DGMM (Directorate General of Migration Management, Turkey) (2016). Goc Istatistikleri. http://www.goc.gov.tr/icerik/goc-istatistikleri_363_378. Accessed: 4/12/16.

Dressler, M. (2013). Writing religion: the making of Turkish Alevi Islam. Oxford: Oxford University Press.

Ediev, D. M., & Yücesahin, M. M. (2016). Contribution of migration to replacement of population in Turkey. Migration Letters, 13(3), 377.

Eurostat (2016). First time asylum applicants in the EU-28 by citizenship, Q2 2015 – Q2 2016.png http://ec.europa.eu/eurostat/statistics-explained/index.php/File:First_ time _asylum_applicants_in_the_EU-28_by_citizenship,_Q2_2015 _%E2%80%93 _Q2_ 2016.png. Accessed 12/12/2016.

Genç, H. D., & Öner, N. A. Ş. (2016). Stuck in the Aegean: Syrians leaving Turkey face European barriers. In: Sirkeci, I. and Pusch, B. (eds), Turkish Migration Policy, London: Transnational Press London, pp.127-148.

Gül, E. & Çevik, B. (2015). 2013 Verileriyle Türkiye'de İllerin Gelişmişlik Düzeyi Araştırması. Is Bankasi. https://ekonomi.isbank.com.tr/UserFiles/pdf/ar_07_2015.pdf Accessed: 01/10/16.

HRW (1996). Syria, The Silenced Kurds. https://www.hrw.org/reports/1996/Syria.htm. Accessed 29/9/2016.

Issa, T. (Ed.). (2017). Alevis in Europe: Voices of Migration, Culture and Identity. London, New York: Routledge.

Kaya, A. (2015). Islamisation of Turkey under the AKP rule: Empowering family, faith and charity. South European Society and Politics, 20(1), 47-69.

Keeley, B. (2015). Income Inequality: The Gap between Rich and Poor, Paris: OECD Publishing. DOI: http://dx.doi.org/10.1787/9789264246010-en.

Kirişçi, K. (1996). Is Turkey Lifting the 'Geographical Limitation'?—The November 1994 Regulation on Asylum in Turkey. International Journal of Refugee Law, 8(3), 293-318.

Kosnick, K. (2004). 'Speaking in One's Own Voice': Representational Strategies of Alevi Turkish Migrants on Open-Access Television in Berlin. Journal of Ethnic and Migration Studies, 30(5), 979-994.

Kulu-Glasgow, I., & Leerkes, A. (2013). Restricting Turkish marriage migration? National policy, couples' coping strategies and international obligations. Migration Letters, 10(3), 369.

Lievens, J. (1999). Family-forming migration from Turkey and Morocco to Belgium: The demand for marriage partners from the countries of origin. International Migration Review, 33(3), pp. 717-744.

Lordoğlu, K., & Aslan, M. (2015). Araştırma - Saha Notları: Beş Sınır Kenti ve İşgücü Piyasalarında Değişim: 2011-2014. Göç Dergisi, 2(2), 249-267.

Martin, P.L. (1991). The unfinished story: Turkish labour migration to Western Europe: with special reference to the Federal Republic of Germany (Vol. 84). Geneva: ILO.

Martin, P.L. (2016). Wither US migration. Migration Letters, 13(2):295-306.

Martin, P.L. & Sirkeci, I. (2017). Recruitment, remittances, and returns. In: Reinert, Kenneth A. (Ed.). *Handbook on Globalisation and Development*. Cheltenham, UK; Northampton, MA, USA: Edward Elgar, chapter 18, pp. 569-603.

Massicard, É. (2013). *The Alevis in Turkey and Europe: identity and managing territorial diversity*. London, New York: Routledge.

McDowall, D. (1996). *Modern History of the Kurds*. New York: IB Tauris.

Milan, F. F. (2016). Turkey: What Hides Behind a Failed Coup Attempt. *The RUSI Journal*, 161(4), 28-32.

Öner, N. A. S., & Genç, D. (2015). Vulnerability leading to mobility: Syrians' exodus from Turkey. *Migration Letters*, 12(3), 251-262.

Pusch, B. & Sirkeci, I. (2016). Introduction: Turkish migration policy at a glance. In: Sirkeci, I. and Pusch, B. (eds), *Turkish Migration Policy*, London: TPLondon, pp.9-22.

Reniers, G. (1999). On the history and selectivity of Turkish and Moroccan migration to Belgium. *International Migration*, 37(4), 679-713.

Sağıroğlu, A.Z. (2016). Turkey's migration law and policy: is it a new era? In: Sirkeci, I. and Pusch, B. (eds), *Turkish Migration Policy*, London: Transnational Press London, pp.41-54.

Scherbov, S., Mamolo, M., et al. (2016). European Demographic Datasheet 2016. http://www.populationeurope.org/. Accessed: 01/10/2016.

Shankland, D. (2003). *The Alevis in Turkey: the emergence of a secular Islamic tradition*. London, New York: Routledge.

Sirkeci, I. (2000). Exploring the Kurdish population in the Turkish context. *GENUS, an International Journal of Demography*, 56(1-2): 149-175.

Sirkeci, I. (2003a). Migration from Turkey to Germany: an ethnic analysis, *New Perspectives on Turkey*, 2003(28-29): 189-208.

Sirkeci, I. (2003b). *Migration, ethnicity and conflict: the environment of insecurity and Turkish Kurdish international migration*. PhD Dissertation, University of Sheffield.

Sirkeci, I. (2004). Iraqi International Migration: Potentials for the Post-war Period, *Population Review*, 43(1): 37-49.

Sirkeci, I. (2005a). Diaspora: Turkish. In: M. Gibney and R. Hansen (eds.) *Immigration and Asylum from 1900 to the Present*, Santa Barbara: ABC-CLIO, pp.607-610.

Sirkeci, I. (2005b). War in Iraq: environment of insecurity and international migration, *International Migration*, 43(4): 197-214.

Sirkeci, I. (2006a). The Environment of Insecurity in Turkey and the Emigration of Turkish Kurds to Germany. New York: Edwin Mellen Press.

Sirkeci, I. (2006b). Ethnic conflict, wars and international migration of Turkmen: evidence from Iraq, *Migration Letters*, 3(1): 31-43.

Sirkeci, I. (2009). Transnational mobility and conflict. *Migration Letters*, 6(1), 3-14.

Sirkeci, I. (2013). Population Change and Migration in Europe and the UK. In: Drew, J. & Bond, M. (eds). *The UK & Europe: Costs, Benefits, Options. The Regent's Report*. London: Regent's University London, pp.16-26.

Sirkeci, I. & Cohen, J. H. (2016). Cultures of migration and conflict in contemporary human mobility in Turkey. *European Review*, 24(3): 381-396.

Sirkeci, I. & Esipova, N. (2013). Turkish migration in Europe and desire to migrate to and from Turkey. *Border Crossing*, 3(1), 1-13.

Sirkeci, I. & Martin, P. L. (2014). Sources of Irregularity and Managing Migration: The Case of Turkey. *Border Crossing*, 4(1-2), pp.1-16.

Sirkeci, I. & Martin, P.L. (2016). Editorial: The Migration Conference and 13 years of Migration Letters. *Migration Letters*, 13(3):329-332.

Sirkeci, I. & Zeyneloğlu, S. (2014). Abwanderung aus Deutschland in die Türkei: Eine Trendwende im Migrationsgeschehen? In: Alscher, S. & Krienbriek, A. (eds.) *Abwanderung von Türkeistämmigen: Wer verlässt Deutschland und warum?* Germany: BAMF, pp.30-85.

Sirkeci, I., Cohen, J. & Can, N. (2012). Internal mobility of foreign-born in Turkey. In: Finney, N. & Catney, G. (eds.) *Minority Internal Migration in Europe*. Farnham: Ashgate, pp.175-193.

Sirkeci, I., Cohen, J. H., & Yazgan, P. (2012). Turkish culture of migration: Flows between Turkey and Germany, socio-economic development and conflict. *Migration Letters*, 9(1), 33-46.

Sirkeci, I., Seker, B.D., & Caglar, A. (eds.) (2015). *Turkish Migration, Identity and Integration*. London, UK: Transnational Press London.

Sirkeci, I., Bilecen, T., Costu, Y., Dedeoglu, S., Kesici, M.R., Tilbe, F., Unutulmaz, K.O. (2016). *Little Turkey in Great Britain*. London: Transnational Press London.

Sözen, Ü.S. (2016). Fragile balance of EU-Turkey readmission agreement. In: Sirkeci, I. & Pusch, B. (eds), *Turkish Migration Policy*, London: Transnational Press London, pp.149-168.

Thielemann, E. R., Williams, R. and Boswell, C. (2010). *What system of burden-sharing between Member States for the reception of asylum seekers?* PE 419.620. European Parliament, Brussels, Belgium.

White, P. J., & Jongerden, J. (Eds.). (2003). *Turkey's Alevi enigma: a comprehensive overview*. Leiden: Brill.

World Bank (2016). World Development Indicators. Last updated: 14/10/2016. data.worldbank.org.

Yazgan, P., Utku, D. E., & Sirkeci, I. (2015). Syrian crisis and migration. *Migration Letters*, 12(3), 181-192.

Yeğen, M. (2007). Turkish nationalism and the Kurdish question. *Ethnic and Racial Studies*, 30(1), 119-151.

PART 5: MIGRATION POLITICS, LAW AND ORGANISATIONS

Essential Reading:

Pusch, B., & Sirkeci, I. (2016). Introduction: Turkish migration policy at a glance. *Turkish Migration Policy*, London: TPLondon, 9-22.

Agustín, Ó. G., & Jørgensen, M. B. (2013). Immigration and civil society New ways of democratic transformation. *Migration Letters*, 10(3), 271-276.

Bendel, P. (2005). Immigration Policy in the European Union: Still bringing up the walls for fortress Europe?. *Migration Letters*, 2(1), 21-32.

Marshall, R. (2014). The case for a foreign worker advisory commission. *Migration Letters*, 11(1), 65-78.

Further Readings

Agustín, Ó. G. (2013). Politics of civility: the case of the Association of Undocumented People of Madrid. *Migration Letters*, 10(3), 288-298.

Ambrosini, M. (2013). Fighting discrimination and exclusion: Civil society and immigration policies in Italy. *Migration Letters*, 10(3), 313-323.

Naujoks, D. Multilateralism For Mobility: Interagency Cooperation In A Postpandemic World. In *COVID-19 and Migration: Understanding the Pandemic and Human Mobility* (pp. 183-193). Transnational Press London.

Öner, S. (2015). The role of Turkish community organisations in Berlin: Their role in Turkey-Germany and Turkey-European Union relations. In *Politics and Law in Turkish Migration* (pp. 155-169). Transnational Press London.

Bendel, P. (2015). But it does move, doesn´ t it? The debate on the allocation of refugees in Europe from a German point of view. *Border Crossing*, 5(1), 25-32.

Manco, A., & Gerstnerova, A. (2016). Migrant associations as alternative jobs providers: Experience of Turkish and sub-Saharan communities in Belgium. *Border Crossing*, 6(1), 1-15.

Abrantes, M. (2013). Voices: migrant domestic workers and civil society. *Migration Letters*, 10(3), 324-332.

Şanli, S. (2019). Contribution of NGOs to the Integration of Syrian Immigrants in Mardin. In *Anthropological Perspectives on Transnational Encounters in Turkey: War, Migration and Experiences of Coexistence* (pp. 59-72). Transnational Press London.

Şekercioğlu, S. (2018). *Civil Society Impact on the EU Climate Change Policy*. Transnational Press London.

Eroğlu, D. (2015). The Making of Immigration Policies in Turkey: An analysis of the Law on Foreigners and International Protection Drafting Process. Sirkeci, I. Elçin, D., Şeker, G.(eds.), *Politics and Law in Turkish Migration*. London: Transnational Press London, 25-38.

Lee, C. C. (2006). Refugee Policy is a Realist's Nightmare: The Case of Southeast Asia. *Migration Letters*, 3(2), 137-149.

Çınar, E. (2018). The Readmission Agreement of Turkey. *Border Crossing*, 8(2SI), 571-581.

Yucesahin, M. M., Adalı, T., & Türkyılmaz, A. S. (2016). Population policies in Turkey and demographic changes on a social map. *Border Crossing*, 6(2), 240-266.

Aras, N. E. G., & Mencütek, Z. Ş. (2015). The international migration and foreign policy nexus: the case of Syrian refugee crisis and Turkey. *Migration Letters*, 12(3), 193-208.

Aker, D. Y. (2020). Hülya Kaya (2020). The EU-Turkey Statement on Refugees: Assessing its Impact on Fundamental Rights. *Migration Letters*, 17(6), 863-864.

Sağıroğlu, A. Z. (2016). Turkey's migration law and policy: is it a new era?. In Sirkeci, I. and Pusch, B. (eds.) *Turkish Migration Policy* (pp. 41-54). Transnational Press London.

Butera, A. C., & Ertorer, S. (2020). Restrictive Asylum Policies and Reflections in the Labour Market: The Cases of Italy And Turkey. In *Current Challenges in Migration Policy and Law*, 9.

CHAPTER 14
Turkish Migration Policy at a Glance

Barbara Pusch and Ibrahim Sirkeci

Turkish migration policy from a historical perspective

Due to the large-scale migration from Turkey to Europe in general and Germany in particular Turkey has primarily been regarded as a migrant-sending country until recently. This image of Turkey characterizes, however, just one aspect of the Turkish migration history. Only since 2011 with the large influxes of Syrians and, there is a shift in the perception of Turkey as a destination country. Throughout history though, Turkey has always been a host country for sizeable inward population movements. There were several waves of population movements in the aftermath of the collapse of the Ottoman Empire: According to Karpat, between 1860s and 1922, around 4 million people migrated to Ottoman territories while later, about 1.5 million Muslims "were forced to take refuge in the Ottoman domains" (more or less the territories of modern Turkey) (Karpat, 1985, p.75). According to the Ministry of Resettlement, then Turkey received a total of 870,000 migrants of whom 400,000 were from Greece, 225,000 from Bulgaria, 120,000 from Yugoslavia, 120,000 from Romania and 10,000 from other Balkan countries (İçduygu & Sirkeci, 1999, p.259).

Along with individually arranged movements, large portion of these migrations were organised as a result of the Lausanne Treaty's compulsory population exchange which took place between 1923 and 1926 (Arı, 1995). This population exchange had an important impact on the nation-building process, which involved transforming a multi-ethnic empire of diverse elements into a homogeneous state. Thus, parallel to the settlement of migrants of Muslim descent, there was the resettlement, displacement of Turkey's non-Muslims who have been largely expelled in the first half century from the new Turkish Republic (Jongerden, 2007).

Kirişçi (2000) argues that full citizenship rights in early Republican period were linked to ethnicity and religion. Alongside the immigrants who were given the right to settle in Turkey, there were also other Muslim groups (such as Muslim Bosnians, Albanians, Tatars etc.) who were able to settle in Turkey due to the 1923 Law of Migration and Resettlement (no. 368), which was a generic law and not specifying any ethnicity-based restrictions. However, with the 1934 Law of Settlement (no. 2510), immigration of non-Turkish persons specified as "those not belonging to Turkish ethnicity, nomadic Gypsies, spies, anarchists, and those expelled from Turkey". The 1934 Law of Settlement which remained in force and was replaced in 2006 by the Law no. 5543 systematically excluded all persons other than Turks. The Law no. 5543 defines migrants [göçmen] as "those who are of Turkish origin and belonging to Turkish culture who came to Turkey, individually or as a group, for settlement purposes and admitted according to this law [Türk soyundan ve Türk kültürüne bağlı olup, yerleşmek amacıyla tek başına veya toplu halde Türkiye'ye gelip bu Kanun gereğince kabul olunanlardır]". Exclusion of certain groups from settlement went hand in hand with other policies. There was, for instance, a law that forbid the practice of more than 72 professions for non-Turkish citizens (Law on Activities and Professions in Turkey Reserved for Turkish Citizens no. 2007). This law remained in force until 2003 and therefore, it is a good example of the Turkish state's attitude towards non-Turkish immigrants until recently.

Erder and Yükseker (2015) argue that the analysis of in- and out-migration movements in the early Republican period has been a taboo for a very long time and has only just recently been broken. Hence the overall knowledge of the experiences and personally perceived mechanism of inclusion and exclusion in the early Republican period is still very limited. However, the analysis of the state politics of the time clearly shows that the homogenization of the population was a major aim (Yeğen, 1999, Jongerden, 2007).

Since the 1980s, migration to Turkey has changed considerably. All in all, we can say that the migration flows towards Turkey has become much more diverse and is not limited to Muslims and/or migrants of Turkish descent. From the 1980s onwards, estimates put the numbers at up to 1 million trans-migrants from Iran, 100,000s of Iraqi migrants, 300,000 Turks from Bulgaria, suitcase traders, circular migrants and clandestine workers from the Eastern European Countries and the former Soviet Union, transit migrants from the Middle East and an increasing number of mainly regular migrants from the Europe and the West. Since 2011, mass migration from Syria characterizes immigration to Turkey and it is likely to be the case for the foreseeable future due to the large numbers that arrived. The number of officially recognized Syrians in Turkey is around 1.8 million along with another 200,000 Iraqis and Kurds. However, it is estimated that approximately 3 million Syrians have fled to Turkey since 2011.

As human mobility patterns shifted over decades, so did the Turkish migration policy. Turkey's international migration regime and relevant policy in the 1960s and 1970s was mainly shaped by demographic pressure, or as Sirkeci (2016) calls it "demographic deficit", which refers to large portion of population in working ages (i.e. 15 and 64) combined with high unemployment rates in a country. Thus Turkish governments of the time were "to seek outlets for the country's labour force abroad. It is not surprising that the goals of the Turkish migration policy were and are to export as many nationals abroad as possible disregarding any possible negative effects such a policy may come to have." (Kubat et al., 1979, p.253). More recently, responding to a reversal of migration flows, in other words, increasing immigration, Turkey's policy focus shifted towards immigrants in Turkey rather than exporting the "excess labour". Due to the fact that immigration in Turkey is in comparison to Europe still perceived as a rather unimportant matter, policy debates have not been well thought. Another important characteristic of the Turkish migration debate is also striking: Contrary to the highly politicied debates on migration in Europe, immigration in Turkey has not become a highly political issue yet. Thus, it is not surprising that migration has not become a subject of populist politics but is rather discussed within small circles of experts and bureaucrats.

Prior to the "Syrian crisis", Turkey has witnessed a relatively liberal debate in forming the current Law on Foreigners and International Protection (no. 6458) which removed some of the earlier restrictions (Eroglu, 2015; Elçin, 2015). All non-Turkish migrants in Turkey - i.e. regular migrants, irregular labour migrants, transit migrants and refugees/asylum seekers - were treated with various regulations based on the laws (and their amended versions) from the early republican period. Needless to say, that this legal framework was out-dated and thus insufficient to manage these new population movements. Besides, Turkey had to adjust its migration policy within the EU-harmonization process. Turkey aims to align its legislation with that of the EU, but it is difficult to speak of a common EU migration policy despite some attempts (Bendel, 2015). On the other hand, Turkey's efforts are limited too as geographical limitation remains intact in the new law. Turkey's comprehensive reform process of migration legislation emerged from this background and resulted in the Law of Foreigners and International Protection (no. 6458). As the Draft Law on Foreigners' Employment submitted to the Turkish parliament in February 2015 indicates, this process is still in flux. However, due to the adoption of various new laws and regulations for foreign nationals in Turkey the legal framework has changed fundamentally in the last few years. It is worthwhile noting, that this reform process is encompassing all groups regardless of their reason of migration and their juridical status.

Results from the MIPEX

The fact that Turkey has started to reform its out dated foreigners' laws is a necessary and appreciable development. However, it is also highly important to evaluate these reforms in order to answer questions such as: What has changes due to these reforms? Where does Turkey stand in an international comparison with its new migration policy?

The recently published MIPEX-data[1] on Turkey is highly important to reflect Turkey's ongoing reform process in migration policy and it provides a framework for international comparison with EU Member States, Australia, Canada, Iceland, Japan, South Korea, New Zealand, Norway, Switzerland and the USA.

Despite Turkey's exemplary humanitarian engagement in admitting refugees, the MIPEX results are sobering, since Turkey is only ranked on place 38 out of 38. Turkey's overall score is only 25 out of 100. Thus we can say that Turkey's legal framework is unfavourable for integration and ranks below the other MIPEX-countries. The implementation of the Law on Foreigners and International Protection, which is praised as important turning point in Turkish migration policy, did not add more than one point on the MIPEX scale.

Non-Turkish citizens have restricted rights and little-to-no state support. As

---

[1] MIPEX stand for Migrant Integration Policy Index. MIPEX is a good tool to answer these questions because it measures policies to integrate migrants in 38 countries. In order to compare migrants' participation opportunities internationally 167 policy indicators have been developed.

outlined in the conclusion of the Turkey report on the MIPEX-webpage, "the policies are unfavorable for labor market mobility, education, and political participation, even compared to other new countries of immigration in Central and Southeastern Europe. Turkey also has the weakest protections against discrimination because a dedicated anti-discrimination law and agency are still lacking and pending approval by Parliament. The country's relative strength, family reunion, is still incompatible with EU law and weak compared to laws in most MIPEX countries. Settled immigrants face not only a slightly unfavorable path to citizenship, as in several new countries of immigration, but also one of the least favorable paths to simply a long-term residence permit, far below EU standards. While the Law on Foreigners and International Protection improved transparency and the rule-of-law, the new family reunion and long-term residence statuses generally formalized existing practices, including new rights, but also new requirements. The new Migration Policies Board still has to create national adaptation strategies and programs and determine the conditions for long-term residence." (http://www.mipex.eu/turkey).

Who is a migrant in Turkey?

As this edited volume deals with migration policy in Turkey, it is self-evident to ask who is referred to as migrant in Turkey. In this context, it has to be stressed that the problem of defining migrants is not merely a "Turkish problem". The question of whom is local/"yerli" or a migrant also comes up in internal migration research since there is no consensus on a single definition of a "migrant" (Anderson & Blinder 2012). Anderson and Blinder (2012) state that categories such as country of birth, nationality and length of stay are fundamental in datasets, and argue that this variety of categories leads to the problem of comparable data. In this context, they also emphasise that this is not simply a technical problem but has various impacts on the public and political debate. Sirkeci and Cohen have been insisting and promoting the use of "mover and mobility and movement" instead of the current terminology of migrant and migration, which, they argue, gained a pejorative meaning turning "immigrant" to a dirty word while also underlining the incapability of the term "migration" to describe the dynamic nature of human mobility (Cohen & Sirkeci, 2011; Sirkeci et al., 2012; Sirkeci & Cohen, 2013). This is perhaps why most recent literature feels obliged to emphasise the fact that migration is a process (Papademetriou, 1985; Massey, 1987; Vertovec, 2003). "Mobility" has been a commonly used term in the latest literature.

Similarly, Erder and Kaşka (2012) note for the concept of "irregular migration" that the meaning of the term "irregular" lacks a discourse on the particular meaning of irregularity in "non-Western" societies such as Turkey. Their remark implies a criticism on the take-over of concepts from the international literature and comprises a call for developing a more specific terminology in order to catch particular historical, social and political contexts.

With these thoughts in mind, we would like to reflect the term "migration" in the Turkish context. A glance at the specific literature reveals that the terms "migrant", "immigrant" and "emigrant" are generally translated as "göçmen" or vice versa. According to the dictionary this is of course completely correct. From the perspective of migration studies, however, this is highly problematic because of the different notions of these concepts.

Apart from that, the specific meaning - or in other words the social perception - of the "göçmen"-concept in the Turkish context has to be taken into consideration: The word "göçmen" comes from the verb "göçmek" and its older form "köcmek". "Köcmek" was used on the one hand for marrying and on the other hand for changing the place of living in general. In Ottoman Turkish the word "hicret etmek" was used to describe this change of places. The people who changed their place of living were called "muhacir". Both nouns "göçmen" and "muhacir" have the same three meanings: They stand for immigrant, emigrant and migrant.

However, in modern Turkish language these concepts are not used in this broad sense. "Muhacir" is mainly used for the historical immigration of people of Turkish descent and/or of Muslim religion to the Ottoman Empire or the young republic respectively. The term "göçmen", however, refers in legal terms and in popular every-day-usage to more recent migration movements of people of Turkish descent and culture. Apart from that, this term refers to both, nationalized and not-nationalized persons of this background. As being a "göçmen" implies certain rights for incorporation in Turkey (such as for instance the right to naturalisation), we have to state an important difference in the "göçmen"-concept in Turkey and in various other countries. The particular meaning of having a "göçmen"-status in Turkey is not only reflected in various academic works (such as for instance by Erder (2000) etc.) but also by the migrants themselves.

Within the Turkish migration regime, the particular "göçmen"-status used to be a privileged status in terms of nationalization and/or incorporate socially by any kind of "Turkishness". Although "Turkishness" is currently not an overall category for incorporation any more (Danış & Parla 2009), it is still a tool for incorporation. Being of Turkish origin and culture still implies not only social but also legal advantages as we see for instance in the Law of Settlement (no. 5543) and the recently submitted Draft Law on Foreigners' Employment. In this context it has to be pointed out first, that the Law of settlement provides the right of settlement to "göçmen" who are of Turkish origin and linked to Turkish culture [Türk soyundan ve Türk kültürüne bağlı], while it does not give this right to foreign nationals, who are of non-Turkish origin and not linked to Turkish culture [Türk soyundan ve Türk kültürüne bağlı olmayan yabancılar]. In the line with this regulation, there also was a simplified naturalization procedure for foreign nationals with "göçmen"-status according to the Citizenship Law (no. 403), which was adopted in 1964. Although simplified naturalization regulations for people with "göçmen"-status (Pusch, 2008 and 2010) were outlawed with the amendment of the Citizenship Law in 2009 (no. 5901), these people remain in an advantageous legal position due their descent. The best proof of this origin-related privilege is the Draft law on Foreigners' Employment, which was submitted to the Turkish parliament in February 2015 (Pusch, 2015a, 2015b). The legal reasoning further states that the indefinite work permit should be mainly granted to foreigners who make investments that support the development of Turkey; are highly qualified foreigners, who strive toward scientific and technological progress; are citizens of the Republic of North Cyprus and other foreigners of Turkish descent who maintain strong linguistic, cultural, and historical ties with Turkey.

These examples clearly indicate a particular understanding of diverse foreigner groups in Turkey. In order to understand these differences, it is important to shed light on the social and cultural distinctions made between "göçmen" and "yabancı" in the Turkish context. "Yabancı" literally means foreigner. From the legal perspective everyone without Turkish citizenship is a "yabancı". However, not all non-citizens perceive themselves or are generally perceived as foreigners in the Turkish context although they technically are foreign subjects. Foreign nationals with some kind of "Turkish background" do not label themselves and are as well not labelled by the majority society as foreigners, even if they are - technically spoken - non-nationals. According to our observations three groups of foreigners are identified as "yabancı" in Turkey. First, short-time stayers with foreign passports such as tourists and foreign posted personnel with their families, who stay in Turkey for a limited time, are labelled as foreigners in Turkey. Secondly, non-Turkish-citizens from Western countries such as retirees, who are mainly in the South-coast and so called "yabancı gelinler", "foreign brides" who are married to a Turkish citizen seem to be regarded as foreigners. As many of them have settled long-term, they are also often referred to as "yerleşik yabancılar", "settled foreigners". With Georg Simmel's definition of stranger in mind – he says: that a stranger is someone who "arrives today and stays tomorrow" (Simmel, 1992: 764) –this term clearly reflects the shortage of terminology. Last but not least it seems that non-nationalized persons of a certain socio-economic status are perceived as foreigners in Turkey, too (Pusch, 2013a).

A glance at the newspapers headlines such as "Yabancılar 723 millyon avro harcadı [Foreigners spent 723 million]" (Zaman, 13.2.2013); "Yabancılar 6 ayda 6 bin dönüm tarım arazisi aldı [Foreigners bought 6 thousand dönüm agricultural land in 6 month]" (Zaman, 13.12.2012); "Yerleşik yabancılar talep edince köy yumurtasının fiyatı fırladı [The price of organic eggs jumped, as the result of demand by settled foreigners]" (Zaman, 11.1.2012); "Yabancılardan gayrimenkule 2 milyar dolar [2 Billion Dollar for real estate from foreigners]" (Hürriyet 17.2.2012); "Yabancılar nereden mülk alıyor? [Where do foreigners buy real estate?]" (Sabah 29.3.2012) suggests a correlation between the usage of the term foreigner and economic activity. Thus the term "yabancı" seems to be related to social class/or perceived social class. This would also partly explain why for example people from Western countries are in general not labeled as "göçmen" in Turkey.

To put it differently: We all know that Turkey's migration experience has evolved over time. Turkey is not only a receiving country of migrants of Turkish descent and culture, the so-called "göçmen" anymore. Within the last 30 years, migration to Turkey has become very heterogeneous and people with different backgrounds, of different countries of origin and different purposes enter the country every year. This change is well reflected by a variety of studies. Although many of these works also point to various aspects of the legal framework the issue of terminology remains rather neglected. Thus for instance the concept "göçmen" is used according to its dictionary meaning for all types of migrants, immigrants and emigrants. In accordance with the international literature several adjectives such as "irregular" or "düzensiz", "undocumented" or "kayıtdışı", "circular" or "mekik", "illegal" or "kaçak", "regular" or "düzenli" are added to specify various migrant groups. In addition, migrants from Western countries who settle in Turkey, are referred to as "yabancı" or "yerleşik yabancı" in line with popular language usage (Pusch, 2013a).

Furthermore, it seems very interesting that within academic overviews on current migration movements to Turkey two groups are often overlooked: returnees from Europe along with the descendants of the first "guest-worker"-generation from Europe, who all experience migration as well and have to incorporate or reincorporate in Turkey although they have a different legal status than most of the newly arriving groups (see Pusch, 2012; Sirkeci & Zeyneloğlu, 2014; Zeyneloğlu & Sirkeci, 2014). In other words, a large number of immigrants with some kind of affiliation to Turkey are often not regarded as part of the diversifying picture of migration to Turkey. This reminds us very much of the "taboo" (see Erder & Yükseker, 2013), to study migration experiences of the so called "traditional migrants" of Turkish descent in former decades. It seems that these groups of migrants are regarded as migrants outside Turkey, even if they are born there, but not when they resettle, settle or partly settle in Turkey (Pusch, 2013b).

Not only there are questions about the meanings and ethical and legal implications of various terms used to refer to different types of "movers", but also there is significant variation in uses and meanings between academic disciplines such as sociology and law. Thus, the debates shared and acknowledged in this edited volume should be read and interpreted bearing in mind these questions on the various terminologies used in legal documents and the literature. By pointing to these issues, we want to raise awareness for a reflected usage of terminology. There are also strong linkages between academic and legal terminology and the popular language usages. In this anthology we want to be a bit more precise. Therefore, when we speak about "Turkish migration policy" we mean policy, regulations, legislations, relevant literature and debates referring to movers in, through and from Turkey.

Migration policy beyond the "Syrian migration crisis"

The "Syrian migration crisis" continues to haunt Turkey and the European Union and warrants a rethinking and overhaul of migration and asylum policies. The attitudes of movers to migration laws are twofold. On the one hand, migration legislation and regulation often follow the patterns and strategies of the movers and on the other hand, movers constantly arrange and rearrange their moves according to the existing rules and regulations. Although this statement seems to be contradictionary at the first glance, it has often been verified in migration history because movers evaluate the legislations and than set up strategies in order to reach their goals. To put it differently: the legislation is the framework of reference for regular or irregular strategies. The irregular movement of masses crossing the

Mediteranean from Turkey to Greece is a vivid example of this interdependence and can be explained by the Turkish and the European migration policy, which does not meet the needs of the refugees.

Ironically, athough the "Syrian migration crisis" was an important factor to accelerate the speed of the implementation of the new Law on Foreigners and International Protection, migration policy remained low priority in Turkey's political agenda. Several developments proof this low importance very clearly: The fact (1) that immigration to Turkey has only been discussed superficially by political actors, (2) that the implementing provisions were published three years after the introduction of the law and (3) that the new law worsens the situation of many immigrant groups, for example the European pensioners, who settle on the South Coast and are generally perceived to have a positive impact on the economy and tourism. This perception of immigration being a negligible matter has also become clear as Turkey's newly formulated migration law has already been revised at the face of large refugee arrivals. This was not predicted by the policy makers who allowed in a liberal set of laws and in several occasions this tone was praised by researchers in the field too. Another key anomaly in Turkish migration policy is that immigration is perceived as a temporary matter, when it is not. Thus there is a risk of overlooking integration issues which often has long term implications. Now with increasing pressure, and "bribery" from the EU, Turkish migration policy is likely to evolve and unfortunately, this evolution is likely to be towards tightening borders. The deals with the EU at the end of 2015 and in March 2016 have tightly linked the migration policy making in Turkey to that of the EU. Given the fragile political environment in the EU regarding migration as well as the UK's "exit" blackmailing, Turkish migration policy may face drastic changes in the near future, particularly regarding the geographical limitation on asylum seekers (i.e. non-Europeans are not allowed to seek asylum in Turkey).

Apart from that at the face of sudden mass influxes from Syria and Iraq, a securitisation note seems to be heard more often. This is perhaps the likely direction for migration policy making in Turkey to take in the near future. This means a series of amendments are likely to follow. Furthermore, recent deals, agreements and negotiations over visa free travel between Turkey and the EU will impose certain amendments. Thus it is still a wide open process for Turkish migration policy.

It is clear that Turkish migration policy is evolving and it is likely to be adjusted given the recent large influxes and practical implications as seen fit by governments. We encourage further research on these dynamics. However, there are also historic gaps in literature. For example, despite the fact that still a large portion of immigrants in Turkey are of Turkish origin (e.g. mostly descendants of Turkish emigrants from Europe and returnees), these new legislations do not refer to these groups which in many sense differ from other immigrants due to their rather privileged legal statuses. This remains an unexploited line of research in Turkish migration policy.

With this book, we aim to shed light on changes in migration policy, determinants beneath these changes, and practical implications for movers and non-movers in Turkey. Nevertheless, one should note that Turkey has only recently faced such a large scale immigration of non-Turkish populations (i.e. Syrians) and the number of foreign born has more than doubled in less than five years from 2011 to 2015. Policy shift from "exporting excess labour" in the 1960s and 1970s to immigrant integration is a drastic but a necessary move. Nevertheless, Turkish migration policy is still far from settled as several chapters in this book point out.

References

Anderson, B. & Blinder, S. (2012). *Who Counts as a Migrant? Definitions and their consequences*. Migration Observatory Briefing, Oxford, UK: Centre on Migration Policy and Society.

Arı, K. (1995). *Büyük mübadele: Türkiye'ye zorunlu göç, 1923-1925*. Istanbul: Tarih Vakfı Yurt Yayınları.

Aybek, C. M., Huinink, J. & Muttarak, R. (2015). Migration, Spatial Mobility, and Living Arrangements: An Introduction. In C.M Aybek & J. Huinink & R. Muttarak (Eds.). *Spatial Mobility, Migration, and Living Arrangements*, (1-19). Switzerland: Springer International Publishing.

Bendel, P. (2015). But it does move, doesn´t it? The debate on the allocation of refugees in Europe from a German point of view. *Border Crossing*, 2015(1), 25-32. Retrieved from http://www.tplondon.com/journal/index. php/bc/ article/ view/508

Büyükkeskin, A. (2012). Yerleşik yabancılar talep edince köy yumurtasının fiyatı fırladı. In *Zaman* (11.01.2012). Available at: http://www.zaman.com.tr/sehir_yerlesik-yabancilar-talep-edince-koy-yumurtasinin-fiyati-firladi_1227926.html (Accessed 21.09.2015)

Cohen, J. H. & Sirkeci, I. (2011). *Cultures of migration: The global nature of contemporary mobility*. Austin: University of Texas Press.

Danış, D. & Parla, A. (2009) Nafile Soydaşlık: Irak ve Bulgaristan Türkleri Örneğinde Göçmen, Dernek, Devlet. *Toplum ve Bilim*, 114, 131-158.

Elçin, D. (2015). The principle of non-refoulement a comparative analysis between Turkish national law and international refugee law. In: Sirkeci, I. Elçin, D., Şeker, G. (eds.), *Politics and Law in Turkish Migration*. London: Transnational Press London, pp.39-50.

Erder, S. & Kaşka, S. (2012). Turkey in the New Migration Era: Migrants between Regularity and Irregularity. In S. Paçaçi Elitok & T. Straubhaar (Eds.), *Turkey, Migration and the EU: Potentials, Challenges and Opportunities*, (113-132). Hamburg: Hamburg University Press.

Erder, S. & Yükseker, D. (2013). Die türkische Migration nach Westeuropa und Migrationsstudien in der Türkei. In: B. Pusch (Ed.), *Transnationale Migration am Beispiel Deutschland und Türkei*, (49-64). Wiesbaden: VS Springer Verlag.

Erder, S. & Yükseker, D. (2015). Challenges for Migration Research in Turkey: Moving Beyond Political, Theoretical and Data Constraints. In A. Biriz Karaçay & A. İçduygu (Eds.) *Critical Reflections in Migration Research: Views from the North and the South*, (35-56). Istanbul: Koç Üniversitesi.

Eroğlu, D. (2015). The Making of Immigration Policies in Turkey: An analysis of the Law on Foreigners and International Protection Drafting Process. In: Sirkeci, I. Elçin, D., Şeker, G. (eds.), *Politics and Law in Turkish Migration*. London: Transnational Press London, pp.25-38.

İçduygu, A. & Sirkeci, İ. (1999). Cumhuriyet Dönemi Türkiye'sinde Göç Hareketleri. In O. Baydar (Ed.). *75 Yılda Köylerden Şehirlere*, (249-268). Istanbul: Tarih Vakfı Yurt Yayınları.

Jongerden, J. (2007). *The settlement issue in Turkey and the Kurds: an analysis of spatial policies, modernity and war*. Leiden, the Netherlands: Brill.

Karpat, K. H. (1985). *Ottoman population 1830-1914: Demographic and social characteristics*. Madison: University of Wisconsin Press.

Kirişçi, K. (2000). Disaggregating Turkish Citizenship and Immigration Practices. *Middle Eastern Studies*, 36(3), 1-22.

Kubát, D., Merhländer, U., Gehmacher, E. (1979). *The Politics of migration policies: the first world in the 1970s*. New York: Center for Migration Studies.

Massey, D. S. (1987). The ethnosurvey in theory and practice. *International Migration Review*, 21(4), 1498-1522.

N.N. (2012). Yabancılar 4 ayda 723 milyon avro harcadı. In: *Haber 32* (23.02.2012). Available at: http://www.haber32.com.tr/ekonomi/haber/yabancilar-4-ayda-723-milyon-avro-harcadi-55850h.html (Accessed 21.09.2015).

N.N. (2012). Yabancılardan gayrimenkule 2 milyar dolar. In: *Hürriyet Ekonomi* (17.02.2012). Available at: http://www.hurriyet.com.tr/ekonomi/19940005.asp (Accessed 21.09.2015).

N.N. (2012). Yabancılar 6 ayda 6 bin dönüm tarım arazisi aldı. In: *Ankara Zaman* (13.12.2012). Available at: http://www.zaman.com.tr/ekonomi_yabancilar-6-ayda-6-bin-donum-tarim-arazisi-aldi_2027997.html (Accessed 21.09.2015)

N.N. (2012). Yabancılar nereden mülk alıyor? In: *Sabah* (29.02.2012). Available at: http://www.sabah.com.tr/ekonomi/2012/03/29/yabancilar-nereden-mulk-aliyor (Accessed 21.09.2015).

Papademetriou, D. G. (1985). Illusions and reality in international migration: migration and development in post-World War II Greece. *International Migration*, 23(2), 211-224.

Pusch, B. (2008). Gefragte und ungefragte Gäste in der Türkei. Zur arbeitsrechtlichen Situation von Ausländern in der Türkei. In B. Pusch & T. Wilkoszewski (Eds.). *Faceten Internationaler Migration in die Türkei. Gesellschaftliche Rahmenbedingungen und persönliche Lebenswelten*, (55-67). Würzburg, Ergon-Verlag.

Pusch, B. (2010). İstenen ve İstenmeyen Konuklar: Türkiye'deki Yabancıların İş Hukuku Karşısındaki Durumu. In B. Pusch & T. Wilkoszewski (Eds.). *Türkiye'ye Uluslarası Göç. Toplumsal Koşullar – Bireysel Yaşamlar*, (75-88). Istanbul: Kitap Yayınevi. (translation of Pusch 2008).

Pusch, B. (2012). Bordering the EU: Istanbul as a Hotspot for Transnational Migration. In T. Straubhaar & S. Paçaci Elitok (Eds.). *Migration Potentials from/ to Turkey*, (167-197). Hamburg: Hamburg Universitesy Press.

Pusch, B. (2013a, 12 April). Mirror Mirror on the Wall Who Is a Migrant of us All?. *Conference "Perceptions of International Migrants in Turkey"*. Istanbul: Istanbul Bilgi University.

Pusch, B. (2013b). Einleitung: Zur Transnationalen Migrationsforschung in der Türkei. In: B. Pusch (Ed.). *Transnationale Migration am Beispiel Deutschland und Türkei*, (11-27) Wiesbaden: Springer VS.

Pusch, B. (2015a, 23 March). Turkey's New Policy on the Employment of Foreigners and its Impact on EU-Citizens. *Hürriyet Daily News* (http://www.hurriyetdailynews.com/turkeys-new-policy-on-the-employment-of-foreigners-and-its-impact-on-eu-citizens.aspx?pageID=449&nID=80026&NewsCatID=396)

Pusch, B. (2015b, 03 March). AB vatandaşı gözüyle yeni yabancı istihdam politikası. *T24*. (http://t24.com.tr/yazarlar/barbara-pusch/ab-vatandasi-gozuyle-yeni-yabanci-istihdam-politikasi,11397).

Simmel, G. (1992). Exkurs über den Fremden. In G. Simmel (1992). *Soziologie. Untersuchungen über Formen der Vergesellschaftung. Gesamtausgabe Bd.11*, (764-771). Frankfurt am Main: Suhrkamp.

Sirkeci, I. (2016). Migration crisis, conflict and Syrians. Invited lecture delivered as part of *ROR-N Lectures*, Institute of Social Anthropology, Austrian Academy of Sciences and University of Vienna, Vienna, Austria, 4 March.

Sirkeci, I., Elçin, D., Şeker, G. (eds.) (2015). *Politics and Law in Turkish Migration*. London: Transnational Press London.

Sirkeci, I. & Zeyneloğlu, S. (2014). Abwanderung aus Deutschland in die Türkei: Eine Trendwende im Migrationsgeschehen? [Migration from Germany to Turkey: reversal of fortunes]. In S. Alscher & A. Krienbriek (Eds.). *Abwanderung von Türkeistämmigen: Wer verlässt Deutschland und warum?* (30-85). Germany: BAMF. Available at: http://www.bamf.de/SharedDocs/Anlagen/DE/ Publikationen/Beitragsreihe/beitrag-band-6-abwanderung-tuerkeistaemmiger.pdf?__blob=publicationFile

Sirkeci, I. & Cohen, J.H. (2013). Not migrants and immigration, but mobility and movement, *Migration Pulse, Migrants Rights, 17 July 2013. Available at:* http://www.migrantsrights.org.uk/migration-pulse/2013/not-migrants-and-immigration-mobility-and-movement.

Sirkeci, I., Cohen, J. H. & Yazgan, P. (2012). Turkish culture of migration: Flows between Turkey and Germany, socio-economic development and conflict. *Migration Letters*, 9(1), 33-46.

Vertovec, S. (2003). Migration and other modes of transnationalism: Towards conceptual cross-fertilization. *International migration review*, 37(3), 641-665.

Yeğen, M. (1999). *Devlet Soyleminde Kurt Sorunu*. Istanbul: Iletisim Yayinlari.

Zeyneloğlu, S. & Sirkeci, İ. (2014). Türkiye'de Almanlar ve Almancılar. Göç Dergisi, 1(1), 77-118.

Laws:

Law on Migration, Development and Settlement no. 368 [368 Sayılı Mübadele, İmar ve İskân Kanunu], dated 8/11/1923. Available at: http://gocdergisi.com/kaynak/1923_ 368sayili_mubadele_kanunu.pdf (Accessed: 29/09/2015).

Law on Settlement no. 2510 [2510 Sayılı İskân Kanunu], dated 14/06/1934. Available at: http://gocdergisi.com/kaynak/1926_885sayili_iskan_kanunu.pdf. (Accessed: 29/09/2015).

Law on Activities and Professions in Turkey Reserved for Turkish Citizens no. 2007 [2007 Sayılı Türkiye'deki Türk Vatandaşlarına Tahsis Edilen Sanat ve Hizmetler Hakkında Kanun], dated 11/6/1932. Available at: http://www.hukuki.net/kanun/2007.13.text.asp. (Accessed: 17/09/2015).

Citizenship Law no. 403 [403 Sayılı Türk Vatandaşlık Kanunu], dated 11/2/1964. Available at: http://www.nvi.gov.tr/Files/File/Mevzuat/Yururlukten_Kaldirilanlar/Kanun/pdf/ turk_vatandasligi_kanunu.pdf. (Accessed: 17/09/2015).

Law on Settlement no. 5543. [5543 Sayılı İskân Kanunu], dated 19/9/2006. Available at: http://gocdergisi.com/kaynak/2006_5543_sayili_iskan_kanunu.pdf. (Accessed: 29/09/2015).

Citizenship Law no. 5901 [5901 Sayılı Türk Vatandaşlık Kanunu], dated 29/5/2009 Available at: http://www.resmigazete.gov.tr/eskiler/2009/06/20090612-1.htm. (Accessed: 17/09/2015).

Law on Foreigners and International Protection no. 6458 [6458 Sayılı Yabancılar ve Uluslararası Koruma Kanunu], dated 11.04.2013. Available at: http://gocdergisi.com/kaynak/2013_yabancilar_ve_uluslararasi_koruma_kanunu.pdf. (Accessed: 29/09/2015).

Draft Law on Foreigners Employment [Yabancı İstihdamı Kanunu Tasarısı] submitted to the Turkish parliament on 9/2/2015. Available at: http://www.alomaliye.com/2015/yabanci-istihdami-kanun-tasarisi.pdf (Accessed 16/9/2015).

Websites:
http://www.mipex.eu/turkey.

CHAPTER 15

Immigration and Civil Society: New ways of democratic transformation

Óscar García Agustín and Martin Bak Jørgensen

Debates in the political field about "democratic transition" or "democratic transformation" have been related to the shift from authoritative regimes to incipient democracy, especially to account for changes in Eastern Europe, Latin America, and, to some extent, Africa and Asia. Both terms are used to designate the idea of democratization of countries.

The Arab Spring in 2011 strongly activated the notion of democratization. Civil society's strong contestation of dictatorships opened, unexpectedly, a way to democratization – but which sort of democracy? Here it is relevant to distinguish more precisely between "democratic transition" and "democratic transformation". The former entails a change on the basis of the legitimacy of the political system (by means of free elections, new constitution, institutional reforms, etc.) whilst "democratic transformation" "expands the horizons of democracy to popular participation, and inclusive and diverse political modes of participation" (El-Khawaga, 2013).

In this special issue, we consider it essential to understand the potential of "democratic transformation", fostered by civil society, not as a transition to democracy but as a way of deepening democracy. In our understanding democratic transformation is based on the power of organized civil society actors to challenge the institutional order rather than an achievement measured against the main characteristics of representative democracy.

Searching for a suitable definition of "democratic transformation", which is not only restricted to regimes in the process of democratization, we build upon what Rancière (2010) calls the "democratic paradox". According to the French philosopher, democracy means both "democratic government" and a form of social and political life, an excess which is manifested in the extremes from freedom (deriving into mass-individualism) to the power of the people. The paradox consists in the fact that the government needs to reduce both excesses to remain in power. Rancière therefore proposes an alternative way of conceiving democracy.

Derrida distinguishes between a democracy which has reached itself (liberal democracy), and a democracy to come, an infinite openness, the time of a promise, which can never be fulfilled. Rancière accepts this distinction but points out that something is missing: democracy as practice, meaning the political process of subjectivization. Referring to his own work, Rancière offers the following definition:

Democratic practice as the inscription of the part of those who have no part - which does not mean the "excluded" but anybody whoever. Such an inscription is made by subjects who are "newcomers", who allow new objects to appear as common concerns, and new voices to appear and to be heard. In that sense, democracy is one among various ways of dealing with otherness (Rancière, 2010: 60).

Our conception of "democratic transformation" coincides with the idea of democratic practice in the sense that new political subjectivities, alliances between civil society actors, and everyday forms of resistance challenge and change the politics of the democratic governments and broaden the democratic field of social struggle. The practices of social movements and individuals attempting to change policies entail a fight in the name of democracy and create new scenarios for democratic transformations.

The economic crisis, which has affected the European countries severely, albeit to different degrees, has had large consequences in the field of immigration. The impact is clear in countries where economic growth has depended on immigrants, including the informal economy of Southern European countries. Governmental policies are constrained by the politics of austerity (basically reducing spending and cutting public services with the hopes of creating the conditions for future economic growth). Immigrants have experienced higher levels of unemployment than before, the flows of migration have been drastically reduced, and, in the political sphere, radical right-wing parties are gaining terrain in the national parliaments on the basis of blaming integration models and even immigrants for the crisis (Collet, 2011). Following from this development distinctions between deserving and undeserving – who provides a value for society and who does not – are being strengthened and rearticulated across Europe. On the political level this can be seen as a response from governments to appease immigrant-skeptical voters. The growth of anti-immigrant sentiments may also lead to counter-mobilizations from the multitude of actors who challenge this form of exclusion. Such mobilizations and struggles are increasingly transnational and transnationally founded. For example, a demonstration in Hamburg is held in solidarity with the social revolt in Greece (e.g. Contrainfo, 2013).

The turn towards migration policies is exemplified by British Prime Minister David Cameron, who wants to toughen migration policies in order to strengthen the British economy. The solution to the crisis would be to reduce the number of immigrants as well as their rights "by stopping our benefits system from being such a soft touch; by making entitlement to our key public services something migrants earn, not an automatic right; and by bringing the full force of government together to crack down on illegal working" (Cameron, 2013). This position is not an exception and it reflects how governments are influenced by the increasing power of populist parties and movements and their positioning against immigration. A disturbing example is the growth and appeal of the Greek Golden Dawn Party, which has ideological links to neo-Nazi groups and is gaining transnational recognition (Smith, 2012; 2013). On a European level the fact that policies have been adjusted but not substantially changed during the economic crisis (Koehler et al., 2010) confirms the previous tendency towards migration control and stricter measures within national borders.

The role of civil society is currently being discussed in different settings and the importance cannot be underestimated. Civil society engagement even became a key issue at the World Economic Forum in Davos in 2013 (World Economic Forum, 2013a). Mobilizations and contestations are interpreted as a "new" response: as a "breakdown in trust in established institutions" and transformation and restructuring of the established channels is perceived to be problematic: "if we think that the solution is to rebuild trust in those same institutions, we may be missing the signal" (World Economic Forum, 2013b). Former Chief Editor of the Observer, Will Hutton, depicts the ongoing protests as follows: "Capitalism's dead end requires intellectual challengers, social movements and trade union leaders prepared to dare to reimagine their role. We need ferment and protest in civil society" (Hutton, 2013). We argue that the "ferment and protest" pointed to in different contributions of this special issue of *Migration Letters* can be interpreted as attempts to challenge consensus and spur democratic transformation(s).

In contrast to the policies adopted by the governments and a progressive closure, at the social level, of the possibilities of thinking an alternative, it is, in our opinion, relevant to look at democratic transformation undertaken by civil society. In a more open or veiled opposition to government policies, these practices of civil society aim towards a more inclusive, plural, equal or participatory sphere and towards achieving more rights or expanding the notion of citizenship. All of them share, in our opinion, a common vision: improving democracy by *doing* democracy. In this conception of democratic transformation the distinction between migrants and nationals is blurred since both can be part of it.

References

Cameron, David (2013). Speech on immigration. Number 10. 25 March. Available at: http://www.number10.gov.uk/news/david-camerons-immigration-speech/

Collett, Elizabeth (2011). *Immigrant Integration in Europe in a Time of Austerity*. Washington, DC: Migration Policy Institute.

Contrainfo (2013). *Hamburg, Germany: Demonstration in solidarity with struggles in Greece and everywhere*. Available at: http://en.contrainfo.espiv.net/2013/04/22/hamburg-germany-demonstration-in-solidarity-with-struggles-in-greece-and-everywhere/

El-Khawaga, Dina (2013). "Democratic transition vs. democratic transformation". *Egypt Independent*, 10 March. Available at: http://www.egyptindependent.com /opinion/democratic-transition-vs-democratic-transformation

Hutton, Will (2013). "Davos man thrives while the rest of us pay for his excesses". *Observer*, 20 January.

Koehler, Jobst et. al. (2010). *Migration and the Economic Crisis in the European Union: Implications for Policy*. Brussels: International Organization for Migration.

Rancière, Jacques (2010). *Dissensus. On Politics and Aesthetics*. London: Continuum.

Smith, Helena (2012). "Golden Dawn threatens hospital raids against immigrants in Greece". *Guardian*, 12 June. Available at: http://www.guardian.co.uk /world/2012/jun/12/golden-dawn-hospital-immigrants-greece

Smith, Helena (2013). "Greece's neo-Nazi Golden Dawn goes global with political ambitions". *Guardian*, 1 April. Available at: http://www.guardian.co.uk /world/2013/apr/01/greece-golden-dawn-global-ambitions

World Economic Forum (2013a). *The Future Role of Civil Society*. Geneva: World Economic Forum.

World Economic Forum (2013b). *Global Agenda Outlook 2013*. Available at: http://www.weforum.org/content/restoring-values.

CHAPTER 16

Immigration Policy in the European Union: Still bringing up the walls for fortress Europe?

Petra Bendel

Introduction: the Tampere guidelines for a common European immigration and asylum system

In May 2004 the deadlines for the transitional five-year-period of the Amsterdam Treaty (in force since May 1999) ended for those European regulations which were supposed to create a common European asylum and immigration system. The European Council in Tampere, 1999, had agreed on quite an ambitious programme in order to create an "area of freedom, security and justice". Underlining a strong EU commitment to the common values of freedom based on human rights, democratic institutions and the rule of law, the Presidency of the European Council stressed that the European Union's common rights should be guaranteed to its own citizens but, at the same time, must "offer guarantees to those who seek protection in or access to the European Union". An open and secure European Union, therefore, has to be "fully committed to the obligations of the Geneva Refugee Convention and other relevant human rights instruments, and able to respond to humanitarian needs on the basis of solidarity." Also, the Tampere conclusions of the Presidency[1] wanted to ensure the integration into the EU societies of those third country nationals who are lawfully resident in the Union.

In order to reach these overarching aims, according to Tampere, the following policies should be developed: The "Partnership with the countries of origin", the creation of a common European Asylum System, measures to guarantee a fair treatment of third country nationals (that is, citizens of Non-EU-countries), the management of migration flows. These policies were transformed in a catalogue of measures to be taken within a five years period. Apart from one measure[2], a broad set of new and common European Directives and basic principles was actually agreed upon in these last five years.

In November 2004, the European Council in Brussels has adopted a new programme for Justice and Home Affairs, the so-called "Hague Programme" (often nick-named "the vague programme" in Brussels), which sets the political terms of reference for immigration issues for the next five years, but is certainly less ambitious than the Tampere Programme. In addition, we may be in the eve of a new European Constitution, which, if ratified by the Member States, would reinforce the tendencies introduced by the Hague Programme. This seems to be a

---

[1] http://www.europarl.eu.int/summits/tam_en.htm
[2] The Directive on asylum procedures has not yet been formally adopted, but was politically agreed upon in April 2004.

171

good moment to back-pedal and have a close look at the achievements as well as the problems of this European policy.

Transfer of competences from the Member States to the European Union

On the one hand, it is surely true to say that in some important areas national asylum and immigration policy has long become unthinkable without the EU. The Community has gained enormous competence in the delicate area of immigration and asylum policies: With the Treaty of Amsterdam, European law in this area, particularly regarding policies of visa as well as most asylum and refugee issues, is now binding and justifiable, and it is superior to national legislation. National veto power on immigration and asylum policies within the European institutions was gradually reduced and the European Parliament's competences were by and by extended. According to article 67 (2) of the EC Treaty, the Council shall now, after the transitional period that has ended since May 2004, vote to change the decision making rules. It could, then, vote by qualified majority (QMV) and the European Parliament would gain co-decision competences, although, as we will see below, still not in all aspects of immigration. The Hague Programme calls for an adoption of these decision making rules established in the Treaty of Nizza by 1st April 2005 at the latest. The draft EU Constitution, too, determines QMV and the co-decision procedure for all the EU measures on immigration and asylum – except for legal migration.

It is legal migration where, on the other hand, some Member States have continued to insist on retaining their domestic competences. Whereas the UK, Ireland and Denmark have opt-outs from the common immigration, asylum and civil law (Peers, 2004), Germany and its *Bundesländer* in particular (struggling at home for a new domestic immigration law that was finally passed in 2004 and trying to "protect" their national labour markets), have been the most rigid defenders of maintaining domestic competence with respect to labour migration issues. The Hague Programme, therefore, retains unanimous voting and, that way, national veto opportunities, as well as restricted parliamentary rights for legal long-term migration on third-country nationals, the freedom to travel for third-country nationals for up to three months, but also for some other measures, such as the abolition of internal border controls between the member states, standard external border controls, measures of "illegal" migration, "burden-sharing" regarding asylum and family law aspects of civil law. Germany and its *Länder* also succeeded with their position in the European Convention by embodying domestic instead of European responsibility in the draft EU Constitution for those aspects that regulate the numbers of third-country nationals coming to the EU for economic purposes. Access to work for third-country nationals is, of course, a very sensitive issue which, according to the European Commission itself, can only be "put in place progressively".

Goals and measures of EU immigration policies: An evaluation

If we accept, as I propose, that immigration policy can and should follow different (certainly sometimes even contradictory) aims, such as: 1) the restriction and control of immigration, 2) the protection of refugees, 3) the prevention of refugee movements and 4) the integration of migrants or 5) the attraction of special groups of immigrants (for instance, the highly skilled), we have to admit that communication of migration policies in the EU has, so far, concentrated excessively on the control of migration and on combating of irregular migration and on an 'effective removal and repatriation policy', once again stressed in the Hague Programme.

The overarching aspect: Security, restriction and control

Burden sharing between the Member states that accept asylum seekers and refugees by a European Refugee Fund (renewed for the period 2005-2010) and attributing responsibility for examining asylum applications between the member states have always been top on the EU agenda since the 1990s. A common European "Schengen Information System" (SIS I and II) as well as a Visa Information System (VIS) were adopted, an electronic system for the identification of asylum seekers´ fingerprints (EURODAC, in order to determine which country is responsible for an asylum claim) was introduced as well as an image archiving system (FADO) in order to combat "illegal" immigration. The Hague Programme wants the SIS II, VIS and EURODA-systems to be linked. Common Visa regulations have been adjusted, repatriation policies as well as measures relating to border management of the common borders of the European Union, Europol and penalties have been harmonised. Large scale measures against "illegal" immigration and human trafficking have been adopted[3]. This overarching aspect of security and control was still reinforced in migration policy after 9/11 2001 in New York, and after 9/3 2004 in Madrid. The Hague Programme for the next five years once again stresses this: The combat of terrorism is mentioned as the first and central task of the common policies in Justice and Home Affairs. Within immigration and asylum policies, the security aspect is central in the form of border checks and the "fight against illegal immigration", and it is found in many other guidelines issued by the European Council. In order to guarantee more security, the European council invites the European organs and Member States "to continue their efforts to integrate biometric identifiers in travel documents, visa, residence permits, EU citizens' passports and information systems without delay and to prepare for the development of minimum standards for national identity cards". The exchange of law-enforcement information is another important element of common policies. Although control and surveillance of external borders is, of course, still national competence, a specialist border assistance provided by the European Agency for the Management of Operational Co-operation at the External Borders (to be established in May 2005) is envisaged. Moreover, the European Council invites to study the feasibility of a European border guard. Security is surely a legitimate and, up to a certain point, also a necessary group of measures to be taken.

Humanitarian aspects: Protection of refugees

But criticism has to set in at the fact that other aspects, such as the protection

---

[3] This list is not supposed to be complete. For a detailed list of European legislation on immigration and asylum issues comp. the Scoreboard http://europa.eu.int/comm/justice_home. The Hague Programme also invites the Commission to present a yearly (before it was twice a year) scoreboard to the Council on the implementation of the Programme.

of refugees, have so far been comparatively underdeveloped. Although common minimum standards for the reception of asylum seekers (2003/9/EC) and for giving temporary protection in the event of a mass influx of displaced persons (2001/55/EC) were agreed upon, common guidelines for the recognition of the refugee status and for the subsidiary forms of protection offering an appropriate status to any person not covered by the 1951 Refugee Convention, but nevertheless in need of international protection, lack behind the expectations of many NGOs concerned with the fate of refugees. Also, the Directive on asylum procedures, which was agreed upon, but not yet formally adopted, was harshly criticized by human rights groups for its low standards. The Hague Programme even envisages a study for an eventual joint processing of asylum applications *outside* the EU; but the text fails to make clear what that would entail (cf. comment of Steve Peers, 2004a).

Prevention of refugee movements

With regard to the prevention of refugee movements, the European Union has not been too active either: Although cooperation with the countries of origin is said to be a cornerstone of common policies, this cooperation has actually also been largely restricted to control aspects. "Partnership with third countries" is, above all, established in order "to improve [these countries] capacity for migration management and refugee protection, prevent and combat illegal immigration, inform on legal channels for migration, resolve refugee situations by providing better access to durable solutions, build border-control capacity, enhance document security and tackle the problem of return." (Conseil Européen, 2004). At least, the Council endorses the Commission's Communication on improving access to durable solutions and invites the Commission to develop EU-Regional Protection Programmes with the countries of origin.

Integration of migrations living in the EU

Looking at the integration of migrants who are already living in the European Union, the principle of non-discrimination in Article 13 of the Treaty of Amsterdam confers the right to the Council to "take appropriate action to combat discrimination based on sex, racial or ethnic origin, religion or belief, disability, age or sexual orientation." This has led the Council of the EU to adopt a Directive on racial discrimination (2000/43/EC) and a Directive on discrimination in employment (2000/78/EC), a fact that was very surprising for many observers, given the liberal character of the Commission's proposal (Geddes and Guiraudon, 2003). Notwithstanding the importance of this agreement, it is also true that many member states have still not fully implemented the Directives, although the deadline ended in 2003 (Jenaro Tejada *et al.* 2002; Nickel *et al.* 2003).

Family reunification, one of the most important aspects of integration policy and still one of the most outstanding pull-factors for migrants towards Europe, was only agreed upon after long discussions. The respective Directive on Family reunification (2003/86/EC) is now being treated by the European Court of Justice (ECJ), because the European Parliament has claimed infringement of its rights to examine the last version of the Directive and to present comments and observations. Below that action for annulment brought to the ECJ, there are concerns about possible contradictions with the European Convention on Human Rights, particularly with article 8 of the ECHR.

In the meantime, the rights of third-country nationals who are long-term residents (2003/109/EC) were passed in the Council. This Directive is designed to third-country nationals to enjoy a legal status comparable to that of citizens of the member states (Kostakopoulou, 2001).

It is also true that the European Commission has called the Member States for more cooperation to ensure the integration of the immigrants. In addition, it has tried to provide a very complex and coherent European policy-framework for integration (Commission of the European Communities, 2003: 26), including its European Employment Strategy (EES). Nevertheless, progress in these areas has certainly been very slow. In 2003, however, the European Commission launched a number of pilot projects on the integration of migrants, supporting networks and transfer of information and good practices. The integration of third-country nationals into society depends on comprehensive integration policies which include integration into the labour market, education and language skills, housing issues, health and social services, nationality/citizenship and respect for diversity, but all these areas are still part of national legislation. The Hague Programme stresses the necessity to exchange information and experiences, but does not touch domestic competences. It does call the Member States and the European institutions to develop common basic principles underlying a coherent European framework on integration.

Legal migration

National competence is, above all, retained in the area of legal migration, especially with regard to the attraction of specific groups of migrants. This is true although the European Commission has presented a very interesting proposal on common European policies (COM 2003/336 final) that emphasizes the importance of the economic potential of migrants and their integration.

Although the need for migration into certain sectors and regions of the EU is openly recognised by the European Commission and the European Council, and although the Member States themselves see the necessity to foster migration in order to cope with bottlenecks with regard to particular professional qualifications and demographic changes, there is still no genuine European labour market and, therefore, no common interest in widening the common policies in this area.[4] The Directive proposed in July 2001 by the European Commission (COM (2001) 386) determining common definitions, criteria and procedures for third-country nationals working in the European Union had, in principle, respected the member states´ discretion to limit economic migration domestically. It had proposed a very interesting possibility to attract migrants quickly in accordance with economic and demographic necessities and interests, but, due above all to Germany's opposition,

---

[4] It is true that intra-EU migration from the new EU countries could also help to alleviate the effects of demographic distorsions and professional necessities in the future. However, it is anticipated that migration from countries such as Poland, the Czech Republic, Hungary, Slovenia, and Estonia would have temporary rather than permanent character.

has not been discussed any more in the Council of Ministers since 2002. The Commission should have presented a Green Paper on labour migration in October 2004, but did only recently, at the beginning of 2005 (COM 2004: 811).

In its Hague Programme, the European Council pays some lip services to the importance of legal migration for a "knowledge-based economy in Europe, in advancing economic development, and thus contributing to the implementation of the Lisbon strategy." But at the same time, it fails to mention the principles laid down by the European Council in Tampere, such as: the treatment of third country nationals comparable to nationals, the equal treatment of long-term residents as near as possible to the treatment of nationals (cf. Peers, 2004a). It also emphasizes "that the determination of volumes of admission of labour migrants is a competence of the Member States." Taking into account the outcome of discussions on the Green Paper on labour migration, best practices in Member States and its relevance for implementation of the Lisbon strategy, it nevertheless "invites the Commission to present a policy plan on legal migration including admission procedures capable of responding promptly to fluctuating demands for migrant labour in the labour market before the end of 2005" (Conseil Européen, 2004). This could possibly lead to resume at least some aspects of the "frozen" Directive proposal on labour migration. Most recently, the new Commissioner and the new President of the Commission, José Manuel Barroso, re-opened the discussion on the necessity of creating an economic migration system, necessity which is still strongly debated in some of the Member States with high levels of unemployment (but, nevertheless, gaps in the labour markets of some specific segments). For the end of 2005, the Commission plans to present a new political plan for a common migration policy for labour migration.

Conclusion: A backward step

As we have seen, border control, sanctions for human trafficking and return policies are still the most important bricks in the walls of "fortress Europe", a fortress that seems tempted to extend its walls even beyond its own borders – as in the case of the debate about holding centers in North Africa, opened by British Prime Minister Tony Blair and re-warmed by the German interior minister Otto Schily.

Following the terrorist assaults of New York and Madrid and making justice to the more conservative political changes in the European countries' governments and, subsequently, of the Council, the Hague Programme has once again restricted priorities to the security aspects of migration, and to measures that reinforce restriction and control. But taking into account the five criteria developed in this study, restriction and control will certainly not provide for a comprehensive and modern approach to migration in the European Union. With its "vague programme", the European Council relapses far behind the predecessor's of Tampere programme, which would at least try to regulate prevention of refugee movements, protection of refugees and integration of migrants within the EU.

References

Conseil Européen- Bruxelles, 04 & 05 novembre 2003, Conclusions de la Présidence, http://europa.eu.int /rapid/pressReleses Action.do?reference=DOC/04/5&format=HTML&aged =0&language=EN&gui Language=en [Accessed 10 november 2004].

Favell, Adrian (1998) "The Europeanisation of immigration politics", *European Integration online Papers* (Eiop) Vol. 2 (1998), No. 10; http://eiop.or.at/eiop/texte/1998-010a.htm.

Geddes, Andrew (2003) "Still Beyond Fortress Europe? Patterns and Pathways in EU Migration Policy", *Queen's Papers on Europeanisation*, No. 4/2003.

Geddes, Andrew and V. Guiraudon (2003) "Anti-discrimination Policy: The Emergence of a EU Policy Paradigm amidst Contrasted National Models", Paper for the workshop Opening the Black Box: Europeanisation, Discourse, and Policy Change, November 23-24, 2002, Oxford, England.

Guiraudon, Virginie (2001) "The EU "garbage can": Accounting for policy developments in the immigration domain", paper presented at the 2001 conference of the European Community Studies Association in the panel "Immigration and the Problems of Incomplete European Integration", Madison Wisconsin, 29 May-1 June 2001.

Guiraudon, Virginie (2003) "The constitution of a European immigration policy domain: a political sociology approach", *Journal of European Public Policy*, 10(2): 263-282.

Jenaro Tejada, Elena, I. Carles-Berkowitz, I. Chopin (2002) *Ohne Unterschied! Umsetzung der Richtlinie zur Anwendung des Gleichbehandlungsgrundsatzes*, Überblick und Vorschläge, Brussels.

Kostakopoulou, Theodora (2001) "Invisible Citizens: Long-term Resident Third Resident Third Country Nationals in the EU and their Struggle for Recognition", in R. Bellamy and A. Warleigh (eds.) *Citizenship and Governance in the EU*, London and New York: Continuum, pp. 180-205.

Kostakopoulou, Theodora (2002) "Integration, Non-EU Migrants in the European Union: Ambivalent Legacies and Mutating Paradigms", *Columbia Journal of European Law*, 8(2): 181-201.

Nickel, Rainer, A. Coomber, M. Bell *et al.*, *Racism as a crime (n.y.), European Strategies to combat racism and xenophobia as a crime*, Brussels.

Niessen, Jan (2001) "Overlapping Interests and Conflicting Agendas: The Knocking into Shape of EU Immigration Policies", *European Journal of Migration and Law*, 3, pp. 419-434.

Peers, Steve (2002) "Key Legislative Developments on Migration in the European Union", *European Journal of Migration and Law*, 4, pp. 339-367.

Peers, Steve (2004) Statewatch Briefing. Vetoes, Opt-outs, and EU Immigration and Asylum Law, prepared for Statewatch by Professor Steve Peers, University of Essex, revised version: 8 November 2004, http://www.statewatch.org/news /2004/nov/eu-immig-opt-outs2.pdf. [Accessed 10 November 2004]

Peers, Steve (2004a) *Statewatch: The "Hague Programme"*. Annotation of final version, approved 5.11.2004. Annotated by Professor Steve Peers, University of Essex), http://www.statewatch.org/news/2004/nov/hague-programme-final.pdf. (rev. 10 november 2004)

Pro Asyl (2002) *Der lange Weg zu einem europäischen Asylrecht, Materialien*, Frankfurt a. M. September.

Salt, John (2001) "Current Trends in International Migration in Europe", *Council of Europe, CDMG*, (2001) 33, November.

CHAPTER 17

The Case for a Foreign Worker Advisory Commission

Ray Marshall

Introduction

This paper outlines the case for an independent Foreign Worker Advisory Commission (FWAC) to assemble and develop data and research to assist the administration and Congress make better and more timely decisions on employment-based migration (EBM), a relatively small (14% in 2010) component of total immigration.[1] The FWAC also would recommend the numbers and composition of temporary foreign workers (TFW) admitted each year, which constituted about 1.7 million (of 46.5 million) US foreign visitors in 2010.[2]

Until the 1980s and 1990s, United States migration policies were similar to those of other immigration nations in that immigration was heavily family based. But with globalization, other nations shifted more to economic immigration, mainly EBM, while the US continued to provide most (over 60%) of its immigrant visas for family reunification and fewer (less than 20%) for economic and employment purposes. This divergence occurred because most other countries—especially Canada and Australia—responded to globalization by adopting value-added (productivity and quality) competiveness policies that stressed upgrading workers' skills and minimizing wage competition that would lead to lower and more unequal wages for workers in high-income countries.

Immigration supports domestic economies by providing skills not readily available in domestic labour markets, compensating for declining native labour force growth, and contributing to creativity, innovation, and entrepreneurship, all critical requirements for value-added economic policies.

Immigration has positive impacts if foreign workers (a) complement, not substitute for, domestic workers or depress wages and working conditions and (b) successfully integrate into labour markets and societies. Unsuccessful integration, by contrast, can lead to deadly and disruptive racial, ethnic, and religious conflicts. The challenge for migration managers, therefore, is to ensure that foreign worker flows maximize the enormous potential advantages of migration while minimizing the disadvantages, which requires increasingly sophisticated data, research and metrics more readily available in other immigration countries than in the United

---

[1] The ideas in this paper come from my experiences with and study of employment-based migration in the United States and other countries, especially Canada, Australia, and the United Kingdom (see Ray Marshall 2011).
[2] These are admissions data, which have been inflated in the past few years by DHS counting methods. For example, Mexican workers living in Mexico and entering the US every day with H-2A visas, as during the Arizona vegetable harvest, are counted as an admission every day that they enter the US.

States.

The case for a foreign worker advisory commission

An essential agency to help ensure an effective EBM system is an independent research, evaluation, and advisory body to give legislators and migration officials objective, evidence-based advice about such matters as labour shortages, whether migration is the most sensible way to fill those shortages, and the characteristics of foreign workers most likely to succeed. A commission can also make recommendations to better match the supply of foreign workers with job vacancies, evaluate the employment implications of immigration reform proposals, and assess how to balance the interests of workers, employers, and the nation.

There is, therefore, growing support for an independent migration commission, including from the Independent Task Force on Immigration and America's Future, co-chaired by Lee Hamilton and Spencer Abraham; the Council on Foreign Relations' (CFR) Task Force on U.S. Immigration Policy, co-chaired by Jeb Bush and Thomas McLarty III; the Brookings-Duke Immigration Policy Roundtable; and the Migration Policy Institute (Papademetriou et al. 2009).

There is, in addition, ample precedent for such entities. As the CFR task force observed:

> Although immigration is every bit as important as trade for the US economy, the institutional expertise on immigration policy is a fraction of that of the trade world. Trade policymakers call on a staff of several hundred economists and other experts at the independent US Trade Commission for background investigations into the effects of trade on specific industries and segments of the economy (Council on Foreign Relations (2009:93).

Structure and purpose

The FWAC's structure and composition should ensure independence, professionalism, and credibility. Members should be appointed by the President and confirmed by the Senate, and the President should appoint the chair. Commissioners must have expertise in migration-related disciplines, be supported by a professional staff, and be authorized to commission research and support advisory networks. The FWAC would develop data and research, supplemented by input from trade, occupational, industry, labour, professional, and regional organizations, and the public.

Specific mandates

A US FWAC would have three specific mandates:

(1) Provide data, research, advice, and recommendations on foreign worker matters to Congress and the President.

(2) Recommend more rational and flexible flows of foreign workers. With present US policies, changing foreign worker quotas – some of which were established over two decades ago – requires highly contentious and inflexible Congressional action unsupported by credible data and analyses. This

process cannot meet the changing needs for foreign workers in dynamic, diverse, and highly competitive labour markets.

(3) Conduct and commission research to improve EBM. It would be extremely bad policy, for example, to expand temporary foreign worker flows before fixing the seriously flawed existing programs, assessing the labour market impact of pending reforms, and developing both effective processes to determine labour shortages and better market tests for qualified Americans.

The FWAC would elevate EBM on the national policy agenda; reduce political conflict over immigration; and increase public support for this important function, provided, of course, that the system was sufficiently transparent and well managed to convince the public that federal immigration authorities were promoting national interests as well as those of the principal stakeholders.

It is important to specify that the FWAC would not make final decisions about annual EBM compositions and levels; this is a political responsibility best left to elected officials. The commission would make recommendations, which Congress could modify, reject, or allow to take effect in a specified time, as is now done, for example, with the annual goals for refugees. Similarly, the commission would provide data, research, and advice to the federal officials responsible for EBM, but would not administer foreign worker programs.

Policy context

To be most effective, the FWAC should operate within a system that included:

A. *Clear goals.*

The most sustainable goals would be to (a) minimize wage competition and maximize value added and (b) promote broadly shared prosperity. A migration system guided by these objectives would clearly be better than one either based on direct cost, mainly wage, competition or guided by macro or per-capita economic growth with little regard for distributional effects.

B. *High-level federal responsibility.*

The advantages of having high-level federal EBM responsibility include:

Better coordination between migration and other economic and social policies. Without coordination, employers and public officials too often neglect this important activity and substitute migration for education, training, and other functions. Coordination also highlights sensible alternatives to the importation of foreign workers.

Greater visibility for employment-based migration.

Strengthened protection of foreign and domestic workers. This is more likely if a Department of Labor official has responsibility for EBM, but the FWAC could facilitate the process by formulating and evaluating innovative approaches to worker protections or faster and more flexible adjustment of foreign workers to domestic labour markets.

C. *Policies and programs to ensure that migrants are successfully integrated into labour markets and communities.* This requires that foreign workers succeed on the job, have adequate English-language skills, and understand and accept American values, institutions, and laws.

D. *An effective immigration management system.* Administrative efficiency, in turn, requires clear *accountability* for outcomes, which is greatly facilitated by high-level federal EBM responsibility. Administrative efficiency would facilitate the flexible adjustment of foreign worker flows to the needs of American employers. The FWAC could, in addition, provide the data and analyses to continuously improve EBM programs.

E. *Well-designed immigration law.*

One of the most glaring defects of US migration policy is that it is not based on transparent, fair, enforceable, sensible, or evidence-based legislation. As a result, these laws not only have been ineffective, but have produced serious unintended consequences.

Resolving disputes over labour shortages

One of the FWAC's major responsibilities would be to identify and measure labour shortages, currently a very contentious issue. There is basic agreement over broad trends, but strong disagreement over specific shortages. Indeed, there is not even a generally accepted definition of shortages.

College-educated workers

Based on current economic and demographic trends, most analysts project a strong demand for college graduates, partly because of the need for higher cognitive skills in a more competitive and knowledge-intensive economy and partly because slack labour markets and declining real wages for college graduates enable employers to hire overqualified workers. The McKinsey Global Institute, for example, projects a 2020 deficit of 1.5 million workers with bachelor's degrees (Manyika et al. 2011). Workers with lower levels of education will continue to face higher unemployment, partly because employers prefer college graduates for many jobs that do not actually require college-level competencies.

The absence of agreed-upon definitions and measures makes it difficult to resolve disagreements over shortages. As evidence for shortages of college-educated workers, for example, employers, politicians, and editorial writers often cite the rapid exhaustion of the annual 85,000 H-1B visa allotment. This, however, is evidence of a high demand for indentured foreign workers willing to accept below-market wages, not a shortage of skilled workers. Moreover, a large percentage of H-1B visas is captured by multinational outsourcing firms, which do not have a US labour shortage because their business models largely exclude American workers, depending instead on the importation of low-wage workers from India and other developing countries. Ron Hira, a leading authority on these visas, concludes: "There are only two reasons that firms hire H-1Bs instead of Americans: 1) an H-1B worker can legally be paid less than a US worker and 2) the H-1B worker learns the job and then rotates back...home...and takes the job with him."(Hira 2013a and 2013b).

Business, academic, and media commentators likewise often grossly understate the supply of available foreign workers by focusing on particular visa limitations rather than the total supply of migrant workers. Thus, despite the 85,000 limitation, approximately 130,000 H-1B visas were granted each year between 2006 and 2012,[3] and H-1B workers who have exhausted their six-year eligibility can remain in the United States while awaiting permanent residency but are not counted as H-1B visa renewals. In addition, an annual average of 71,330 L visas for intra-company transfers (which have no numerical limit, but compete with H-1Bs and are authorized to work in the US for five to seven years) were granted between 2008 and 2012.[4] There is thus a large (probably over one million), but unfortunately unknown, number of college-educated temporary foreign workers in the United States at any time.

This supply is augmented by significant numbers of international students who remain in the United States after completing their studies on Optional Practical Training (OPT) visas for 12 months for each degree; science, technology, engineering and mathematics (STEM) graduates are eligible for an additional 17 months (i.e., 29 months total).

Advocates for increasing visas for college-educated workers, or "stapling green cards to their diplomas," often argue that it is irrational for the United States to educate foreign students and force them to leave after they graduate (see for example, Wadhwa 2008). However, according to work by Michael Finn for the National Science Foundation, about two-thirds of foreigners who receive US science and engineering PhDs stay in the United States for 10 years or longer (Finn 2012:1). Finn concludes: "The data…do not support the view that the best and the brightest have been returning home because of visa difficulties in the United States" (2012:13)

Focusing on a particular visa category is misleading because there are alternative ways for former students to acquire permanent residence. For example, Mark Rosenzweig (2006) found that in 2003 56% of foreign graduates who acquired green cards did so by marrying US citizens while only 20% were sponsored by employers.

Other evidence casts doubt on a general shortage of college-educated workers: high unemployment and underemployment rates for college graduates, a more than doubling of the unemployment rate for science and engineering workers between 2007 and 2010 (from 2.6% to 5.6%), stagnant or declining real median incomes for college-educated workers, the difficulty many graduates—including STEM majors—have finding jobs in occupations for which they are trained, the fact that about two-thirds of engineering graduates work in non-engineering fields, and the large percentage (almost half, according to some assessments) (Beaudry et al. 2013)

---

[3] http://travel.state.gov/visa/statistics/nivstats/nivstats_4582.html; http://www.travel.state.gov/ pdf/ FY12 AnnualReport-TableXVIB.pdf; http://www.travel.state.gov/pdf/FY08-AR-TableXVI(B).pdf
[4] Ibid.

of college graduates in jobs that do not require college degrees.

According to one assessment, an increase in foreign-born scientists who will work for relatively low wages by American standards has contributed to a glut of science and engineering PhDs and has caused "a growing aversion of America's top students...to enter scientific careers. Increasingly, foreign-born technical and scientific personnel on temporary visas staff America's university labs and high-tech industries" (Benderly 2013).

Richard Freeman, a leading authority on science and engineering labour markets, also rejects the assertion that there are shortages of qualified workers in these fields. He argues that "huge increases in supply [of foreign students] make these careers less attractive to the native-born." Moreover, "the potential that the country will experience a genuine labour market shortage seems remote... (Freeman 2007:7-8)."

Thus, although media and business reports often warn of "looming" general shortages of science and engineering graduates, there are ample grounds for scepticism because these claims usually evaporate under objective scrutiny. Most such assessments confirm Michael Teitelbaum's conclusion: "...no one who has come to the question with an open mind has been able to find any objective data suggesting 'shortages' of scientists and engineers" (Teitelbaum 2007).

For migration management purposes shortages must be defined with much greater precision. If properly measured, there could well be shortages of college-educated workers in some specific fields and geographic locations, but advocates for larger foreign worker flows rarely, if ever, present credible evidence about the duration or size of shortages, the occupations involved, the geographic distribution, or other characteristics needed to determine if it were sensible to use immigration to overcome those shortages.

Less-skilled workers

It likewise is highly questionable that the United States faces a general shortage of workers with sub-baccalaureate education. The McKinsey research cited earlier, for example, projects 2020 surpluses of 5.9 million high school dropouts and 800,000 high school graduates (Manyika et al. 2011:39).

Furthermore, wage and employment data do not suggest a general shortage of less-skilled workers. The unemployment rate of young high school graduates was 21% in 2011, more than double that of young college graduates. And the real median income for male high school graduates 25 and older fell 11.5% between 2000 and 2009; it fell 16.3% for those with 9 to 12 years of education and no diploma (Marshall 2012: 376-387).

For a variety of reasons, most other high-income immigration countries greatly restrict the number of less-educated temporary foreign workers (LETFW). First, low-income workers generally have negative fiscal implications for countries with costly health care, social support and education systems (Rowthorne 2008:560). Second, these countries have generally adopted value-added economic strategies to avoid low-wage jobs (with 25 per cent of its jobs classified as low wage, the United

States had the highest proportion of such jobs among the OECD countries surveyed; Denmark, with 8.5 per cent, had the lowest) (Gautie and Schmitt 2010). These countries also import more college-educated workers in order to minimize the political, economic, and social consequences of growing inequality of wealth and income (Aydemir and Borjas, 2008 and Marshall 2011). Most high-income countries likewise give preference for work requiring less education to resident youth, older people, and other qualified workers. Foreign workers are imported in highly restricted categories and for specific time periods, like summer jobs, agricultural harvesting, holiday maker programs, and other jobs for which domestic workers are not available at the times and places where they are needed.

A significant negative deterrent to importing LETFWs is their vulnerability to exploitation. Indeed, even countries like Canada and Australia, with strong worker protections and labour market institutions, have found it difficult to protect the LETFWs or the domestic workers with whom these migrants compete. Their inherent vulnerability makes it hard to enforce typical complaint-driven labour protection regimes (Marshall 2011 and Nakache and Kinoshita 2010). It is, in addition, hard for countries to prevent LETFWs from becoming unauthorized immigrants.

Those who advocate a large new LETFW or "guest worker" program likewise focus on the caps for particular visas, like the H-2b, and ignore other ways authorized foreign workers enter the United States, especially via permanent immigrant visas for purposes of family reunification, which are more than triple those issued for economic purposes. According to the Mexican Migration Project, for example, in 2010, 517,000 Mexicans entered the United States as authorized temporary workers, while net illegal immigration from Mexico had fallen to virtually zero (Castaneda and Massey 2012).

Finally, it is hard to imagine general labour shortages of less-educated workers in the future when we already have a large supply of unemployed and underemployed low-income workers who would be the main losers from a large-scale LETFW program. If we adjust the status of millions of unauthorized immigrants along with their immediate family members, as we should, the United States could have a continuing flow of less-educated workers. A value-added, shared-prosperity strategy would give high priority to improving opportunities for these and other low-wage workers, not to importing people to compete with them.

Again, there might be specific shortages of less-educated workers that migrants could sensibly fill, but this will not be revealed by current methodologies, data sources or market processes. An independent professional agency is needed to produce much better data, measurements, and labour market assessments before we change the limits on LETFWs. We should, however, reform existing programs to more effectively meet employers' legitimate needs while protecting the interests of foreign and domestic workers and the public.

Defining and Measuring Shortages

A major cause of the controversies over labour shortages is the absence of agreed-upon definitions and measures, permitting antagonists to make their case with assertion instead of objective evidence. A major mandate for the FWAC therefore would be to build consensus for definitions and measurements to help adjust the flow of migrants to jobs that cannot sensibly be filled by domestic workers.

The commission should start by benchmarking international experiences and adapting them to American conditions. While all immigration nations have developed shortage concepts to guide EBM, the definitions and processes developed by the UK's Migration Advisory Committee (MAC) are particularly transparent, well thought out, and evaluated.

In performing its calculations, MAC identifies four labour shortage categories:

1. **Cyclical**, when, especially during periods of rapid economic growth, wages or suitable labour supplies cannot keep pace with rising demand because of market frictions like "sticky wages."

2. **Structural,** when occupational or sectoral labour supplies do not match demand for reasons unrelated to economic cycles. If there are no market adjustment restrictions, rising wages should ultimately overcome these shortages.

3. **Public sector wage restraints** can cause long-run shortages because wages are not allowed to rise enough to attract resident workers to these occupations. In the UK, as in the US, this kind of shortage is common in education, research, and social and health care where public employers rely heavily on foreign workers who find these wages and conditions attractive.

4. **Rare skills shortages** occur when there are global shortages of workers with the skills demanded, either because of small numbers with specific innate abilities or because those skills are attained in connection with innovations that have not yet reached the country experiencing the shortages.

In identifying and measuring specific job or occupational shortages, MAC uses a top-down, bottom-up methodology. Top-down statistics on particular occupations checked against submissions from employers, unions, statistical agencies, and others at the national, regional and local levels. Top-down statistics provide rigor and continuity, while the bottom-up assessments help refine the top-down data, which are always too general and less timely and specific than needed for migration decisions. This process permits continuous refining and updating and is greatly enhanced by information technology.

MAC uses the concept of **dovetailing** to identify shortages confirmed by both the top-down and bottom-up evidence. This is an important step because top-down indicators do not by themselves provide incontrovertible evidence for or against a shortage. For example, not all job titles within an occupation showing a shortage might be in short supply, and top-down evidence might conceal shortages within particular job titles. Before adding an occupation to the shortage occupations list (SOL), MAC applies a *sensibility test*, asking if migration is the most sensible way to overcome the shortage. This test forces an extensive examination of alternatives to migration. If, for example, employers are not making adequate efforts to recruit and train resident workers, the occupations applied for will not be added to the SOL.

It should be noted, however, that the SOL is not used for all EBM categories. Tier 2 of the UK's points-based migrant worker program is for skilled workers with a job offer and is the main component of the British EBM system. Tier 2 has five routes: shortage occupations (SO), resident labour market test (RLMT), intra-company transfers (ICT), sportspeople and ministers of religion. The advantages of an SO occupation is that it gains the applicant enough points (70) for entry: 50 for being on the SOL and 10 each for mandatory English language competency and income support requirements.

Migrants entering through the RLMT, the most important non-ICT route, get 30 points for a job offer and an additional 40 points from the mandatory 20 points, qualifications (5-15 points) and prospective earnings (5-15 points). As the name implies, employers using the RLMT must test the market to ensure that no British workers are available for the jobs.

Since the ICT route (comparable to L-1 visas in the US) has been very problematic, MAC helped the UK Border Agency devise a new system to identify, eliminate, and prevent abuses. In reforming the much-criticized L-1 visa program, the United States could benefit from the British ICT experience.

MAC's work has produced a number of advantages:

1. It has made decisions more evidence-based, thereby improving the government's ability to meet labour market needs while promoting the national interest and protecting foreign and domestic workers.

2. The top-down, bottom-up methodology has improved the data used to measure labour shortages, as well as for labour market and EBM research. Because they participate in the bottom-up process, stakeholders are more inclined to accept MAC's methods and recommendations.

3. MAC's transparency and credibility has depoliticized contentious debates over whether or not there are shortages (Martin and Ruhs 2011).

4. The transparency of the process, driven by the UK's national interest in value-added economic policies, has caused economic migration to have broad public acceptance, though other migration categories remain extremely contentious.

5. The sensibility test has forced better coordination between migration, education, health, economic, and social policies.

A Response to Critics

Employers often contend that they, not an appointed commission, are better suited to select foreign workers to meet their needs. However, the power to select foreign migrants should not be delegated to employers who, even according to competitive business doctrine, are unlikely to protect the interests of workers or the nation. Instead, adjusting foreign worker flows is a sovereign responsibility best left to the legislative and executive branches. A professionally staffed, properly resourced FWAC would enable Congress to optimize migration policies' benefits for workers, employers, and the nation while simultaneously easing the divisiveness this issue generates.

Of course, an effective migration policy must respond to employers' legitimate interests in recruiting foreign workers for jobs that cannot be readily filled by domestic workers at prevailing wages, benefits, and working conditions. And the FWAC, like the British MAC, would seek active input from employers and other labour market participants. Indeed, managing foreign worker flows effectively would include policies that induce as much self-regulation by employers and workers and their organizations as is consonant with the national interest. And EBM programs recognize employers' interests by giving major credit for job offers and characteristics employers value.

A US Chamber of Commerce official opposes a commission because, he argues, "It would never be able to determine shortages in a timely manner that reflects the always-changing realities of the market place"(Greenhouse 2013:1). The issue, however, is not perfection, but whether a commission could help significantly improve the existing system. Logic, as well as experience in other countries, leaves little doubt that a commission could make the current migration selection process, with congressionally mandated caps, more flexible, timely, transparent, and useful. Moreover, the process would calculate the kind of persistent shortages the Chamber and other employer organizations complain about, not less important temporary shortages. As noted, moreover, shortage calculations would be only one of the FWAC's functions. Shortage lists accelerate the migrant hiring process by making it possible avoid time-consuming market tests for available resident workers.

Finally, an independent commission can help resolve disputes about whether or not there are shortages of qualified domestic workers. It clearly would not be good policy to accept employers' or domestic workers' word for whether or not there are shortages. Indeed, there are few, if any, objective academic, foundation, or non-profit analysts of immigrant labour markets using generally acceptable methodologies and appropriate data. Given the subject's growing importance for workers, employers, labour market and education institutions, more objective and evidence-based analyses benefit all parties—especially where, as proposed here, all parties have an opportunity to make their case based on evidence produced by sound methodologies.

Some sceptics doubt that the FWAC could avoid being politicized or captured by special interests. That challenge deserves serious analysis, discussion, and debate. It would be particularly useful to examine why some US and foreign commissions and boards have been more politicized and co-opted than others.

However, the evidence suggests that independence could be strengthened by creating a highly professional, evidence-based culture, as, for example, the Bureau of Labor Statistics, the International Trade Commission, and the Federal Reserve Board have done. Independence also is strengthened through selecting highly respected professional members who serve for long, staggered terms that do not coincide with those of any administration, and ensuring a high level of visibility, transparency, and professionalism in the commission's deliberations.

This does not mean that the FWAC's deliberations, as emphasized earlier, can or should be divorced from politics. Not only must decisions about immigration reconcile conflicting interests, but also is a sovereign responsibility. That is the reason the final decision on the FWAC's recommendations should be left to democratic political processes.

Concluding remarks

An independent, professional FWAC should be an important component of comprehensive immigration reform. Indeed, the FWAC should be established and operational before any substantive changes are made in current foreign worker programs. The United States should, however, immediately improve the enforcement of the rights of foreign and domestic workers, simplify and modernize administrative procedures, and strengthen data relevance and reliability.

A note on the 2013 bipartisan Senate immigration reform bill

The Senate reform bill provides for a Bureau of Immigration and Labor Market Research (BILMR), located in the Department of Homeland Security (DHS), to perform some of the functions I propose for the FWAC, but would restrict its recommendations to a three-year W visa, renewable for an additional three years, for non-seasonal LSTFWs "or guest workers." I believe my proposal for a FWAC is superior for the following reasons:

1. An independent commission would have greater autonomy and visibility than a DHS bureau.

2. Even if this entity remains a bureau, it should be located in the Department of Labor and given at least as much independence as the Bureau of Labor Statistics. As stressed in this paper, employment-based migration is a labour market, not a law enforcement of national security, function.

3. The BILMR's responsibilities should extend to all EBMs, not just the new W visa. It is logical to have a separate non-seasonal, non-agricultural visa, but W visas should not be issued until an objective case is made for them, employers have tested the domestic labour markets, and there are adequate protections for foreign and domestic workers.

4. The name of the BILMR would more appropriately be the Bureau of Migration and Labor Market Research; TFWs are migrants, not immigrants, though a strong case can be made for allowing all migrants to earn immigrant status.

References

Aydemir, A. and Borjas, G. (2008). "A Comparative Analysis of the Labor Market Impact of International Migration: Canada, Mexico, and the United States," *Journal of the European Economic Association*, 5(4):663-708.

Beaudry, P., Green, D. and Sands, B. (2013). *The Great Reversal in the Demand for Skills and Cognitive Tasks*, National Bureau of Economic Research Working Paper No. 18901, March 2013.

Benderly, B.L. (2013). "The Real Science Gap," *Miller-McCune*, February 12, 2013.

Castañeda, J.G. and Massey, D.S. (2012). "Do-It-Yourself Immigration Reform." *New York Times*, June 2, 2012.

Council on Foreign Relations (2009). *Task Force on US Immigration Policy, US Immigration Policy*. New York, N.Y.: Council on Foreign Relations.

Finn, M. (2012). "Stay Rates of Foreign Doctorate Recipients from U.S. Universities, 2009," Oak Ridge Institute for Science Education Program, January 2012.

Freeman, R. (2007). "The Market for Scientists and Engineers," NBER *Reporter*, November 2007, pp. 7-8.

Gautié, J. and Schmitt, J. (2010). *Low-Wage Work in the Wealthy* World. New York, N.Y.: Russell Sage Foundation.

Greenhouse, S. (2013). "Business and Labor United," *New York Times*, February 8, 2013, p. B-1.

Hira, R. (2013a). "Top 10 users of H-1B guest worker program are all offshore outsourcing firms," Economic Policy Institute blog. February 14, 2013, http://www.epi.org/blog/top-10-h1b-guestworker-offshore-outsourcing/.

Hira, R. (2013b). E-mail correspondence to Ray Marshall, dated February 14, 2013.

Manyika, J. et al. (2011). *An Economy That Works.* McKinsey Global Institute. http://www.mckinsey.com/Search. aspx?q=James%20Manyika%20et%20al.,%20An%20Economy%20that%20Works.

Marshall, R. (2011). *Value-Added Immigration: Lessons for the United States from Canada, Australia, and United Kingdom.* WDC: Economic Policy Institute.

Marshall, R. (2012). "Can We Restore Broadly Shared Prosperity?" *Work and Occupations,* vol. 39, 4, 2012, pp. 376-387.

Martin, P.L. and Ruhs, M. (2011). "Labor Shortages and U.S. Immigration Reform: Promises and Perils of an Independent Commission," *International Migration Review* 45 (1).

Nakache, D. and Kinoshita, P.J. (2010). *The Canadian Temporary Foreign Worker Program: Do Short-Term Economic Needs Prevail over Human Rights Concerns?* Montreal, Canada: Institute for Research on Public Policy.

Papadimitriou, D.G., Meissner, D., Rosenblum, M.R., and Sumption, M. (2009). *Harnessing the Advantages of Immigration for a 21st-Century Economy: A Standing Commission on Labor Markets, Economic Competitiveness, and Immigration.* WDC: Migration Policy Institute, May 2009.

Rosenzweig, M. (2006). "Global Wage Differences and International Student Flows." In: Carol Graham and Susan M. Collins, (eds.) *Brookings Trade Forum 2006: Global Labor Markets.* Washington, D.C.: Brookings Institution, 2006.

Rowthorne, R. (2008). "The Fiscal Impact of Immigration on the Advanced Economies," *Oxford Review of Economic Policy,* vol. 24, no. 3.

Teitelbaum, M. (2007). Statement to the Subcommittee on Technology and Innovation, Committee on Science and Technology, U.S. House of Representatives, November 6, 2007.

Wadhwa, V. (2008). "America's Other Immigration Crisis," *Journal of the American Enterprise Institute,* July/August 2008.

PART 6: CITIZENSHIP, INTEGRATION, AND DIASPORAS

INTEGRATION

Essential Reading:

Biffl, G., & Martin, P. L. (2018). Migration and Integration: Austrian and California Experiences with Low-Skilled Migrants. *Border Crossing, 8*(1), 30-39.

Unutulmaz, K. O. (2017). Integration of Syrians: Politics of integration in Turkey in the face of a closing window of opportunity. In *Turkey's Syrians: Today and Tomorrow* (pp. 213-236). Transnational Press London.

Further Readings

Bianco, R. L., & Chondrou, G. (2019) Social Inclusion Processes for unaccompanied minors in the city of Palermo: Fostering Autonomy through a New Social Inclusion Model. In *Unaccompanied Children: From Migration to Integration*, Edited by Işık Kulu-Glasgow, Monika Smit and Ibrahim Sirkeci.141-158.

Fischer, C. (2020). Manifestations and Contestations of Borders and Boundaries in Everyday Understandings of Integration. *Migration Letters, 17*(4), 531-540.

O'Brien, P. (2019). Bordering in Europe: Differential Inclusion. *Border Crossing, 9*(1), 43-62.

Osmandzikovic, E. (2020). Integration of Displaced Syrians in Saudi Arabia. *Border Crossing, 10*(2), 91-110.

Palat, M. (2014). Integration prospects of Turkey into European Structures and Turkish Immigration to Germany. *Border Crossing, 4*(1-2), 32-40.

Palop-García, P., & Pedroza, L. (2020). Beyond Emigrant Voting: Consultation as a Mechanism of Political Incorporation from Abroad or not all Emigrant Consultative Bodies are Born the Same. *Migration Letters, 17*(1), 139-146.

Psoinos, M., & Rosenfeld, O. (2018). Developing the understanding of migrant integration in the EU: implications for housing practices. In *Migration Policy in Crisis*, edited by Ibrahim Sirkeci, Emília Lana de Freitas Castro, Ülkü Sezgi Sözen , 115.

Ricucci, R. (2016). Learning by sharing and integration of second-generation: the Italian case. *Migration Letters, 13*(2), 193-202.

Stephens, C. S. (2016). Acculturation contexts: Theorizing on the role of inter-cultural hierarchy in contemporary immigrants' acculturation strategies. *Migration Letters, 13*(3), 333-349.

Tewolde, A. I. (2020). Reframing Xenophobia in South Africa as Colour-Blind: The Limits of the Afro Phobia Thesis. *Migration Letters, 17*(3), 433-444.

Tol, G. (2012). Macroenvironmental factors affecting integration Turks in Germany and the Netherlands. *Migration Letters*, *9*(1), 25-32.

CITIZENSHIP

Essential Reading:

Aker, D. Y. (2020). Introduction. In *Citizenship and Naturalization Among Turkish Skilled Migrants*. London: Transnational Press London. 1-6.

Bauder, H. (2018). Westphalia, migration, and feudal privilege. *Migration Letters*, *15*(3), 333-346.

Schwarz, T. (2016). Naturalisation policies beyond a Western focus. *Migration Letters*, *13*(1), 1-15.

Further Readings

Utku, D. E., & Sirkeci, İ. (2020) Ethics of commodified (golden) citizenship. *Journal of Economy Culture and Society*, (62), 365-380.

Hoyo, H. (2016). Nationals, but not full citizens: Naturalisation policies in Mexico. *Migration letters*, *13*(1), 100-115.

Scherschel, K. (2011). Dearly Deported: Social Citizenship of Undocumented Minors in the US. *Migration Letters*, *8*(1), 67-76.

Leung, M. (2016). 'One country, two systems','one city, two systems': Citizenship as a stage for politics of mobility and bordering practices in Hong Kong. *Migration Letters*, *13*(1), 49-63.

DIASPORAS

Essential Reading:

Brettell, C. B. (2006). Wrestling with 9/11: Immigrant Perceptions and Perceptions of Immigrants. *Migration Letters*, *3*(2), 107-124.

Féron, É. (2020). Embracing Complexity: Diaspora Politics as a Co-Construction. *Migration Letters*, *17*(1), 27-36.

Further Readings

Arslan, Z. (2016). The Alevi Diaspora: Its emergence as a political actor and its impact on the homeland. *Border Crossing*, *6*(2), 342-353.

Aydın, Y. (2016). Turkish diaspora policy: transnationalism or long-distance nationalism?. In *Turkish Migration Policy* (pp. 169-182). Transnational Press London.

Ozturk, B. B., & Hoyo, H. (2020). Introduction to the special issue: Politics, policies and diplomacy of diaspora governance: New directions in theory and research. *Migration Letters*, 17(1), 1-6.

Caruso, C. (2018). The Syrian diaspora in London through the transnational lens: a distinctive contribution to contemporary public space and citizenship. *Border Crossing*, 8(2), 409-432.

Kranz, D. (2020). Towards an Emerging Distinction between State and People: Return Migration Programs, Diaspora Management and Agentic Migrants. *Migration Letters*, *17*(1), 91-101.

Mateos, P. (2020). Mexican-us asymmetrical diaspora policies in the age of return migration. *Migration Letters*, *17*(1), 147-153.

Schaefer, C. (2019). "The body overseas, but the heart remains in China"?– China's diaspora politics and its implications. *Border Crossing*, *9*(1), 29-42.

Tigau, C., Pande, A., & Yuan, Y. (2017). Diaspora policies and co-development: A Comparison between India, China and Mexico. *Migration Letters*, *14*(2), 189.

CHAPTER 18

Migration and Integration: Austrian and California Experiences with Low-Skilled Migrants

Gudrun Biffl and Philip L. Martin

Austria and EU

Austria had a labor force of 4.4 million in 2015, almost 19 percent foreign born, including 60% who were from other EU countries. Many of the migrants from other EU member states in Austria are highly skilled, but they are not always employed according to their skills, particularly migrants from the new European Union Member States (EU-MS). The language barrier is one major reason for down-skilling, and another is the large difference in wages between Poland and other source countries and Austria, which attracts teachers and other professionals to jobs in Austrian tourism and care services, even if they lack training for these lower-than-average wage jobs. Austria has required non-EEA (European Economic Area) migrants since 1996 to have skills, so Austrian employers take advantage of free mobility of labor within the EU and recruit some EU-migrants from Central European countries for low-paid jobs with difficult working conditions.

Most low-skilled migrants in Austria are from former guest-worker countries, and today most arrive via family migration from former Yugoslavia and Turkey. Turkish migrants tend to work in the production of textiles and consumer goods as well as in retail trade, while those from ex-Yugoslavian are more often found in the construction sector, transport and cleaning services.

Given free mobility of labor within the EU, national governments can in principle only regulate the entry of third country migrants. Most EU governments limit non-EU entries to skilled or highly skilled migrants, so refugee migration has become a major source of low-skilled labor to supplement workers who arrive via family migration. Irregular migration is fairly small, and includes over-stayers who face difficulties getting their status regularized. Such persons, who may not access social welfare payments but have access to shelters and emergency health and care services, may work irregularly in agriculture and domestic services. (Biffl, 2017 a/b)

The employment outcomes of migrants are highly correlated with their educational attainment. The employment rate is highest for citizens of the EU-15 (77%), largely Germans, followed by migrants from the EU-12 at 70%, and much lower for persons from former Yugoslavia (61%) and Turkey (46%). The low employment rate of Turks reflects a low employment rate of Turkish women, often women from rural Turkey who marry Turkish men settled in Austria and stay at home. [1] The combination of low skills and traditional ethnic-cultural behavior patterns results in Turks having the highest unemployment rates (16.4% in 2015), compared to the national average of 5.7%, and even lower for Austrians and EU-15 citizens, 4.8 and 5% respectively). The unemployment rate of unskilled workers was 11.9% in 2015. (Biffl, 2017d)

The poverty rate of low-skilled migrants is significantly higher than of natives, 41% for third country migrants after transfer payments, as compared to 10% for natives. While Austria's overall performance on the Social Justice Index 2016 (Schraad-Tischler and Schiller, 2016) exceeds the EU average, it scores badly on socioeconomic factors despite ensuring access to its labor market. Austria ranks among the bottom third in the EU for the education attained by foreign-born students.

The educational attainment of the children of migrants is higher than their parents, especially low skilled parents, but their competence in reading, writing, mathematics and science is significantly lower than for natives. The PISA surveys indicate that the gap has narrowed since 2000, an improvement that may reflect a declining inflow of unskilled migrants and an increasing share of medium to high-skilled migrants.

Refugees tend to have the worst employment performance of any migrant group. (Dumont et al 2016) In Sweden, a country which has taken large numbers of refugees from the Middle East since the Gulf War in 1990, only 39% of all refugees who arrived between 1999 and 2007 found employment after 5 years of residence, and those who found jobs did not use their education and qualifications. In many cases there was intense competition among migrants for Swedish jobs. (Bevelander and Irastorza 2014)

Refugees resettled in Austria may access the labor market without any waiting period, but asylum seekers who enter and apply for asylum on Austrian territory must wait until the Austrian government determines their identity and whether the person qualifies for protection, which may take several years. The Austrian federal government provides benefits worth 980 EUR a month to adult asylum seekers, including group accommodation, health insurance, pocket money, and clothing allowances, and incurs administrative costs to provide this support.

Costs are much higher for unaccompanied minors, 3,692 EUR a month, because they need special accommodations and support such as language training and education. Upon recognition as a refugee, the person may register with the employment service, which pays basic income support, provides skills and language training, and offers subsidies to employers willing to hire those granted refugee status.

Access of asylum seekers to the Austrian labor market has changed. Since 2003 asylum seekers awaiting a decision on their applications are allowed to work only

---

[1] A Muslim orthodoxy has emerged, resulting in a withdrawal of a rising share of Turkish women from the labor market. Many women are wearing more traditional clothing including the scarf, which tends to reduce their employment opportunities.

in temporary jobs in agriculture and tourism or as self-employed. The EU Reception Conditions Directive of 2013, which replaced the Council Directive 2003/9/CE, aimed to ensure more harmonized standards of reception conditions by 20 July 2015, including access to the labor market after 9 months. Austria has implemented the Directive but continues to deny those waiting for decisions full access to the labor market.

Asylum seekers in Austria under 25 may access apprenticeship programs in shortage occupations for the whole period of training plus the legally obliged duration of continued employment, an average 3 months. This new regulation went into effect 2017, replacing one that required the training to be terminated if the asylum claim was rejected, since rejected asylum seekers were to leave Austria immediately. However, many rejected asylum seekers remained as irregular migrants, finding informal employment with no option for a red-white-red-card[2] to be employed in a labor-shortage occupation.

Asylum seekers over 25 may work after three months into asylum procedures in occupations with seasonal employment contracts, agriculture and forestry as well as tourism, and may work as self-employed in non-regulated commercial or noncommercial activities. The Integration Act, which passed the Council of Ministers in March 2017[3] and came into effect October 2017, allows legal employment for asylum seekers in the household sector.

Asylum processes have taken on average 6-8 months for the initial decision plus appeal. If refugee status is not granted, subsidiary protection may be granted in cases where refoulement is not feasible, at first for one year with possible renewal; after five years, the person can apply for humanitarian settlement. More than 90% of the asylum seekers from Syria are recognized as refugees, compared to 50% from Afghanistan. But most rejected Afghanis receive subsidiary protection, which allows them to access employment and apprenticeships without any restrictions.

Few of the current wave of refugees and foreigners with subsidiary protection can find a regular job without upskilling or retraining. Austria introduced a one-year integration program in 2017 that requires refugees to participate in language training and other integration measures in order to receive support services and welfare payments; refugees receiving public support must also do community and voluntary work until they are job ready.

Participation in community work does not affect the regular labor market, but allows the establishment of social ties with the local community and teaches local work practices. Similar introductory courses have been established in the Nordic countries, where support services are offered in combination with penalties if job and training offers are not accepted. (Brochmann and Hagelund 2011)

In 2015, the Austrian government spent 480 million EUR (0.14% of GDP) on asylum seekers, most for basic income support. In 2016, the amount rose to 1.3

---

[2] This is a settlement permit for third country citizens which came into effect 2011. For more see: http://www.migration.gv.at/en/types-of-immigration/ permanent-immigration/
[3]   https://www.facebook.com/notes/sebastian-kurz/integrationsgesetz-im-ministerrat-beschlossen/1297736166984720

billion EUR (0.38% of GDP) despite a 50% drop in the number of asylum seekers. The increased asylum budget was due to the large numbers of asylum seekers waiting for a decision and the crossover from the asylum system to the welfare benefit system, which is closely linked to the labor market support system that offers education and training and language courses. In 2017 the total additional budgetary costs are estimated to some 1.2 billion EUR (0.37% of GDP). While GDP growth is expected to increase as a result of the increased labor supply and public expenditure on refugees (+0.6 percentage points in 2016 and again in 2017), GDP per capita is expected to decline (-0.4 percentage points). (Berger et al., 2016; Biffl, 2017c)

Germany in July 2016 enacted an integration law that went into effect in August 2016 that requires recognized refugees to remain in particular regions to receive benefits, as was done for German Aussiedler until 2009. In addition, permanent residence visas are granted only to recognized refugees who fulfill all the requirements of the one-year-integration phase, that is, they must participate in language and cultural orientation classes and accept job offers commensurate with skills. In addition, the requirement that German employers give preference to Germans or EU citizens to fill job vacancies was suspended for three years, easing the transition of newcomers into the labor market.

However, the low education levels of newcomers prompted the head of Germany's employment agency to say that the asylum seekers who arrived in 2015 "are not the work force that the German economy needs." Frank-Juergen Weise predicted that, under the current integration plan, 10 percent of those granted asylum might be able to find regular jobs within a year, and half within five years. Such predictions prompted calls for adoption of faster access into the German labor market, even at lower wages (John and Martin, 2017).

California and US

California had a labor force of 19.1 million in 2015, including 27 percent who were born abroad (Employment Development Department, 2017). The foreign-born workers in California include highly educated Chinese and Indians associated with innovative industries in Silicon Valley as well as Mexicans and Central Americans with little education who are employed in agriculture, construction, and services that range from hotels and restaurants to health care and janitorial services.

The US is a nation of immigrants. Foreign-born US residents are almost a seventh of the 320 million Americans (Cohn, 2017). Over half of the international migrants in the US are Hispanic, including 28 percent who were born in Mexico and five percent each who were born in China, India and the Philippines. Almost half of the foreign-born are naturalized US citizens, reflecting the trend of more immigrants arriving from countries that allow or encourage dual nationality (Lopez and Radford, 2017). Less than 20 percent are non-Hispanic whites, and half of those five and older report speaking English well.

Foreign-born residents are concentrated: a quarter, 10.5 million, was in California in 2014, followed by 4.5 million each in New York and Texas, so that these three states included almost half of all immigrants (Lopez and Radford, 2017).

Over 27 percent of California residents are migrants, as are 23 percent of New York residents. Over half of Miami's residents were born outside the US, as were 40 percent of Los Angeles residents.

Migrants generally and unauthorized foreigners in particular divide Americans. A Pew poll in summer 2016 found that Republicans tend to give priority to enforcement to reduce illegal migration, while Democrats believe the government should prioritize legalizing some unauthorized foreigners in the US (Pew Research, 2016). Candidate Donald Trump made opposition to illegal migration one of the hallmarks of his campaign, and President Trump has called for a wall on the Mexico-US border and stepped upped the enforcement of laws against illegal migration in the US (Martin, 2017).

The 11 million unauthorized foreigners generate similar divisions. Gallup polls in recent years found that slightly more people think the US government should focus on dealing with unauthorized foreigners in the US rather than halting the inflow of unauthorized foreigners, 51 to 45 percent in June 2016 (Gallup, 2017). When asked in June 2016 what should be done with unauthorized foreigners in the US, over 80 percent of Americans favored allowing them to become immigrants and eventually US citizens if they meet certain requirements.

The number of unauthorized foreigners rose rapidly in the late 1990s and again after recovery from the 2000-01 recession, and peaked at over 12 million in 2007 before declining after the 2008-09 recession to 11.1 million in 2014 (Krogstad, Passel, and Cohn, 2017). The unauthorized include 5.9 million Mexicans, 1.7 million Central Americans, and 1.5 million Asians.

About eight million unauthorized foreigners, 73 percent, are in the US labor force (Krogstad, Passel, and Cohn, 2017). The stock of unauthorized foreigners fell nine percent between 2007 and 2014, while the stock of unauthorized workers fell less than four percent, suggesting that the unauthorized without jobs were most likely to be deported or to leave the US on their own. Unauthorized workers were 10 percent of Nevada's labor force in 2014, nine percent in California, and eight percent in Texas.

The US labor force also includes 20 million legal foreign-born workers. US government data collected from households do not distinguish between authorized and unauthorized foreign-born workers but, among all foreign-born workers, the labor force participation rate (LFPR) was higher than for native-born workers, 65 compared with 62 percent in 2016, and their unemployment rate was lower, 5.0 versus 4.3 percent (Bureau of Labor Statistics, 2017).

There is a striking difference between the LFPR of foreign-born men and women. The LFPR of foreign-born men, 78 percent in 2016, was higher than for US-born men, 67 percent, while the LFPR of foreign-born women, 53 percent, was lower than for US-born women, 58 percent (Bureau of Labor Statistics, 2017). Some of these differences reflect the fact that a higher share of the foreign-born are in the 25 to 54 age group, which is marked by high LFPRs for men and lower LFPRs for women with children.

The US has an integration-via-private-sector jobs policy, meaning that newly arrived migrants are expected to use family and social networks to find jobs and housing to support themselves without government assistance (Siskin, 2016). Unauthorized foreigners are generally barred from federal social safety net programs, and legal immigrants cannot receive most means-tested federal benefits until they have worked in the US at least 10 years or 40 quarters; some can become naturalized US citizens after five years, shortening the bar on welfare benefits.

The US migrant-integration-via-private-sector jobs policy has several effects. First, the availability of jobs gives migrants what they most want, a job offering higher wages than they could earn at home. Second, employers become advocates for low-skilled migrants, often arguing that they would have to close their businesses without them. Some employers benefit from the availability of migrants desperate for low-wage jobs, as in agriculture (Martin, Hooker, Aktar, and Stockton, 2016).

The third effect of integration-via-work is to reduce public opposition to migrants because they are associated with hard work rather than welfare benefits. Fourth, the children of migrants who see their parents working very hard in low-wage jobs may be inspired to get sufficient education to get a better US job. Many children of low-skilled migrants educated in the US reject their parents' first jobs.

There are also major drawbacks to the US integration-via-private-sector jobs policy. First, since many social safety net programs are linked to work, workers in low-wage jobs may lack access to health insurance, pensions, and similar work-related benefits, making them "working poor," that is, employed (sometimes full time) but with poverty-level wages. Second, children in working poor families may be tempted to drop out of US schools to work and increase the family's income because of their parents' low earnings, a short-term income-support strategy that may reduce the child's long-term earnings. Third, some (minority) children of migrants may believe that the US system discriminates against them, and identify with Blacks, Hispanics, and others who often drop out of the labor force and sometimes turn to crime.

Conclusions

Integrating low-skilled migrants poses tradeoffs. Austria and most European countries tend to invest in newcomers, providing them with skills so that they do not put downward pressure on wages when they enter the labor market. Many low-skilled jobs have disappeared in Europe, and there are already native workers seeking those that remain, so governments want to limit migrant-native worker competition at the bottom of the labor market.

The Austria-Europe approach is to invest in newcomers first and hope that the outcome is a more skilled labor force that can justify high wages. However, this requires an investment of public funds upfront, since many newcomers arrive with little education and few skills. The US-strategy is different. By expecting newcomers to be self-supporting upon arrival, migrants are encouraged to go to work even in low-wage jobs. On the one hand, the US policy gets many newcomers into jobs, but leaves many migrants among the working poor, employed but not earning more than the poverty line.

There is a sharp contrast between the European no-work and the American no-welfare policies toward newcomers. It is difficult to determine which policy is better, but the difference highlights the tradeoff between investing in newcomers to provide them with language and job training so that they can fill middle-skill jobs, or making the first priority to get newcomers into jobs even at very low wages.

References

Berger, Johannes, Biffl, Gudrun, Graf, Nikolaus, Schuh, Ulrich, Strohner, Ludwig. (2016). Ökonomische Analyse der Zuwanderung von Flüchtlingen nach Österreich, Monograph Series of the Danube University Krems. https://www.donau-uni.ac.at/imperia/md/content/department/migrationglobalisierung/forschung/schriftenreihe/berger_2016_oekonomische_analyse_flucht.pdf

Bevelander, Pieter and Nahikari Irastorza (2014). *Catching up. The labor market integration of new immigrants in Sweden.* Washington, DC. And Geneva: MPI and ILO. http://www.migrationpolicy.org/research/catching-labor-market-outcomes-new-immigrants-sweden

Biffl, Gudrun. 2017a. Europe's Challenge: Integrating Low-skilled Migrants. Paper presented at UC Davis April 17.

Biffl, Gudrun. 2017b. Migration and Labor Integration in Austria. *SOPEMI Report on Labor Migration, Austria 2014-15.* http://www.donau-uni.ac.at/imperia/md/content/department/migrationglobalisierung/forschung/sopemi/biffl-sopemi -2015.pdf

Biffl, Gudrun. 2017c. Chancen und Risiken der Flüchtlingszuwanderung für die Wirtschaft (Opportunities and challenges of refugee inflows for the economy). WISO (Wirtschafts- und Sozialpolitische Zeitschrift) 39. Jg. (2016), Nr. 3: pp109-124. http://www.isw-linz.at/wiso/

Biffl, Gudrun. 2017d. Flüchtlinge: Herausforderung für die Erwachsenenbildung (Refugees: Challenge for the Lifelong Learning System in Austria). Journal of Adult Education (MEB) June 2017, Nr. 31. https://erwachsenenbildung. at/magazin/17-31/03_biffl.pdf

Brochmann, Grete and Anniken Hagelund. 2011. Migrants in the Scandinavian Welfare State. The emergence of a social policy problem. Nordic Journal of Migration Research. https://www.degruyter.com/downloadpdf/j/njmr. 2011.1.issue-1/v10202-011-0003-3/v10202-011-0003-3.pdf

Bureau of Labor Statistics. (2017). Foreign-born Workers: Labor Force Characteristics Summary. https://www.bls .gov/ news.release/forbrn.nr0.htm

Cohn, D'Vera. 2017. 5 key facts about U.S. lawful immigrants. Pew Research. http://www.pewresearch.org/fact-tank/2017/08/03/5-key-facts-about-u-s-lawful-immigrants/

Dumont, Jean-Christophe, Liebig, Thomas, Peschner, Jorg, Tanay, Filip, Xenogiani, Theodora. (2016). How are refugees faring on the Labour Market in Europe? A first evaluation based on the 2014 EU Labour Force Survey ad hoc module. Working Paper 1, 2016. OECD and EC. http://ec.europa.eu/social/main.jsp?catId=738&langId=en&pubId=7921&type=2&furtherPubs=yes

Employment Development Department. (2017). Labor Market Information. http:// www.edd.ca.gov/About_EDD/Quick_Statistics.htm#LaborMarketInformation

Gallup Poll. (2017). Immigration. http://www.gallup.com/poll/ 1660/ immigration.aspx

John, Barbara and Philip Martin (2017). Flüchtlinge müssen arbeiten! FAZ. 10.1.17 http://www.faz.net/aktuell/politik/inland/fluechtlinge-in-deutschland-erwartet-ein-massnahmen-marathon-14611012.html?printPagedArticle =true#pageIndex_2

Krogstad, Jens, Jeffrey Passel, and D'Vera Cohn. (2017). 5 facts about illegal immigration in the U.S. Pew Research. http://www.pewresearch.org/fact-tank/2017/04/27/5-facts-about-illegal-immigration-in-the-u-s/

Lopez, Gustavo and Jynnah Radford. (2017). Statistical Portrait of the Foreign-Born Population in the United States. Pew Research. http://www.pewhispanic. org/2017/05/03/statistical-portrait-of-the-foreign-born-population-in-the-united-states-2015/

Martin, Philip. (2017). Election of Donald Trump and Migration. *Migration Letters.* Vol 14. No 1. http://www.tplondon.com/journal/index.php/ml/ article/ view/846

Martin, Philip, Brandon Hooker, Muhammad Aktar, and Marc Stockton. (2016). How many workers are employed in California agriculture. *California Agriculture.* Vol 71 No 1. http://calag.ucanr.edu/archive/?article =ca.2016a0011

Pew Research. (2016). On Immigration Policy, Partisan Differences but Also Some Common Ground. http://www.people-press.org/2016/08/25/on-immigration-policy-partisan-differences-but-also-some-common-ground/

Schraad-Tischler, Daniel and Christof Schiller. (2016). Social Justice in the EU – Index Report 2016, Social Inclusion Monitor Europe. Bertelsmann Stiftung, Gütersloh. https://www.bertelsmann-stiftung.de/fileadmin/files/ BSt/Publikationen/ GrauePublikationen/Studie_NW_Social-Justice-Index_2016.pdf

Siskin, Alison. (2016). Noncitizen Eligibility for Federal Public Assistance: Policy Overview. CRS. https://fas.org/sgp/crs/misc/RL33809.pdf.

CHAPTER 19

Integration of Syrians: Politics of integration in Turkey in the face of a closing window of opportunity

K. Onur Unutulmaz

Introduction

Integration has become one of the most popular concepts in today's daily, political, and academic discussions. Countries of all sorts with a large number of immigrants and sizable communities with 'immigrant-origins' are now conceptualising several issues and challenges related to immigration and the ensuing ethnic and cultural diversity as matters of integration. While both what they mean by the term and how they are trying to achieve it vary widely, the political nature of the whole process and the hegemony of the concept of integration are beyond discussion.

This chapter, firstly, provides a brief selective analytical background for the significance of the concept of integration by describing how the current 'backlash against diversity' has come into being. Secondly, the concept of integration is discussed briefly with reference to some common facets that could be identified in effective integration schemes. Thirdly, integration of Syrian communities in Turkey is discussed as a particularly big challenge. Lastly, the chapter makes a case for urgency in adopting a sound integration vision and creating effective integration policies in Turkey. Relatively low level of politicisation of immigrant integration issue is then discussed as a context conducive to develop such policies. Finally, the ways in which this politicisation has been rapidly changing recently and the restrictive impact of such politicisation over controversial issues on governance is discussed.

A Conceptual Background: Integration and Its Discontents

Backlash against Diversity

It seems evident that in Turkey, like in many other countries, international migration has become more visible, politically salient, and controversial than ever. However, contrary to a quite common perception of immigration growing exponentially with every passing year as a major aspect of world's apparent globalisation (Ghemawat 2011), the share of international migrants in world population remains low at 3.4 per cent despite an increase over the last few decades (Sirkeci, 2017, 129). Similarly, de Haas (2005, 2008) repeatedly suggests that the public outcry and intensified debates over international migration are often influenced by myths rather than facts: a myth of growing, unstoppable invasion of immigrants draining national sources and abusing the welfare state.

These myths, ever so masterfully exploited by extreme right political movements, have become the ideological justification to what has been termed a 'backlash against diversity' (Grillo 2005; Vertovec et al. 2010). The actual dynamics that created this backlash, particularly in the Western European context, were manifold and, in fact, a separate inquiry would be necessary to understand it in each different national context. There are, however, some common factors that contributed in the emergence of such a backlash can be identified. As can be seen below, many of these factors and dynamics are inter-related and they are caused by various other important factors. Yet, it would be beneficial to underline these factors anyway:

Emergence of super-diversity in the West: While probably no human society has ever had complete ethnic and cultural homogeneity, the level of diversity in the contemporary Western societies seems to be unprecedented in history. It also differs from its historical precursors in essence as well since it is marked by "a dynamic interplay of variables, including: country of origin (comprising a variety of possible subset traits such as ethnicity, language, religious tradition, regional and local identity, cultural values and practices), migration channel, and legal status (including myriad categories determining a hierarchy of entitlements and restrictions)" (Vertovec 2007, 7). While the idea that "unstoppable floods of immigrants are invading all Western countries" is a myth (Haas 2008), the fact that Western societies have become such visibly super-diverse is one of the reasons why this myth exists and has so much traction. It needs to be also remembered that a vast majority of mass immigration in Western European countries occurred in the latter half 20th century, following the end of the Second World War. Thus, the most intense immigration flows that would change the European social fabric forever, took place in a rather short amount of time which, coupled with some other factors described below, significantly adds to the identity concerns of Europeans citizens.

End of post-war economic boom and economic crises: In line with "inter-group conflict" theories, immigration and diversity seemed to cause the perception of threat and negative attitudes towards immigrant and minority groups particularly when the groups seem to compete for same scarce resources (Blalock 1967; Olzak 1992; Quillian 1995). Therefore, when the economy is in a dynamic growth period where unemployment is low and the immigrants usually fill jobs that are deemed undesirable by the natives, such perceptions of threat and emergence of negative stereotypes are not very likely. It is when economy is in stagnation and unemployment levels are high, however, that such negative developments become more likely. Indeed, the fact that the backlash against diversity has intensified in 1980s and 1990s appear to confirm this prediction. While until mid-1970s European economies had displayed dynamic growth rates with very low unemployment rates as they were undergoing a largely US-sponsored economic reconstruction in the aftermath of WWII, following 1974 OPEC crisis the economic growth came to a halt and unemployment soared (Eichengreen 2007; Aldcroft 2001). Therefore, the end of post-war economic boom and occurrence of periodic large-scale crises need to be highlighted as a significant factor contributing in the politicization of migration and emergence of a strong societal backlash against diversity in many European countries.

Demographic factors- Ageing and declining populations: Another important component of the contemporary backlash against migration-related diversity is the demographic transformation the Western world has been undergoing. There are three main aspect of this transformation that had caused significant concerns related to cultural and national identities in different countries. The first is the changing demographic profiles of the native populations in the West related to decreasing fertility rates. As it is well known, in order for a population to remain stable the fertility rate needs to be 2.1 which is called the 'replacement level'. Fertility rate can be defined as the total number of children that are born to a woman over her lifetime. When we look at the fertility rates in Europe, we see that in all European countries the rate is well beyond the replacement level (Coale and Watkins 1986; Fargues 2011). In fact, the average total fertility rate in the EU-28 is 1.58 while it gets as low as 1.3 in many countries (see Table 1).

It should also be pointed out that the fertility levels in Europe used to be much higher a few decades ago. When we look at 1960s and 1970s, for instance, the fertility rates in many European countries appear to be well above the replacement level. In 1990s and 2000s, however, this demographic shift seems to have become very apparent which means that literally all Western European countries and most others in other parts of the continent have demographically decreasing populations (Coale and Watkins 1986) (Table 1).

Another important implication of the falling fertility rates is that the structure of existing populations is also undergoing a remarkable structural change. This process is called ageing and it involves the shrinking of younger strata of the population while the older age groups are getting progressively more crowded (Alvardo and Creedy 1998; Davoudi, Wishardt, and Strange 2010; Walker and Maltby 1997). In fact, while the number of new individuals joining the society is continuously decreasing due to aforementioned fall in the fertility rates, the number and share of older people in the population tends to increase due to a corresponding fall in the mortality rates. In other words, while less and less babies are being born, less and less people die due to improved life standards, advancements in medicine, and overall lowered risk of death in the contemporary developed world. This shift has many significant implications for the countries concerned. For example, due to growing elderly population and declining population in working ages, welfare systems face a challenge because contributions to welfare funds and pension funds decline. Hence the systems face funding crisis in serving inactive populations. Moreover, because changing such demographic indicators is considerably difficult if not impossible, impact of these demographic transitions are projected to continue in the near future (Davoudi, Wishardt, and Strange 2010; Alvardo and Creedy 1998) (Figure 1).

These two demographic trends, i.e. low fertility and ageing of populations, have been somewhat countered by mass immigration (Alvardo and Creedy, 1998). In other words, through immigration mostly young and economically active individuals arrive in these countries to offset the impact of low fertility as shown in Syrian case by Yucesahin and Sirkeci (2017). Moreover, immigrant communities in most countries tend to have a higher fertility rate than the host society which further helps offset the ageing (Coleman 1994). However, all these demographic trends have given rise to serious anxieties about identity amongst host societies who seemingly perceive their ethnic, cultural, and national identities to be under risk. Extreme far-right political leaders exploit this idea that due to continuing (and "unstoppable") immigration flows and very high fertility rates of immigrant communities, they will become the majority in the near future which will make the current dominant ethnic group (in the host country) a minority in their own lands (Unutulmaz 2012).

Table 1: Total Fertility Rates in Europe, 1960-2015

	1960	1970	1980	1990	2000	2010	2013	2014	2015
EU-28 ([1])	2.58	2.36	1.87	1.66	1.46	1.62	1.55	1.58	1.58
Belgium ([2])	2.54	2.25	1.68	1.62	1.67	1.86	1.75	1.73	1.70
Bulgaria	2.31	2.17	2.05	1.82	1.26	1.57	1.48	1.53	1.53
Czech Republic	2.09	1.92	2.08	1.90	1.15	1.51	1.46	1.53	1.57
Denmark	2.57	1.95	1.55	1.67	1.77	1.87	1.67	1.69	1.71
Germany	2.37	2.03	1.44	1.45	1.38	1.39	1.42	1.47	1.50
Estonia ([3])	1.98	2.17	2.02	2.05	1.36	1.72	1.52	1.54	1.58
Ireland	3.78	3.85	3.21	2.11	1.89	2.05	1.96	1.94	1.92
Greece	2.23	2.40	2.23	1.39	1.25	1.48	1.29	1.30	1.33
Spain	2.86	2.84	2.20	1.36	1.23	1.37	1.27	1.32	1.33
France ([1])	2.85	2.55	1.85	1.77	1.89	2.03	1.99	2.01	1.96
Croatia	2.29	1.98	1.88	1.63	1.39	1.55	1.46	1.46	1.40
Italy	2.37	2.38	1.64	1.33	1.26	1.46	1.39	1.37	1.35
Cyprus	3.50	2.61	2.35	2.41	1.64	1.44	1.30	1.31	1.32
Latvia	1.94	1.96	1.86	2.02	1.25	1.36	1.52	1.65	1.70
Lithuania	2.56	2.40	1.99	2.03	1.39	1.50	1.59	1.63	1.70
Luxembourg	2.29	1.97	1.50	1.60	1.76	1.63	1.55	1.50	1.47
Hungary	2.02	1.98	1.91	1.87	1.32	1.25	1.35	1.44	1.45
Malta	3.62	2.03	1.99	2.04	1.70	1.36	1.38	1.42	1.45
Netherlands	3.12	2.57	1.60	1.62	1.72	1.79	1.68	1.71	1.66
Austria	2.69	2.29	1.65	1.46	1.36	1.44	1.44	1.47	1.49
Poland ([4])	2.98	2.20	2.28	2.06	1.37	1.41	1.29	1.32	1.32
Portugal	3.16	3.01	2.25	1.56	1.55	1.39	1.21	1.23	1.31
Romania	2.34	2.89	2.43	1.83	1.31	1.59	1.46	1.52	1.58
Slovenia	2.34	2.23	2.06	1.46	1.26	1.57	1.55	1.58	1.57
Slovakia	3.04	2.41	2.32	2.09	1.30	1.43	1.34	1.37	1.40
Finland	2.72	1.83	1.63	1.78	1.73	1.87	1.75	1.71	1.65
Sweden	2.17	1.92	1.68	2.13	1.54	1.98	1.89	1.88	1.85
United Kingdom	2.69	2.44	1.90	1.83	1.64	1.92	1.83	1.81	1.80
Iceland	4.29	2.81	2.48	2.30	2.08	2.20	1.93	1.93	1.80
Liechtenstein	:	:	:	:	1.57	1.40	1.45	1.59	1.40
Norway	2.85	2.50	1.72	1.93	1.85	1.95	1.78	1.75	1.72
Switzerland	2.44	2.10	1.55	1.58	1.50	1.52	1.52	1.54	1.54
Montenegro	3.60	2.74	2.24	2.08	1.72	1.70	1.73	1.75	1.74
FYR of Macedonia	3.84	3.16	2.49	2.21	1.88	1.56	1.49	1.52	1.50
Albania	6.49	4.91	3.62	2.98	2.16	1.65	1.70	1.79	1.67
Serbia	2.5	2.3	2.1	1.8	1.48	1.40	1.43	1.46	1.46
Turkey	6.30	5.56	4.36	3.08	2.48	2.04	2.08	2.17	2.14

([1]) 2014 and 2015: break in series.   ([3]) 2015: break in series.
([2]) 2014: break in series.   ([4]) 2000 and 2010: break in series.

Sources: World Bank and Eurostat. Available at *http://ec.europa.eu/eurostat/statistics-explained/index.php/Fertility_statistics* and *https://data.worldbank.org/indicator/ SP.DYN.TFRT.IN/* (last accessed on 19.10.2017)

Figure 1: Population Pyramids EU-28, 2016 and 2080

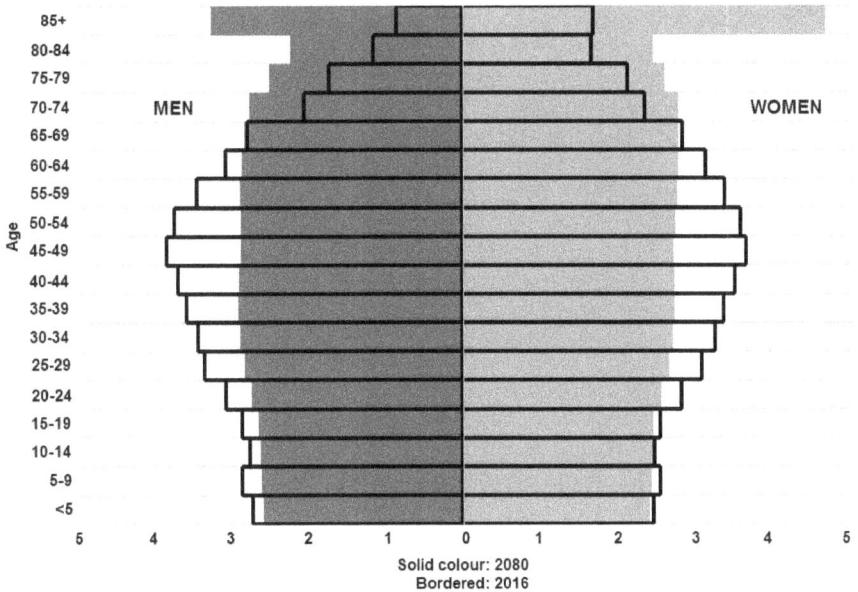

Solid colour: 2080
Bordered: 2016

Source: Eurostat. Note. 2016: provisional estimate. 2080 projections (EUROPOP2013).
Available at http://ec.europa.eu/eurostat/statistics-explained/index.php/Population_structure_and_ageing

Securitization of migration in post 9/11 world: A further development which significantly exacerbated the backlash against diversity in the Western world in general and in Europe in particular was the impact of the September 11 terrorist attacks in the US (Bourbeau 2011; Buonfino 2004). These attacks, which involved hijacking of commercial airplanes and crashing them to the twin towers of World Trade Center in New York as well as to Pentagon, were carried out by the fundamentalist terrorists and this created a global reaction. Most significant was the reaction of the US who declared a war against the global Islamic terror (Bourbeau 2011, 106). The truly tragic terminology used by the American administration provided ample opportunity for xenophobes and Islamophobes by referring to the perceived religious aspect of the attacks and their perpetrators (Saeed 2016). What is more, George W. Bush, then the President of the US, went so far as to use the term 'crusades' when referring to their fight against these Islamist terrorists. This was beginning of a period with intensified debates over the 'clash of civilizations' (Huntington 1992) where individuals of immigrant origin would now be confronted with questions about their loyalty and allegiances to the host countries even more frequently (Bourbeau 2011; Aksoy 2006).

The Concept of Integration

As a result of all these and some other factors, the aforementioned backlash against diversity, liberal immigration policies, and multiculturalist social frameworks were created. The rise of populist and/or nationalist politics that we are witnessing today, a particular defining characteristic of which is an anti-immigration discourse, can also be seen as the continuation of the above-summarised processes. Another outcome of the above-discussed factor has been the growth, both in prominence and popularity, of the concept of integration (Castles et al. 2002; Favell 1998). Integration emerged as a very useful notion that symbolizes a compromising position for the liberal democrats: although they were not prepared to partake in the anti-immigrant and xenophobic fervour of the far right, they conceded the necessity on the part of immigrants to make an effort to become a part of the society and share at least some basic societal values. Therefore, integration was meant to reject both the assimilationist demands put forth by the far right, on the one hand, and the too expansive multicultural rights granted previously by countries like the UK and the Netherlands, on the other (Unutulmaz 2017). This undoubtedly positive sounding concept that seems to be simultaneously able to soothe the general public's above described anxieties and provide policy-makers with a vague, hence flexible, vision to mobilize people and resources in adopting policies managing diversity (Unutulmaz 2012, 2017, Favell 1998, 2001).

The concept of integration has become an almost universal point of reference in public, academic, and political debates (Castles et al. 2002; Unutulmaz 2017). As suggested above, it is possible to identify many points of criticism against the inherent vagueness of the concept as well as the tendency it seems to embody for many people to put a disproportionate responsibility on the shoulders of immigrants. Some people even suggest that integration is nothing but a sugar-coated version of assimilation (Vasta 2009, 2007). Differences in political visions of what should integration mean and how should it be achieved notwithstanding; it needs to be pointed out that the basic yearning for effective integration policies seems to be a fairly justified one. That is if we define integration policies as the ones to create a framework in which newcomers are provided with necessary opportunities for becoming fully functional members of the society who are bound with the rest of the society by feelings of mutual belonging and shared values.

What is 'the Best' Integration Policy?

There have been explicit efforts for constructively managing ethnic and cultural diversity as well as integration programmes in most countries receiving mass immigration for the past several decades (Unutulmaz 2017). Moreover, there have been an extremely wide-ranging set of visions, policies, institutional frameworks, legal precautions, and political instruments used in these countries. Surely, one may be inclined to look at these different policies to try to measure them with respect to their effectiveness and identify 'the best one'. Such an endeavour, however, would be futile for several reasons. First, the integration visions, i.e. what is meant by the concept and hence what the policy objectives are, are ultimately political constructs that emerge through intricate processes in each context (Unutulmaz 2012). Therefore, the effectiveness and overall success of each integration policy needs to be assessed in reference to its own objectives and vision. In other words, it would be analytically fallacious to compare the effectiveness of different integration policies with so diverse visions.

Secondly, integration policies are not adopted or implemented in a vacuum.

They are rather the products of lengthy historical processes in terms of both how the question of integration is posed and how it is responded. In other words, the very understanding of what needs to be done and how are shaped by the social, political, legal, and institutional structure of a country that had been shaped for over centuries. What some authors call "national philosophies of integration" emerge in a dynamic interplay with the rest of public philosophies of such countries (Favell 1998).

Lastly, even if it were possible to recognize a policy or a specific programme to be perfectly effective or the best compared to all others with similar stated objectives, this would not automatically mean that the same policy would work in other contexts in the same way. In other words, just as the policy is dependent on the political vision and historical context, so would its outcomes be dependent on the context. While an integration policy might work perfectly in one country, in whatever way 'the perfect' is defined; it may just cause more problems in another country.

Does that mean it is of no use to look at the experiences in other countries to come up with some useful tips on how to develop effective integration policies? Certainly not. In fact, what is suggested here is that the context and its peculiarities are to be taken into account before defining not only the answers but, perhaps more importantly, the questions. It is appropriate and potentially very useful, to review the existing integration policies as well as the literature on these policies, to try to highlight common elements in the effective policies. There are two key aspects in integration policy debates: first, the vision of integration (essential features) and instruments used in realising the vision.

The essential features of successful integration policies include, firstly, an emphasis on the requirement of fostering a common identity and sense of belonging among immigrants and the host society members. Particularly in the above described context of securitised immigration debates and backlash against diversity, this emphasis of creating certain common norms and values gluing the whole society together in all of its complexity and diversity came to dominate the agenda. Secondly, a solid and explicit rejection of assimilation as a political objective is now an invariable and essential aspect of effective integration policies. This may sound somewhat tautological yet it is not: the conceptual vagueness of integration coupled with the negative reaction against contemporary diversity have meant that certain 'integration policies' could mostly concentrate on immigrants' acquisition of new values, norms, and knowledge even at the expense of their existing ones. More recently, however, integration policies are built on the solid understanding that people could adopt a strong identity (of belonging to the host society) without forfeiting their existing cultural norms and values. Lastly, a common element of successful integration initiatives is a strong emphasis on mainstreaming. Mainstreaming refers to a strategy of preventing social marginalisation of immigrants and minorities by bringing them closer to the centre of society. In other words, mainstreaming immigrants means making every effort to make them and their culture a part of the mainstream society and culture instead of pushing them towards a socially and culturally isolated position. Mainstreaming can also be described as making minorities a part of 'us' rather than 'them' or 'others', both in the eyes of the host society and the immigrants themselves[1] (see Figure 2).

Figure 2: Common Elements in Effective Integration Policies

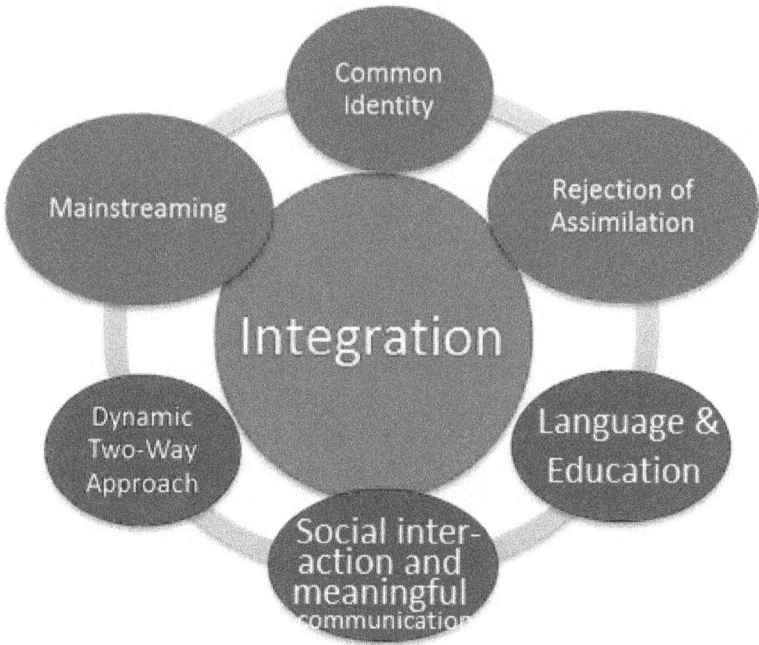

Source: Created by the author based on the discussion presented above. The green circles represent essence-related objectives and blue ones potential instruments.

There are also instrumental aspects of effective integration policies. Firstly, the vital importance of language instruction for newcomers and their children could not be over-stressed. The countries with well-developed language instruction programmes that include language support throughout school life of immigrant children are more successful in effective integration (SIRIUS 2013). Equally important is creating an education system, which does not accommodate diversity in a passive manner, but places diversity at the centre of the system to try to maximise potential benefits of it. This perspective is reflected in the multicultural composition of the teaching staff and the curriculum as well as incorporation of cultural elements such as religious festivals (of immigrant groups) in the education system (Brown 2015; Crul 2004). Secondly, it needs to be emphasised that effective integration policies appear to require adopting a dynamic two-way and multilateral approach, instead of a top-down and static perspective (Castles et al. 2002, 11). The latter considers integration as the responsibility, or rather obligation, of the immigrants to integrate into the society, which would be facilitated by national integration policies. By adopting a dynamic two-way and multilateral approach,

---

[1] See for instance, https://www.gov.uk/government/publications/2010-to-2015-government-policy-community-integration

integration is understood as a mutual process of adaptation for all segments of the society. Lastly, increasing the volume and quality of social interaction between different segments of society, particularly including immigrants and minorities is important. Both for creating common values and norms and for ensuring mainstreaming of minority cultures, this is of critical importance (see Figure 2).

Why are Integration Policies Particularly Essential in Turkey?

It is clear that integration policies, as generally defined above, are essential for any country with an ethnically and culturally diverse population. It should further be underlined, however, that effective integration policies are even more vital in today's Turkey (Şeker, Sirkeci, and Yüceşahin 2015; Sirkeci, Şeker, and Çağlar 2015; Erdoğan 2014). Before elaborating on the various risks and challenges as well as opportunities and potential benefits specific to the Turkish case, it would be useful to very briefly reiterate the context in Turkey.

Turkey has faced a very quick and unprecedented insertion of mass immigration. In the course of less than six years, more than 3 million Syrian refugees have arrived in Turkey. According to the official figures released by the Directorate General of Migration Management (DGMM), there were more than 2.9 million Syrians who are registered as 'persons under temporary protection' (see Figure 3). This is obviously a mass population movement making Turkey the country with the largest refugee population in the world (IOM 2015: 2). While Turkey has long been a country of immigration as well as emigration, the immigration of Syrians has certainly been unmatched with respect to its volume, pace, and complexity (Erdoğan and Kaya, 2015). Moreover, it needs to be remembered that this immigration was perceived to be temporary for a long time, which had meant that no systematic or long-term preparation for their effective integration existed. As it is discussed in the below section on increasing politicisation of the issue, it has only recently been acknowledged that at least a significant part of the Syrians will be permanent residents in Turkey.

In addition to the large volume of the Syrian immigrant community, its demographic and socio-economic profile also makes it imperative for Turkey to develop effective policies and mechanisms for integration. Some key statistics are worth mentioning in the context of a discussion over integration. The first and foremost is the fact that the Syrian community in Turkey is very young. Almost half (45.6%) of all registered Syrians are under the age of 18, with around 350 thousand are between the ages of 0 and 4 indicating that they were either born in Turkey or moved here as infants. When we look at the young age group of under the age of 35, it constitutes a staggering 78% of the whole Syrian population (see Table 2). Therefore, this very young population should be integrated into the social, economic, legal structures in Turkey very carefully. This is in line with our analyses of the Syrian demographics overall (see Chapter by Yucesahin and Sirkeci in this book; also Yucesahin and Sirkeci, 2017).

Secondly, it needs to be pointed out that the socio-economic and educational attainment levels of the Syrians in Turkey are quite low. The existing information on the educational attainment levels of Syrians indicates that almost half (46%) of them are either illiterate or literate but not graduate of any formal schools. The combined ratio of those who are graduates of primary and secondary schools are around 28% while there is no information on more than a quarter of the community (see Figure 4).

Figure 3: Number of Officially Registered Syrians in Turkey, 2011-2017

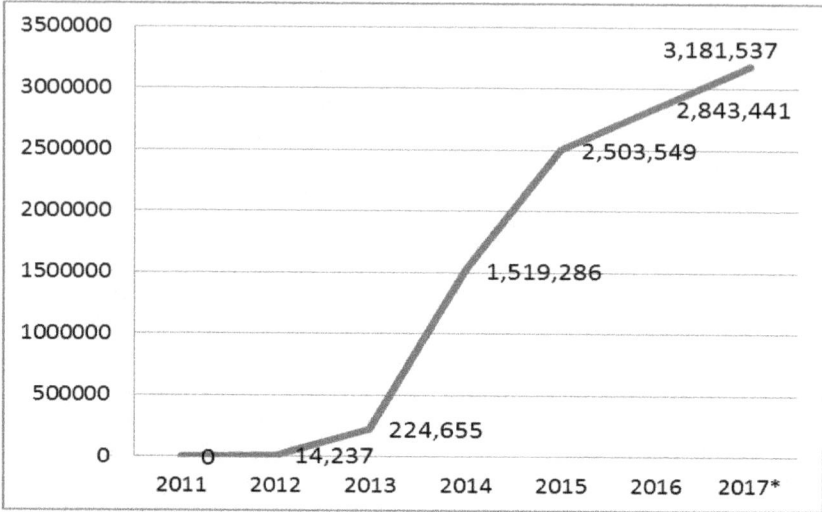

Source: DGMM Official Web Page (*by the date 14.09.2017)
http://www.goc.gov.tr/icerik6/gecici-koruma_363_378_4713_icerik (last accessed on 20.09.2017)

Table 2: Syrians Under Temporary Protection by Age and Gender

Yaş Grubu	Erkek	Kadın	Toplam	%
0-18	695.334	637.020	1.332.354	
0-4	179.572	166.898	346.470	
5-9	216.619	204.180	420.799	45.6
10-14	164.380	151.693	316.073	
15-18	134.763	114.249	249.012	
19-34	535.813	416.830	952.643	
19-24	243.368	187.117	430.485	
25-29	158.471	124.262	282.733	32.6
30-34	133.974	105.451	239.425	
35-59	283.718	256.479	540.197	
35-39	95.266	78.849	174.115	
40-44	67.047	62.765	129.812	
45-49	51.727	47.539	99.266	18.4
50-54	41.689	39.398	81.087	
55-59	27.989	27.928	55.917	
60 +	47.728	51.121	98.849	
60-69	32.439	33.228	65.667	
70-79	11.213	12.800	24.013	3.4
80-89	3.499	4.376	7.875	
90 +	577	717	1.294	
TOPLAM	1.562.593	1.361.990	2.924.583	100

Source: DGMM Official Web Page
http://www.goc.gov.tr/icerik6/gecici-koruma_363_378_4713_icerik (last accessed on 15.04.2017, age breakdown for the 14.09.2017 figure not available)

The studies conducted on Syrians as well as reports produced by the NGOs working in the field overwhelmingly suggest that socio-economic profile of the population tends to be low with majority of them suffering from economic problems (Erdoğan 2014; Icduygu 2015; Kirisci 2014; Emin 2016). The low educational attainment and skill repertoires coupled with rampant economic problems experienced by the Syrian population in Turkey further complicate the question of integration as well as making it vital for the social and economic stability in the country.

Figure 4: Syrians in Turkey According to their Educational Attainment

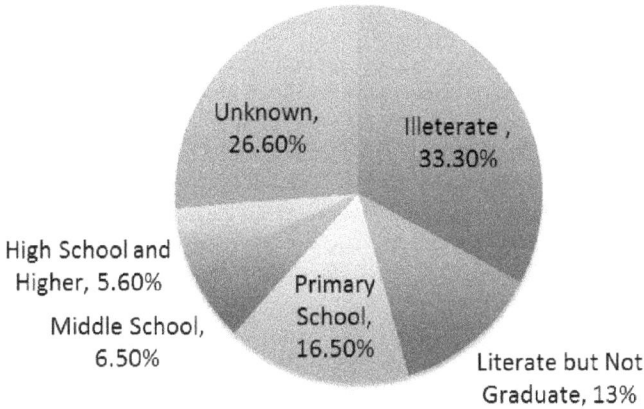

Source: Ministry of Development, March 2016[2]

Figure 5: Syrians in Turkey According to Where They Live

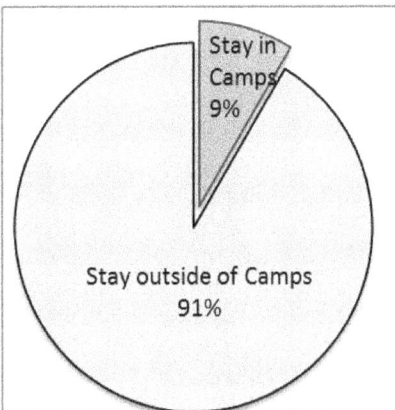

Source: DGMM Official Web Page: http://www.goc.gov.tr/icerik6/gecici-koruma_363_378_4713_icerik (last accessed on 15.04.2017)

Last but not least, the fact that a huge majority of Syrians are not only scattered across Turkey but also are leading quite mobile lives frequently moving from one city to another further accentuates the necessity of well-designed and standardised

---

[2] Figures are obtained by Prof. Murat Erdogan from the Ministry and used with his permission.

integration policies at the national level. Out of the 2.9 million registered Syrians, more than 2.7 million live as dispersed to all 81 provinces of Turkey, only 254 thousand live in camps, which corresponds to around 9% of the population (see Figure 5).

This mobile and scattered living situation of the Syrian community in Turkey naturally makes it more difficult to manage them as well as ensuring smooth provision of public services such as education and health to Syrians as well as the wider society.

Politics of Immigration and Integration in Turkey: A Fleeting Window of Opportunity

Politicization of immigration and integration policies, which could be defined as the process through which issues related to immigration and immigrants move upwards in political salience and importance, has a tremendous impact on how integration matters are handled in a given context. In Turkey, ethnic and cultural diversity have always been at the centre of political debates. Further, it can be argued that, in terms of its historical experiences and legal, institutional and social structure, Turkey is not well prepared to manage suddenly emerging "super-diversity" (Vertovec 2007). It has been a migration country for a long time, yet the mass Syrian immigration has caught the country off guard. Besides, ethnic and cultural diversity has never been welcomed in the country, which was established on very strong republican ideals of a unified nation embodied in the imagination of a modern Turkish citizen. While Turkey failed in handling the 'Kurdish question', a basic question of integration remains unanswered: how to foster a sense of belonging among a minority ethnicity to the country while retaining their distinctive ethnic and cultural identity? How can they be integrated in all national public institutions and economy while responding to their cultural demands? How will they be integrated into national education while granting them the very basic right of education in mother tongue?

Now the questions remain the same: How can a nation which has struggled for decades with a similar question without success be expected to effectively deal with an emerging Syrian diaspora?' Yet, surprisingly, Turkish government as well as the wider Turkish society appears to be much more welcoming and constructive in responding to the various challenges arising from the presence of Syrians. The government appears keen on establishing a longer-term integration vision and strategy. While this issue is regularly covered in annual Migration Reports published by the DGMM-Directorate General of Migration Management there have also been projects commissioned by the DGMM and conducted by the International Organisation for Migration (IOM) and United Nations High Commissioner for Refugees (UNHCR) for this specific purpose[3]. In everyday life, too, one can be surprized to see how relatively easily, for instance, Arabic is incorporated in official plates on hospital walls or public transportation system while any use of Kurdish

---

[3] One of the most relevant such projects is the "Project to Support Development of Turkey's Harmonization Policy" which includes a "Harmonization Strategy Document and National Action Plan" (for details, see: http://www.goc.gov.tr/icerik6/uyum-strateji-belgesi-ve-ulusal-eylem-plan)i-gelistirme-komisyonu-1-toplantisi-gerceklestirildi_350_359_9031_icerik)

language would have created a public uproar. Why, then, does it seem easier at the moment to take constructive steps towards Syrians and what are the implications?

While the answer to the first question requires a sophisticated comparative historical analysis of Turkey's Kurdish question and the displacement caused by the Syrian crisis; a large part of the answer seems to be related to the fact that the Kurdish question in Turkish politics is extremely securitised while the case of Syrian refugees appears to enjoy a much lower, yet increasing, level of securitisation (Aydin 2003, 176-179). In fact, there are studies which empirically substantiate the argument that 'the peace process' between the Turkish government and the PKK made some significant progress when the AKP government was able to 'de-securitize' the Kurdish issue and this process came to the brink of utter and complete breakdown when the issue became 're-securitized' (Geri 2016; Weiss 2016). As it is the case with the Kurdish question in Turkey and Muslim immigrants and refugees in many European countries, the heightened political debates and security-oriented perception of an issue significantly reduces the ability of policy-makers to effectively govern it (Bourbeau 2011, 18-30).

In democratic systems this usually works in the following way: an issue comes to occupy a very central place in the political agenda, any action the policy-makers take will be more closely followed by public and reported by the media, they immediately become more politically risky, any move they make will also be criticized and abused by their political opponents, the policy-makers will become more and more reluctant to move, they face increasing pressure to move in the meantime, the prospects of approaching elections will further make policy-makers who wish to be re-elected move with more caution, and so on and so forth (Balzacq 2011; Rychnovska 2014). Politicization of an issue has the additional politically destructive and dangerous effect of polarizing the society. Usually, the more politicized it is, the stronger will the people feel about it and more bitter the polarization will be (Hammerstad 2012). In cases of certain ethnic communities and social groups being in the centre of such debates, this polarization tends to create victimization of certain groups as well as an increase in social perils of racism and xenophobia. This has been certainly the case with politicization of immigration and integration issues (Bourbeau 2011).

It is possible to argue that the issue of Syrian refugees has not been politicized to the extent that it makes it difficult for the policy-makers to effectively produce solutions to different challenges including integration. It is, however, becoming increasingly clear that the issue is moving rapidly upwards in the political agenda in Turkey and it is only a matter of time before it reaches a fully politicized status. In the following, an analysis is presented on why this issue has been able to escape the fate of politicization and securitization in the Turkish context. Next, the quickly transforming social and political dynamics will be listed to suggest that Turkey has indeed a small window of opportunity before the issue will move to become a much more difficult one to manage.

Why has the issue of Syrian refugees not been politicized in Turkey?

To clarify, it is not argued here that the issue of Syrian refugees in Turkey has not been political at all. Of course it has always been so and it still is. The point is, however, it has not been very central in political discussions so far and it has not created a significant social polarization for the majority of time it has existed. Now, the situation is changing, yet what were the reasons that shielded this issue to become such an important and controversial political debate?

Firstly, the humanitarian aspect of the open door policy, i.e. extending a helping hand to a neighbouring people who are devastated by civil war and escaping violence, has shielded it from initial harsh criticisms. The presentation of the policy with strong reference to this humanitarian motivation has effectively silenced any opposing views and prevented the issue to be perceived as a polarizing political preference. Any comment made on the government policies or Syrian refugees themselves have had to first acknowledge the difficulty of the situation, nobility of Turkey's response which has humanitarian responsibility, communicate a message of sympathy, and only then could proceed to criticize one or the other aspect of the policies' implications.

Secondly, an enormously influential factor complementing the humanitarian aspect has been the perception of temporariness. In fact, the presentation of the policy as a humanitarian response based on good conscience and historical sense of responsibility was mostly as effective as it had been because it was also presented to be a temporary nuisance. Accordingly, the Syrians were displaced by a civil war and political oppression which were to come to an end in Syria soon with an upcoming change of government/regime. All the Syrians would then happily go back to their countries and Turkey would have been a country which has delivered what it seems to be promising in the region and it would obtain more influence. Indeed, in the initial stages of the Syrian crisis, the Turkish government seems to have been expecting the crisis to be over in a short few months. This perception was also reflected in the official discourse for the initial couple of years when the Syrian movers were called 'guests' and not given any other stable official status.

Thirdly and perhaps most importantly, the heavy political investment of a strong government seems to have shielded the issue from being easily manipulated. The above described political calculation of a swift transfer of power in Syria became the cornerstone of AKP government's foreign policy. While the calculation has proven to be wrong in the 6th year of the civil war with no change in Syrian government seems viable, admitting this would harm the credibility of government as a whole. Therefore, the AKP government, which has had a strong electoral support and a single party government for over a decade, has been the main actor framing the discussions related to Syrians in Turkey. It needs to be added that media outlets in Turkey have been under a significant level of pressure and all the mainstream media channels are now largely under the control of government. Therefore, the way all the news and information concerning the Syrians are framed has been under the control of government, too. In many Western countries where the aforementioned backlash against diversity and the rise of far-right political currents on anti-immigrant discourses have been witnessed, there are considerable media coverage of anti-immigrants views and inflammatory stories (Brookes 1999; Khosravinik 2009; Holland 2010; Clare and Abdelhady 2010). Particularly many tabloid newspapers have been able to exploit such increasing xenophobic and anti-immigrant sentiments. When we look at the mainstream media outlets, this has mostly not been the case in Turkey.

Closing window of opportunity: politicization of Syrian migration in Turkey

It seems apparent, however, that the issue of Syrian immigrants in Turkey has recently been undergoing a quick process of politicisation. The first reason accounting for this is related to the growing numbers and visibility of this community in Turkey. As stated earlier, more than 90% of around 3 million Syrian refugees live across all 81 provinces of Turkey.[4] Therefore, in all these cities their visibility in the daily life has been progressively increasing over the past few years. This increasing visibility coupled with a growing economic stagnation and increasing unemployment rates are likely to contribute to a rising anti-immigrant (i.e. anti-Syrian in Turkey) sentiment.

Secondly, there is a growing realisation that Syrians' presence in Turkey will not be temporary as it was initially expected, but rather a significant proportion would be very likely to be permanent. When the immigrants were perceived to be temporary asylum-seekers who would return to their homes as soon as the war finishes, the level of tolerance of the host society is expectedly higher (Erdoğan 2014). Not preparing the mentality of society for the long-term presence of immigrants would be very harmful and this is one of the reasons accounting for the quick politicisation of the issue in Turkey.

Thirdly, the intense political atmosphere in Turkey over the past few years inflamed by a series of local and national elections as well as, most recently, a constitutional referendum caused an increase in politicisation of the issue. This is mostly because, considered in conjunction with the political investment of the governing party in this issue, during every election campaign certain gossips and conspiracy-theories surface about government plans to have Syrians vote in the elections. It has been assumed that, since it was the AKP government under the leadership of Recep Tayyip Erdogan that applied the open-door policy towards the Syrians, they have a great sympathy toward him and that they would vote for his party[5].

Fourthly, several politicians from major opposition parties have recently started to use anti-immigrant discourses to gain political support. In a widely popular speech, Sinan Ogan an MP from the ultranationalist National Action Party (*Milliyetçi Hareket Partisi*-MHP) created public uproar by suggesting that while the Turkish

---

[4] By the way, it is important to underline that Turkey has always been home to a small Arabic speaking minority, especially in the southern provinces (Sirkeci, 2000; Sirkeci, 2006) and Sirkeci argues that this might be one of the reasons why Syrians (outside camps) have been dispersed around the country so easily because there are Turkish citizen friends and perhaps relatives with whom they may want to be nearby.

[5] For some examples, see: "Will the Syrians vote? A Response from the Government" http://www.haber7.com/guncel/haber/2264173-suriyeliler-oy-kullanacak-mi-hukumetten-cevap ; "Will 10 Thousand Syrians Cast Their Votes in the Referendum? Deputy Prime-Minister Answered"http://t24.com.tr/haber/basbakan-yardimcisi-cevapladi-10-bin-suriyeli-referandumda-oy-kullanacak-mi,386349 ; "Will Syrians Vote in the Referendum?" http://odatv.com/referandumda-suriyeliler-oy-mu-kullanacak-0802171200.html ; "Will the Syrians Vote?" https://www.cnnturk.com/video/turkiye/suriyeliler-oy-kullanacak-mi

soldiers were fighting in Syria (in the context of the Shield of Euphrates Operation), Syrian young men were harassing Turkish women by their gazes on Turkey's Mediterranean beaches[6]. Similar remarks came from a Deputy Chairman of the main opposition Republican People's Party (*Cumhuriyet Halk Partisi*-CHP), Ozturk Yilmaz[7]. Other politicians have made similar comments, albeit not using an as strongly racist, patriarchal, and provocative language. Obviously, such comments echo those of similar ones made by political figures such as Geert Wilders of the Netherlands or Nigel Farage of the UK, among others, indicating how strongly the issue is entering into the political arsenal of particularly nationalist politicians.

Concluding Remarks

Managing ethnic and cultural plurality and/or superdiversity against a backlash of declining multiculturalism and increasing securitisation of migration and integration is an extremely complex challenge. While there is a wide range of integration policies and programmes implemented in different countries, it is possible to identify some common key features in devising effective integration policies and mechanisms. Integration of more than 3 million Syrians now living all around Turkey is not only an inevitable public policy challenge, but it is vital for the social and political stability in the future. Turkey needs to act urgently as it has a quickly closing window of opportunity due to relatively low level of politicisation of the issue of Syrian migration. It has been shown that while many of the factors that prevented politicisation of the issue in the Turkish context are still prevalent, the issue is quickly becoming a divisive political issue exploited by nationalist politics.

The well-known tendency of far right political circles to exploit people's fears does not change the fact that international human mobility brings with itself a number of risks and challenges that really need to be addressed. It is true that the language and discourse people use with respect to immigration and immigrants do carry significant political implications. Therefore, one should be very careful while talking about 'terror and immigrants' or 'crime rates at times of mass immigration'. However, this does not necessarily mean that various risks related to human mobility should be ignored. Instead, they should be openly addressed in a politically careful and constructive fashion so that they cannot be exploited for racist or discriminatory purposes manipulating ignorance and fears.

One particular risk facing countries without effective integration mechanisms is that of marginalizing particularly younger immigrants and future generations born to immigrant families. Dramatic examples of this were seen in Europe. What was common in the dramatic incidents erupted in the suburbs of Paris in 2005 and in the very heart of London in 2011 was the image of young people clashing with

---

[6] "While they were staring at Turkish girls at beaches…" (Hurriyet, 3 March 2017, http://www.hurriyet.com.tr/sinan-ogandan-soke-eden-sozler-40383629 ; Sozcu, 3 March 2017, http://www.sozcu.com.tr/2017/gundem/sinan-ogan-suriyeliler-sahilde-turk-kizlarini-dikizliyor-1712208/)

[7] "Our Mehmets are becoming martyrs in Syria while Syrians are strolling around with Turkish girls" (Hurriyet, 31 January 2017, http://www.hurriyet.com.tr/mehmedimiz-el-babda-sehit-olurken-suriyeliler-turk-kizlariyla-geziyor-40352135 ;Sozcu, 1 February 2017, http://www.sozcu.com.tr/2017/gundem/mehmedimiz-suriyede-sehit-oluyor-suriyeliler-turk-kizlariyla-geziyor-1653857/)

police, harming public properties, and displaying a complete disregard for the public order and law. Another commonality was that most of these young people were coming from immigrant and minority communities. In the aftermath of the 2011 riots in London, the overwhelming feeling was that these young people have been left at the margins of society without any feeling of belonging or ownership and the solution was to give these young people a steak in the society. The way to do that was suggested to involve improving community engagement and cohesion, giving these young people hopes and dreams, and let them get involved in meaningful social interactions (Riots Communities and Victims Panel 2011). This is just another way of describing an effective integration policy.

As it has been argued in detail above, the young Syrian community in Turkey, a significant part of whom has been traumatised by the on-going bloody conflict, makes this risk even more crucial. Therefore, Turkey needs to adopt effective integration policies and programmes that:

- aim to create a common denominator in terms of shared norms and values which in time would create a base of a common identity;

- absolutely and clearly reject assimilation as a political objective and respect the cultural and ethnic identity of all immigrants; and,

- emphasise mainstreaming of its immigrant population by adopting a welcoming approach to cultural diversity.

In order to realise these general objectives, a wider perspective change is necessary. In other words, the above listed policy objectives could not be achieved in themselves through adoption of any particular set of legislation or establishment of any institutions. Their existence could only be hoped when, and only when, a long-term transformation of mentality and vision takes place. Lastly, it is argued and needs to be underlined again that Turkey has a brief window of opportunity where the issue of Syrian immigrants is not completely politicized and abused by extremist political movements.

References

Aksoy, A. (2006) . Transnational Virtues and Cool Loyalties: Responses of Turkish-Speaking Migrants in London to September 11. *Journal of Ethnic and Migration Studies* 32 (6): 923–46. doi:10.1080/13691830600761487.

Aldcroft, D. H. (2001) . *The European Economy 1914-2000.* 4th ed. London and New York: Routledge.

Alvardo, J., & Creedy, J. (1998) . *Population Ageing, Migration and Social Expenditure.* Edward Elgar Publishing.

Aydin, M. (2003). Securitization of history and geography: understanding of security in Turkey. *Southeast European and Black Sea Studies* 3 (2)

Balzacq, T. (2011). A theory of securitization. In Balzacq, T. (ed.) *Securitization Theory: How security problems emerge and dissolve.* London and New York: Routledge

Blalock, H. M. (1967) . *Toward a Theory of Minority Group Relations.* New York: John Wiley and Sons.

Bourbeau, P. (2011) . The Securitization of Migration: A Study of Movement and Order. London and New York: Routledge.

Brookes, R. (1999). Newspapers and National Identity: the BSE/CJD crisis and the British press. *Media, Culture and Society* 21 (2)

Brown, C. S. (2015) . The Educational, Psychological, and Social Impact of Discrimination on the Immigrant Child. Washington DC: Migration Policy Institute.

Buonfino, A. (2004) . Between Unity and Plurality: The Politicization and Securitization of the Discourse of Immigration in Europe. *New Political Science* 26 (1): 23–49.

Castles, S., Vasta, E., Vertovec S., & Korac, M. (2002) . *Integration: Mapping the Field.* Oxford: COMPAS, University of Oxford.

Clare, M. & Abdelhady, D. (2016). No longer a waltz between red wine and mint tea: the portrayal of the children of immigrants in French newspapers (2003-2013). *International Journal of Intercultural Relations.* 50

Coale, A.J., & Watkins, S.C.. (1986) . *The Decline of Fertility in Europe*. Princeton: Princeton University Press.

Coleman, D. A. (1994) . Trends in Fertility and Intermarriage among Immigrant Populations in Western-Europe as Measures of Integration. *Journal of Biosocial Science* 26 (1): 107–36.

Crul, M. (2010) . How Do Educational Systems Integrate? Integration of Second Generation Turks in Four Institutional SettingsIn . Harvard University.

Davoudi, S., Wishardt, M., & Strange, L. (2010). The Ageing of Europe: Demographic Scenarios of Europe's Futures. *Futures* 42 (8).

Eichengreen, B. J. (2007). *The European Economy since 1945: Coordinated Capitalism and Beyond*. Princeton: Princeton University Press.

Emin, M. N. (2016). Türkiye'deki Suriyeli Çocukların Eğitimi: Temel Eğitim Politikaları. SETA.

Erdoğan, M. M. (2014). *Syrians in Turkey: Social Acceptance and Integration Research*. Ankara: Hacattepe University Migration and Politics Research Centre.

Erdoğan, M. M. & Kaya, A. (2015). *Türkiye'nin Göç Tarihi: 14. Yüzyıldan 21. Yüzyıla Türkiye'ye Göçler*. İstanbul: İstanbul Bilgi Üniversitesi Yayınları.

Fargues, P. (2011). International Migration and the Demographic Transition: A Two-way Interaction. *International Migration Review* 45 (3): 588–614.

Favell, A. (1998). Philosophies Of Integration: Immigration and The Ideal Of Citizenship In France and Britain. Basingstoke: Macmillan.

Favell, A. (2001). Citizenship Today: Global Prespectives and Practices. In *Integration Policy and Integration Research in Europe: A Review and Critique*, edited by T. Alexander Aleinikoff and Doug Klusmeyer. Washington, DC: Brookings Institute.

Geri, M. (2016). The securitization of the Kurdish minority in Turkey: ontological insecurity and elite's power struggle as reasons of the recent re-securitization. *Digest of Middle East Studies*

Ghemawat, P. (2011). *The World 3.0: Global Prosperity and How to Achieve It*. Boston: Harvard Business Review Press.

Goodhart, D. (2004). Too diverse? *Prospect* 95

Grillo, R. D. (2005). Backlash against Diversity? Identity and Cultural Politics in European Cities. University of Oxford *COMPAS Paper*.

Haas, H. d. (2005). International Migration, Remittances and Development: Myths and Facts. *Third World Quarterly* 26 (8): 1269–84.

Haas, H. d. (2008). The Myth of Invasion: The Inconvenient Realities of African Migration to Europe. *Third World Quarterly* 29 (7): 1305–22.

Hammerstad, A. (2012). Securitization from below: the relationship between immigration and foreign policy in South Africa's approach to the Zimbabwe crisis. *Conflict, Security and Development*. 12 (1)

Holland, J. (2010) Shooting the Messenger: Mediating the public and the role of the media in South Africa's xenophobic violence. *Africa Development*. 35 (3)

Huntington, S. P. (1992). The Clash of Civilizations? *Foreign Affairs* 72: 22–49.

Icduygu, A. (2015). *Syrian Refugees in Turkey: The Long Road Ahead*. Istanbul: Migration Policy Institute.

IOM. (2015). *World Migration Report 2015*. International Organization for Migration.

Khosravinik, M. (2009). The representation of refugees, asylum seekers and immigrants in British newspapers during the Balkan conflict (1999) and the British general election (2005). *Discourse and Society*. 20 (4)

Kirisci, K. (2014). Syrian Refugees and Turkey's Challenges: Going Beyond Hospitality. Washington DC: Brookings Institute.

Olzak, S. (1992). *The Dynamics of Ethnic Competition and Conflict*. Stanford, CA: Stanford University Press.

Quillian, L. (1995). Prejudice as a Response to Perceived Group Threat: Population Composition and Anti-Immigrant and Racial Prejudice in Europe. *American Sociological Review* 60 (4): 586–611.

Riots Communities and Victims Panel. (2011). *After the Riots: The Final Report of the Riots Communities and Victims Panel*. http://webarchive.nationalarchives. gov.uk/20121003195935/http:/riotspanel.independent.gov.uk/wp-content/uploads/2012/03/Riots-Panel-Final-Report1.pdf.

Rychnovska, D. (2014). Securitization and the power of threat framing perspectives. *Perspectives* 22 (2)

Saeed, T. (2016). Islamophobia and Securitization: Religion, Ethnicity and the Female Voice. Palgrave Macmillan.

Şeker, B. D., Sirkeci, I., & Yüceşahin, M. M. (2015). *Göç ve Uyum*. London: Transnational Press London.

SIRIUS. (2013). European Policy Network on the Education of Migrant Children and Young People with a Migrant Background- Literature Review. SIRIUS Network.

Sirkeci, I. (2017). Turkey's refugees, Syrians and refugees from Turkey: a country of insecurity. *Migration Letters*, 14(1), 127-144.

Sirkeci, I. (2000). "Exploring the Kurdish population in the Turkish context", GENUS, an International Journal of Demography, 56(1-2): 149-175.

Sirkeci, I. (2006). The Environment of Insecurity in Turkey and the Emigration of Turkish Kurds to Germany. New York: Edwin Mellen Press

Sirkeci, I., Şeker, B. D., & Çağlar, A. (2015). *Turkish Migration, Identity and Integration*. London: Transnational Press London.

Unutulmaz, K. O. (2012). Gündemdeki Kavram: Göçmen Uyumu- Avrupa'daki Gelişimi ve Britanya Örneği. In *Küreselleşme Çağında Göç: Kavramlar, Tartışmalar*, edited by Aslı Sirin and Suna Gulfer Ihlamur. Istanbul: Iletisim Yayinlari.

Unutulmaz, K. O. (2017). Batı Dünyasında Farklılıkların Yönetimi Ve Azınlıkların Entegrasyonu. In *21. Yüzyılda Din ve Uluslararası İlişkilerde Dönüşüm*, edited by Filiz Çoban. Istanbul: Nobel Yayınları.

Vasta, E. (2007). Accommodating Diversity: Why Current Critiques of Multiculturalism Miss the Point? University of

Oxford COMPAS Working Papers.

Vasta, E. (2009). Accommodating Diversity: Understanding Multiculturalism. *Confluence*, 1–2.

Vertovec, S. (2007). New Complexities of Cohesion in Britain: Super-Diversity, Transnationalism and Civil-Integration. London: Commission on Integration and Cohesion.

Vertovec, S., Wessendorf, S. & others. (2010). Multiculturalism Backlash: European Discourses, Policies and Practices. Routledge.

Walker, A., & Maltby, T. (1997). *Ageing Europe*. Bristol: Open University Press.

Yucesahin, M.M. and Sirkeci, I. (2017). Demographic gaps between Syrian and the European populations: What do they suggest?, *Border Crossing*, 7(2): 207-230.

CHAPTER 20

Citizenship and Naturalization Among Turkish Skilled Migrants

Deniz Yetkin Aker

Introduction

There have been many studies about the concept of citizenship; nevertheless, as Joppke argues, "one of the biggest lacunae in the literature" is what people associate with the concept (Joppke, 2007: 44). In addition, naturalization is the procedure of citizenship acquisition for several reasons, such as gaining political rights. Although some scholars posit that non-citizens have several rights just as citizens do (such as, Bloemraad, 2000; Soysal, 1996), as Wallace-Goodman points out, for immigrants "naturalization is still the key to full rights of citizenship" (Wallace- Goodman, 2010: 3). Despite all the rights and benefits associated with citizenship acquisition, not all immigrants (can or want to) obtain the host country's citizenship. Especially since 1982, many studies (such as Bloemraad, 2002; De Voretz & Pivnenko, 2005; Yang, 1994 and Vink & Dronkers, 2012) dwell on the naturalization processes and policies to understand reasons of such variance in citizenship acquisition rates and dissimilarities in citizenship regulations among nations (Bloemraad, 2000: 13).

With these discussions in mind, this study focuses on three main questions: What does citizenship mean for immigrants? Why do some immigrants decide to acquire host countries' citizenship while others do not? Do citizenship and migration policies of countries (such as Canada and Germany) are related to the decision-making process of immigrants? More specifically, the objective of the study is to investigate high-skilled and business Turkish immigrants (HSBTI) who moved to Germany and Canada between 2000 and 2010: Unlike the existing literature, this study focuses on high skilled and business Turkish immigrants as a whole and compares their views (skilled migrants as the most desired category by developed countries such as Canada, OECD, 2013: 34) living in two countries with very different migration and citizenship policies.

There are several reasons why this study revolves around high-skilled and business immigrants moved to Canada and Germany between the years of 2000-2010: First of all, in this century, post-war immigration and globalization transform the meaning of citizenship, and changes in the concept of citizenship affect immigrants the most.

Secondly, among categories of immigration, the study focuses on high skilled and business immigrants. In this century, there is an increasing competition for high- skilled immigrants among countries such as Canada and Germany. Especially over the period 2000–2010, both Canada and Germany have introduced new immigration and citizenship policies considering the recent needs of the market, thereby increasing the number of high-skilled immigrants. Besides, the EU member states compete with countries such as the United States and Canada for high-skilled Turkish migrants (Koser-Akcapar & Yurdakul, 2009: 139).

The global integration of markets for goods, services, and capital requires an increase in the number of international immigrants. To promote free trade and investment, countries need to manage higher levels of migration. According to OECD statistics, in the current century, developed countries such as Canada prefer to attract high -skilled and business migrants (OECD, 2013: 34). Many countries (such as Canada and Germany) prefer to become guarantors for not all categories of migration but high-skilled migration. The reason is that those immigrants are not high in numbers and it would be less likely to have political resistance by their citizens toward highly skilled immigrants (Hollifield, 2004: 902).

Since skilled migration is related to economic class or economic migration, the present study uses Castles' categorization of high-skilled and business immigrants (Castles, 2000: 270) that incorporates "managers, executives, professionals, technicians or similar, who move within the internal labour markets of transnational corporations and international organizations or who seek employment through international labour markets for scarce skills" (Castles, 2000: 271) as well as international students (OECD, 2013: 34).

Canada allows high -skilled individuals to migrate to the country through the "economic class" and it has continuously increased since 1999 (Statistics Canada, 2012). Most importantly, almost 60 % of all the immigrants who moved to Canada fall into this economic category. (Challinor, 2011) Similarly, in the last century, migration - especially economic migration- to Germany has increased, mostly from other European Union countries. For instance, in 2011 the migration flow increased by 23% from the previous year (Federal Statistical Office of Germany, 2013: 20) and in 2008, almost half of the EU-residents migrated to Germany for employment-related reasons (OECD, 2013: 254). Besides, to improve the governance of international migration, states categorize immigrants as, for instance, temporary labour migrants and high-skilled and business immigrants Castles, 2000: 270).[1]

To question the effect of policies of country of destinations, the study selects only Turkish migrants from that category: Turkey has mostly sent immigrants after the 1950s. Since the 1990s, Turkey has both sent and received immigrants and it has been accepted as a key player on the Eurasian immigration flow both as a country of origin, as a destination, and a transit country. Since the early 2000s, almost 4000 of Turkish university graduates and skilled workers have moved to countries such as Australia, Canada, the US, and European countries every year (Icduygu, Kaya, & Tokuzlu, 2013). However, not all of the high-skilled and business Turkish immigrants decide to acquire host country's citizenship. For instance, there

---

[1] For further examples of categorization and detailed discussions on the concept citizenship, please see, for instance, The Oxford Handbook of Citizenship, eds. Ayelet Shachar, Rainer Bauböck, Irene Bloemraad, and Maarten Vink (2017).

is a decrease in naturalization rates of Turkish nationals in Germany (Kaya, 2009: 49). It is very crucial to understand the variance in their decision-making process for citizenship acquisition.

Another reason why Germany and Canada are selected as two cases is that the citizenship and migration policies of Canada are generally categorized as multiculturalist while the citizenship and migration policies of Germany are categorized as restricted (Howard, 2005: 710). The citizenship acquisition system in Canada is generally considered an immigrant-friendly system with its easy legal and administrative procedures. For instance, while the naturalization rate in Canada is 89 percent, in Germany it is 37 percent (Banulescu-Bogdan, 2012). Besides, the citizenship policies of Canada and Germany (as well as Turkey) have been changing dramatically during the twenty-first century, which is the period of focus in the study.

Canada is known for its multicultural citizenship policies[2] and differs from Germany, which has a restrictive citizenship policy, although the country has attempted to change it into a more moderate one recently (Howard, 2005: 710). This study uses the Citizenship Policy Index, developed by Marc Morjé Howard (2005), to categorize and analyze the differences of Canadian and German migration and citizenship policies. As Howard (2006) argues, considering citizenship only as a legal status might cause deviation from several existing debates, in which the term citizenship is used as a substitute for civic engagement and similar concepts (Howard, 2006: 444). However, considering citizenship as a legal concept may provide a more focused comparison (Howard, 2005: 717). Howard explains:

> The Citizenship Policy Index (CPI) is based on a simple additive formula, with 2 points for each of the three criteria, allocated in the following way: Citizenship by birth is coded as either 0 (not allowed) or 2 (allowed). Residency requirement for naturalization is coded as follows: countries that require at least ten years are coded 0 (difficult); those that require six to nine years of residence are coded 1 (medium); and those that require five years or less are coded 2 (easy). Acceptance of dual citizenship for immigrants is coded as either O (naturalized citizens must relinquish their prior citizenship) or 2 (naturalized immigrants can retain their previous citizenship) (2005: 717).

In this index, citizenship policies of countries that have zero 0 to one 1 point are categorized as restrictive; two to four points are categorized as medium; and five to six points are categorized as liberal. (Howard, 2005: 710) By using this formula, it is argued that the result for a contemporary period of Canada is liberal, with six points, where citizenship by birth is allowed (+2), residency requirements for naturalization is three years (+2), and dual citizenship for immigrants is accepted (+2).

---

[2] Multiculturalist policies and bilingualism were introduced as a solution against growing Québec nationalism and as a solution toward conflict between the French and English majority and other European immigrants who came to the country in the twentieth century. (Elrick, Jeniffer. 2007. "Country Profile: Canada," Focus Migration (8). Available online at: http://focus-migration.hwwi.de/Canada.1275.0.html? &L=1, [Last Access, 14 December 2013]).

In the study of Howard (2005: 710-12), the contemporary period result of Germany is accepted as medium with three points and zero in 1980. According to Howard, there is a liberal direction of change in Germany CPI score results. In 2000 a new German law was introduced, and this new law affected its CPI score. With this law, Germany's minimum residency requirement is diminished from fifteen to eight years and permission for citizenship by birth is allowed. The second change is the most noteworthy one since it changes the long history of the blood-based definition (*jus sanguinis*) of national membership in Germany. According to this amendment, children belong to any nationality, who are born in Germany and whose parents (at least one of them) have residence permit at least for eight years, are allowed to get German citizenship automatically. These children are also allowed to hold dual citizenship until adulthood; later they should decide which citizenship they want to hold until the age of 23. Briefly, although the new German citizenship law agrees to the concept of *jus soli,* which is a remarkable change from the concept of *jus sanguinis,* this right may be cancelled for those who do not want to renounce their other citizenship (Howard, 2005: 710-12).

This study considers German citizenship policy as restricted. First of all, such linear explanations cannot cover the complexity of citizenship policy changes (Goodman 2010: 757). Moreover, this recent change in 2000 may facilitate German citizenship acquisition and allow automatic naturalization by birth for the second and third generations (Faist, Gerdes and Rieple, 2004: 929). However, German nationality legislation is still very restrictive with its principle of preventing dual nationality (Faist, Gerdes and Rieple, 2004: 926-27). Suppose the CIVIX (civic integration requirements) index prepared by Goodman (2010) is used (0 to 6, 'thick' citizenship requires many content to citizenship vs. 'thin' citizenship requires minimal content such as country knowledge or language) with CPI (citizenship policy index). In that case, German citizenship policies can be considered as restrictive with its mandatory language and integration courses (Goodman, 2010: 759) and Canadian citizenship policies liberal/multiculturalist (or 'enabling' according to Goodman's terminology).

The main data sources of this study include country statistics and current literature, legal texts, country reports of Germany and Turkey, as well as in-depth, semi-structured face-to-face interviews (snowball method, only a few of them were through email or Skype, interview questions are provided in APPENDIX 1) conducted in Germany and Canada. The study sample includes immigrants whose country of origin is Turkey, and who moved from larger Turkish cities between 2000 and 2010 as high-skilled and business immigrants to Canada and Germany with visa (for the Canadian case with permanent residency and for the German Case (generally) with temporary residency).

Interviews with community leaders were also conducted and a series of activities organized by Turkish immigrants were attended (such as Anniversary celebrations of the March 18 Çanakkale Victory) to obtain general information about the Turkish community. The continuous collaboration was formed with some of the associations such as Turquebec (The Turkish Quebec Cultural and Friendship Association) and in Berlin such as Allmende. In total, 157 interviews were conducted in 6 months (in March 2011-September 2011, German Academic Exchange Service [DAAD] and the Scientific and Technological Research Council of Turkey [TUBITAK] support the author with scholarship for the field researches of this study in Canada and Germany); the data analysis consists of 48 interviews from Germany and 64 interviews from Canada, which fit the aim of the study (List of Case summaries are provided in APPENDIX 2).

Interviews are analyzed using the content analysis method. Codes and categories are used for data analysis. While codes are assigned during data analysis, the text is the source of categories. (Hsieh and Shannon, 2005; 1277 and 1286) In order to analyze data with this technique, interviews were transcribed and coded as text. The software program Nvivo is used for coding and analysis of the data. After studying the qualitative data from Canada and Germany, many important points related to tree nodes were found. These points, raised by Turkish migrants, were used as branches of tree nodes.

It is expected that immigrants' naturalization decisions and conceptualization of citizenship are related to countries' migration and citizenship policy approaches (such as restricted or multiculturalist). With respect to high-skilled and business Turkish immigrants, this study put forwards the view that host country citizenship and migration policy (whether it is restricted or multicultural); economic, social and political benefits and costs of host country's citizenship; and individuals' conceptualization of citizenship (as a sense of belonging or commodity) influence their naturalization decisions. In this sense, theoretical frameworks for the concept citizenship and for citizenship acquisition will be presented. After a review of Canadian and German citizenship and migration policies, data analyzes will be detailed and critically discussed.

CHAPTER 21

Westphalia, Migration, and Feudal Privilege

Harald Bauder

Introduction

In the 1990s, scholars and practitioners were optimistic that globalization would result in open borders or that borders would vanish altogether (Ohmae, 1990). In this way, humanity would continue along the path towards liberation that it has strived for since the Enlightenment. This optimism was premature. Borders between nation states are far from open today (Paasi et al., forthcoming); many borders are actually tightening, and thousands of migrants have died trying to cross international borders (International Organization for Migration, 2018). Apparently, we cannot shake off the ghosts of migration control that have haunted humanity for centuries if not millennia (O'Dowd, 2010).

In this paper, I interrogate the claim that migration controls enforce the continuation of feudal principle within the modern Westphalian order of sovereign states. I derive this claim from scholarship that has examined privileges of citizenship acquired at birth (e.g. Shachar, 2009). More than three decades ago, Joseph Caren articulated an argument in support of open borders suggesting that citizenship without free migration is a birth-right akin to a feudal privilege: "Citizenship in Western liberal democracies is the modern equivalent of feudal privilege – an inherited status that greatly enhances one's life chances" (Carens, 1987: 252). Western liberal democracies, in this context, refer to states that generally aim to uphold individual political and civic rights and freedoms, and that possess democratic forms of government. Migration has played varying roles in these states. For example, settler states such as Australia, Canada, New Zealand, and the United States have a history of Indigenous displacement and often genocide that was facilitated by selective European immigration. Conversely, many European countries have an emigration history and currently struggle with accepting immigration.

Despite their differences, Western liberal democracies tend to define membership and belonging in terms of citizenship, which entitles a person to enter and remain in the national territory. The lack of citizenship subjects a person to migration controls. In this context, Carens proposed that "[t]he current restrictions on immigration in Western democracies – even in the most open ones like Canada and the United States – are not justifiable. Like feudal barriers to mobility, they protect unjust privilege" (1987: 270). I suggest that there are striking similarities in the way in which this moral injustice has been enshrined in legal frameworks in the feudal Westphalian territorial state and today's liberal democracies.

Power has always regulated people's mobility. European feudal rulers tended to control the exit of their subjects, while liberal democracies today control the entry of foreigners. However, is it fair to argue that little has changed in this respect between European feudalism and today's liberal democracies? To address this question, I examine the Treaties of Osnabrück and Münster (aka the Westphalian Treaties) to uncover possible links between migration controls and emerging sovereign territorial states. Although the sovereign territorial state was not created solely by the Westphalian Treaties, these treaties occupy a prominent and important position on the path that saw Europe move from its feudal past towards today's global order based upon territorial sovereignty. The Treaties can thus provide clues as to how the migration of people was interpreted at that time with respect to territorial state sovereignty.

My analysis suggests that the Westphalian Treaties generally envisioned that people are not free to migrate and therefore regulated some aspects of cross-border migration. In the feudal past, it was up to the sovereign to decide who can leave or enter a territory. In the modern liberal state, migration policy – rather than arbitrary decisions by the sovereign – has become the central instrument to control population movement. In this way, migration policy maintains an order that is based on the privilege of birth and location. However, rather than bonding subjects to the sovereign, it bonds them to the state and excludes those who were not born with the privilege of citizenship.

In the sections below, I first review the "Westphalian model" (Krasner, 2000) and the concept of territorial sovereignty in relation to human migration. Then I examine the contents of the Westphalian Treaties. Thereafter, I discuss the Westphalian model in an ongoing era a migration that followed after feudalism and that has been driven by technological innovations, transportation advancements, and demographic developments. I conclude by linking the discussion back to my original claim that migration controls maintain feudal principle.

The Westphalian Model

The concept of sovereignty bridges feudal and modern political orders. Jean Bodin has been credited for the "first systematic modern use of the term 'sovereignty'" (Prokhovnik, 2008: 41). He wrote in the 16th Century that "there are none on earth, after God, greater than sovereign princes, whom God establishes as His lieutenants to command the rest of mankind" (Bodin, 1955[1576]: n.p.). According to Bodin, the sovereign possesses

> the power to make law binding on all his subjects ... [which] includes all other rights of sovereignty, that is to say of making peace and war, of hearing appeals from the sentences of all courts whatsoever, of appointing and dismissing the great officers of state; of taxing, or granting privileges of exemption to all subjects, of appreciating or depreciating the value and weight of the coinage, of receiving oaths of fidelity from subjects and liege-vassals alike, without exception of any other to whom faith is due. (Bodin, 1955[1576]: n.p.)

Various enlightenment philosophers elaborated on the concept of sovereignty (Bartelson, 1995; Prokhovnik, 2008). There was disagreement, however, concerning what exactly sovereignty entailed and whether it would be associated with territory and at which scale. John Locke linked sovereignty to the free and rational individual (Prokhovnik, 2008: 81), Baruch Spinoza (1900[1883-1884]: n.p.) applied the concept to Dutch city-states and provinces; Jean-Jacques Rousseau (2003 [1762]: 20) tied sovereignty to "the body of the nation;" and Immanuel Kant (1977[1797]) and Georg Wilhelm Friedrich Hegel (1979[1820]) located it within the legal state (*Rechtsstaat*). The "Westphalian model" associates sovereignty with the territorial state. In this case, a sovereign – which can be represented by a monarch, a dictator, a ruling party, or a democratically elected government – does not rule directly over people but over people within a bounded territory.

The migration of people into or out of a sovereign's realm of authority received considerable attention from the early theorists of sovereignty, especially in the context of the European colonization of territories outside of Europe; hospitality rights – i.e. the right to enter a territory – legitimated European colonization (Cavallar, 2002). While some theorists, such as Immanuel Kant (1946[1795]) qualified that hospitality rights may not justify conquest and colonialization, others, such as Samuel Pufendorf, suggested that sovereigns may very well deny hospitality to visitors (Cavallar, 2002: 201-208). Enlightenment philosophers thus not only disagreed about whether and in which way sovereignty relates to territory, they were also ambiguous about the rights to enter or leave a territory vis-à-vis the sovereign's right to deny migration.

The Westphalian model did not spring from the theoretical musings of enlightenment philosophers but developed in light of efforts to enshrine existing configurations of privilege and authority in a general political framework for a new Europe. Joseph Camilleri and Jim Falk explain that the enlightenment philosophers' theories of sovereignty "became essentially exercises in abstraction. … By divorcing themselves from the historical context, even though they themselves were often a direct response to prevailing political and socioeconomic conditions, these formulations acquired an air of unreality" (Camilleri and Falk, 1992: 23). Rather than being an abstraction, territorial state sovereignty is an "instrument of the dominant social order" (Camilleri and Falk, 1992: 23). Assuming such a perspective, Thomas Biersteker and Cynthia Weber (1996: 3, parenthesis in original) conclude:

> The modern state system is not based on some timeless principle of sovereignty, but on the production of a normative conception that links authority, territory, population (society, nation), and recognition in a unique way and in a particular place (the state). Attempting to realize this ideal entails a great deal of hard work on the part of statespersons, diplomats, and intellectuals … The ideal of state sovereignty is a product of the actions of powerful agents.

Westphalian territorial sovereignty is an instrument to rule over populations that reside in a territory. Controlling who enters and leaves a given territory is an important aspect to maintain this rule.

The Westphalian Treaties

Prior to the emergence of the modern territorial state in Europe, the medieval rule of empire, feudal lords, and the church generally lacked "territorial fixity and exclusivity" (Sassen, 2008: 27). Political authority was generally directed towards people; and privilege, rights, and obligations were framed in terms of class or cast, not territory. The Westphalian model of territorial state sovereignty is the result of a long and complex process (Sassen, 2008; Foucault, 2007). In this section, I explore how territorial state sovereignty relates to authority over migration and migrants at the time when the Westphalian model emerged.

The Treaties of Osnabrück and Münster were signed in 1648 and together comprised the Westphalian Peace. These treaties are often regarded a milestone towards the establishment of territorial state sovereignty, which became the dominant political organizing framework in Europe and eventually around the globe. The exact historical significance of these treaties is disputed (Kegley and Raymond, 2002; MacRae, 2005). Benno Teschke challenges the "myth" that the birth of the modern nation-state can be pinpointed to an exact location and time, and argues that the modern nation-state developed in an ongoing dialectical process in conjunction with capitalism (Teschke, 2003). Stephen Krasner (2009), too, suggests that the Treaties of Osnabrück and Münster merely reaffirmed many of the principles that already existed, and aspects of the modern state are credited to the Treaties although they were not formulated in these treaties and did not become international practice until centuries later. Furthermore, territorial state sovereignty has always been compromised by force and coercion, voluntary contracts and international conventions, and capitalist interests (Krasner, 2009). This view is shared by Brendan Simms (2011), who rejects the common conception that the Peace of Westphalia enshrined the sovereign principle that "interference in the internal affairs of another state would be impermissible" (90). Rather, Simms suggests, "the historical reality is that states had always intervened in each other's domestic affairs" (2011: 91). It is not my aim to argue for or against the historical significance of the Westphalian Treaties. Rather, I use the Treaties as a particular occasion – a snapshot in time – to assess whether and in which way control over migration has been associated with sovereignty in the emerging territorial state. While I do not claim to know what the negotiators of the Treaties were seeking to achieve, the outcomes of the negotiations provide legal texts that gain insights into legal and political practice in Central Europe at the time.

The primary purpose of the Treaties of Osnabrück and Münster was to end the Thirty-Years War that had devastated large parts of Europe. To achieve this purpose, much of the contents of the Treaties covered the return and redistribution of territory and possessions between the warring parties. In addition, the Treaties spelled out important political concepts and organizing principles for the German princely states. They specified that the German states possess a considerable degree of freedom "to exercise their territorial right in both political and religious matters" (*Westphalia Treaties from October 24th*, 1648: Article VIII, Paragraph 1) and they granted significant autonomy to states to make and enforce laws and policies that apply in their territories. Although the idea of legal autonomy had been included in the founding document of the Holy Roman Empire, the Golden Bull of 1356, and German princes already possessed the right to sign treaties (Krasner, 2009: 15), the Treaties of Osnabrück and Münster reinforced this legal autonomy and the state's right to forge alliances and sign treaties with other states. By restricting, in particular, the influence of the Holy Roman Empire and the Pope, the Treaties granted

> sovereign authority on every German prince ... territorial states were legally permitted to interact with each other without interference by a higher authority. They could now freely manage their domestic affairs and their diplomatic relationships. (Kegley and Raymond, 2002: 131)

By constraining external political influences, the Treaties elevated the authority of German princes while questioning the sovereignty of the Emperor and the church.

Nevertheless, the Treaties also limited state sovereignty (Krasner, 2009: 15). Article VIII, Paragraph 2 of the Treaty of Osnabrück, for example, stipulates that alliances among German states must not go against the German Emperor and observe the oath to the Emperor and the Empire (*Westphalia Treaties from October 24th, 1648*). This Treaty (e.g. Article VII) also constrained the authority of sovereigns by protecting their subjects' religious rights and by prohibiting arbitrary actions against religious groups.

An important feature of the Treaties of Osnabrück and Münster is that they preserved the established systems of ruling. The Treaty of Osnabrück speaks, for example, of "electors", "princes", and "estates" of the Roman Empire (*"electores, principes et status Imperii Romani"*) who act on behalf of their subjects (*Westphalia Treaties from October 24th, 1648*: Article VII). In fact, the Treaties declared the practices and mechanisms of how sovereigns enforce domination over their subjects a largely internal matter beyond the authority of other sovereigns, the Pope, or the Emperor. Territorial sovereignty thus protects a sovereign's privilege to rule against other claims of authority. According to Kegley and Raymond (2002), the Treaties "went too far in liberating states from moral restraints" (4) and set "back development of the concept of human rights for centuries" (104). Instead, it presented territorial states – not the individual or communities – as the basic political unit and legal entity to which international law applies. Centuries later, international legal convention continued to speak of the state as "a sole person in the eyes of international law" (*Montevideo Declaration of 1933*: Article 2).

In terms of migration, Krasner (2000) observes that it would be inaccurate to associate the Westphalian model of sovereignty with cross-border migration. Rather, this model fixes claims of authority to geographically-bounded territory at the scale of the state. The Westphalian model is thus about territorial autonomy, not regulating migration. The often-celebrated achievement of the Westphalian model lies precisely in framing political authority in territorial terms in opposition to the direct bondage between subjects and a feudal authority.

Based on the assumption that people are not free to migrate, the Treaty of Osnabrück explicitly *enabled* migration: it ensured that subjects of a religious denomination that differs from the sovereign's denomination are permitted to emigrate (*Westphalia Treaties from October 24th, 1648*: Article V, paragraph 30); it protected the property of emigrants (*Westphalia Treaties from October 24th, 1648*:

Article V, Paragraph 36); and it regulated the return of refugees of war (*Westphalia Treaties from October 24th, 1648*: Article V, Paragraph 37). In this way, the Treaty affirmed the right to emigrate with family and belongings for religious motives (*beneficiun emigrandi*). In addition, it granted safe passage by land and water to persons (vassals and subjects alike) for the purpose of trade (*Westphalia Treaties from October 24th, 1648*: Article IX, Paragraph 2). Furthermore, the Treaty restricted the amount of exit fees the sovereign is allowed to charge (*Westphalia Treaties from October 24th, 1648*: Article V, Paragraph 37). Thus, the Westphalian Treaties did not entirely concede control over cross-border migration to the state as a purely internal matter but rather established rules of migration that could be applied between states.

The Treaties of Osnabrück and Münster regulated cross-border migration as an exception to the general practice of denying people the right to cross territorial borders. The pre-Westphalian feudal rulers, indeed, tended to tightly control the mobility of their subjects (Anderson, 2013). Although in the early Westphalian state in Europe, long-distance migration was not the mass phenomenon that it became in later centuries, rural-to-urban migration was a common practice through which rural peasants escaped feudal bondage and pursued economic opportunities. Feudal lords were therefore keen to impose exit controls (Schwarz, 2008). Correspondingly, the early Westphalian model assumed that people were not free to migrate. Thus, territorial rule was practically synonymous with rule over a fixed population.

In this sense, the Westphalian model changed little in respect to migration: people became subjects by being born on state territory and the unauthorized departure from this territory "was tantamount to treason" (Zollberg, 1994: 160); entry was controlled to prevent the infiltration of enemies and invaders. Aristide Zolberg (1994: 160) calls this rationale "pre-liberal." In the next section, I will discuss how controlling migration has continued to serve as a mechanism of rule over people based on the circumstances of their birth. States – including today's liberal democracies – have evoked this mechanism especially as populations acquired greater capacity to migrate.

The Westphalian Model in an Era of Migration

The Westphalian model of territorial rule gained prominence in the 19th and 20th Centuries in Europe and subsequently in other parts of the world, and it is now firmly engrained in the global geopolitical imagination. John Agnew (1994; 2002: 53) refers to this geopolitical imagination as the "territorial trap," which expresses the normalization of the sovereign territorial state as a universal political organizing principle.

While the Treaties of Osnabrück and Münster assumed that populations are largely immobile and did not explicitly concede control over human migration to the princes, migration controls later became a fundamental feature of territorial state sovereignty (Krasner, 2009). Legal scholars from the mid-19th Century to early 20th Century tended to argue that "no state has a legal duty to admit aliens, and that ... the sovereign state may set limits and specify conditions to entry" (Cavallar, 2002: 388). The idea that the territorial state possesses a monopoly over regulating cross-border migration has subsequently become an important aspect of the territorial trap. Today, the sovereign state's control over cross-border migration is rarely questioned: "in an international state system that still regards sovereignty as its most fundamental principle, no traveler can presume that receiving states will grant access to their soil" (Torpey, 2000: 163).

Over the centuries, sovereign states have maintained policies, laws, and control mechanisms of migration that reflected "extreme diversity" (Fahrmeir et al., 2003: 2). Some territorial states have been concerned about controlling *emigration* to prevent the departure of subjects obligated to perform military service or to block the exodus of skills, knowledge, and labour. In the early 18th Century the Kingdom of Württemberg curbed mass emigration of impoverished families destined for Eastern Europe by denying them exit visas, and Prussia's Frederick William I even authorized the death penalty to prohibit the unauthorized departure of peasants (Torpey, 2000: 58, 64). In the 20th Century, the socialist states of the "Eastern Block" prohibited the unauthorized departure of citizens. A recent study shows that the regime of the German Democratic Republic killed an estimated 327 people at its border to the Federal Republic of Germany between 1949 and 1989 (Staadt und Schroeder, 2017). Today, repressive regimes, such as Cuba and North Korea, continue to deny exit to their citizens.

The increasing number of states following liberal principles of governance no longer deny their citizens the liberty to leave. The United Nations enshrined this principle in Article 13.2 of the Universal Declaration of Human Rights, which states: "Everyone has the right to leave any country, including his own, and to return to his country" (United Nations, 1948). Only in exceptional cases – e.g. when a person is expected to stand trial or intends to join enemy forces – will liberal states impose travel bans that deny the right to leave (e.g. Council of Europe, 2013).

Modern states, however, have devised other ways to tie their subjects to the state. Nationalism, for example, attaches subjects to the nation imagined as a sovereign community (Anderson, 1991). The indoctrination into nationalism, however, does not necessarily require members of a national community to remain on sovereign territory. In fact, nationalism can be quite effective in binding expatriates to the nation (Gamlen, 2008). Overall, in liberal democracies, citizens tend to be formally free to leave state territory temporarily or permanently.

Entry controls have alternatively become a preferred mechanism for population control. States claim their sovereignty when they deny non-citizens access to their territory or when they permit only temporary or conditional entry through visas and work-permit. Immigration and naturalization policies, too, tend to be highly restrictive and selective. By way of exclusion, modern liberal democratic states assert control over their citizenry (Torpey, 2000). This practice evolved roughly over the last century.

During the second half of the 19th Century, states across Europe actually liberalized cross-border migration. Within the Holy Roman Empire, the *Pass-Card Treaty* (*Passkartenvertrag*) of 1850 standardized passports between most German states and eased inter-state mobility. Simultaneously, the requirement to possess visas to enter other states was relaxed or abolished. Similar policies facilitating inter-state migration were enacted by other European countries, including Belgium, England, France, the Scandinavian countries, and Switzerland (Torpey, 2000: 75-81). During this period, the United States permitted the influx of large numbers of migrants, especially in light of the country's rapid industrialization (Fahrmeir et al., 2003). While the Page Act and other exclusionary legislation and policies enabled the US government to deny racialized non-Europeans, the mentally ill, and other undesired groups entry into the country, these laws and policies did not quantitatively limit immigration.

Around World War I (WWI), states increased their control of cross-border migration (Sauvy, 1949; Torpey, 2000). Several factors led to this development: First, due to the war, borders were tightened to prevent enemies from crossing into and defectors from fleeing state territory. The corresponding technical and bureaucratic advances in population monitoring and surveillance made during WWI subsequently became permanent fixtures of states' effort to regulate cross-border migration. Second, with the entrenchment of nationalism among the fighting states "distinguishing between friend and foe on the basis of national background had become common-sense practice and ideology" (Wimmer and Glick Schiller, 2002: 315). The territorial boundary of the state now became the defining marker of migrants' identities, making it more difficult for migrants to belong. In this way, border-controls marked a territory to defend in the fist place. Third, the war disrupted economic globalization that characterized the pre-war period; and the post-war recovery was followed by the Great Depression, during which controlling migration became a way for states to regulate their national economies. Reflecting on these developments three decades after WWI had ended, Alfred Sauvy (1949: 22) observed:

> before the war of 1914, there was little opposition to international migration in Europe. The essential distinction between tourists and the workers was not clearly defined as it is today, with the result that barriers to migration were of a political, public safety, or health order, rather than of economic order.

In light of rising unemployment after the war, national trade unions pushed for migration controls to protect national labour markets from foreign competition.

WWI war losses, however, also created labour shortages in some regions and occupations. Corresponding bilateral and international treaties permitted the recruitment of workers from other countries to fill these shortages. For example, between 1919 and 1926, France signed labour mobility treaties with Poland, Italy, Czechoslovakia, Luxembourg, and Yugoslavia. Such treaties established important principles of regulating cross-border migration (Sauvy, 1949). On the one hand, they granted migrants equal treatment in terms of pay, social privileges, and taxation. On the other hand, they further enshrined the idea that sovereign states could deny or facilitate entry into their territory based on their own criteria, which often included a migrant's occupation, skills, wealth, and 'racial' markers.

More regulations were put in place after World War II. International agreements, such as the World Trade Organization's General Agreement on Trade in Services (Mode 4) or Chapter 16 of the North American Free Trade Agreement, which came into force in 1995 and 1994 respectively, have tended to grant business persons and entrepreneurs, wealthy elites, highly-educated professionals, and other privileged workers entry into the territories of counties in the Global North. In Europe, a series of treaties and agreements regulating labour mobility culminated in Article 45 of the Treaty of the Functioning of the European Union, which entered into force in 2009, and which enshrined the freedom of movement among workers within the European Union. Corresponding developments expanded migrant rights. The establishment of the European Court of Human Rights, for example, has obliged member states to grant rights typically associated with citizenship to non-EU citizens. The concept of postnational citizenship expresses this expansion of migrant rights in the wake of a strengthening human rights discourse throughout the postwar period (Soysal 1994).

These developments seem to suggest that territorial states are partially surrendering control over migration. However, exclusionary migration regulations that deny or only conditionally grant entry to state territory have remained firmly in place (Andreas and Snyder 2000). The countries of the Global North disproportionately deny migrants from the Global South entry into their territories; or they grant only temporary and probationary access in the form of visas and work permits (Lenard and Straehle, 2012). The US's Bracero Program, which was in place from 1942 to 1964, Germany's guest worker program, which existed from the 1950s to 1970s, and Canada's ongoing Temporary Foreign Workers Program exemplify how states grant territorial access to workers without extending equal social, political, or economic rights, or the right to remain in the country. Many of the states that participate in international agreements facilitating the mobility of privileged workers, block the entry of less privileged classes or permit entry only through highly restrictive programs that impose residency limitations, curb migrants' rights, or bond migrants to particular jobs or employers (Sharma, 2006; Vosko et al., 2014). These restrictive migration policies create a vulnerable and exploitable underclass of migrants. The selective conferring of status categories based on country of citizenship thus enforces an "international segmentation of labor" (Bauder, 2006: 10-34) that disadvantages some workers based on the national citizenship they most likely acquired at birth (Samers, 2010).

In many other cases, cross-border mobility is strictly denied. While the European Union has opened its borders internally between member states, it closed its "external" border. The almost 3,000 human deaths in the Mediterranean Sea in 2016 alone attest to the brutality with which migration controls are enforced (International Organization for Migration, 2018). The United States has controlled migration at its southern border with Mexico in a comparably forceful manner (Nevins 2002). In this way, entry controls maintain a system of "global apartheid" based on racism (Sharma, 2005; van Houtum, 2010). This system is maintained by legal practice that continues to frame the right to entre and remain in a state – like under feudalism – as a condition of the circumstances of a person's birth.

Conclusion

The above discussion follows a line of critical scholarship that sees the Westphalian model as a historically and geographically specific instrument of political rule (Agnew, 2005; Painter, 2010; Sassen, 2013). The control of human migration is a critical element of maintaining this rule. In this sense, there are parallels between European feudalism and contemporary liberal democratic states. The often-praised achievement of the Westphalian model was to reject the feudal bondage of people in favor of rule over territory; controlling migration into state territory, however, effectively continues an aspect of the feudal way of ruling (Carens, 1978).

Nevertheless, there are decisive differences. Pre-liberal rulers tightly controlled the mobility of their subjects, especially their departure. The Treaties of Osnabrück and Münster still assumed that people were not free to cross borders but that sovereigns possess control over their subjects' mobility. The Treaties therefore specified general rules of cross-border mobility that apply to particular populations and situations. The liberal-democratic Westphalian state differs in that it controls especially the migration (and the circumstances of visitation and residency) of non-subjects. Thus, the feudal logic of rule through direct bondage was replaced with rule through exclusion. In both cases, privilege is a matter of circumstances of birth: both privileged feudal ruler and the citizen of countries in the Global North, and unprivileged feudal peasants and citizen of countries in the Global South, are born into their situations. Nevertheless, while feudal lords possessed supreme authority over their subjects, the citizens of the Global North exercise their privileges in a less direct manner. In the liberal democratic states of the Global North today, migration controls in the name of sovereignty preserve the birth privileges of citizens by facilitating a system of global apartheid and enforcing an international segmentation of labour that disadvantages those born in the Global South. Although modern racism and labour segmentation under capitalism are a far stretch from feudalism, birth privilege remains at the core of social and political order.

References

Agnew, J. (1994). "The Territorial Trap: The Geopolitical Assumptions of International Relations Theory". *Review of International Political Economy*, 1: 53-80.
Agnew, J. (2002). *Geopolitics: Re-visioning World Politics*. London: Routledge.
Agnew, J. (2005). "Sovereignty Regimes: Territoriality and State Authority in Contemporary World Politics". *Annals of the Association of American Geographers* 95 (2): 437-461.
Anderson, B. (1991). *Imagined Communities: Reflections on the Origin and Spread of Nationalism*. Revised Edition ed. London: Verso.
Anderson, B. (2013). *Us and Them? The Dangerous Politics of Immigration Control*. Oxford: Oxford University Press.
Andreas, P. and Snyder, T. (eds.) (2000). *The wall around the West: State boundaries and immigration controls in North America and Europe*. Lanham, MD: Rowman and Littlefield.
Bartelson, J. (1995). *A Genealogy of Sovereignty*. Cambridge: Cambridge University Press.
Bauder, H. (2006). *Labor movement: How migration regulates labor markets*. New York: Oxford University Press.
Biersteker, T. and Weber, C. (1996). "The Social Construction of Sovereign Identity". In: T. Biersteker and C. Weber (eds.) *State Sovereignty as Social Construct*, Cambridge: Cambridge University Press.
Bodin, J. (Abridged, 1955[1576]). *Six Books of the Commonwealth* (Les Six livres de la République), Book I., M. J. Tooley (trans.). Accessed December, 22 2016, http://www.constitution.org/bodin/bodin_1.htm.
Camilleri, J. A. and Falk, J. (1992). *The End of Sovereignty? The Politics of a Shrinking and Fragmented World*. Aldershot, England: Edward Elgar.
Carens, J. H. (1987). "Aliens and Citizens: The Case for Open Borders". *Review of Politics*, 49: 251-273.
Cavallar, G. (2002). *The Rights of Strangers: Theories of International Hospitality, the Global Community, and Political Justice since Victoria*. Aldershot, UK: Ashgate.
Council of Europe. (2013). *The Right to Leave*. Accessed Dec. 28, 2017,

https://www.coe.int/t/commissioner/source/prems/prems150813_GBR_1700_TheRightToLeaveACountry_web.pdf.

Fahrmeir, A., Faron, O. and Weil, P. (2003). "Introduction". In: A. Fahrmeir, O. Faron and P. Weil (eds.) *Migration control in the North Atlantic World*, pp. 1-7, New York: Berghahn Books.

Foucault, M. (2007). *Security, Territory, Population: Lectures at the Collège de France 1977-1978*, G. Burchell (trans.). New York: Picador.

Gamlen, A. (2008). "The emigration state and the modern geopolitical imagination". *Political Geography*, 27 (8): 840-856.

Hegel, G. W. F. (1979[1820]). *Grundlagen der Philosophie des Rechts*. Accessed December 22, 2016, http://www.zeno.org/Philosophie/M/Hegel,+Georg+Wilhelm+Friedrich/Grundlinien+der+Philosophie+des+Rechts.

International Organization for Migration (2018). Missing Migrants Project. Accessed Jun. 13, 2018, https://missingmigrants.iom.int/.

Kant, I. (1946[1795]). *Zum ewigen Frieden*. Accessed 22 December 2016, http://gutenberg.spiegel.de/buch/zum-ewigen-frieden-8301/1

Kant, I. (1977[1797]). *Metaphysik der Sitten*. Accessed December 22, 2016, http://www.zeno.org/Philosophie/M/Kant,+Immanuel/Die+Metaphysik+der+Sitten.

Kegley, C. W. Jr and Raymond, G. A. (2002). *Exorcising the Ghost of Westphalia: Building World Order in the New Millennium*. Upper Saddle River, NJ: Prentice Hall.

Krasner, S. D. (2000). "Compromising Westphalia". In: D. Held and A. McGrew (eds.) *The Global Transformations Reader: An Introduction to the Globalization Debate*, 126, Cambridge, UK: Polity Press.

Krasner, S. D. (2009). *Power, the State, and Sovereignty: Essays on International Relations*. London: Routledge.

Lenard, P. T. and Straehle, C. (eds.) (2012). *Legislated inequality: Temporary labour migration in Canada*. Montreal-Kingston: McGill-Queen's University Press.

MacRae, A. (2005). "Counterpoint: The Westphalia Overstatement". *International Social Science Review*, 80.3: 159-160.

Montevideo Declaration of 1933, "Article 2". Accessed January 4, 2017 http://www.cfr.org/sovereignty/montevideo-convention-rights-duties-states/p15897.

Nevins, J. (2002) *Operation Gatekeeper: The rise of the "illegal Alien" and the making of the U.S.-Mexico Boundary*. New York: Routledge.

O'Dowd, L. (2010). "From a 'Borderless World' to a 'World of Borders': 'Bringing History Back in'". *Environment and Planning D: Society and Space*, 28 (60): 1031-1050.

Ohmae, K. (1990). *Borderless World: Power and Strategy in the Inter-linked World Economy*. Harper Business, New York.

Paasi, A., Prokkola, E. K., Saarinen, J., Zimmerbauer, K. (eds.) (Forthcoming). *Borderless worlds - for whom? Ethics, moralities and (in)justice in mobilities* (working title). London: Routledge.

Painter, J. (2010). "Rethinking Territory". *Antipode*, 42.5: 1090-1118.

Prokhovnik, R. (2008). *Sovereignty: History and Theory*. Charlottesville, VA: Imprint Academic.

Rousseau, J. J. (2003 [1762]). *On the Social Contract*, G.D.H. Cole (trans.). Mineola, NY: Dover.

Samers, M. (2010). *Migration*. London: Routledge.

Sassen, S. (2013). "When Territory Deborders Territoriality". *Territory, Politics, Governance*, 1.1: 21-45.

Sassen, S. (2008). *Territory, Authority, Rights: From Medieval to Global Assemblages*, 2nd ed. Princeton: Princeton University Press.

Sauvy, A. (1949). "European migrations: Regulations and treaties". *Annals of the American Academy of Political and Social Sciences*, 262 (1): 22-30.

Shachar, A. (2009). *The Birth Lottery: Citizenship and Global Inequality*. Boston: Harvard University Press.

Sharma, N. (2005). "Anti-trafficking rhetoric and the making of a global Apartheid". *NWSA Journal*, 17 (3): 88-111.

Sharma, N. (2006). *Home economics: Nationalism and the making of 'migrant' workers in Canada*. Toronto: University of Toronto Press.

Simms, B. (2011). "'A False Principle in the Law of Nations': Burke, state sovereignty, [German] liberty, and intervention in the Age of Westphalia". In: *Humanitarian Intervention*, 89-110, D. J. B. Trim (eds.) Cambridge: Cambridge University Press.

Soysal, Y. N. (1994). *Limits of citizenship: migrants and postnational membership in Europe*. Chicago: The University of Chicago Press.

Spinoza, B. (1900[1883-1884]). *A Theologico-Political Treatise*. Originally published as volume 1 of *The Chief works of Benedict de Spinoza* by G. Bell and Sons, (London,). Accessed December 22, 2016, http://www.sacred-texts.com/phi/spinoza/treat/tpt00.htm.

Staadt, J. and Schroeder K. (eds.) (2017). *Die Todesopfer des DDR-Grenzregimes an der innerdeutschen Grenze 1949–1989*. Frankfurt am Main: Verlag Peter Lang.

Teschke, B. (2003). *The Myth of 1648: Class, Geopolitics, and the Making of Modern International Relations*. London: Verso.

Torpey, J. (2000). *The invention of the passport: Surveillance, citizenship and the state*. Cambridge, UK: Cambridge University Press.

United Nations. (1948). *Universal Declaration of Human Rights* http://www.un.org/en/universal-declaration-human-rights/ (accessed Dec. 28, 2017)

van Houtum, H. (2010). "Human blacklisting: the global apartheid of the EU's external border regime". *Environment and Planning D: Society and Space*, 28: 957-976.

Vosko, L., Preston, V. and Latham, R. (eds.) (2014). Liberating temporariness? Migration, work and citizenship in an era of insecurity. Montreal and Kingston: McGill Queen's University Press.

Westphalia Treaties from October 24th (1648). Acta Pacis Westphalicae. Supplementa electronica, 1). Accessed January 9, 2018, http://www.pax-westphalica.de/ipmipo/.

Wimmer, A. and Glick Schiller, N. (2002). "Methodological nationalism and beyond: Nation-state building, migration and the social sciences". *Global Networks*, 2 (4): 301-334.

Zollberg, A. (1994) "Changing sovereignty games and international migration". *Indiana Journal of Global Legal Studies*, 2(1): 153-170.

CHAPTER 22

Naturalisation Policies Beyond a Western Focus

Tobias Schwarz

Naturalisations: taking the alienage-nationality nexus to investigate national politics of belonging

At the core of the nation-state principle, which by now encompasses the whole globe, stands the assignment of each individual to (usually only) one nation-state. Foreigners have to naturalise in the country of destination if they want to become equal members at least nominally. Only through the acquisition of nationality[1] can they gain access to most citizenship rights, most notably the security of residence and the right to vote. From the perspective of the national state administration, an equal legal status for every member of the population resident within national territory is often seen as necessary to maintain social cohesion. Nevertheless, to incorporate foreigners as equal members of society can pose a threat to the unity of the imagined nation, especially when the new members are perceived as ethnically or culturally different. Therefore criteria must be set as to who belongs and who does not. Naturalisation is the legal process of acquisition of a nationality, not automatically at birth, but later in life (and then usually in substitution for or in addition to an existing nationality). From the perspective of a particular state, to naturalise means to confer on an individual a legal membership status.[2] The usual requirements are to be of legal age, to be lawfully present inside the country, and to have resided there for a minimum duration; the latter can vary considerably, e.g. from one year in the case of Portuguese wishing to naturalise in Brazil, to as much as 25 years in Qatar. The period of residency requirement is often lower for a spouse or a child of a national and for former nationals, and sometimes also for those seen as co-ethnics (indeed, it may even be that naturalisation is only possible for those categorized as of the same "race", see Ludwig, this issue). These basic requirements are usually accompanied by proof of "good conduct" (operationalized as a clean criminal record), often (but not always) by possession of a permanent residency permit, and sometimes by the demonstration of either a minimum economic self-sufficiency or, on the contrary, an outstandingly high economic contribution by the applicant (as in a two-tier immigration systems like in Hong Kong and Singapore, see Leung and Mathews/Soon in this issue). Additional naturalisation requirements

---

[1] Nationality, in accordance with international law, is understood as the legal relationship between individuals and states. In some domestic legal systems this meaning is subsumed under the term *citizenship* (Bauböck et al., 2006: 2). Some scholars prefer to avoid the term *nationality*, because in some languages it connotes ethnicity, and utilize *citizenship* instead. Yet, "citizenship is a legal identity oriented inwards to rights and obligations within the state, while nationality is a state-certified membership oriented outwards to other states" (FitzGerald 2005: 172). In line with latter definition, the term *nationality* is preferred here to solely express the formal membership of an individual in a state.

[2] The word "natural" in the term *naturalization* originally expressed the acquisition of a status equal to that acquired by birth. It hence symbolically underlines that someone is being made a "natural" member of a state, while in fact the global state system and its concomitant membership regulations are anything but natural or self-evident.

are proficiency in (one of) the official language(s) and/or country knowledge (which may or may not be rigorously tested – again, as in Singapore). Alongside these requirements for regular naturalisations, many states allow for "special naturalisation" at the discretion of the executive for those with exceptional achievements in favour of the country (in the past, often war heroes; today, football stars and other athletes). What is more, an increasing number of states "sell" their nationality to rich foreigners if the latter invest large amounts of money inside the respective country, whereby some or all other requirements are waived (Dzankic, 2012; van Fossen, 2007; see Ramtohul in this issue on investor citizenship in Mauritius).

Naturalisations are more than just one aspect of the complex national "politics of belonging", to borrow a term coined by Brubaker, among others.[3] Unlike nationality at birth, naturalisation is neither automatic nor random (i.e. not determined by place of birth or status of the parents, or a combination of both), but must be brought about deliberately. To a varying degree, the person concerned can influence her naturalisation, or at least it is dependent on the activity and some characteristics of the individual. Therefore, the way naturalisations are organized in any society offers a particular opportunity to gain clues as to which criteria are assumed to be relevant for the respective definition of national belonging. Apart from the fact that naturalisations help draw the boundaries of a symbolic membership status, they are made explicit (as laws), and the rules governing these policies have been controversial issues in many places in recent years. This makes them a prime subject for the study of national policies of belonging. The works gathered in this special issue follow this line of argument and share a common perspective on the acquisition of nationality: they investigate what forms of relationships and affiliations are privileged over others; what ideals of collectivity and solidarity are seen as legitimate; and what assumptions of difference and foreignness impede national belonging.

With transnational migration on the rise (Glick Schiller, 2008), research on migration patterns and migrant incorporation has increasingly managed to overcome the limitation of a sole focus on national policies and of the concomitant state-focused theory-building (also termed *methodological nationalism*, Wimmer & Glick Schiller, 2003). Yet the tendency to include developments that transcend national containers should not lead to a neglect of nation-state powers – or, in other words: there is no sign that the global state system has actually reached a post-national order (see Favell, 2006; Hansen, 2009; Weil, 2012). On the contrary, formal nationality does still matter, because the nation-state "remains the decisive locus of membership even in a globalizing world; struggles over belonging in and to the nation-state remain the most consequential forms of membership politics" (Brubaker, 2010, p. 76). Here it is not necessary to repeat all arguments in this regard; suffice it to mention the most notable consequences of national membership. It is certainly true that foreign permanent residents often enjoy rights

---

[3] See Crowley (1999); Anderson et al. (2011); Yuval-Davis (2011). Brubaker argues that the (negotiations of) criteria to define membership in a nation-state are, obviously, closely related to negotiations of rights and obligations as citizens, but nevertheless "the politics of citizenship *in* the nation-state can be distinguished analytically from the politics of belonging *to* the nation-state" (Brubaker 2010: 64).

similar to those of nationals, such as access to the labor market and to social security. But political activity by foreigners is strongly restricted in most countries, and voting rights are usually reserved for citizens.[4] Another important aspect, yet often ignored by scholars, is the security of residence. Even permanent residents are subject to forced removal if they're convicted of a crime, or sometimes even if they rely on welfare benefits.[5] Only nationals are protected from being physically removed from the territory.[6]

Empiric research on naturalisation

During the last decade, nationality policies in many countries (most visibly perhaps in Western Europe) have attempted to attach more symbolic weight to the procedure of naturalisation. Through introducing language- or country-knowledge tests and inventing new rituals, such as citizenship oaths or ceremonies, amendments to nationality laws have striven to attach more profound meaning to the process of becoming a citizen.[7] In this process, national administrations are inspired by the practices of other states, and even copy each other outright, to the extent that there is some convergence, for instance in the use of naturalisation tests and ceremonies in the Western world.[8]

But what is happening in other regions? In Singapore, to name an example of a country successfully attracting international migrants, the public policy of immigrant admission and naturalisation explicitly trains would-be citizens in national values and history using a naturalisation procedure called the "citizenship journey". The prime importance given to naturalisations as a means to shape national populations is not unique to this South East Asian country, as the articles in this special issue show. This is illustrative of the need to analyse naturalisation policies beyond the "classic" countries of immigration. With regard to western countries, scholarly interest in naturalisation has during the last decade entered into a theoretical debate on whether negotiations of nationality and naturalisation (law) can be explained by understandings of nationhood, or whether they are primarily shaped by structural conditions like demographic or economic patterns or institutional configurations, or are temporary and alterable outcomes of momentary political decisions. As much as the theorizing of nationalism has profited from the broadening of perspectives through non-Western cases and concepts during the 1990s (Chatterjee, 1986; Tønnesson & Antlöv, 1996; Chakrabarty, 2000), research on naturalisations as a way of approaching concepts of nationhood and politics of

---

[4] Many states exclude all foreigners from the ballot boxes; in most cases non-citizen voting rights are confined to local elections or the active suffrage (Hayduk, 2006). When studying 25 democratic states in 2003, Earnest (2003) found full equation of foreigners with nationals in only two countries: New Zealand and Uruguay.

[5] Kanstroom frames this as "post-entry social control" (Kanstroom, 2012: 28–49). On deportation in general see Anderson et al. (2013).

[6] Accordingly, deprivation of nationality has been put on the agenda again in some European states since 9/11; see Gibney (2013) on the policy of denaturalisation in the UK; on denaturalisation in German history see Gosewinkel (2001: 369–420); in the US, Weil (2013).

[7] This has been interpreted as attempts to make national membership "thicker", e.g. to make representations of particular national histories and cultures more distinguishable from each other (Kostakopoulou, 2006; Goodman, 2012).

[8] On the transfer of the concept of citizenship ceremonies between the UK, Canada, and Australia see Damsholt (2008) and Byrne (2014).

national belonging can profit from expansion beyond a Western focus.

In line with this observation, this introduction argues that theories of naturalisation have been largely derived from interaction with cases in the West. It will go into the ethnocentric bias of much of the universalizing comparative research on naturalisations, and will argue that particularly the evaluation of restrictive naturalisation policies has so far been biased by a Western focus. Explicitly restrictive naturalisation (and more generally, nationality) policies are not confined to the West, but are a feature of boundary maintenance in other regions of the world, too. Such ethnic or economic exclusivity is often not taken into account by Western scholars, much in line with the neglect of non-Western racism in immigration restrictions (see Webb, 2015). Many cross-national (implicitly or systematic) comparisons are tilted towards taking the West as the measuring rod. The cases examined in this special issue substantiate this finding: ethnically exclusive nationality laws in Liberia and Israel; selective two-tier regimes of immigrant incorporation in Hong Kong and Singapore, typical of the South-East Asian striving economies; investor citizenship schemes which are much more common in the Global South than in the North, exemplified by the case of Mauritius; and Mexico, whose norms assign naturalized Mexicans the status of "second-class citizens".

Universal explanations of nationality and naturalisation policies

Since Rogers Brubaker's comparative study of nationality in France and Germany, published in 1992 (Brubaker, 1992), many studies have engaged with the question of how to make sense of varying patterns of nationality law in different, primarily Western, nation-states. Some scholars are currently searching for theoretical models that universally explain nationality policies, including naturalisation law and practice (for an overview on comparative approaches that come up with "causal explanations" of such variations see Janoski, 2013, p. 386). Such a quest for universal explanations is challenging; firstly because its theoretical tools are developed from Western perspectives; secondly because the universalist approach relies primarily on quantitative data that are currently not available for most regions of the globe.

Lack of research beyond the West

Comparative studies of naturalisations, which strive to explain policy differences, are still dominated by studies on Western polities.[9] Their theoretical tools are developed from academic perspectives of the "classic" West (the "West of the Cold War", see Lewis & Wigen, 1997: 50). Its main focus has so far been on "settler-colonial" countries (Bashford, 2014: 34) or the "classic immigration

---

[9] Some studies that explain naturalisation policies primarily take laws and regulations into account (in political science, this is called the *output* of a policy). As an example, a comparative study on the EU discusses the reasons why naturalisation tests were introduced, see van Oers et al. (2010). For other studies, the driving question is to explain variations in naturalisation rates across different countries by relating the numeric *outcomes* to their respective specific legal setups (Weil, 2001), or to the structure of their immigrant populations (Bloemraad, 2006 compared the US and Canada). This is also frequently done as a comparison of naturalisation rates between different groups within the population of one country; see on the USA Bloemraad and Ueda (2006); on Germany Street (2014). Yet other studies combine outputs and outcomes; for instance by taking into account the "Five Dimensions of Implementation" by Huddleston (2013: 3).

countries" (Castles & Miller, 2009: 250), while for instance countries of emigration have not been "adequately" addressed (FitzGerald, 2005: 171). From a global perspective, this is still fragmentary, as most research has been done on comparatively few cases, almost all of them OECD member states.[10] Such a theory, with its origins in the North, must be tested against Southern perspectives, but not as derivations of "normal" Northern models. Scholars have pointed rightly to the problem of "projecting North Atlantic perspectives and understandings onto data from the rest of the world" (Connell, 2011: 288). Only if existing theories prove to be applicable to the naturalisation policies of Mexico, Singapore, or Mauritius (to mention just a few examples), can they then be applied globally with some degree of confidence.

Because of its focus on the West, much of the existing literature produces regionally specific theoretical elements that lead to a distorted picture with regard to access to nationality, both at birth and later in life, and theoretically disprivileges divergent cases in other regions of the world. I will look at a few extreme cases beyond the "classic" West to illustrate how the resulting overall picture is misleading. The model derived from the context of (Western) Europe and USA/Canada/Australia is necessarily distorted, because its main structuring principle is the placement of national policies along a continuum from closed to open.[11] In this regard, the ethnically selective nationality policies of Eastern Europe have recently been compared to those of (other) EU countries, resulting in them being considered relatively closed (Sievers, 2009). However, from a global perspective they have to be placed closer to the center of an imagined continuum between open and closed, because in such an extended perspective the region near the "closed" pole would be populated by policies that make acquisition of nationality after birth almost impossible. This includes states that set the minimum time of residence required for naturalisation very high (for instance, between 20 and 25 years in the Arab Gulf States, see van Waas, 2014: 11) or leave naturalisation decisions at the discretion of the administration, with very low factual outcomes, as in the case of China (on the right of abode as an approximation to nationality in Hong Kong, see Leung, this issue). Other Asian countries are also close to this pole, the most so perhaps Japan (Refsing, 2003), and Taiwan (Low, 2013). More generally speaking, ethnic selectivity is a well-founded principle of immigration and nationality policies in Southeast Asia (Asis & Battistella, 2012), making naturalisation preferences for co-ethnics in Eastern Europe appear anything but extreme. Another non-European benchmark with pointedly ethnically selective nationality law is Israel (like Japan, a country very ambiguously located at the margin of "the West", and discussed more at length below). In other words: most comparative models are still fragmentary, from a global perspective, and tilted towards Western Europe, USA/Canada, and Australia.

---

[10] Among the most prominent of such works are Bauböck (1994); Bauböck et al. (2006); Bloemraad (2006); Brubaker (1992); Janoski (2010); Joppke (2010); Howard (2009); Huddleston and Niessen (2011); Dumbrava (2014).
[11] Even if such a one-dimensional model is increasingly amended to include other dimensions, as outlined above, the criterion of closedness-openness remains present in all of them.

Lack of data for systematic comparisons beyond the West

Alongside the descriptive conclusion that there is a Western bias in the work on naturalisations, it also seems that there is a lack of will to look beyond the West. So far most works on nationality policy (and on naturalisations in particular) have deliberately chosen to focus on the USA, Canada, and Australia, and on the former colonial powers, France and the UK – or, more recently, on a growing number of EU member states. This is because those countries are pictured as the main destinations of international migration today (Castles & Miller, 2009: 4). Regions beyond them are rarely integrated into comparative research designs, and little has so far been published in a comprehensive and comparative way about naturalisation policies and practices throughout the world.[12]

It is obvious why so many authors dedicate time to the study of the USA, Canada, Australia, and the EU: research on nationality follows the policy-driven perspective of how to manage migration and immigrant incorporation in those countries – and hence is well funded. But numbers count in another way too: the (un-)availability of statistical data is one mayor inhibitor of systematic comparisons on a global scale. Inspired by the quest to *explain* naturalisation policies, the methodology used in index-based comparative design makes differing nationality policies comparable by reducing the particularities of the cases they study to a limited set of numerically comparative variables (for instance by counting the years of residence required, or assigning the value of 0-5 for levels of language requirements, etc.). The calculated results are later interpreted (or "measured") by placing them on a scale that ranges, for example, from open to closed, or from liberal to restrictive. After the data have been computed, the national policies to be compared can be related to each other (or "ranked") according to their degree of closure/openness.

The ongoing academic interest in large scale comparative works based on numerical indexes leads to continuously growing sample sizes and to a matrix of comparison that is continuously becoming more complex. In an article in 2013, Maarten Vink and Rainer Bauböck compared the naturalisation laws of 36 European states. For their comparative scale, they defined a set of twelve indicators which include both ordinary naturalisation, and acquisition through "special ties", for instance for co-ethnics; and they included loss of nationality inside as well as outside the territory of a state, i.e. through voluntary acquisition of another nationality, and through prolonged residence abroad (Vink & Bauböck, 2013: 626). Vink and Bauböck admit that the explanatory value of a model as complex as theirs is limited, and that they primarily demonstrate the great "empirical variety of regimes in Europe" (Vink & Bauböck, 2013: 641).

The practical problem this sort of "measuring" (Huddleston, 2013) of naturalisation policies from a large-scale comparative perspective faces is that reliable data are only available for proportionately few countries. It is already not

---

12 Two exemptions are edited volumes that add to the 'usual suspects' the Baltic states, Russia, South Africa, Japan, Israel, and Mexico (Aleinikoff and Klusmeyer, 2000), and the EU enlargement states of the 2000s and Turkey (Bauböck et al., 2009) respectively.

an easy task to compare policy outputs (i.e., the regulations on paper) when each and every norm must first be translated accurately, not from the languages of the former European empires, but from Malay, Chinese, or Azerbaijani, into a lingua franca to allow comparison. But even more so it is no wonder that index-based comparisons cover states that publish statistics on the outcome of naturalisation policies (i.e., the numbers of naturalisations, naturalisation rates, rejected applications, etc.). The latter is currently not the case for most countries in Latin America, Africa, or Asia, hence those regions simply cannot be incorporated into complex comparative grids. As a consequence, it will continue to be difficult to test this descriptive modelling against cases from non-Western regions. Thus, relying primarily on quantitative data so far impedes the implementation of a truly global perspective.

The case studies and heuristic comparisons of this special issue

The argument made so far is that universal comparison is difficult to accomplish on a global scale and has not yet advanced very far, even if the comparative designs derived in and for the West are becoming ever more elaborate. Nevertheless, studies with a Western bias can provide stimulating input for research beyond "the West", though they have to be adjusted and expanded, and some arguments might be partially dropped in the process.

The contributions in this special issue study naturalisations in order to better understand the broader societal constellations they reflect. They are directed at distinctive features of singular cases they want to understand, and allow for comparison not with the aim of universalizing theory-building, but only in a heuristic sense. In-depth case studies like these have the advantage of analysing naturalisations in their respective contexts, and therefore allow for a better understanding of particularities – which would, in turn, not be visible without comparisons with other cases and general trends.

Studies on regions beyond the West

Studies with a broader regional focus can still productively draw on theories derived from Europe. Many colonies of Western powers became independent states only in the course of the 20th century. Particularly with regard to the relatively short independent history of the post-colonial states in Africa, Asia, and the Caribbean, studies on them take into account the historical "making of" nationality law, for instance through decolonization (see the contributions in Ko, 1990). When post-colonial states became independent of Western dominance, they also gained sovereignty over the decision as to who would be considered a member of the new nation. But their legal definitions of membership were often informed by the knowledge and the worldviews of their (former) colonial administrators. This was for instance the case when South (-East) Asian countries drafted their first post-colonial immigration legislations by copying outright norms regarding the selection and prohibition of immigrants from US, Australian, and other "Western" laws;[13] or when countries that emerged from the British empire received direct instructions

---

[13] As examples see "the postcolonial immigration acts of Malaysia, Singapore, Fiji, Brunei, Papua New Guinea, and more" (Bashford, 2014: 40).

from British expert commissions on how to draft their own constitutions and their new nationality laws (Hassall, 1999: 53). Christopher Lee also returns to the role of nationality law in the formation of the (British) colonial state in Africa, and concludes that his analysis of how the colonial form of *jus sanguinis* helped to maintain a distinction between the categories of "native" and "non-native" amended the "ethnic state model that has predominated conventional understandings of the state in Africa" (Lee, 2011: 521–522).

Other countries in Asia were never (formally) under European colonial dominance (like China and Thailand), but fit into a general description of Asian countries as less likely to accept immigrants as permanent members of their societies, and hence as restricting access to legal membership status. As migration of less skilled migrants is seen as merely temporary, long-term integration is not considered necessary, and family reunification and naturalisation is ruled out (Asis & Battistella, 2012: 32), while highly skilled professionals are usually sought after and their permanent residence is encouraged, including in some cases the provision of investor citizenship.[14]

Due to its location off the east coast of Africa and as part of the Indian Ocean rim, the island of Mauritius is located at a unique crossing point of different regional influences, and has seen many migration flows passing by throughout its (modern) history. Its society, today a middle-income economy, is deeply marked by the consequences of the colonial labor regime, with a white elite (formerly the plantation owners) still in control of much of the land, while the larger, poorer parts of the population are ethnically mixed, of African and Indian ancestry. Like many African countries Mauritius became independent in the 1960s, and has subsequently adopted a restrictive immigration policy, which has allowed low-skilled migrant workers to enter only temporarily, and only with a work permit tied to a particular contractor. This regime is currently partially opening, based on the "selling" of residency/citizenship to rich foreigners who invest in the country. As Ramtohul's study shows (this issue), in line with similar schemes in other parts of the world, this commodification of nationality is solely directed at attracting money, not people. Accordingly, the integration of such individuals was no issue when the immigration and naturalisation laws were amended in the 2000s to allow citizenship to be sold, and the problematic social impacts of such schemes became visible only later. Certainly, naturalisation in Mauritius is not seen as the final step of a process of integration, nor is it considered important to encourage the naturalized new citizens to become equal members of society. On the contrary, the rich investors are perceived (and maybe erroneously so) as a mobile transnational elite, without social ties to Mauritius and with no interests in political (or other) rights that come with Mauritian nationality.

Singapore is an example of a state that not only enables immigrant incorporation by a selective naturalisation policy, mentioned above as typical for many Asian states, but also outright forces the desired immigrants to stay and

---

[14] Such a two-tiered system with significantly differing rights accessible to the two different groups is practiced in India, Bangladesh, Thailand, Malaysia, Singapore, Indonesia, the Philippines, and other countries (Asis and Battistella, 2012: 38).

become legally equal citizens. During its fifty years of independence, the city-state relied on selective import of immigrant labour in line with its meritocratic vision of society, and thereby managed successfully to strengthen its economic capacity. The relevant policies were selective, normatively excluding less-skilled immigrant labourers from permanent incorporation and offering highly skilled immigrants an exclusive access to nationality and full citizenship rights. Up until today, the granting of nationality to desired immigrants is not only a means to meet economic objectives, but can also be interpreted as an ongoing process of symbolic nation-building. Soon/Mathews (this issue) show how the state's effort to anchor foreign talents to the nation by granting them Singaporean nationality is in turn canonizing supposedly key national values, like multiculturalism and individual entrepreneurship. They are communicated to new citizens during the recently created *Singapore Citizenship Journey*, the core element of the naturalisation procedure, and in turn foster a specific understanding of what Singaporeanness means.

In Hong Kong, a selectively two-layer regime, very similar to the policy in Singapore, is in place. "Foreign talents" are desired immigrants, while less-skilled and less-educated workers are rejected, to the extent that even family reunion is not provided for. But in addition to a very short period of independence from British colonialism, Hong Kong shows another particularity: its incomplete sovereignty due to the influence of China. Hong Kong was designed by the colonial state, and is still envisioned by the political elites as a mere "economic machine", not a society, a community of people with social rights (see Leung, this issue). This brings with it the neoliberal logic of an optimal composition of immigrant population, and the potential for the city to grow through foreign talents. As an example, foreign domestic workers are excluded by law from the right of abode, and hence from other rights of permanent residents – including the right to work without being tied to a particular employer, the right to vote, and the right to reunite with family members from abroad. In this way, a large segment of less-skilled, poorly educated, and overwhelmingly female foreign immigrant population is deprived of even long-term legal incorporation into Hong Kong society.

As has been mentioned above, some of the naturalisation policies discussed in this special issue are even more restrictive, most strikingly the exclusive norms in Israel and Liberia, where naturalisation is only possible for those belonging to a racially or religiously defined group. In Israel the Jewish religion is seen as the basis of the state, and this conception is consequentially carried forward into the norms of nationality. The Law of Return considers every Jew a member of the Jewish "people", which predates the State of Israel. This results in both the unusual conception of complete equality between domestic-born and immigrant Jews, even before naturalisation of the latter, which "reverses the common hierarchy between a native citizen and a new immigrant" (Shachar, 2000: 396), and also in an even more pronounced difference between Jewish and non-Jewish immigrants to Israel. Kranz (this issue) is not concerned with immigrant Jews "returning" to Israel, but instead looks at the normative treatment of *non*-Jewish immigrant partners/spouses of Jewish Israeli citizens. They can only obtain a residency permit at the full discretion of the Ministry of the Interior, and this permit furthermore remains dependent on their continued partnership with the Israeli citizen. By taking into account the status of children born to non-Jewish foreign mothers, and Jewish Israeli fathers, the lack of civil marriage, and the normative value of family unity and parenthood, Kranz evaluates the particularly tight provisions on permanent residency and naturalisation accessible to spouses and non-married partners of Jewish Israelis, and thus analyses the self-understanding of the Israeli state (and probably nation, too) as Jewish.

Another state based on explicit ethnic exclusivity is Liberia. Its nationality law defines only those of "negro descent" as eligible for Liberian nationality, with the effect of ensuring enduring exclusion from the citizenry for large, and in no way marginal, parts of the immigrant population. This is outlined by Ludwig (this issue) with reference to the descendants of immigrants from Lebanon. Their parents arrived in Liberia from the late 19th century onwards, and as they were (and still are) classified as non-black, they cannot naturalize to become Liberian nationals. Even though born inside the country, their everyday rights are severely curtailed because their status as foreigners prevents them from buying land, among other restrictions. Ludwig concludes that not only was Liberia's national identity modelled around the freed African American slaves who founded the country in the mid-19th century, but that the racialized concept of African ancestry continues to plays a pivotal role in today's hegemonic understanding of who the Liberian state and society should include.

Mexico is included in this special issue as an example from the Americas, a region known for its long republican history (starting in late 18th or early 19th century), and its inclusive *jus soli* regime (i.e., membership of immigrants relies on territory, not ancestry). In Mexican nationality law, however, the border drawn symbolically between full-fledged insiders and the less privileged is located within the citizenry, as Hoyo (this issue) shows. He points to the many legal restrictions naturalized Mexicans have to face, including being barred from many governmental positions and "security-sensitive" occupations, such as becoming the crew member of a merchant vessel. Hoyo concludes that in order to understand why in Mexico the naturalized are not seen as "authentic Mexicans". His study must be both historiographic and take into account the specific context. The "Mexicans only" doctrine in many fields of domestic policy, and most of all where nationality is concerned, he sees as being related to the deeply entrenched ideology of Revolutionary Nationalism, installed by the ruling party PRI, which became almost interchangeable with the Mexican state in the course of its 70-year rule. The strict defense against any "foreign intervention" that the PRI called for was obviously directed against their overpowering neighbour, the USA. When taken into account, these two aspects – the unequal relations between Mexico and the USA, and the former's Revolutionary Nationalism – go a long way toward explaining much of the "protective" nationality policy in Mexico up to the present day.

The compilation of studies in this special issue constitutes an exemplary extension of existing publications on this matter, because it includes selective nationality regimes in new(er) countries of immigration, ranging from the "two-tier system" in Hong Kong and Singapore to "citizenship for sale" in Mauritius; the collection also includes "liberal classics" like Mexico, as well as cases of ethnic/racial/religious exclusivity like Liberia and Israel. The cases investigated in this special issue thus enable heuristic comparisons among them. To reach a genuinely global perspective means not to treat the Global South separately from global entanglements by confining ones interest to "authentic Southern" perspectives only – much less to "*the*" Southern perspective – as this would lead to an additional segregation, similar in consequence to the classic area-studies approach, and would bring with it the "danger of introducing gross generalisations and reinforcing stereotypes" (as remarked by Bakewell and Jónsson with regard to the study of "African migration", Bakewell & Jónsson, 2013: 478). But it is also necessary to let a wider variety of cases speak for themselves, and not to study them as mere deviations from a "global norm" (which is, in fact, if anything a *Northern* norm). This might produce fruitful discussions and possibly new theoretical insights from a genuinely global perspective.

Acknowledgements

The preparation of this special issue was made possible by funding through the Institutional Strategy of the University of Cologne within the German Excellence Initiative.

References

Aleinikoff, T. A., & Klusmeyer, D. B. (Eds.). (2000). *From migrants to citizens: Membership in a changing world*. Washington, D.C.: Carnegie Endowment for International Peace.

Anderson, B., Gibney, M. J., & Paoletti, E. (2011). Boundaries of belonging: deportation and the constitution and contestation of citizenship. *Citizenship Studies, 15*(5), 543–545.

Anderson, B., Gibney, M. J., & Paoletti, E. (Eds.). (2013). *Immigrants and Minorities, Politics and Policy. The Social, Political and Historical Contours of Deportation*. New York, NY: Springer.

Asis, M. M. B., & Battistella, G. (2012). Multicultural Realities and Membership: States, Migrations and Citizenship in Asia. In L. A. Eng, F. L. Collins, & Yeoh, Brenda S. A. (Eds.), *Migration and diversity in Asian contexts* (pp. 31–55). Singapore: Institute of Southeast Asian Studies.

Bakewell, O., & Jónsson, G. (2013). Theory and the Study of Migration in Africa. *Journal of intercultural studies, 34*(5).

Bashford, A. (2014). Immigration restriction: rethinking period and place from settler colonies to postcolonial nations. *Journal of Global History, 9*(01), 26–48.

Bauböck, R. (Ed.). (1994). *Public policy and social welfare17. From aliens to citizens: Redefining the status of immigrants in Europe*. Aldershot: Avebury.

Bauböck, R., Ersbøll, E., Groenendijk, K., & Waldrauch, H. (Eds.). (2006). *IMISCOE research. Acquisition and loss of nationality: Policies and trends in 15 European states*. Amsterdam: Amsterdam Univ. Press.

Bauböck, R., Perchinig, B., & Sievers, W. (Eds.). (2009). *IMISCOE research. Citizenship policies in the New Europe* (Expanded and updated ed.). Amsterdam: Amsterdam University Press.

Bloemraad, I. (2006). *Becoming a citizen: Incorporating immigrants and refugees in the United States and Canada*. Berkeley: Univ. of California Press.

Bloemraad, I., & Ueda, R. (2006). Naturalization and Nationality. In R. Ueda (Ed.), *Blackwell companions to American history: Vol. 15. A companion to American immigration* (pp. 36–57). Malden, Mass: Blackwell.

Brubaker, R. (1992). *Citizenship and Nationhood in France and Germany*. Cambridge/MA.

Brubaker, R. (2010). Migration, Membership, and the Modern Nation-State: Internal and External Dimensions of the Politics of Belonging. *Journal of Interdisciplinary History, 41*(1), 61–78.

Byrne, B. (2014). *Making citizens: Public rituals and personal journeys to citizenship*. Basingstoke: Palgrave Macmillan.

Castles, S., & Miller, M. J. (2009). *The age of migration: International population movements in the modern world* (4. ed.). New York: Guilford Press.

Chakrabarty, D. (2000). *Provincializing Europe: Postcolonial thought and historical difference. Princeton studies in culture/power/history*. Princeton, N.J: Princeton University Press.

Chatterjee, P. (1986). *Nationalist thought and the colonial world: A derivative discourse?* Delhi: Oxford Univ. Press.

Connell, R. (2011). Sociology for the whole world. *International Sociology, 26*(3), 288–291.

Crowley, J. (1999). The politics of belonging - some theoretical considerations. In A. Geddes & A. Favell (Eds.), *Contemporary trends in European social sciences. The politics of belonging. Migrants and minorities in contemporary Europe* (pp. 15–41). Aldershot: Ashgate.

Damsholt, T. (2008). Making Citizens: On the Genealogy of Citizenship Ceremonies. In P. Mouritsen (Ed.), *Constituting communities. Political solutions to cultural conflict* (pp. 53–72). Basingstoke: Palgrave Macmillan.

Dumbrava, C. (2014). *Nationality, citizenship and ethno-cultural belonging: Preferential membership policies in Europe. Palgrave studies in citizenship transitions*. Basingstoke: Palgrave Macmillan.

Dzankic, J. (2012). *The Pros and Cons of Ius Pecuniae: Investor citizenship in comparative perspective.* EUDO Citizenship Observatory (EUI Working Papers, 14). Retrieved from http://hdl.handle.net/1814/21476

Earnest, D. (2003). *Voting Rights for Resident Aliens: A Comparison of 25 Democracies: Paper presented at the annual meeting of the North Eastern Political Science Association.* Retrieved from http://www.allacademic.com/meta/p89774_index.html

Favell, A. (2006). The Nation-Centered Perspective. In M. Giugni & F. Passy (Eds.), *Program in migration and refugee studies. Dialogues on migration policy* (pp. 45–56). Lanham: Lexington Books.

FitzGerald, D. (2005). Nationality and Migration in Modern Mexico. *Journal of Ethnic and Migration Studies, 31*(1), 171–191.

Gibney, M. J. (2013). 'A Very Transcendental Power': Denaturalisation and the Liberalisation of Citizenship in the United Kingdom. *Political Studies, 61*(3), 637–655.

Glick Schiller, N. (2008). Transnationality. In D. Nugent & J. Vincent (Eds.), *A Companion to the Anthropology of Politics* (pp. 448–467). Malden, MA: Blackwell Pub.

Goodman, S. W. (2012). Fortifying Citizenship: Policy Strategies for Civic Integration in Western Europe. *World Politics, 64*(4), 659–698.

Gosewinkel, D. (2001). *Einbürgern und Ausschließen. Die Nationalisierung der Staatsangehörigkeit vom Deutschen Bund bis zur Bundesrepublik Deutschland.* Göttingen: Vandenhoeck & Ruprecht.

Hansen, R. (2009). The poverty of postnationalism: Citizenship, immigration, and the new Europe. *Theory & Society, 38*(1), 1–24.

Hassall, G. (1999). Citizenship in the Asia-Pacific: a Survey of Contemporary Issues. In A. Davidson & K. Weekley (Eds.), *Globalization and citizenship in the Asia-Pacific* (pp. 49–70). New York, N.Y: St. Martin's Press.

Hayduk, R. (2006). *Democracy for all: Restoring immigrant voting rights in the United States.* New York, NY: Routledge.

Howard, M. M. (2009). *The politics of citizenship in Europe.* Cambridge, New York: Cambridge University Press.

Huddleston, T. (2013). *The naturalisation procedure: measuring the ordinary obstacles and opportunities for immigrants to become citizens.* EUDO Citizenship Observatory (EUI RSCAS Policy Paper, 16). Retrieved from http://hdl.handle.net/1814/28122.

Huddleston, T. & Niessen, J. (2011). *Migrant Integration Policy Index (MIPEX) III.* Retrieved from http://www.mipex.eu/sites/default/files/downloads/migrant_integration_policy_index_mipexiii_2011.pdf.

Janoski, T. (2010). *The ironies of citizenship: Naturalization and integration in industrialized countries.* Cambridge: Cambridge Univ. Press.

Janoski, T. (2013). Micro- and macro-explanations of naturalization. In S. J. Gold & S. J. Nawyn (Eds.), *Routledge international handbook of migration studies* (pp. 380–395). London, New York: Routledge.

Joppke, C. (2010). *Citizenship and immigration.* Cambridge: Polity.

Kanstroom, D. (2012). *Aftermath: Deportation law and the new American diaspora.* Oxford, New York: Oxford University Press.

Ko, S. S. (Ed.). (1990). *Nationality and international law in Asian perspective.* Dordrecht, Boston, Norwell, MA, U.S.A.: M. Nijhoff.

Kostakopoulou, D. (2006). Thick, Thin and Thinner Patriotisms: Is This All There Is? *Oxford Journal of Legal Studies, 26*(1), 73–106.

Lee, C. J. (2011). Jus Soli and Jus Sanguinis in the Colonies: The Interwar Politics of Race, Culture, and Multiracial Legal Status in British Africa. *Law & History Review, 29*(2), 497.

Lewis, M. W., & Wigen, K. E. (1997). *The Myth of Continents: A Critique of Metageography.* Berkeley: University of California Press.

Low, C. C. (2013). Taiwanese and German Citizenship Reforms: Integration of Immigrants without Challenging the Status Quo, 1990–2000. *European Journal of East Asian Studies, 12*(2), 269–294.

Refsing, K. (2003). *In Japan, but not of Japan.* In C. Mackerras (Ed.), *Asia's transformations. Ethnicity in Asia* (pp. 48–63). London, New York: RoutledgeCurzon.

Shachar, A. (2000). Citizenship and Membership in the Israeli Polity. In T. A. Aleinikoff & D. B. Klusmeyer (Eds.), *From migrants to citizens. Membership in a changing world* (pp. 386–433). Washington, D.C.: Carnegie Endowment for International Peace.

Sievers, W. (2009). 'A call to kinship'? Citizenship and migration in the new Member States and the accession countries of the EU. In R. Bauböck, B. Perchinig, & W. Sievers (Eds.), *IMISCOE research. Citizenship policies in the New Europe* (pp. 439–457). Amsterdam: Amsterdam University Press.

Street, A. (2014). My Child Will Be a Citizen: Intergenerational Motives for Naturalization. *World Politics, 66*(2), 264–292.

Tønnesson, S., & Antlöv, H. (Eds.). (1996). *studies in Asian topics: Vol. 23. Asian forms of the nation.* Richmond, Surrey: Curzon Press.

van Fossen, A. (2007). Citizenship for Sale: Passports of Convenience from Pacific Island Tax Havens. *Commonwealth & Comparative Politics, 45*(2), 138–163.

van Oers, R., Ersbøll, E., & Kostakopoulou, D. (2010). Mapping the Redefinition of Belonging in Europe. In R. van Oers, E. Ersbøll, & D. Kostakopoulou (Eds.), *A Re-definition of Belonging? Language and integration tests in Europe* (pp. 307–331). Leiden: Nijhoff.

van Waas, L. (2014). A Comparative Analysis of Nationality Laws in the MENA Region. *SSRN Electronic Journal.* Retrieved from http://ssrn.com/ abstract=2493718.

Vink, M. P., & Bauböck, R. (2013). Citizenship configurations: Analysing the multiple purposes of citizenship regimes in Europe. *Comparative European Politics, 11*(5), 621–648.

Webb, A. K. (2015). Not an Immigrant Country? Non-Western Racism and the Duties of Global Citizenship. *Theoria: A Journal of Social & Political Theory, 62*(142), 1–25.

Weil, P. (2001). Access to citizenship: A comparison of twenty five nationality laws. In T. A. Aleinikoff & D. B. Klusmeyer (Eds.), *International migration publications. Citizenship today. Global perspectives and practices* (pp. 17–35). Washington, D.C: Carnegie Endowment for International Peace.

Weil, P. (2012). From conditional to secured and sovereign: The new strategic link between the citizen and the nation-state in a globalized world. *International Journal of Constitutional Law, 9*(3-4), 615–635.

Weil, P. (2013). *The sovereign citizen: Denaturalization and the origins of the American Republic.* Philadelphia, Pa.: Univ. of Pennsylvania Press.

Wimmer, A., & Glick Schiller, N. (2003). Methodological Nationalism, the Social Sciences, and the Study of Migration: An Essay in Historical Epistemology. *International Migration Review, 37*(3), 576–610.

Yuval-Davis, N. (2011). *The politics of belonging: Intersectional contestations.* Los Angeles: SAGE.

CHAPTER 23

Wrestling with 9/11: Immigrant Perceptions and Perceptions of Immigrants

Caroline Brettell

At 2:30 p.m. on September 11, 2001, an email from the President of the India Association of North Texas (IANT), located in Dallas, Texas, was distributed to all members of the organization. It announced a special candlelight vigil for the following evening at the India Association office to "show our support to the nation, condemn terrorists, and pray for the victims."

Approximately 200 people of Indian origin gathered at 7 p.m. on September 12. After the Pledge of Allegiance, the President-elect of the Association called for the Indian community to stand with the President of the United States and with their fellow Americans against the terrible act of international terrorism. In his remarks, the President of IANT described India as a place where people had learned to get along with one another despite their incredible diversity of languages and religions. This, he said, is what he hoped for the world. Representatives from various religious communities followed these two speakers, offering prayers appropriate to their respective faiths. Small candles were distributed and lit. When the prayers and candlelight vigil had concluded the President stated that he planned to fast until $25,000 was raised for the American Red Cross. Within 15 minutes about $30,000 had been pledged. A few weeks later, at a gathering in Thanksgiving Square, an ecumenical chapel in downtown Dallas, a check for $116,000 was presented to Congressman Martin Frost.

While some immigrants, like the Asian Indians who assembled the day after 9/11 to express their support for the victims and their sense of belonging to the United States, have been only mildly inconvenienced by the events of 9/11, others have had their lives torn apart. In another part of the Dallas metropolitan area, three weeks after 9/11, a gas station/convenience storeowner from the Indian State of Gujarat named Vasodev Patel (a Hindu) was hard at work. A man walked in, expressed anger at what had happened in New York City, and shot and killed Mr. Patel. His wife Alka and two children were left to pick up the pieces. Several years later Alka still struggles, not only to keep the store afloat, working 15 hours a day 7 days a week, but also to raise her children without a father.

Soon after 9/11, a research project to study new immigration into the Dallas-Fort Worth metropolitan area was launched.[1] A questionnaire, administered to 600

---

[1] The project, "Immigrants, Rights and Incorporation in a Suburban Metropolis", was funded by the Cultural Anthropology Program of the National Science Foundation (BCS 003938). Other co-principal investigators involved with the project are James F. Hollifield, Dennis Cordell, and Manuel Garcia y Griego. Any opinions, findings, and conclusions or recommendations expressed in this paper are those of the author and do not necessarily reflect the

immigrants across five different immigrant populations (Asian Indians, Vietnamese, Mexicans, Salvadorans, and Nigerians) between 2003 and 2005, included the following question: 'How has the attack on the World Trade Center on September 11, 2001 affected your position as an immigrant in the United States?' In this article I discuss some of the responses to this question. However, before addressing these data, I briefly review broader policy, behavioral, and attitudinal changes after 9/11 that have influenced the lives of US immigrants as well as shaped the debate on immigration reform during the spring and summer of 2006.

The Post 9/11 Immigrant Environment
In the years prior to the attacks of 9/11, the immigration debate primarily focused on the economic, fiscal, demographic, and cultural impact of the unprecedented level of immigration the United States has experienced in recent decades. While these issues will continue to be important, terrorism has now been added to the debate (Camarota 2002:44).

Several changes put into effect since 9/11 have affected the lives of immigrants in the United States. In the months immediately following the terrorist attack many thousands of undocumented workers, including individuals whose visas had expired, were rounded up, arrested, and deported. Increasingly, immigrant households in the U.S. are composed of individuals with different immigration and citizenship statuses and hence some families have been split apart as a result of some of these arrests and deportations. As borders have tightened many undocumented immigrants, largely Mexicans, have chosen not to take the risk of traveling to their home villages to visit their families because of the fear of not being able to reenter the US.

Perhaps better known is the policy implemented soon after 9/11 that required all adult males from specific, largely Muslim, countries to register at local immigration offices. While this action failed to turn up terrorists, it too led to the deportation of many individuals who were out of visa status for one reason or another. It has also resulted, according to a report issued by the Migration Policy Institute (2003), in the progressive alienation of US Arab and Muslim communities and the weakening, rather than strengthening, of the relationship between these immigrants and their adopted country. Attorney General John Ashcroft called for non-citizens, all 17.8 million of them, to report changes of address within ten days of their movement. If they failed to do so, they too would face deportation and/or prosecution. While almost impossible to implement, this policy has led to further discomfort among legal immigrants in the United States. In view of all these activities, many people have come to the conclusion that the war on terrorism has been transformed into a war on immigrants and on those seeking political asylum. In their report "Securing Our Borders" Little and Klarreich (2005) argue that immigrants have become scapegoats—which they always have been during times of economic crisis but which they have now become in a time of heightened security.

More generally, immigration laws are being enforced more aggressively. Audits

views of the National Science Foundation.

of places of work have increased to establish employer compliance on I-9 and H-1B visas. In several cities local police officers are engaged in a debate with immigration authorities about whether or not they should ask questions about immigration status when they arrest foreign nationals. The police have always argued that they do not want to enforce immigration laws because it might hamper their crime fighting efforts at the local level. People might be afraid to report crimes if they feel this will put them in jeopardy. Entry regulations have also been tightened. There are stricter background checks for visa applicants, fees have been raised, and the wait time for a visa is longer. The result has been a decline in the number of tourist and business visas issued.

Foreign students and refugees have also been impacted. Universities and schools have had to adopt tighter regulations. Between 2001 and 2003, the number of student visas declined by 26 percent. The number of refugees, particularly from countries like the Sudan and Somalia that have been linked to terrorism, has also declined (Orrenius 2003). In other words, immigration regulation in the post 9/11 world has affected all visa categories. This is in part a result of the realization that terrorists, even those who were involved in incidents prior to 9/11, have taken advantage of a host of visa categories for entry to the United States (Camarota 2002).

The 9/11 Commission's Final Report, released in July of 2004, includes several recommendations related to immigration. For example, it alludes to detectable false statements on visa applications as well as false statements made to broader officials. It refers to immigration laws that were violated once the perpetrators were in the US, including overstaying visas or not showing up at the schools that had issued them student visas. Among the recommendations in the report related to immigration were 1) the development of a more comprehensive screening system that might include biometric identifiers; 2) the integration of US border security; 3) more uniform standards for the issuance of birth certificates and drivers licenses; 4) addressing the illegal immigration issue; 5) bridging state and local law enforcement agencies into the mix on immigration control (National Commission on Terrorist Attacks Upon the United States 2004).

In late summer of 2005 two reports highlighting the connection between immigration and national security were released. One, titled "Immigration and Terrorism; Moving Beyond the 9/11 Staff Report on Terrorist Travel", was authored by Janice Kephart, counsel for the 9/11 Commission (Kephart 2005). Like the 2002 report cited above, it points to the widespread terrorist violations of immigration laws and calls for much stricter enforcement. The second, titled "Keeping Extremists Out: The History of Ideological Exclusion and the Need for Its Revival" (Edwards 2005), calls for the restoration of policies that would allow aliens to be excluded or deported for overt acts as well as for radical affiliations or advocacy. 'At every stage of American history,' the author writes, 'immigration has exposed this nation to ideological threats. We should learn from our long experience and once again err in favor of American security' (Edwards 2005: 26).

Given this climate and the connections that fill reports such as those just cited, it is no wonder that immigrants themselves, no matter what their status, feel particularly vulnerable. Indeed, after 9/11 naturalization requests increased. The Immigration and Naturalization Service (INS; now United States Citizenship and Immigration Services-USCIS) reported that during the first eight months of the 2002 fiscal year (which began in October of 2001) naturalization applications were 65 percent higher than in the previous year. In the single month of May of 2002 the number of applications was 121 percent higher than in the previous year. And yet despite the increase in applications the approval process has become much slower.

The vulnerability that immigrants feel is reinforced by national polls that demonstrate that the response of Americans to immigrants is mixed. A New Jersey poll released on July 4, 2002 (The Star-Ledger/Eagleton-Rutgers poll) showed that people had become more opposed to immigration as a result of 9/11.[2] But it also showed that while in the abstract respondents opposed current immigration policies and want it reduced, on a day-to-day basis they see no problem with individuals with whom they have contact in their own neighborhoods. In this survey 59 percent of New Jersey residents thought that current immigration levels should be decreased—and of these 24 percent thought it should be stopped entirely. Fifty-two percent said they were more opposed to immigration now (in 2002) than before the attacks while only 38 percent said that the attacks had no effect on their attitudes. Fifty-six percent of respondents recommended reducing immigration levels for Middle Easterners in particular, and 21 percent of these wanted Middle Eastern immigration stopped altogether. But when asked about the impact of recent immigration on local life, the majority saw very little effect. Nearly two-thirds stated that recent immigrants have not had much effect on job opportunities, crime, or the quality of life in general.

In a telephone survey conducted in DFW in the fall of 2004, we asked a series of questions about immigration. There were 500 foreign-born respondents and 500 native born respondents. Of the foreign born, 318 (63.6%) were from Mexico, 36 (7.2%) from India, 18 (3.6%) from China (excluding Hong Kong and Taiwan), 17 (3.4%) from El Salvador, and the rest (in totals of 11 down to 1) were from a range of countries (22.2%). The native born were asked if they considered themselves white, African-American, Hispanic or Latino, Asian American, or some other ethnic background. Of the 500 native-born respondents, 375 (75%) said they were white, 62 (12.4%) African American, 51 (10.2%) Hispanic or Latino, 5 (1%) Asian, and 6 (1.2 %) of some other ethnic background. One respondent declined to give his/her ethnicity. Respondents were asked to place their responses to the question on a scale from 1-5 with 1 indicating that the statement did not correspond at all with what they thought to 5 where it corresponded exactly to what they thought.

The responses from the foreign born are included in Table 1 and those for native-born in Table 2. Not surprisingly the native born expressed much more concern about or ambivalence toward immigration than did the foreign-born and yet the responses do not reflect a strong anti-immigrant sentiment. If one looks at

---

[2] This poll is available online under the Star-Ledger/Eagleton-Rutgers Poll, Eagleton Institute of Politics (http:// slerp. rutgers. edu). Clearly such polls are time sensitive. Polls taken in the spring of 2006 as immigration reform has heated up on Capitol Hill yield different responses.

the proportion who answered 4 or 5 to the questions (closer to the statement matching what they think 'exactly'), the native born recognize that immigrants contribute to the growth of the local economy (46.2%); they bring skills and talents to the city (50.6%); and they offer cheap labor (54.8%). Just under 50 percent also see immigrants strengthening American culture and only 23 percent leaned strongly toward the view that immigrants take more than they contribute. They did not perceive immigrants as contributing significantly to crime nor to the burden on public services. However, all this said, almost 41 percent of the native born expressed disagreement with the idea of admitting more legal immigrants in the coming years.

Table 1: Foreign Born (N=500) responses to questions on attitudes toward immigration (as a % of the total responses) (1=Not at All; 5=Exactly)

	1	2	3	4	5	No Opinion	Refused
Immigrants strengthen American Culture	6.8	8.4	20.2	19.2	36.8	7.8	0.8
Immigrants generally take more than they contribute to the American economy	49.2	13.6	14.6	7.0	9.6	5.2	0.8
In the next ten years, the government should admit more legal immigrants	5.8	7.2	18.8	16.2	43.4	7.8	0.8
There is a great deal of discrimination against immigrants in the US	8.2	11.6	16.6	16.6	42.4	3.6	1.0
The growth of the immigrant population in the DFW area is a good thing	2.6	3.4	19.2	22.2	48.2	3.8	0.6
Immigrants make the city's economy grow	1.4	3.4	13.4	19.6	60.2	1.4	0.6
Immigrants bring lots of skills and talents to the city	2.6	3.4	17.4	21.8	51.2	3.0	0.6
Immigrants bring lots of cheap, low-wage labor to the city	6.0	5.0	15.4	12.4	58.0	2.6	0.6
Immigrants are a burden on public services	42.2	21.0	17.2	7.4	6.4	5.0	0.8
Immigrants cause a lot of crime	29.6	29.6	22.2	7.0	6.0	4.6	1.0

(DFW Telephone Survey, Fall 2004)

This latter question, the question about the growth of the immigrant population in the DFW area being a good thing, and the question stating that immigrants make a city's economy grow generated the greatest disparities between the native born and the foreign born. Almost 60 percent of the foreign born supported the admission of more legal immigrants in the next ten years (compared with just under 30 percent of the native born). Over 70 percent of the foreign born (compared with only 37 percent of the native born) thought that the growth of immigration in DFW was a good thing. Close to 80 percent of the foreign born (compared with 46 percent of the native born) tended to agree that immigrants make the city's economy grow.

For immigrants themselves the reality of America has changed. While many of the interviewees in the DFW study shrugged off the question about 9/11, saying it had not affected them personally, there were others who acknowledged an impact, whether directly or indirectly, whether concrete or more elusive. Several noted a general suspicion of immigrants in the months immediately following 9/11, while others pointed to a specific impact on people from the Middle East, but not on them. Several commented that it had made travel more difficult. But there were responses that illustrate some common themes. It is to these that I now turn.

Table 2: Native born (N=500) responses to questions on attitudes toward immigration (as a % of the total responses; 1=Not at All; 5=Exactly)

	1	2	3	4	5	No Opinion	Refused
Immigrants strengthen American Culture	11.2	11.2	27.8	22.2	25.0	2.4	0.2
Immigrants generally take more than they contribute to the American economy	31.4	21.8	20.0	9.6	13.4	3.8	0.0
In the next ten years, the government should admit more legal immigrants	23.2	17.6	26.8	13.8	16.0	2.4	0.2
There is a great deal of discrimination against immigrants in the US	17.0	11.8	30.2	20.8	17.4	2.8	0.0
The growth of the immigrant population in the DFW area is a good thing	10.0	15.2	35.4	19.0	18.2	1.8	0.4
Immigrants make the city's economy grow	9.8	12.6	28.4	23.6	22,6	2.6	0.4
Immigrants bring lots of skills and talents to the city	8.0	10.2	28.6	30.0	20.6	2.2	0.4
Immigrants bring lots of cheap, low-wage labor to the city	7.0	8.6	26.6	23.8	31.0	2.6	0.4
Immigrants are a burden on public services	23.8	24.0	25.6	11.8	11.6	3.0	0.2
Immigrants cause a lot of crime	31.6	33.0	19.6	5.8	6.6	3.2	0.2

(DFW Telephone Survey, Fall 2004)

'It makes me feel that the country is not safe'

Many immigrants and refugees come to the U.S. looking for a way of life that is more peaceful and secure. 9/11 shattered some of these dreams of safe haven. As one Nigerian put it, "If the U.S. isn't secure, what place is secure?" A Salvadoran commented that she felt like she was back in El Salvador where she saw people being murdered. The feeling of being robbed of a sense of security was most strongly voiced by Vietnamese immigrants, many who came to the U.S. in the 1970s and 1980s to escape the harshness of the communist regime.

"I grew up in a war zone. The attack made me think about my childhood. But how could something like this happen here, in such a powerful country?

I can understand war and violence in a poor weak country like Vietnam. But why here in a powerful country like the U.S.?"

In the period immediately after the attack Asian Indians were particularly worried about their safety because they were not sure that Americans could distinguish them from Arabs or that they understood about their dress. Women chose not to wear their saris and salwar kameezs in public. Reported one female respondent: "It was scary; people were telling us not to wear Indian clothes to go out because people might hurt us. There were Indians who were killed. People also told us not to wear the red dot." A male respondent remembered going down to pick up the mail in the complex where he lived and someone had stuck up a notice saying 'foreigners go home'.

That was unsettling. But at the same time there was a tall man in the grocery store who said to me 'you are Indian, right?' I nodded and he said that he wanted to apologize ahead of time for all the people who would think me Middle Eastern.

Indian Muslims were especially distressed:

It has made it more difficult for me to come out a say that I am a Muslim. Sometimes I embrace the opportunity but I have to be careful. I have to explain to people that the people who did this are extremists, just like those who kill abortion doctors. They are doing crazy things and trying to justify it….. There are US people who think that Islam is a religion that tells people to commit suicide. It was much easier before 9/11. There was general discrimination but now it is targeted and there is this fear of outsiders and of people who look different.

This sentiment was also voiced by Nigerian Muslims, although several admitted that Americans could distinguish them from Arabs because they were decidedly African in appearance.

The second observation made by Indians was about terrorism more generally. They noted that they have lived with this kind of violence in their own country and now perhaps Americans would better understand what it means. But at the same time they acknowledged that they had come to the US to escape the terrorism with which they grew up.

It was a humbling thing but I was never afraid. The benefit is that terrorism is now a global issue. India has been dealing with terrorism for years and it was a local issue. But now that it has hit the US it has become global.

Another respondent offered some advice. "Terrorism comes from frustration so you have to work to help people, to create liberties, to change the structure. That is the way you will stop it." Even Nigerians commented on their familiarity with the oppression that breeds terrorism. "We grew up with that…Muslim fundamentalism is common in one part of our country."

'Now you need a good social security card!'

The second biggest concern among immigrants was the impact of 9/11 on the

US economy. Indeed this impact was probably heightened because of the prosperity of the 1990s—the higher you are, the harder you fall. Many Indians came to the area in the 1990s on H-1B visas to fuel the booming technology industries. But as the years after 9/11 progressed and the technology bubble burst many lost their jobs. Some had no alternative but to return to their home country. Others were simply left looking for work elsewhere. A Vietnamese respondent had this to say.

> The attack damaged the American economy and caused a recession. Because of this I lost my job with Nokia and we lost a lot of money, and can no longer afford health insurance. I have to act as the doctor for my family, because we cannot afford to go to the doctor. I blame the terrorists for hurting the American economy, and thereby hurting me and my family.

Salvadorans and Mexicans were particularly concerned about the impact on employment as well as on their ability to even find work because papers are now more carefully scrutinized. Said one Mexican: "The economy has deteriorated. Many people are left with no jobs. Before the towers fell you could find work anywhere. Now you have to have a good social security card." A Salvadoran woman reinforced this assessment. "Employment is down, factories are closing. After that day, my son lost a job working as an electrician when the company closed." Another Salvadoran noted that some jobs are now closed to non-US citizens. He said he had wanted to apply for a job installing security systems in the airport. He met all the qualifications but because he was not a citizen he could not have the job. A Mexican respondent who arrived after 9/11 observed that those who came before were able to find work. "When I arrived there was this check of documents. [They were] much more exacting (*mas requisitos*)." Many Mexicans felt that they were being viewed as and treated like terrorists.

Immigrants have aggressively entered the small business sector and they too have felt the economic impact of 9/11. In the year after 9/11, for example, those in the travel business whose revenues derive to a large extent from arranging travel for their countrymen to the homeland, witnessed a sharp decline in business which only gradually picked up as the distance from that day became longer. A Salvadoran woman who owns a salon said that her business had declined, particularly since the start of the war in Iraq. She noted that many of her Mexican friends and clients have returned to their country for the duration. A Mexican contractor said that after 9/11 his building contracts dwindled. Before that date he had fifteen workers and at the time of the interview he could only afford to employ six. Asian Indian entrepreneurs expressed similar concerns. One reported having to lay off five employees. After 9/11, he observed, people just stopped spending. A Nigerian entrepreneur reported that his import/export business has been all but impossible. "I cannot tell you how long it takes to get the simplest shipments like cassava into the country. They check every little thing."

'I felt prouder to be an American'; and yet!

In their effort to raise funds for the American Red Cross the Indians in North Texas were trying to demonstrate their embrace of the United States and their patriotism. Other immigrants also commented that the events of 9/11 had stirred powerful feelings of identifying with America. One Vietnamese respondent who had served in the South Vietnamese army had this to say:

> The attack made me very angry, nationalistic, and patriotic. I wanted to get back in my fighter and go attack the terrorists. I even called the USAF and volunteered to fight, but they said I was too old. Americans have a very short memory. Soon they will forget about the attack, but Al Qaeda has a long memory. They will strike again.

Another observed:

> The people who did this are crazy fanatics. The have no morals. The attack made me more patriotic and made me want to support the government. We must be more attentive to national security. There is an old Vietnamese proverb that says--It is too late to close the gates (or make a fence) when the cows already have gotten out.

A Mexican immigrant said: "I always felt I was a Mexican. I was never patriotic toward the US. I would not put my hand on my heart when hearing the National Anthem. Seeing the response of others after 9/11 ignited a patriotism that I did not feel before." A Salvadoran said that 9/11 affected "his sense of belonging in the society." He reported feeling "more unified with other Americans." And a Nigerian put it this way: "The attack has not affected me as an immigrant, but as an American. I wondered what did I do for people to attack me like this? What should I be doing differently?"

> Others noted that the events of 9/11 prompted them to become a citizen and thereby express loyalty to the United States. Some expressed concern about the openness of the United States. "I cried," said one Asian Indian woman.

> I just thought about the goodness of this country. I do not want to see it happen again. This is a great nation but it has had troubles because of its goodness and leniency. Perhaps there would not have been this trouble if the US had not let so many people in.

And yet there were those who readily criticized some of the policies of the US and viewed 9/11 as a wake-up call for Americans who choose to ignore the rest of the world. "There are things to be critical about," commented one Indian male.

> The US government supported the overthrow of Allende in 1973 and a lot of people were massacred and there was no complaint. The US needs to see things from a global perspective. This is not to say that what happened on 9/11 was not horrible but Americans are so individualistic in their perception. They are also misinformed. There is not all this anti-Americanism out there. The actions are not the entire Muslim world. It is just some people using religion as a pedestal for politics.

In other words, some respondents expressed grave concerns about how 9/11 has distorted the American perception of Islam. Others put the event into a more global perspective. For example, one Vietnamese respondent said that although he feels sorry for those who lost their lives and for the families (he had made a contribution to the 9/11 fund) he nevertheless thought that the US had overreacted. "Look at what happened in Vietnam, where many more lives (millions) were lost. This war in Vietnam was a much greater tragedy for the people of Vietnam." A Nigerian noted that while immigrants feel sorry about the people who died and about the attack, they also recognize that the US has some culpability. "If you keep imposing selfish policies on the world, then what else can you expect?"

'There is a certain suspicion of immigrants'

By far the greatest concern was about the impact on immigration itself—the tightening of regulations that has affected all visa categories. It is harder to enter as a student, something that the Vietnamese are increasingly trying to do and that Indians and Nigerians have been doing for some time. It is harder to sponsor family members—the delays are exceedingly long. Said one Vietnamese respondent, "My mother tried to sponsor my brother to come here. It's been five years of paperwork and we still don't know when it will happen - especially now." Others have observed that it is harder for their relatives to get a tourist visa to attend a wedding in this country. A Nigerian said that his family has been refused visas every time they have applied. "There is a general mistrust of foreigners. That incident has ruined people's lives."

An Indian student who applied to come to the US soon after 9/11 reported the following experience.

I got a US visa reject on my first attempt to come here to study. But I was determined to come to US, so I applied for the second time, but still got rejected. Then I applied for the third time and thought this would be my last attempt to do so. …..I was called for an interview and then they gave me the visa. I am still shocked as to why I got the visa rejected on the first two occasions. I had everything proper. But then I thought it might be due to September 11.

A Nigerian student reported that now at the end of each year he has to have documents confirmed and signed by university officials. If he leaves the state, he must inform officials of his whereabouts. There is a lot of trouble, he said, if he does not tell people he has changed his address or where he is going.

Some Hispanics noted how the events of 9/11 had put a halt on some changes in immigration legislation that were progressing—specifically the talks between George W. Bush and Vicente Fox about undocumented workers that were initiated early in 2001. Said one Mexican, "I had hopes that we would arrive at a more just immigration policy, but due to the attacks it has been delayed." Another said, "Bush abandoned the promises of amnesty that he had made and this has created disillusion among immigrants." Clearly these issues were put back on the table in the spring of 2006 and Hispanics across the country, legal and undocumented, responded with a loud voice. But it took five years for the US government to return to the discussion.

Some Salvadorans noted that the opportunities available to immigrants became more limited because both laws and attitudes had changed. One respondent said that this had particularly affected illegal immigrants. Indeed many noted that crossing the border takes more time and that documents are more carefully scrutinized. Many Mexicans said that they were not even trying to travel to Mexico because they feared not being able to return to the US. Said one Mexican, "Nothing has changed for me, but for my wife yes. She is undocumented and cannot return to Mexico without the risk of having complications to return to this country."

Respondents across all groups recognized that the attitudes toward immigrants/foreigners had changed, with heightened discrimination "against brown and black people." A Nigerian respondent commented, "The September 11th attack affected all foreigners. People no longer trust foreigners and we have no privacy. The government watches us all the time." A Salvadoran respondent observed that 9/11 has affected people from the Middle East the most, but also Latinos. "People are now more suspicious of immigrants, who are viewed as possible terrorists." Another Salvadoran observed that "People look at you differently, thinking that because you are an immigrant you might also be something else." An Indian respondent noted that he was most afraid of hate crime. "Whenever you are a minority somewhere you are blamed for things that go wrong." Several noted that their rights were being limited and some commented that they had moved forward toward citizenship because they feared the anti-immigrant hostility.

Conclusion

Several years have passed since the events of 9/11, 2001. Most people, native and foreign born, have stored the horrors of that day deep in their memory and do not confront it on a daily basis as they did in the immediate aftermath. But it is not entirely forgotten for it marks a political and economic turning point for the United States. As Mattingly, Lawlor and Jacobs-Huey (2002:743) have argued, the September 11 tragedy is "an astonishing and unthinkable breach....In public discourse and for many Americans personally, it has split time into a "before" and "after." '

For immigrants in particular the country changed, both as it was and is imagined, and as it is lived. Immigration reform is back on the table but the debate is not only about numbers (how to solve the problem of the large pool of undocumented workers), but also very much about political and economic security. As recent reports indicate, it is also about national belonging, rights, and citizenship—all issues of deep concern to the foreign born who, no matter where they originate from, may feel a little less sure about their future in the so-called nation of immigrants.

References

Camarota, Steven (2002) 'The Open Door: How Militant Islamic Terrorists Entered and Remained in the United States, 1993-2001.' Washington, DC: Center for Immigration Studies (www.cis.org/articles/2002/Paper21/terrorism2.html).

Edwards, James R. Jr. (2005) 'Keeping Extremists Out: The History of Exclusion and the Need for Its Revival.' Washington, DC: Center for Immigration Studies (www. cis. org/ articles/ 2005/ back1005.html).

Kephart, Janice (2005) 'Immigration benefits and Terrorism: Moving Beyond the 9/11 Staff Report on Terrorist

Travel.' Washington, DC: Center for Immigration Studies.

Little, Cheryl and Kathie Klarreich (2005) 'Securing Our Borders: Post-9/11 Scapegoating of Immigrants.' Miami: Florida Immigrant Advocacy Center.

Mattingly, Cheryl, Mary Lawlor, and Lanita Jacobs-Huey (2002) 'Narrating September 11: Race, Gender, and the Play of Cultural Identities,' *American Anthropologist* 104: 743-753.

Migration Policy Institute (2003) 'America's Challenge: Domestic Security, Civil Liberties and National Unity after September 11.' http://www.migrationpolicy.org.

National Commission on Terrorist Attacks Upon the United States (2004) *The 9-11 Commission Report.* Washington, DC: Government Printing Office.

Orrenius, Pia (2003) 'U.S. Immigration and Economic Growth: Putting Policy on Hold,' *Southwest Economy* 6:1-9.

PART 7: TURKEY'S MIGRATION EXPERIENCE

Essential Reading

Yazgan, P., Utku, D. E., & Sirkeci, I. (2015). Syrian crisis and migration. *Migration Letters*, 12(3), 181-192.

Yüceşahin, M. M., & Sirkeci, I. (2017). Demographic gaps between Syrian and the European populations: What do they suggest. *Border Crossing*, 7(2), 207-230.

Sirkeci, I., & Esipova, N. (2013). Turkish migration in Europe and desire to migrate to and from Turkey. *Border Crossing*, 3(1), 1-13.

Further Readings

Akkoyunlu, S. (2012). Intervening opportunities and competing migrants in Turkish migration to Germany, 1969-2008. *Migration Letters*, 9(2), 155-175.

Altintop, N. (2014). Barriers versus promotion: Culturally sensitive healthcare for elderly Turkish migrants in Austria and Germany. *Border Crossing*, 4(1-2), 41-46.

Atac, I. (2014). Determining Turkish migration to Austria The role of migration policy. *Migration Letters*, 11(3), 275-287.

Geraci, A. (2020). "Out of Sight, Out Of Mind". Managing Migration Flows With Turkey as a "Safe Third Country"?. In *Current Challenges in Migration Policy and Law* (pp. 91-104). Transnational Press London.

Glazar, O. (2014). Turkish migration in Europe: EU accession and migration flows. *Migration Letters*, 11(2), 245-257.

Pötzschke, S. (2015). Mobilities of Turkish migrants in Europe. In *Turkish Migration, Identity and Integration* (pp. 11-21). Edited by Ibrahim Sirkeci, Betül Dilara Şeker and Ali Çağlar. Transnational Press London.

Sievers, W., Atac, I., & Schnell, P. (2014). Turkish migrants and their descendants in Austria Patterns of exclusion and individual and political responses.

Sirkeci, I., Cohen, J. H., & Yazgan, P. (2012). Turkish culture of migration: Flows between Turkey and Germany, socio-economic development and conflict. *Migration Letters*, 9(1), 33-46.

CHAPTER 24

Syrian Crisis and Migration

Pinar Yazgan, Deniz Eroglu Utku, Ibrahim Sirkeci

Introduction

In this issue, we aimed to shed some light on the Syrian refugee crisis which seems to shake European common policy on migration and asylum. However, it seems focus is still on raising walls, strengthening borders, and futile categorisations of movers as 'refugees' and 'economic migrants'. As well put in a recent interview, "managing international migration is not a matter of controlling borders; it is a question of transnational peace" (Bardakci, 2015). People will continue fleeing the environments where they feel insecure and Europe will continue to face large influxes from neighbouring countries in trouble.

The 2015 summer of tragedy is about to turn into a nightmare as we approach to winter while conflict in Syria continues and more and more Syrians try to reach Europe. Since mid-Summer, there has been a surge in number of refugees arriving in Europe, mostly through unauthorized channels and the death toll on Turkish and Greek shores reached drastic levels. Only after the body of Aylan Kurdi, a small Kurdish child from Syria, found on a beach in Bodrum, a popular tourism destination, ordinary people and governments in Europe began discussing and offering help, albeit inadequate as yet. The common question is why now so many Syrians are desperately leaving the region, mostly through and from Turkey? How many more "refugees" will come to Europe? Are these "refugees" or "economic migrants"?

Let's begin with the last question: First of all, in our conflict driven culture of migration model (Sirkeci, 2009; Cohen and Sirkeci, 2011; Sirkeci and Cohen, 2016), all human mobility is down to some kind of a conflict. Conflict is defined in a very broad sense which includes latent tensions and disagreements on the one end and goes to armed and violent clashes (e.g. wars) on the other. This is to say, migration is initiated by discomforts, difficulties, restrictions, clashes, and finally violence and wars at the country of origin. People only decide to move when they see that given conflict as a threat, an environment of insecurity, which is unmanageable. This also allows us to factor in potential conflicts arise as people move from one place to another, including the transit areas. Thus migration changes in response to these new challenges *en route* and in destinations. This is the dynamic nature of human mobility, which can be helpful to understand why suddenly so many Syrians are also desperate to leave Turkey, a country welcomed them in millions in the first place.

The second question about refugee versus economic migrant is utterly unhelpful. The difference between a refugee and an economic migrant is "imagined". In fact, most economic migrants have some story of difficulty driving them to other countries whilst all refugees have an obvious economic cause along with the immediate threat they are escaping from. Therefore countries or political parties trying to address the current crisis by sifting through the registration documents and trying to categorize people as refugees and not so refugees are in a futile play. This futile play is what we have seen over and over again. People move away from difficulties and once this experience of movement/migration is established, accumulated over time, a culture of migration emerges and that is what leads continuous migration from certain parts of the world even after the root causes have disappeared. There are hundreds of studies, qualitatively showing that there are almost always multiple motivations for migration. More to the point, these motivations may change over the course of the move as people move spatially and over time. For example, economic motivations may become secondary when movers face extreme discrimination in a country or a very positive welcome by a tiny and poor country may not be enough when there are no means to survive. Therefore, these people must be recognized as migrants who perceive greater risks and dangers at home. The response should cover improving economic, political, and cultural wellbeing. Mending just one aspect will not settle the issue.

Nevertheless, the root causes in Syria are unlikely to disappear soon. Long before the current violence, this was a country of multifaceted problems: unemployment, income inequality, suppression of minorities, suppression of opposition is just a few issues to name. If one wants economic drivers for migration, the average GDP per capita in Syria has been about a third of −or less- that is in Turkey, and about a tenth of the averages in most European countries. This means even without the current violence, there were adequate reasons for many Syrians to leave. The violence is perhaps providing an opportunity framework to facilitate the process. We should not also forget that the conflict migration is not a Syrian problem, it is a wide spread issue and the responses to this must be transnational and comprehensive in nature. We mean, offering more blankets and tents here and there will only sooth the upset of the giver but will not alleviate the much deeper issues countries like Syria are facing. Therefore, any effort to manage migration has to focus on securing livelihoods for people in their home countries. Syrian migration will continue for the foreseeable future just like Iraqi emigration and Afghan emigration continues; after a while it may slow down but Europe must accept to live with sizeable Syrian immigrant communities from now on. If there is no settlement about the crisis in Syria these outflows will remain to be strong for a long while.

The first question is critical and more investigation is needed to answer fully. For instance, why so many Syrians are desperate to leave Turkey now? Syrian refugees have been coming to Turkey in large numbers since the early 2011. By mid-2014, estimations had already shown the number of Syrians in the country were well over 1.6 million officially and over 2 million unofficially. What did change? The official numbers reached 2 million since then and anecdotal evidence is there that some local conflicts between Syrians and natives arose. Germany's announcement to admit half a million Syrians per year is clearly an incentive, but there were already a large number of Syrians leaving Turkey long before. One question comes to mind is the potential impact of the agreement signed between Turkey and the EU on 16 December 2013 on "the readmission of persons residing without authorization"[1] which is ratified by Turkey on 25th June 2014. When signed, it was expected that the agreement is fully implemented in three years. That means in 2016, this agreement may come into force fully. What would be the implication for so many Syrians as well as others who reaches Europe through Turkey? Article 4, paragraph 1(c) of the agreement states: [Turkey shall readmit … such persons who] "illegally and directly entered the territory of the Member States after having stayed on, or transited through, the territory of Turkey". We are not sure, of course, if this is a widely known fact among Syrian movers who reside in Turkey. However, migration literature offers enough accounts on myths of migration referring to the ways in which people make decisions to move based on hearsay – often good stories relayed by past movers. Thus, we believe if a hint of the facts about this agreement reached to Syrian communities, a reaction would be in order. Yet, the question remains: Do Syrians fear of being sent back if they delay their onward moves any further as we approach to 2016, the year of implementation? Could this be one of the reasons behind the 2015 upsurge in desperate efforts risking so many lives to reach European Union territories? These are the two questions worth investigating further to understand the recent peak of the European crisis in dealing with a truly transnational phenomenon.

The crisis

Syrian crisis was not expected and began to produce refugees in April 2011. Now 4 years on, there are estimated to be over 6 million displaced about two thirds of whom headed abroad, most arrived in neighbouring countries. Today, the UNHCR reports 2.1 million registered Syrians in Egypt, Iraq, Jordan and Lebanon, more than 24,000 Syrian refugees registered in North Africa and 1.95 million registered Syrians in Turkey (http://data.unhcr.org, 06.09.2015). In order to understand the whole picture, we also need to consider Syrian refugees who cannot able to register to the officials and/or try irregular ways to stay in other countries. This number is not stable as Syrians continue to stream into different countries.

Since the environment of human insecurity[2] in Syria gives no signs to change in the foreseeable future, it seems that large-scale refugee movements from this country will continue. Thus, Syrian's intensifying refugee crisis together with human tragedies in the Mediterranean Sea diverted public as well policy makers' attention to the subject. Particularly, policy makers whose main focus on possible impacts of refugees on their country became to discuss humanitarian aspect of the topic and they also emphasised the importance of a collective responsibility in the field.

Migration is not a popular or pretty topic. It is easy to cry in front of your TV set when witnessing these tragedies. It is harder to stand up and take responsibility. What we need now is the collective courage to follow through

---

[1] For the full text of the agreement see: http://gocdergisi.com/kaynak/.
[2] Environment of insecurity is defined and discussed in (Sirkeci, 2006)

with concrete action on words that will otherwise ring empty[3]

The world's attention turned to Syrian crisis and the refugee question caused by the proxy war in the Syria very recently. However, Syrian migration is not a new phenomenon. The difference is the volume and transnational effect of Syrians today is particularly high. Barrout (2008) conveys that the number of emigrants along with the relatives who left the country before 1922 were around 500,000 while this number increase to 4,180,444 by 2007 (as cited in Mehchy and Mahadi Doko, 2010:2). The Syrian refugees today already reached half of these numbers.

Both Middle East countries and countries outside of this region received considerable number of immigrants from Syria in different   time   periods (Mehchy and Mahadi Doko, 2011; Chalcraft, 2009; Gualteri, 2004; Hourani and Shedadi, 1992). Political environment of Syria has long motivated Syrians to move other countries as they felt political oppression and insecurity (Beitin, 2012; Fargues and Fandrich, 2012). This country has been unstable; it has experienced chain military coups from the very beginning of its foundation. Syria experienced more than 20 military interventions over the following years of the first coup d'état happening in 1949 (Beshara, 2013:21).

In addition to political turbulence, economic motivations were also strong to pave the way for migration flows from Syria. Until the 1960s and 1970s, emigration from Arab countries was mainly to Europe and the USA (Mehchy and Mahadi Doko, 2011). In addition to this, Lebanon was a popular destination country for Syrians. Workers preferred this country because of the visa convenience for physical closeness of the country (Winckler, 1997:109). Intra-regional migration trend intensified in the second half of the 1970s as job opportunities in the oil producing countries of the Middle East increased (Winckler, 1997). Lebanon still received large numbers of Syrian workers as there were labour shortage resulted by civil war (1975-1989) (MPC Team, 2013), but Gulf countries appeared as new attractive destinations for the Syrian economic immigrants. As a result of this trend, remittance became an important part of Syrian economy. According to the Syrian government source, this country received two billion dollars remittance from expatriate Syrians in 2007 (Seeberg, 2012:10).

Until 2011, the literature mainly emphasised economic consideration motivated emigration from Syria. However, 2011 has been a turning point year for Syria as both volume and nature of migration from this country changed dramatically. Following popular uprisings against dictatorships in several Arab countries, many Syrians poured into the streets to protest Bashar al-Assad government. Street protests evolved into a civil war that would cause an enormous refugee influx later on.

As the number of Syrians seeking asylum in neighbouring countries as well as in Europe increases, issues related to this topic have become more diverse and complicated. Currently, Syrian question is not only a matter of foreign policy for

---

[3] European Commision Press Release, 06 August 2015. http://europa.eu/rapid/press-release_STATEMENT-15-5480_en.htm

the states; the future of Syrian refugees is also on top of the agenda.

While the world has been witnessing 'the worst refugee crisis since World War II' (Amnesty International, 2015), somewhat surprisingly there is limited literature on Syrian refugee crisis. Rather than academic studies empirically focusing on the issue, it is more common to see field works conducted by regional and international human rights organisations and the specialized agencies of national and international organisations (e.g. Amnesty International, 2014, 2015; IRD&UNHCR Report, 2013; Ajluni and Kawar, 2014; International Crisis Report, 2014).

When we examine at the studies and the reports, much focuses on the situation of Syrians in host countries and policy responses, the economic impact of refugees on host areas and the access of rights in these places .They mainly concentrate on three countries that receive the largest numbers of refugees: Turkey, Lebanon and Jordan.

The first wave of studies descriptively reveals the issue, policy responses of host countries to Syrians and public attitudes towards their new neighbours (Naufal, 2012; Özden, 2013; Dinçer et.al. 2013; Refaat, 2013; Döner et al., 2013; Thorleifsson, 2014; Achilli 2015). While they inform the situation in the camps -as long as they can have access and collect data-, it is also possible to sense the relation between the non-camp refugees and local people. In addition to this, some of them underline the reluctance of states to grant definite status to those have fled the Syrian conflict and complicated results of this policy. (Özden 2013; Aranki and Kalis 2014).

As the duration and cost of Syrians in host countries increase, scholars diverted their attention to investigate the impact of Syrians on the countries in political, social and economic terms (Al, Kilani, 2014; Orsam, 2015; Berti, 2015; Stave and Hillesund, 2015; Akgündüz et al., 2015). While the impact studies claim to approach from the social and political aspects of refugee question, much focus is placed on the financial cost of refugee hosting. In this regard, the importance of international cooperation and burden sharing/responsibility sharing initiatives are emphasised as a remedy to deal with the question (see Kirisci, 2014; Bidinger et al., 2014).

In addition to these groups, another wave of research conducts specific sectorial analysis of rights of Syrian refugees. The right of education (Christophersen, 2015; Ahmadzadeh et al., 2014; Education Sector Working Group, 2015), healthcare (Murshidi et al., 2013; El Khatib et al., 2013) and the right of work (ILO, 2015; Bidinger, 2015) are important areas which Syrians face obstacles to access in the countries they seek international protection. These studies try to attract attention on these fundamental rights.

Besides neighbouring countries, studies that scrutinise European countries began to appear as the number of Syrians aiming to reach these countries increase. While these studies investigate the responses and practices of European countries, they also suggest the European countries to take more responsibility in terms of providing reception and protection facilities and sharing burden of other host countries (Miller and Orchard, 2014; Fargues, 2014). More studies discussing the policy responses of European countries towards Syrian refugees and situation of these people in Europe's refugee-hosting countries are expected since there has been visible awakening in these countries after publication of drowned Syrian boy Aylan Kurdi's devastating picture.

Although analytical reports have been relatively bourgeoning regarding Syrian refugees in host countries, it is more difficult to find those endeavours for non-Syrian refugees. However, more than 5 hundred Palestinian refugees that have been living in 12 refugee camps in Syria found themselves in the middle of another conflict when the civil war broke out in 2011 (UNRWA, 2015:2). Once again, we see different organisations' regional reports on showing vulnerable position of Palestinians from Syria in new host countries (ANERA Report, 2013; European Commission, 2015). In addition to these reports, some studies explore that the situation of Palestinians fleeing Syria conflict is even worse than citizens of Syrians as they cannot have rights that Syrians can (White, 2013; Morrison, 2014). Therefore these studies undercover case of the Palestinians from Syria and that shows particular importance of investigating this.

As the discussion above illustrates, Syrian refugee issue is related to variety of areas, which are still in need of a deep analysis on conflict and migration nexus, humanitarian protection, refugee burden sharing, mass influxes and public opinion formation, refugee health care and refugee integration support with different aspects. The main reason for this is it is a dynamic process therefor the situation and legal status of Syrians in host countries change constantly. Also, attitudes towards the case keep changing. Spreading refugee tragedies through media has pushed the policy makers' attention to this subject although they opt for closing their eyes for a long time. Public opinion towards Syrian refugees has become a salient topic as the length of their stay in the countries extend. Social and cultural dimensions of refugee hosting is yet left untouched in the literature therefore more empirical research is required to analyse the possible different impacts of refugees.

Taken all together, in this special issue dealing with Syrian crisis and its impact on migration, we aim to approach the subject from variety of angles. In this regard, not only state policies and priorities are illustrated, but also rights and lives of Syrians in host societies are critically discussed. By doing so, we try to open an academic discussion that questions 'the future impact of the Syrian crisis on the scope and scale of this human mobility'.

References

Achilli, L. (2015). Syrian Refugees in Jordan a Reality Check Policy brief. Migration Policy Centre, EUI.

Ahmadzadeh, H., M. Çorabatır, J.A. Husseini, L. Hashem and S. Wahby (2014). Ensuring quality education for young refugees from Syria. Refugee Studies Centre. University of Oxford.

Ajluni, S. and Mary K. (2014). The impact of the Syrian Refugee Crisis on the Labour Market in Jordan. International Labour Organisation Regional Office for the Arab States. http://www.ilo.org/wcmsp5/groups/public/---arabstates/---ro-beirut/documents/publication/wcms_242021.pdf (access: 05.07.2015).

Akgündüz, Y.E et al. (2015). The Impact of Refugee Crises on Host Labor Markets: The Case of the Syrian Refugee Crisis in Turkey. *IZA Discussion Papers*, No: 8841.

Al-Kilani, S. (2014). A duty and a burden on Jordan. *Forced Migration Review*. 47: 30-31.

Amnesty International (2014). Left Out in the Cold: Syrian refugees abandoned by the international community http://www.amnesty.eu/content/assets/Reports/Left_Out_in_the_Cold_Syrian_Refugees_Abandoned_by_the_International_Community_final_formatted_version.pdf (access: 19.10.2015).

Amnesty International (2015). The Global refugee Crisis. A conspiracy of Neglect. http://www.amnestyusa.org/sites/default/files/p4575_global_refugee_crisis_syria.pdf (19.09.2015).

Amnesty International (2015). World leaders' neglect of refugees condemns millions to death and despair https://www.amnesty.org/en/latest/news/2015/06/world-leaders-neglect-of-refugees-condemns-millions-to-death-and-despair/ (access : 15.09.2015).

ANERA Report (2013). Palestinian Refugees from Syria in Lebanon. Volume:4. http://www.anera.org/wp-content/uploads/2013/04/PalestinianRefugees FromSyriainLebanon.pdf (access: 18.09.2015).

Bardakci, S. (2015, 26 August). Ibrahim Sirkeci interview: "Bu göçün artıları olabilir", *Al Jazeera Turkish*. Available at: http://www.aljazeera.com.tr/haber/bu-gocun-artilari-olabilir (Accessed 1 Sept. 2015).

Barrout, J. (2008). *External Migration in Syria* (in Arabic)

Beitin, B. K. (2012). Syrian Self-Initiated Expatriates: Emotional Connections from Abroad. International Migration, 50(6), 1-17.

Berti, B. (2015). The Syrian Refugee Crisis: Regional and Human Security Implications. *Strategic Assessment* 17(4):41-53.

Beshara, A. (2013). *Lebanon: The Politics of Frustration - The Failed Coup of 1961*. Routledge, London.

Bidinger, S., A. Lang, D. Hites, Y. Kuzmova, E. Noureddine, S. Akram (2015). Protecting Syrian Refugees: Laws, Policies and Global Responsibility-Sharing. Boston University School of Law https://www.bu.edu/law/central/jd/programs/clinics/international-human-rights/documents/FINAL FullReport.pdf (accessed: 18.09.2015).

Bidinger, S. (2015). Syrian Refugees and the Right to Work: Developing Temporary Protection in Turkey. http://www.bu.edu/ilj/files/2015/01/Bidinger-Syrian-Refugees-and-the-Right-to-Work.pdf (access: 17.09.2015).

Chalcraft, J. (2009). *The invisible cage: Syrian migrant workers in Lebanon*. Stanford University Press.

Christophersen, M. (2015). Securing Education for Syrian Refugees in Jordan. International peace Institute. http://www.ipinst.org/wp-content/uploads/ 2015/05/IPI-E-pub-Securing-Education-for-Syrian-Refugees.pdf (access:17.09.2015).

Cohen, J., and Sirkeci, I. (2011). *Cultures of Migration, the Global Nature of Contemporary Mobility*. University of Texas Press, Austin, USA.

Dalia A. and Olivia K. (2014). Limited legal status for refugees from Syria in Lebanon. *Journal Forced Migration Review*. Issue 47. Pages 17- 18.

Dinçer, O. B., V. Federici, E. Ferris, S. Karaca, K. Kirişci and E. Özmenek Çarmıklı. (2013). Suriyeli Mülteciler Krizi ve Sonu Gelmeyen Misafirlik. Brooking Enstitüte and USAK

Döner, P., A. Özkara, R. Kahveci (2013). Syrian refugees in Turkey: Numbers and emotions. *The Lancet*. 382(9894): 764.

Education Sector Working Group (2015). Access to Education For Syrian Refugee Children and Youth in Jordan Host Communities.

El-Khatib, Z., D. Scales, J. Vearey, B. C. Forsberg (2013). Syrian refugees, between rocky crisis in Syria and hard inaccessibility to healthcare services in Lebanon and Jordan. *Conflict and Health*, 7:18.

European Commision Press Release, (06 August 2015). http://europa.eu/ rapid/press-release_STATEMENT-15-5480_en.htm (access: 02.09.2015).

European Commission 2015. Lebanon Syria Crisis. http://ec.europa.eu/echo /files/aid/countries/factsheets /lebanon_ syrian_crisis_en.pdf (access :15.07.2015).

Fargues, P. & C. Fandrich (2012). Migration after the Arab Spring, MPC. Research. 2012/9.

Fargues, P. (2014). Europe must take on its share of the Syrian refugee burden, but how? Migration Policy Centre; Policy Briefs; 2014/01.

Gavin, D. W. (2013). Conflict in Syria Compounds Vulnerability of Palestine Refugees, *Forced Migration Review*, no. 44 (September 2013): 79.

Gualtieri, S. (2004). Gendering the Chain Migration Thesis: Women and Syrian Transatlantic Migration, 1878-1924. *Comparative Studies of South Asia, Africa and the Middle East*, 24(1): 67-78.

Hourani A., N. Shehadi (Eds.) (1992). *The Lebanese in the world a century of emigration* London: Centre for Lebanese Studies.

ILO: International Labour Organisation (2015). Access to work for Syrian refugees in Jordan: A discussion paper on labour and refugee laws and policies. International Labour Organization Regional Office for Arab States.

International Crisis Group (2014). The Rising Costs of Turkey's Syrian Quagmire http://www.crisisgroup.org/ ~/media/Files/europe/turkey-cyprus/turkey/230-the-rising-costs-of-turkey-s-syrian-quagmire.pdf (access:15.09.2015).

Kirişci K. (2014). Syrian Refugees and Turkey's Challenges - http://www.brookings.edu/~/media/research/files/reports/2014/05/12-turkey-syrian-refugees-kirisci/syrian-refugees-and-turkeys-challenges-may-14-2014.pdf(15.09.2015).

Mehchy Z., A. Mahadi Doko (2011). General overview of migration into, through and from Syria, *CARIM Analytic and Synthetic Notes* 2011/41.

Miller, A., and C. Orchard (2014). *Forced Migration Policy Briefing 10: Protection in Europe for Refugees from Syria*. Oxford: Refugee Studies Centre, Oxford Department of International Development.

MPC Team Migration Policy Centre Team (2013). Syria: The Demographic-Economic Framework of Migration The Legal Framework of Migration. The Socio-Political Framework of Migration. www. migrationpolicycentre. eu/docs/ migration_ profiles/Syria.pdf (access:15.09.2015).

Morrison, L. (2014). The vulnerability of Palestinian refugees from Syria. *Forced Migration Review, Special issue.: The Syrian Crisis, displacement and Protection*. Issue 47.

Murshidi, M. M., M. Q. B. Hijjawi, S. Jeriesat, A. Eltom (2013). Syrian refugees and Jordan's health sector. *The Lancet*, 382 (9888): 206–207.

Naufal, H. (2012). Syrian Refugees in Lebanon: the Humanitarian Approach under Political Divisions. MPC Research Report 2012/13.

Orsam (2015). The Economic Effects of Syrian Refugees on Turkey. http://www.orsam.org.tr/en/enUploads/

Article/Files/201519_rapor196ing.pdf (18.09.2015).

Özden. Ş, (2013). Syrian Refugees in Turkey, MPC Research Reports 2013/05

Refaat MM, Mohanna K. (2013) Syrian refugees in Lebanon: facts and solutions. *Lancet* 382: 763–764.

Seeberg, P. (2012). Migration and non-traditional security issues in the MENA-region. The case of pre-revolt Syria. Center for Mellemøststudier.

Sirkeci, I. (2006). *The Environment of Insecurity in Turkey and the Emigration of Turkish Kurds to Germany*. New York: Edwin Mellen Press.

Sirkeci, I. (2009). Transnational mobility and conflict. Migration Letters, 6(1): 3-14.

Sirkeci, I. and Cohen, J. H. (2016). Cultures of migration and conflict in contemporary human mobility in Turkey. European Review, Vol. 23, No.3 (forthcoming).

Stave, S. E., Hillesund, S. (2015). Impact of Syrian Refugees on the Jordanian Labour market a preliminary analysis / ILO. Regional Office for Arab States and Fato.

Thorleifsson, C. (2014). Coping Strategies among self-settled Syrians in Lebanon. *Forced Migration Review, Special issue: The Syrian Crisis, displacement and Protection.* 47: 23.

UNHCR and IRD (International Relief and Development) Report (2013). Jordan Home Visits Report 2014 - Living in the shadows http://unhcr.org /jordan2014urbanreport/home-visit-report.pdf (access: 09.09.2015).

UNRWA (2015). http://www.unrwa.org/syria-crisis#Syria-Crisis-and-Palestine-refugees (accessed: 09.09.2015).

Winckler, O. (1997). Syrian Migration to the Arab Oil-Producing Countries, *Middle Eastern Studies*, 33(1), 107-118.

UNHCR (2015). http://data.unhcr.org. (accessed: 6.09.2015).

CHAPTER 25

Demographic Gaps Between Syrian and the European Populations

M. Murat Yüceşahin and Ibrahim Sirkeci

Introduction

At least 6 million 148 thousand Syrians have been uprooted as a result of the crisis and conflict ongoing since 2011 in Syria. As of 6 August 2017, 5,165,502 have crossed the borders into neighbouring countries of Turkey, Lebanon, Jordan and Iraq whilst 983,876 moved further to Europe (UNHCR, 2017). A similar volume of population has been displaced within Syria too. This practically makes Syria one of the worst displacement cases in the history as more than half the contemporary population is displaced. Turkey with a long land border with Syria as well as historic links between populations, particularly in border provinces appeared as a favourite destination for Syrians who escape the conflict. As conflict grew and spread, in 2012 and onwards, a sharp increase in the number of Syrians arriving in Turkey was observed (Yazgan *et al.*, 2015; Sirkeci, 2017a). When Lebanon receiving proportionally the largest share of Syrian movers, Jordan, Egypt, and Iraq have also accommodated sizeable populations seeking refuge. Unlike the early days of the conflict when most movers preferred neighbouring countries, in later years, an increasing number of Syrians destined to Europe. There can be and are many factors moderating this behaviour. We can cite economic opportunities, democratic environment, as well as aspirations and cultures of migration among these factors. Certain political manoeuvres such as the German Chancellor Merkel's welcoming message in 2015 have also played a role.

In countries where sizeable Syrian communities emerged, debates about integration of movers have also been heightened in academia and general public. Being host for the largest population of Syrian movers, Turkey saw an exponential increase in academic interest in Syrians and migration in general. Nevertheless, most, if not all, of the research projects publicized have drawn conclusions based on small and non-representative samples. In the meantime, official data and summary releases remained primitive. Despite some interesting qualitative studies transpiring narratives of Syrian movers and non-movers in Turkey, there is a grave need for comprehensive analysis of trends in Syrian populations before attempting any conclusions about the future of this particular group and integration issues in waiting in Turkey and elsewhere.

Differences in demographic patterns and trends are as important as socio-economic and cultural differences between the movers and the non-movers in countries of destination. Nevertheless, apart from limited and often poor remarks that appear in discourses of politicians and in media, there has been no analysis of the demographic differences and projections for the future.

This sudden rise in interest in Syrians has resulted in an exponential growth in the number of research with poor quality, questionable methodologies, and controversial as well as unreliable analyses. This warrants robust and reliable analyses using representative and good quality data –as available. Our aim in this study is to offer a comprehensive analysis of Syrian population and demographic trends with reference to Demographic Transition Theory. Hence we may contribute to this gigantic task of filling the void with quality information. In this study, first, we delineate the demographic trends and changes in Syrian population from 1950 to 2015. Then we look at the projected trends from 2015 to 2100. We contrast these with the trends from selected key destination countries, Germany, Turkey and the United Kingdom. These analyses are based on the data from the World Population Prospects (UN, 2016). The conceptual point of reference for the analyses is Demographic Transition Theory which guides us in understanding the demographic changes which will be reflected in Syrian mover populations in destination countries in medium to long term.

Demographic Transition

The demographic transition is generally believed to be an unfinished process in the developing or less developed world, where rapid population growth is prevalent (Newbold, 2010). Mortality rates in the developing world have fallen rapidly from the mid-20th century, particularly due to much improved health provisions and technologies, better care and nutrition. However, fertility rates largely remained above the replacement level, and on average approximately three children per woman were reported. The rates in sub-Saharan Africa have been much higher than the average.

Within the "developed" world[1], shifts in mortality and fertility rates occurred towards the end of the 19th century and in early 20th century in relation to the Industrial Revolution and major improvements in public health provision. These led to a rapid decline in infant mortality rates while increasing the life expectancy (Bongaarts and Watkins, 1996; Weeks, 2002; Weinstein and Pillai, 2001; Rowland, 2012; Yaukey et al., 2007). In all developed countries today, fertility rates have been low for long enough to see populations in many developed countries are nearing to the end of the age transition, which brings up the challenge of population aging as a major concern. Populations in developed countries are largely characterized by relatively slow rates of population growth, low fertility levels, and controlled immigration. Some countries in Europe, and particularly in Eastern Europe, have been experiencing negative population growth rates for a while. In other words, their populations are on decline. According to the Population Reference Bureau projections, for example, Latvia's current population of 2.3 million will shrink to 1.9 million by 2050, thanks to low fertility levels. Germany's population, currently 82 million, is projected to decline to 71.4 million by 2050 (Newbold, 2010: 23). Due to its population momentum effect, Turkey's population is projected to increase until 2045-50. However, negative population growth attributed to low fertility rates

---

[1] Here we are using "developed countries" to refer to highly industrialised countries with high average incomes.

is projected for the second half of the 21st century. However, this transition in fertility and mortality was observed in the 19th century and in the beginning of the 20th century in developed countries.

Despite the effectiveness of the global demographic transition, especially in the second half of the twentieth century (Reher, 2004; Caldwell, 2001; Caldwell and Caldwell, 2001), today there are still significant demographic differences between countries and population groups across the world. Undoubtedly, our understanding of the demographic transition is deepened through comparing populations, especially between migrant sending and receiving countries. Every country or population experiences demographic transition in a unique fashion characterised by their own historic, social, cultural, economic and technological transitions (Lestheaghe, 1983; Coale and Watkins, 1986; Watkins, 1987; Caldwell and Caldwell, 2001). Therefore, no rate or percentage change can be deemed 'high' or 'low', and no set of characteristics can be considered 'more developed' or 'less developed', or 'traditional' or 'modern', for instance, without comparisons with other populations (Rowland, 2006: 120).

Concepts and theories, such as the demographic transition, provide a general comparative framework for research. These comparisons are necessary to draw conclusions and improve our understanding. Comparing data for different populations, at national, regional or local levels, is essential in gauging whether populations are distinctive, how much they have changed through time and whether their characteristics are adequately understood. Hence we can identify and explain the structural characteristics and changes in demographic trends over time.

The age and sex structure of a population is a commonly overlooked aspect of the social structure, yet it is one of the most influential drivers of social change in human society. The number of people at each age and of each sex is important to understand how a society is organized and how it operates (Rowland, 2012). The age composition is determined by the interaction of three demographic processes. Population movements can have a sizable impact, since movers tend to be concentrated in particular age groups and, in addition, movement is often selective of sex and age. Males in working ages are often more likely to move and this may have a significant impact on population change (Rowland, 2012; Newbold, 2010). Mortality has the smallest short-run impact on the age distribution. When mortality declines suddenly (as is the case in less developed countries), it turns the population to be more youthful and makes it grow rapidly. At the same time, a decline in mortality influences the sex structure by resulting in an increasingly larger number of females than males in older age groups (due to the fact that females usually have longer life expectancy than males and hence share of females in older age groups increases). Changes in fertility generally produce the biggest changes in a society's age structure, regardless of the level of mortality. High fertility, in general, results in a young age structure whereas low fertility leads to ageing of population.

Demographers examine the population processes that are likely to have an impact on future age and sex structure of a population based on various population projection scenarios. At the same time, examining past population trends allows us to understand behaviours of cohorts over time and in relation to social events and changes. Population projections help us to identify the direction of change. For example, it is possible to understand how a youthful population structure turns to an ageing population over time by examining the past demographic transition records of many developed countries. What matters is how fast or slow this transition takes place. These changes in age and sex structures of a population have a bearing on political, economic and social stability.

Countries with significant negative or positive net migration will face a change in age and sex structure of their populations after a while. For instance, it is useful to examine population movements and demographic transition in Germany, United Kingdom, USA, and Canada as these countries are characterised by strong net migration flows over a long period.

Overall, it is possible to spot the full variety of age groups among the movers. However, young adults are overrepresented among international and internal movers. For example, USA sees more inflows than outflows but those moving abroad are generally older than those arriving in the USA. This would certainly have, albeit a small, impact on age structure (Bouvier et al., 1997; Weeks, 2002). In the short run, the volume of young population declines in places marked by net emigration whereas in places of net immigration, the share of the young age groups increases in the total population. In the long run, the impact of migration is felt most in fertility patterns. This is due to the fact that most migrants are in prime reproductive ages (15-49 years old).

Therefore, movers' demographic features can be important for the receiving countries. Being concerned of the impact of population movements on demographic transition, many developed and developing countries have altered their population policies from anti-natalist to pro-natalist perspectives. More specifically, many developed countries have been applied a controlled or selective immigration policy within a pro-natalist perspective (Yüceşahin et al., 2016). Pro-natalist policies promote fertility to ensure population growth. By doing so, they aim to compensate their possible workforce deficit.

Data and Methods

There are no data sources that include country specific demographics of Syrian movers in the receiving countries. Therefore, in this study, we used the United Nations' (UN, 2016) country specific demographics to study the demographic differences among populations assuming that Syrians who moved to other countries would continue with similar demographic behaviour to what can be portrayed for the population of Syria. Here we should note that over time, some convergence is expected in demographic patterns of the movers and local populations. However, since mass Syrian population movements have only emerged in the last six years, the convergence is expected to be limited. To illustrate the demographic transition of Syrian population, we used crude birth rate (CBR) which is the ratio of births to the total population, crude death rate (CDR) which is the ratio of deaths to the total population, total fertility rate (TFR) which is an age-adjusted, period measure of lifetime fertility, derived by summing age specific birth rates in a given year for all ages of childbearing, and life expectancy at birth

(LEB) which is the average number of years of life remaining to a group of persons who reached a given age, as key demographic indicators (for detailed definitions see Siegel and Swanson, 2004). We have also used population distribution by age and sex in 1950, 1980, 2010, and 2015 to explain the changes and transformations in age and sex structure of Syrian population. For this analysis, we selected roughly equal intervals (i.e. 30 years) as 1950, 1980 and 2010. On the other hand, we used the 2015 data for the distribution of population by age and sex in order to present the outflow effects on Syrian population between the 5-year-period from 2010 to 2015.

In the second part of this chapter, we focus on the potential future demographic differences between Syrian and European populations. Based on the current population movements since the beginning of the Syrian crisis, we have selected three destination countries: Germany, Turkey and the United Kingdom. These countries either received a large number of Syrian movers or have been popular destinations for movers in the last three decades. We used several demographic indicators produced by the United Nations (UN, 2016) for the period from 1950 to 2100. These include median age (the age at which a population is divided into two equal sized groups), total fertility rate, child dependency ratio, age dependency ratio and total dependency ratio (dependency ratios are relative size of an age group of interest to the number of persons in a different age group providing support for the former) (see Siegel and Swanson, 2004). We have also produced population pyramids of the four countries for 2015, 2025, 2050 and 2100 to illustrate the changes regarding age and sex distributions.

Background: Demographic Transition in Syrian Population, 1950-2015

Middle Eastern countries saw a shift from high fertility rates and high mortality rates towards lower rates in the second half of the 20th century. Similar to other developing regions, populations in the Middle East have gone through three major demographic stages especially during the second half of the twentieth century, in line with the Demographic Transition Theory (Winckler, 2003). The first is the pre-transition phase probably spanning from the early 20th century to the 1960s marked with high fertility and mortality rates. The second is the early transition phase from the 1960s to the 1990s, with rapid declines in fertility and mortality rates. This period saw high population growth rates (Allman, 1980; Omran and Roudi, 1993; Rashad, 2000). The third is the mid-transition phase from the late 1990s to 2010-15, during which the decline of fertility and mortality rates slowed down (Table 1). Thus, the demographic transition in the Middle East and/or Arab countries of Western Asia in general has been somewhat peculiar. Total fertility rose substantially before it began its historical decline in the 1960s. Life expectancy at birth rose rapidly.

Today in many countries of the Middle East, average total fertility is three or more children per woman. However, in general, fertility rates in Turkey, Tunisia and the Gulf countries are at about replacement level (i.e. 2.1 children per woman). Demographic transition in the Middle East and Near East seems likely to begin and continue at a declining pace, a unique fashion for the region. Syrian population in 1950 was 3.4 million and by 2010, it rose to 21.5 million. According to the United

Nations (UN, 2016) Syrian population is expected to grow to 35 million by 2050. When compared to developed countries, Syrian population growth rate is significantly higher (Douglas, 2010: 50). With the exceptional small increases in 1965-70 and 1990-95 periods, crude birth rate has declined from 50.8 per thousand in 1950-55 to 24.1 in 2010-15. These high fertility rates along with low mortality rates resulted in increasing youth share in Syrian population. Also in general, across the region, crude death rates declined significantly to around 3.5 per thousand by 2005-10 (Table 1; Figure 1). This is even lower than the rates we would find in developed countries. However, by 2010-15, crude death rates increased slightly which is likely to be due to several wars and armed conflicts in the region (Figure 1). Population growth changes in Syria were mostly negative from 1980 to 2015 (Figure 2). This shows that Syrian population growth slowed down and was destabilised due to wars and resulting mass displacements. As shown in Figures 1 and 2, crude death rate increased between 2005-10 and 2010-15 and average annual population growth rate changes turned negative at more remarkable rates. Conflicts and generally uncomfortable living circumstances pushed large segments of Syrian population to move to other countries in the region and beyond (Yazgan et al. 2015; Sirkeci, 2017a). This is particularly evident in the decline since 2010 corresponding to the intensive conflicts since 2011 (Figure 2).

Figure 1. Trends of crude birth rate, crude death rate, and population size in Syrian population from 1950-55 to 2010-15

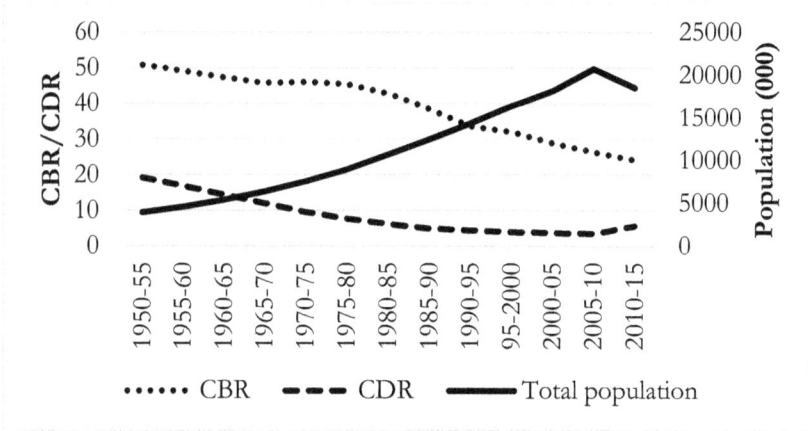

Data Source: UN (2016).

Contrary to many developing countries' experience with declining fertility in the early 1960s, the total fertility rate in Syria only started to decline significantly in the 1980s. Thus, despite rapid fertility transition seen in Syria, birth rates have remained high. The total fertility rate in Syria declined from 6.8 children per woman in 1980-1985 to 3.0 children per woman in 2010-2015 (Table 1).[2] In 1990-1995, the TFR declined to below 5 children per woman for the first time. Therefore three distinct

---

[2] Taleb et al. (2015), with reference to the World Bank data, refer to different rates. For example, they state that total fertility rate was 3.6 in 2000 and declined to 2.9 in 2010.

phases of fertility transition can be seen in Syria: the first is the 'pre-transition phase' spanning from 1950s to the early 1980s with very high fertility rates; the second is the 'early transition phase' from the early 1980s to the mid-2000s, with rapid fertility decline; and the third is the 'mid-transition phase' of the mid-2000s to 2010-2015 period (Figure 3). Approaching to the last phase(s) of the fertility transition, the third phase is characterised by slowing down of the decline in TFR. Unlike slightly below replacement level total fertility rates observed in many developing countries, the projections (UN, 2016) show that Syria's total fertility rate will reach the same levels no earlier than 2035-2040.

Figure 2. Trends in average annual rate of population change in Syrian population, from 1950-55 to 2010-15

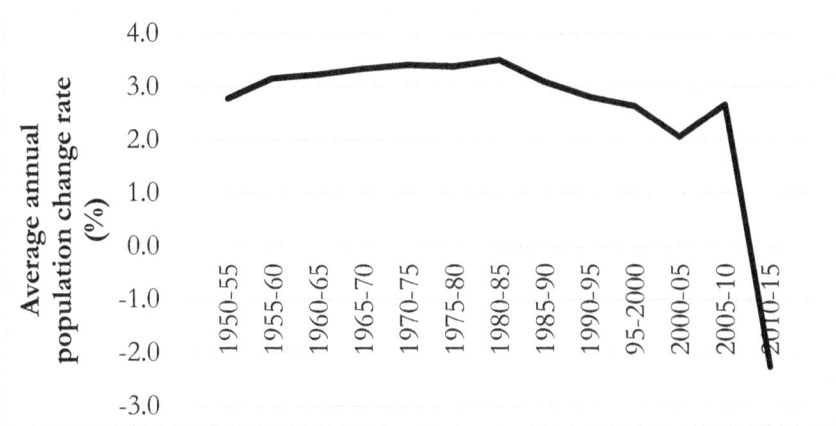

Data Source: UN (2016).

Figure 3. Trends of total fertility rate and life expectancy in Syrian population between the periods of 1950-55 and 2010-15.

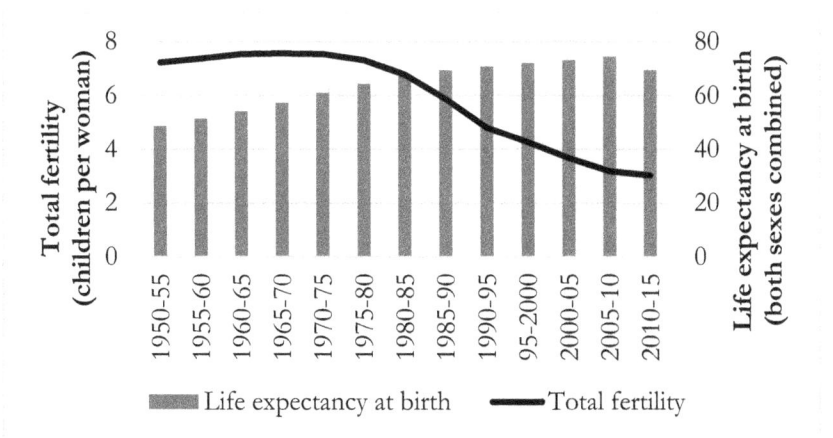

Data Source: UN (2016).

Table 1. Some selected demographic indicators of Middle East countries, from 1950-55 to 2010-15

	1950-55		1980-85		1990-95		2005-10		2010-15	
	CBR	**CDR**	**CBR**	**CDR**	**CBR**	**CDR**	**CBR**	**CDR**	**CBR**	**CDR**
Algeria	50.2	23.1	40.8	9.2	28.8	6.1	23.1	5.1	25.1	5.1
Bahrain	45.0	21.1	33.0	4.1	26.7	3.2	17.0	2.4	15.4	2.3
Egypt	50.6	25.4	39.0	11.4	29.8	7.9	25.2	6.4	28.5	6.2
Iraq	53.3	27.7	39.0	9.9	37.1	6.4	35.5	5.8	35.1	5.3
Iran	50.7	26.8	44.6	13.6	28.1	6.0	18.1	5.1	18.2	4.7
Jordan	47.4	20.4	39.7	6.5	34.0	4.8	28.7	3.9	27.9	3.9
Kuwait	43.7	13.6	36.3	3.6	19.9	2.6	23.2	2.7	20.6	2.5
Libya	51.0	30.6	37.0	6.5	25.4	4.8	22.9	4.8	21.7	5.3
Lebanon	40.2	12.9	28.8	7.2	23.3	6.6	12.7	4.7	15.0	4.6
Morocco	51.3	20.2	36.7	10.0	27.5	6.9	20.8	6.1	21.3	5.7
Oman	49.1	28.3	48.2	8.6	33.4	4.8	21.4	3.0	20.8	2.7
Palestine	45.9	20.0	44.9	6.8	45.7	4.8	34.0	3.7	33.1	3.6
Qatar	47.5	13.4	33.3	2.8	21.4	2.1	13.0	1.7	12.1	1.5
Syria	50.8	19.2	42.8	6.2	33.5	4.4	26.3	3.5	24.1	5.6
S. Arabia	47.8	23.2	42.5	7.2	33.1	4.5	22.6	3.5	20.8	3.4
Tunisia	45.5	26.6	33.1	7.8	22.9	5.8	17.0	6.0	18.4	6.6
Turkey	49.3	24.1	32.8	10.3	24.5	7.8	18.7	5.9	17.3	5.8
UAE	49.1	21.9	30.2	3.5	22.8	2.5	12.6	1.5	11.2	1.5
Yemen	48.4	30.3	54.7	15.1	49.8	11.1	35.8	7.8	33.2	7.1
	NI	**TFR**	**NI**	**TFR**	**NI**	**TFR**	**NI**	**TFR**	**NI**	**TFR**
Algeria	27.1	7.3	31.6	6.3	22.8	4.1	18.0	2.7	19.9	2.9
Bahrain	23.9	7.0	28.9	4.6	23.5	3.4	14.6	2.2	13.0	2.1
Egypt	25.2	6.6	27.6	5.5	21.8	4.1	18.8	3.0	22.3	3.4
Iraq	25.7	7.3	29.1	6.4	30.7	5.7	29.8	4.6	29.8	4.6
Iran	23.9	6.9	30.9	6.5	22.1	4.0	13.0	1.8	13.5	1.8
Jordan	27.0	7.4	33.2	7.1	29.2	5.1	24.8	3.6	24.0	3.5
Kuwait	30.1	7.2	32.7	5.0	17.2	2.4	20.6	2.6	18.1	2.2
Lebanon	27.3	5.7	21.6	3.8	16.8	2.8	8.0	1.6	10.3	1.7
Libya	20.4	7.1	30.5	6.7	20.5	4.2	18.1	2.7	16.4	2.5
Morocco	31.1	6.6	26.7	5.4	20.6	3.7	14.7	2.5	15.5	2.6
Oman	20.8	7.3	39.6	8.3	28.6	6.3	18.4	2.9	18.1	2.9
Qatar	34.1	7.0	30.4	5.5	19.2	3.7	11.3	2.2	10.6	2.1
Palestine	26.0	7.4	38.0	7.1	40.9	6.6	30.3	4.6	29.5	4.3
Syria	31.5	7.2	36.7	6.8	29.1	4.8	22.8	3.2	18.5	3.0
S. Arabia	24.6	7.2	35.3	7.0	28.6	5.6	19.2	3.2	17.4	2.9
Tunisia	18.9	6.7	25.4	4.8	17.1	3.0	11.0	2.0	11.8	2.2
Turkey	25.2	6.7	22.5	4.1	16.7	2.9	12.8	2.2	11.5	2.1
UAE	27.1	7.0	26.7	5.2	20.4	3.9	11.1	2.0	9.7	1.8
Yemen	18.1	7.4	39.6	8.8	38.7	8.2	28.0	5.1	26.1	4.4

Note: CBR: Crude birth rate (per 1,000 people); CDR: Crude death rate (per 1,000 people); NI: Natural increase (per 1,000 people); TFR: Total fertility rate (children per woman).
Source: UN (2016).

One of the important characteristics of the Demographic Transition is the increasing life expectancy depending on the primarily decreases in mortality in contrast to the decreases in fertility in due course. Life expectancy at birth in Syria increased 25.7 years from 1950-1955 to 2005-2010, increasing from 48.7 years to 74.4 years. It is expected to rise to 77.5 years by the 2050s (UN, 2016). Nevertheless, the civil war and conflicts in the country increasing since 2011, life expectancy at birth has declined to 69.5 years in Syria (Figure 3).

When child dependency ratio decreased from 100.8 percent in 1980 to 58.5 percent in 2010 in Syria, old-age dependency ratio also decreased from 6.1 percent to 5.8 percent. However, child dependency ratio bounced back to 63.1 percent and old-age dependency ratio to 6.9 percent in 2015. Total dependency ratio, therefore, decreased from 106.9 percent in 1980 to 64.3 percent in 2010, mainly due to the decrease in child dependency ratio (UN, 2016). The share of the population aged 65 and over first declined from 4.5 percent in 1950 to 3.0 percent in 1980, but increased to 3.5 percent in 2010 and to 4.1 percent in 2015 (UN, 2016).

The types of population pyramids can illustrate the changes through demographic transition. For example, declining mortality makes population younger, since more children survive. This is reflected in wider based pyramids as the proportion of children increases early in the transition and leading young age profiles. Later in the transition, population ageing emerges as fertility declines reduces the share of children. Successive generations then become similar in size, as evident initially in the emergence of 'mature' age structures with similar numbers in parent and child generations. Ultimately 'old' age structures evolve in which the numbers in successive age groups are similar below the advanced ages where mortality is concentrated in post-transitional societies.

In sum, fertility decline has the greatest impact on the percentages in older age groups during the demographic transition, particularly because it reduces the relative numbers of children. In contrast, mortality decline has a smaller effect on the percentages in older age groups, but a dramatic impact on population size, bringing increased numbers through improved survival of infants and children (Rowland, 2012: 99-101). On the other hand, conflicts, wars and out- or in-migrations as a result of these conflicts could have an impact on the population structures because of the deaths, inflows or outflows (Courbage, 1999; Fargues, 2011). There are indirect relationships between demographic structures and economic and political crises (Courbage, 1994) and it was clearly evident in the Syrian case.

Population ageing has come as a rapid change in many developing countries especially in the 2000s. However Syria's population composition has been dominated by younger people. The population pyramids of Syria in 1950 and 1980 show a typical wide-based structure signalling a very young population (Figure 4).

Rapidly declining mortality and high fertility levels made Syria's population younger from 1950 to 1980 (Figure 3 and 4). However, from 1980s because of the rapid decreases in total fertility rates (Figure 3) between 1980 and 2010, shape of the population pyramid for Syria has changed dramatically. Although the pyramid for 2010 shows still a young profile, a narrowing trend on the base can be observed (Figure 4).

It can also be said that the population pyramid of Syria in 2010 was starting to converge to a rectangular shape. However, between 2010 and 2015, probably the most important change was reflected in the fact that the population pyramid turned to an asymmetrical shape. The population pyramid for 2015 shows that the share of female population was higher than that of males in all age groups. For the 2010-2015 period, the two-way transition process was probably the reason for the asymmetrical distribution of population by age and sex in Syria. Undoubtedly, the first reason is the demographic transition. However, the impact of the violent conflicts from 2011 to 2015 is also evident, particularly reflected in the population pyramid for 2015 (Figure 4).

Figure 4. Distribution of Syrian population by age groups and sex, 1950-2015

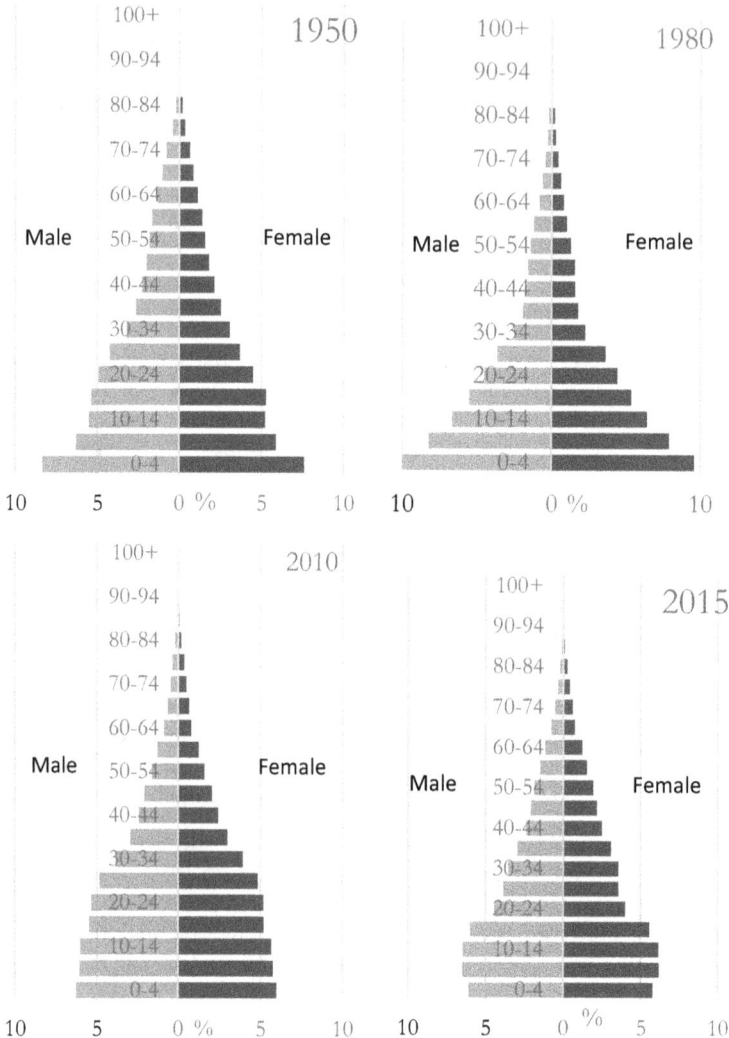

Data source: UN (2016)

Demographic Deficit and Potential Future Impact on Population

In this section, we first briefly examine population patterns in Syria, the United Kingdom, Germany and Turkey to reflect on the differences between Syrian movers and local populations in receiving countries. While the total fertility rates in Turkey and Syria were both very high in the 1950s, Turkish rates are expected to match that of the UK in about 2020 and Germany in about 2050 (Figure 5). Despite similarly declining fertility rates seen in Syrian population, the population momentum is likely to continue to be well above Turkey until the 2050s. In the second half of the century, fertility levels for all four countries are expected to converge at slightly below replacement level.

Different demographic trends are evident in the projections of median age, too (Figure 6). Even if we assume these patterns to remain the same in the long run, i.e. 2100 and beyond, in the near future we expect the largest age group will differ among these four countries. This will be reflected in general population structure. Median age is a measure indicating that the population below and above this age will have 50% equal shares of the total but it does not imply any age concentration (Hobbs, 2004: 158). Median age is 45 in Germany, 40 in the UK, 30 in Turkey and just above 20 in Syria (Figure 6). In other words, when Syria just step into "middle age" group, Turkey, Germany and the UK are in the "ageing" group with median ages above 30. When we do not expect radical changes in median ages in Germany and the UK, Turkey and Syria are likely to see their populations rapidly ageing in the coming decades. Significant differences between the three countries and Syria are likely to remain until the end of the century.

Figure 5. Total fertility rates in selected countries: 1950-2100

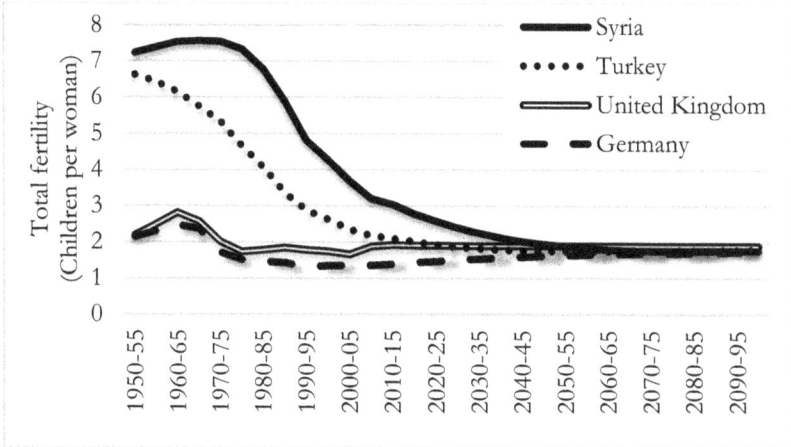

Data Source: UN (2016).

Age profile differences between the four selected countries can also be seen through the child and old-age dependency ratio patterns. These are shown in Figures 7 and 8, respectively. Old-age dependency ratio is also a socio-economic indicator because it reflects the working age population. Figure 7 roughly shows that Turkey will converge with the UK in around 2040 and with Germany in about 2065 regarding child dependency ratios. However, Syrian population will reach to similar levels only towards the end of the 21st century.

Share of the population under 15 in Syria has started to decline in about the same period as it did in Turkey but this was reversed towards the 1980s, since when it has been in decline. This fluctuation can also be explained by the conflicts in the Middle East as Syria has historically received significant number of movers from neighbouring countries in trouble. Those aged 15-64 comprised 48.3 percent of population in Syria in 1980 and this figure rose to 60.5 percent by 2010. These trends in age structure of Syrian population needs to be taken into account when it comes to services such as child care, schooling, and job creation in the countries and areas of destination.

Figure 6. Median age trends in selected countries: 1950 – 2100

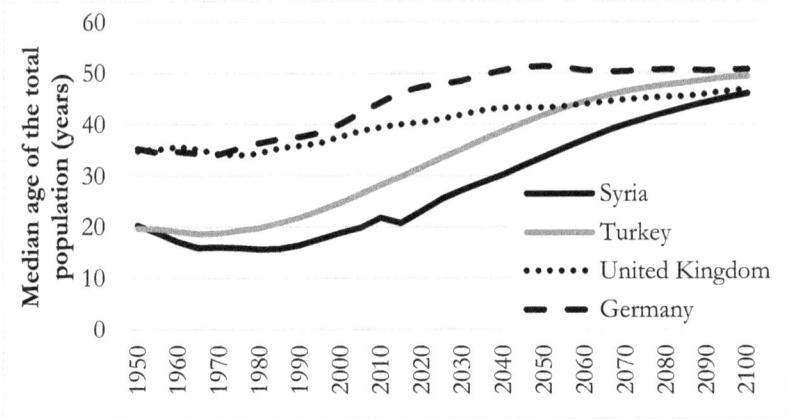

Data Source: UN (2016).

Figure 7. Child dependency ratios, 1950-2100

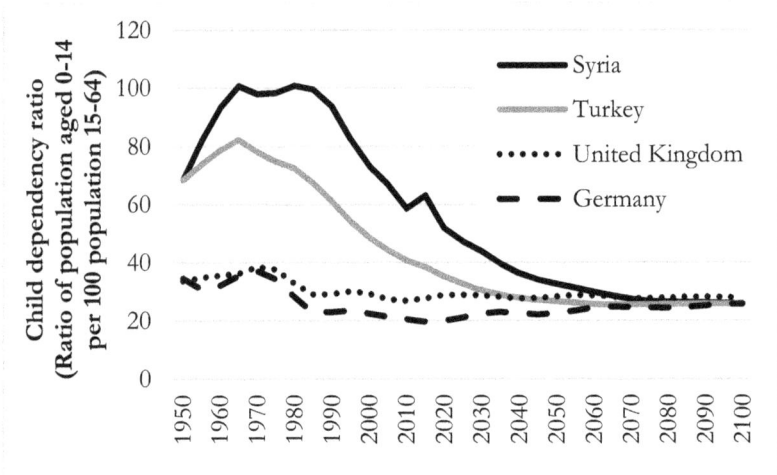

Data Source: UN (2016).

288

Figure 8 shows ratios of elderly population against those in working ages. The period from 1950 to present day is characterised by high percentage of people in working ages both in Turkey and Syria. This is also called "demographic window of opportunity". However, this period will end after the 2040s as the volume of 15-64 aged population will decline. For both countries, population aged 65 and over has been on the rise since 1980. However in Germany and the United Kingdom this decline had started long time ago and the demographic window of opportunity was closed. In 1980, the ratio of old-age dependency was 2.9 percent. It rose to 3.7 percent by 2010 and expected to reach 12.9 percent by 2050. As we have shown in Figure 8, this represents a large gap between Syrian population and populations of receiving countries. Projections indicate that difference will only fade away at the end of the 21st century.

Figure 8. Old-age dependency ratios, 1950-2100

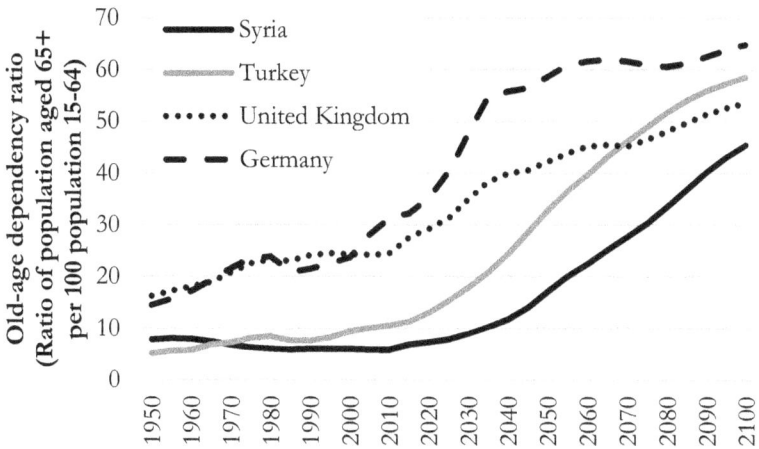

Data Source: UN (2016).

In figures 9a to 9d, we present population pyramids for the four selected countries. Different shapes of population pyramids and changes expected over time support our argument above. It is clear that a significant decline is expected in working age populations in Germany and the United Kingdom. Turkey's age and sex structure is also expected to converge rapidly with the trends seen in these two developed countries. It is important to note that all age groups up to 35-39 are about the same size in Turkey. Nevertheless, Syria differs from other three countries with its very large children and adolescent age groups. Over the course of the century, Syrian population is expected to be transformed into a shape similar to developed countries. Turkey's population will be ageing faster than others while children population will further shrink in Germany and the United Kingdom.

Figure 9a. Population pyramids for Syria, 2015-2100

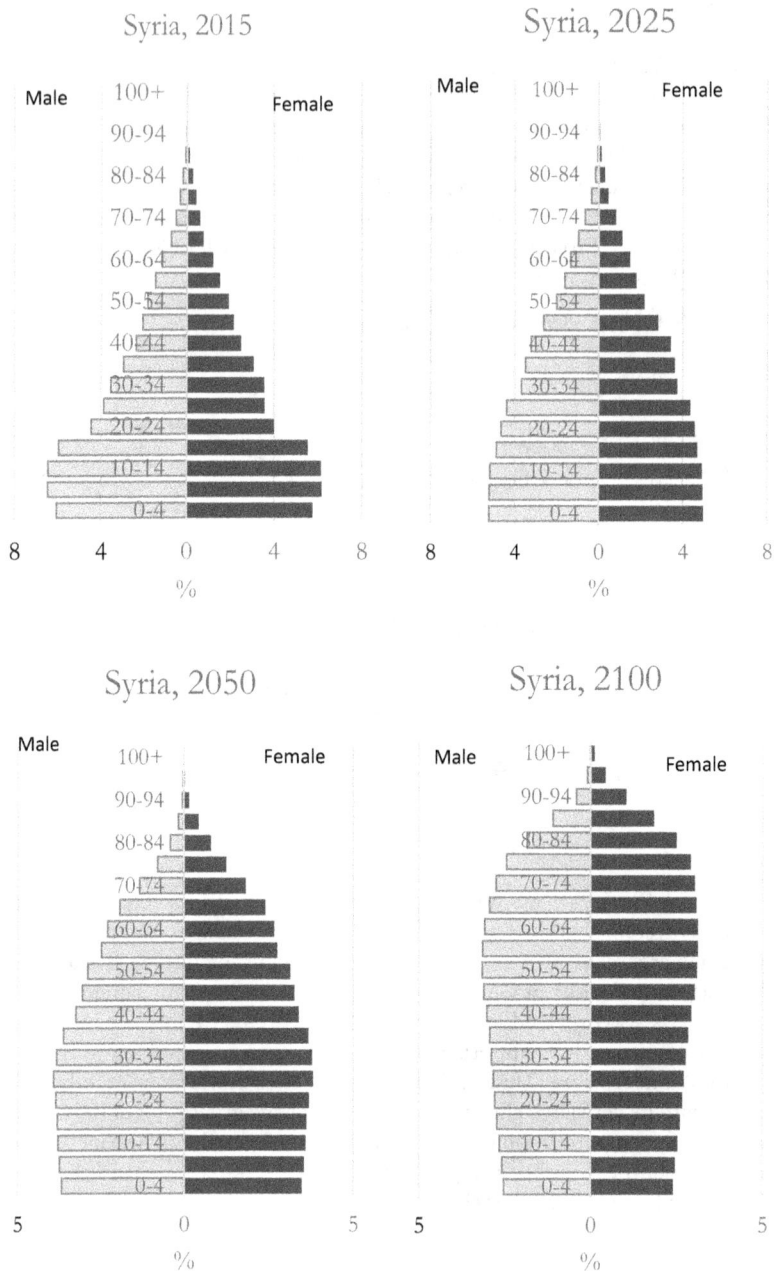

Syria, 2015

Syria, 2025

Syria, 2050

Syria, 2100

Data source: (UN, 2016)

Figure 9b. Population pyramids for Turkey, 2015-2100

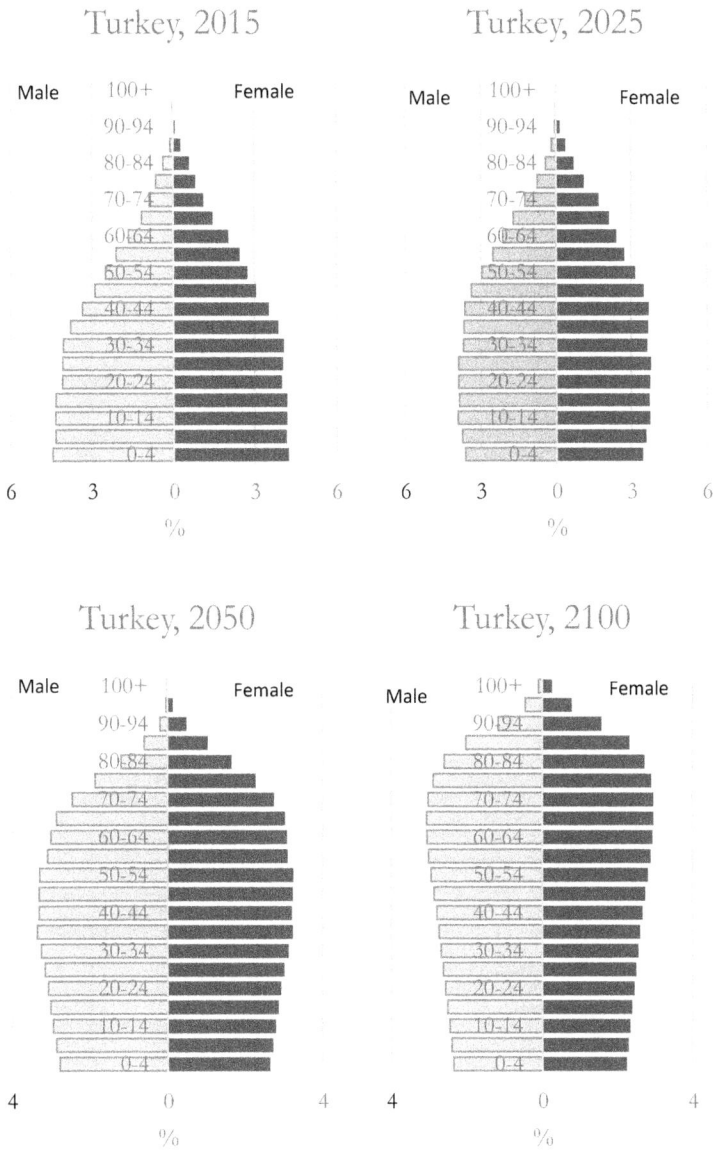

Data source: (UN, 2016)

Figure 9c. Population pyramids for Germany, 2015-2100

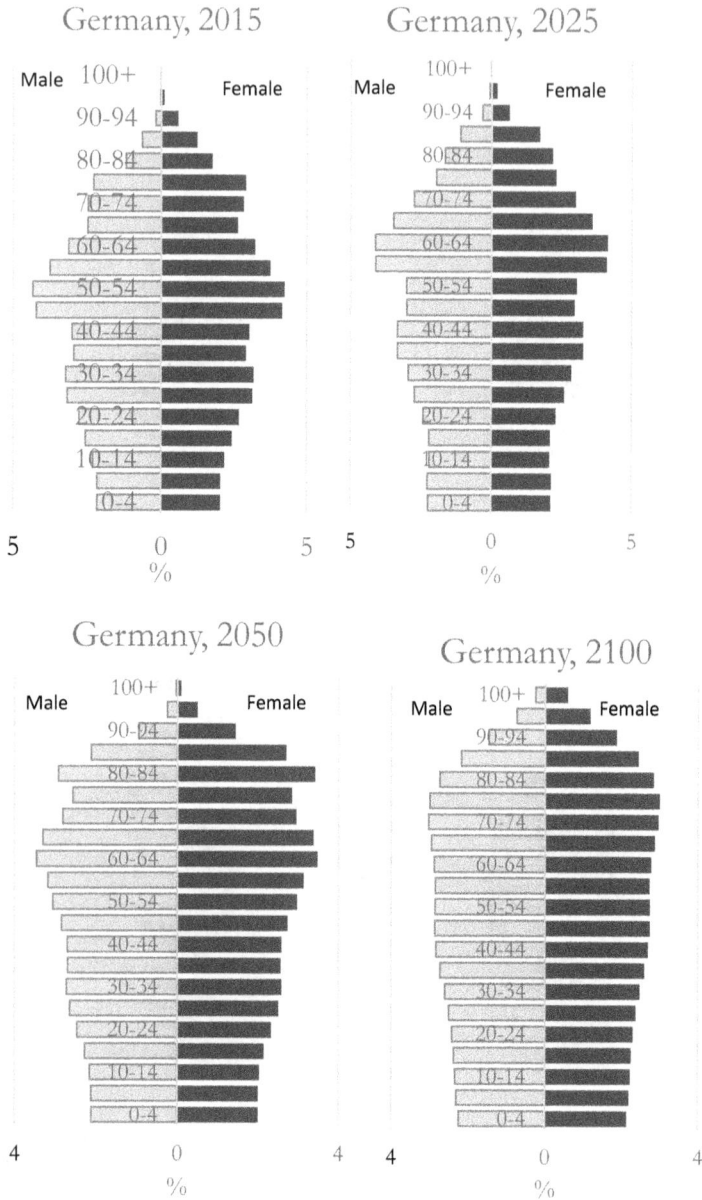

Data source: (UN, 2016)

Figure 9d. Population pyramids for United Kingdom, 2015-2100

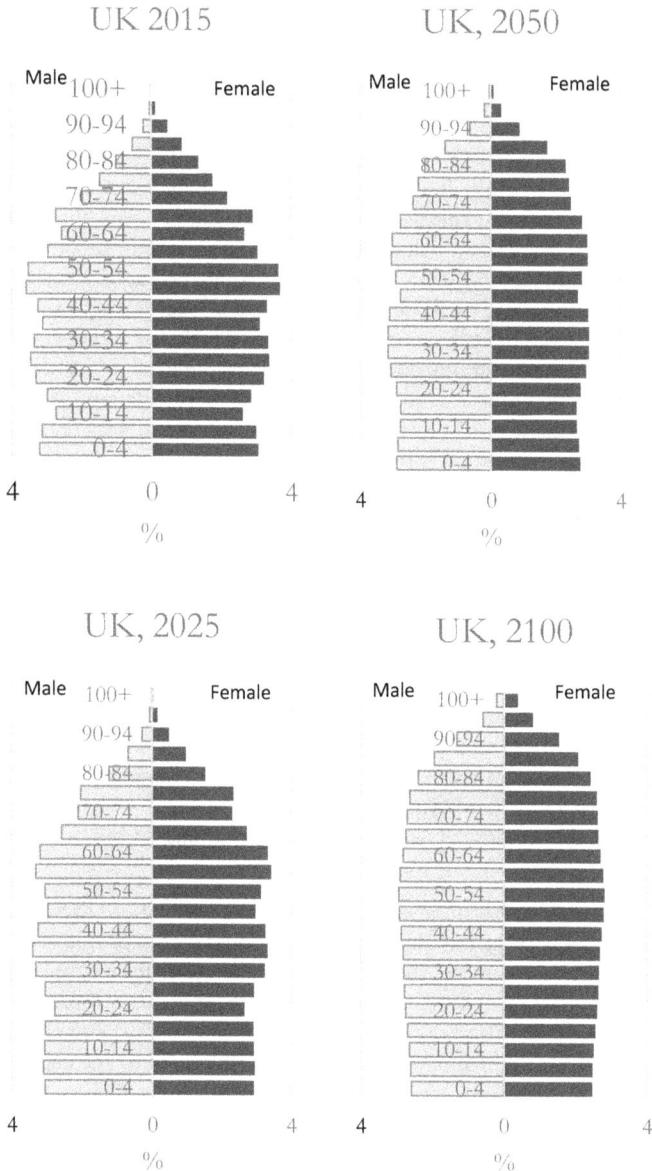

UK 2015

UK, 2050

UK, 2025

UK, 2100

Data source: (UN, 2016)

By 2050, the lower age groups, particularly children, will decline in their share of the total population in all four countries. In the same period, we expect the share of the groups aged 40 and over to gradually increase. However, this process will be much slower for the Syrian population. By the end of the 21ˢᵗ century, we predict that population pyramids will significantly converge as differences in demographic processes and patterns will decrease among these selected countries. Low fertility rates, ageing populations and relatively high mortality rates due to elderly population will characterise the demographic profiles of the countries by the end of the century (Figures 9a to 9d).

Conclusion

According to Demographic Transition Theory, fertility rates have been declining almost everywhere in the world (Reher, 2004). The same theory also suggests that the world population will continue growing as well as rapidly ageing across the countries in the coming years. By 2050, the population aged 65 and over is expected to exceed the share of those under 15 years of age in the world. This means, in terms of economic productivity, especially in developed and developing countries, we will experience serious difficulties in filling the gaps in the working populations due to ageing. In this regard, dynamic immigrant populations with their youthful demographic characteristics offer a potentially beneficial answer, at least for the short term, to this gap in the workforce that is expected to emerge in both the developed and developing countries. Again, our arguments also get strength with the assumption that migration is almost always age and sex selective (Weeks, 2002: 255-257).

We expect the Syrian movers abroad to exhibit very similar demographic behaviours with the population in Syria in the short term, and to converge with the trends in the respective countries of destination in the long-term (also see Sirkeci, 2017a; Sirkeci, 2017b). In this regard, we believe that the analysis of the population trends in Syria is appropriate and beneficial in the absence of reliable, detailed and definitive data on Syrian refugee populations in countries of destination. Our analyses will help interested parties to understand probable demographic trends of these new populations in Turkey, Germany and elsewhere. Hence better understanding of the needs, desires, wants and better planning of public services will be possible.

In our analysis, it is clear that there is a lag between the populations in Syria and the three selected countries in this analysis. Syrian population's profile with its largely young composition resembles that of Turkey in the 1980s for example. This also means that Turkey will benefit from a young population because already more than 3 million Syrians (half of whom are children) moved to Turkey and more Syrians who are likely to join them in the near future as suggested by the culture of migration model (Cohen and Sirkeci, 2011). Nevertheless, while this may mean receiving countries will have additional human resources to exploit by filling the gaps in the labour market and in pension funds, it comes with costs such as additional resources needed for schools, hospitals and other public services. For example, the number of additional school places needed in Turkey might be as high as one million and a large number of Syrian refugee children were still not enrolled at schools as of the end of 2016. Similarly, the number of children born to Syrian refugee mothers in Turkey has probably already exceeded 200,000 as by September 2016, the total number of children born to Syrians was nearly 180,000 according to

Turkey's health ministry (Al Jazeera, 2017). Thus a young profile often means higher birth rates and that much healthcare and prenatal care needed.

As they are likely to stay on and more movers from Syria are to follow (i.e. culture of migration model (Cohen and Sirkeci, 2011; Sirkeci and Cohen, 2016) predicts further mobility even after the initial triggers of mobility disappears over time), one further issue of concern is sociocultural, political and economic integration of Syrian movers in destination countries. For example, in Turkey, despite the presence of a sizeable Arabic speaking minority population prior to the arrival of Syrians, anxieties about the arrival of this large additional Arabic speaking population need to be addressed to avoid conflicts and facilitate cohesion. Different cultural practices including religious nuances need to be understood and accommodated. The process of settlement and integration will be complicated and not without hurdles (Özservet and Sirkeci, 2016).

References

Allman, J. (1980). The demographic transition in the Middle East end North Africa. *International Journal of Middle East Studies*, 12: 277-301.

AlJazeera (2017, January 19). UNICEF: 40% of Syrian children in Turkey not in school. http://www.aljazeera.com/news/2017/01/unicef-40-syrian-children-turkey-school-170119175018121.html (accessed 21/06/2017).

Bongaarts, J. and Watkins, S.C. (1996). Social interactions and contemporary fertility transitions. *Population and Development Review*, 22: 639-682.

Bouvier, L., Poston, D. L. and Zhai, N. B. (1997). Population growth impacts of zero net international migration. *International Migration Review*, 31: 294-311.

Caldwell, J.C. (2001). The globalization of fertility behaviour. *Population and Development Review*, 27: 93-115.

Caldwell, J.C. and Caldwell, P. (2001). Regional paths to fertility transition. *Journal of Population Research*, 18: 91-117.

Coale, A.J. and Watkins, S.C. (1986). *The Decline of Fertility in Europe*. Princeton: Princeton University.

Cohen, J. H., and Sirkeci, I. (2011). *Cultures of Migration: The Global Nature of Contemporary Mobility*. Austin: University of Texas Press.

Courbage, Y. (1999). Economic and political issues of fertility transition in the Arab World—answers and open questions. *Population & Environment*, 20 (4), 353-379.

Courbage, Y. (1994). Fertility transition in Syria: From implicit population policy to explicit economic crisis. *International Family Planning Perspectives*, 20 (4): 142-146.

Douglas, A. P. (2010). *Syria (Modern World Nations)*. New York: Chelsea House Publishers.

Fargues, P. (2011). International migration and the demographic transition: A two-way interaction. *International Migration Review*, 45 (3), 588-614.

Hobbs, F. B. (2004). Age and sex composition. In: *The Methods and Materials of Demography*. Siegel, J.S. and Swanson, D.A. (ed.). Londra: Elsevier Academic Press, pp. 125-173.

Lestheaghe, R. (1983). A century of demographic and cultural change in Western Europe: An explanation of underlying dimensions. *Population and Development Review*, 9: 411-435.

Newbold, K. B. (2010). *Population Geography: Tools and Issues*. Lanham: Rowman & Littlefield Publishers, Inc.

Omran, A. R., and Roudi, F. (1993). The Middle East population puzzle. *Population Bulletin*, 48 (1): 1-40.

Özservet, Y. Ç., and Sirkeci, I. (2016). Editörden: Çocuklar ve göç. *Göç Dergisi*, 3 (1): 1-4.

Rashad, H. (2000). Demographic transition in Arab countries: A new perspective. *Journal of Population Research*, 17(1): 83-101.

Reher, D. S. (2004). The demographic transition revisited as a global process. *Population, space and place*, 10 (1): 19-41.

Rowland, D. T. (2012). *Demographic Methods and Concepts*. New York: Oxford University.

Sirkeci, I. (2017a). Turkey's refugees, Syrians and refugees from Turkey: a country of insecurity. *Migration Letters*, 14 (1): 127-144.

Sirkeci, I. (2017b). Bir güvensizlik ülkesi olarak Türkiye'nin mültecileri, Suriyeliler ve Türk mülteciler. *Göç Dergisi*, 4 (1): 21-40.

Sirkeci, I., and Cohen, J. H. (2016). Cultures of migration and conflict in contemporary human mobility in Turkey. *European Review*, 24 (3): 381-396.

Taleb, Z. B., Bahelah, R., Fouad, F. M., Coutts, A., Wilcox, M., and Maziak, W. (2015). Syria: health in a country undergoing tragic transition. *International journal of public health*, 60 (1): 63-72.

UN (United Nations) (2016). *World Population Prospects, the 2015 Revision Data Base*. United Nations, Department of Economic and Social Affairs, Population Division, USA. Accessed from https://esa.un.org/unpd/wpp/; on 18.09.2016.

UNHCR (2017). Syria Regional Refugee Response. Inter-agency Information Sharing Portal. Accessed from http://data.unhcr.org/syrianrefugees/regional.php; on 12.08.2017.

Watkins, S.C. (1987). The fertility transition: Europe and the Third World compared. *Sociological Forum*, 2: 645-673.

Weeks, J. R. (2002). *Population: An Introduction to Concepts and Issues*. Belmont: Wadsworth Thomson Learning.
Weinstein, J. and Pillai, V.K. (2001). *Demography: The Science of Population*, Boston: Allyn and Bacon.
Winckler, O. (2003). Fertility transition in the Middle East: The case of the Israeli Arabs, *Israel Affairs*, 9: 39-67.
Yaukey, D., Anderton, D.L. and Lundquist, J.H. (2007). *Demography: The Study of Human Population*. Illinois: Waveland.
Yazgan, P., Eroğlu Utku, D. and Sirkeci, I. (2015). Syrian crisis and migration. *Migration Letters*, *12* (3): 181-192.
Yüceşahin, M. M., Adalı, T. and Türkyılmaz, S. (2016). Population policies in Turkey and demographic changes on a social map. *Border Crossing*, 6 (2): 240-266.

CHAPTER 26

Turkish Migration in Europe and Desire to Migrate to and from Turkey

Ibrahim Sirkeci and Neli Esipova

Introduction

According to the Gallup World Poll, nearly 630 million (14%) people desire to move to another country while only about 7.6 per cent of world's adult population are planning to move within a year and only about 3 per cent are already preparing –i.e. applying for visas and booking tickets (Esipova *et al.*, 2011). This last figure is more or less corresponding to the estimated total number of migrants in the World –i.e. around 214 million (3.1%) by 2010 (UN DESA, 2009). About one third (69.8 million) of these migrants are estimated to be in Europe: 1.4 million in Turkey, 6.4 million in Spain, 6.5 million in the UK, 10.8 million in Germany, and 12.3 million in Russian Federation. Nearly half of the worlds' migrants are based in less developed countries and least developed countries - about 98 million. Nevertheless, a high percentage of immigrants in the total population of Europe is a fact, while trends and directions in the near future are unknown. While a reasonable increase in mobility for Turkish citizens within the EU countries is expected, Far Right claims about '75 million Turks roaming around the EU'[1] are unrealistic. Turkey's role as a country of origin for one the largest minority populations in Europe, as a transit country, and as a destination country are of concern to academics, practitioners, and policy makers.

Turkey's European Union (EU) membership adventure began five decades ago and seemingly it will take quite a while until we see a shift. Public opinion polls in Turkey are showing a decline in Turks' interest in membership reflecting the Turks' frustration in this lengthy process. According to the European Commission's progress report on Turkey-EU relationships, by 2012 only one of the 32 chapters of negotiation has been concluded satisfactorily (EC, 2012). The report confirms that Turkey is the sixth biggest trade partner for the EU, and the EU -with 75 per cent of FDIs and 50 per cent of Turkish international trade- is the largest trade partner for Turkey. However, nearly a third of the report is about issues of democracy and human rights violations in Turkey. These demands and criticisms of the EU over Turkey's policies and practices regarding human rights is an example for the conflict (incompatible interests perhaps) between Turkey and Europe. It also means relative deprivation of human rights in the country is a cause for conflict in Turkey. According to our conflict model of migration (Sirkeci, 2006 and Cohen

---

[1] See: http://www.ukip.org/content/latest-news/2413-turkey-not-ready-to-join-eu.

and Sirkeci, 2011), these conflicts are drivers for migration.

Turkey's economy remained strong during the last decade which has been reassuring for her European partners. Nevertheless, it is a common concern that Turkey's EU membership could cause a mass migration from Turkey to Europe where already a large (i.e. between 3 to 5 million) Turkish immigrant population exist. The 10 Eastern European countries' accession to the EU in the mid-2000s caused a great concern when significant numbers of Polish and other Eastern Europeans are believed to have migrated to the UK and elsewhere immediately after the accession agreement came into force (Burrell, 2009, DWP, 2008, Drinkwater *et al.*, 2006). Nowadays a similar anxiety exists regarding Bulgarian and Romanian access to the UK and certain EU countries in 2014.[2]

The Turkish migration regime is better understood from a conflict perspective as described and discussed elsewhere (Sirkeci, 2005a, 2006, 2009a and Cohen and Sirkeci, 2011). The Turkish context of conflict - comprises   socio-economic challenges and difficulties including regional differences, a long term ethnic conflict and troubled minority affairs in Turkey, as well as discrimination, xenophobia, and economic difficulties faced in destination countries. These very broadly defined conflicts along mezzo and micro level conflicts have shaped and moderated the outflows and inflows of migrants in Turkey. Along with conflicts which can be identified as facilitating human mobility, the established networks of migration and developed culture of migration must be considered to understand potentials and trends of future migrations to and from Turkey. In this paper, first Turkey's potential as a country of migration and a source country are discussed in relation to past and current human mobility trends. Then, the 'desire to migrate to and from Turkey' is elaborated using data from the Gallup World Poll.

Turkey: A country of emigration, immigration, and transit

Earlier studies argue that emigration is more likely to be from countries where push factors are strong towards countries where pull factors are strong (Dorigo and Tobler, 1983, Zimmermann, 1996). There is a mature body of literature on the link between migration and wage differentials, development and migration (Piore, 1979, Borjas, 1994, Todaro, Martin, 2012 and 1991). Naturally, people have varying and often multiple motivations for migration. These may be moderated by gender, occupations, educational attainment, and so on. For example, Vujicic *et al.* (2004) identifies gaining experience and upgrading qualifications among top reasons for migration of sub-Saharan African health professionals. Boneva *et al.* (1998), on the other hand, proposed a migrant personality model (within the framework of McClelland's motivational theory (1987). Thus they argue that higher achievement motivation and lower affiliation trigger migration.

Sirkeci (2005, 2006, 2009a) and Cohen and Sirkeci (2011) proposed a model based on understanding a variety of conflicts determining human mobility

---

[2] For example, see: UK will not extend Romania and Bulgaria migration curbs (http://www.bbc.co.uk/news/uk-politics-20287061?print=true); Migration Watch warning on Romanian and Bulgarian immigration (http://www.bbc.co.uk/news/uk-21039087?print=true); Britain is facing new eastern Europe immigration surge (http://www.telegraph.co.uk/news/ uknews/ immigration/9637967/ Britain-facing-new-eastern-Europe-immigration-surge.html).

behaviour as well as indicating the directions characterising the process of migration. Within this model, conflicts of any kind appear as a driver for migration (and non-migration to the same effect). Turkey's migration history can be better understood through the lenses of conflicts in the country and in its neighbourhood. Urbanisation and industrialisation in Turkey played a role in internal and international migration –which we prefer to consider on a continuum (see Cohen and Sirkeci, 2011). While population growth pressurised rural areas, industrialisation appeared to attract people to cities in Turkey. This has coincided with mass migration from Turkey governed by bilateral labour exchange agreements in the 1960s and 1970s.

The conflicts of 1970s and the military intervention in 1980 resulted in hundreds of thousands fleeing Turkey. In the 1980s, at least 503,627 asylum applications were filed by Turkish citizens in the industrialised countries (UNHCR, 2001; Sirkeci, 2006). The war with the PKK began in the mid-1980s and created 309,764 more asylum seekers in the 1990s (UNHCR, 2001); there were a further 203,976 asylum applicants from Turkey in the 2000s. This ethnic conflict is still believed to be one of

> *Asylum seekers from Turkey:*
>
> *In the 1980s: 503,627*
>
> *In the 1990s: 309,764*
>
> *In the 2000s: 203,967*
>
> *In 2010-2011: 13,352*

the drivers for emigration from Turkey as the number of asylum seekers from Turkey was reported to be 6,509 in 2010 and 6,843 in 2011, while an even higher number is expected for 2012 (UNHCR, 2012). According to UNHCR data, by the end of 2011, there were officially 139,779 refugees originating from Turkey along with some 19,000 asylum applications filed in the first 30 months of the 2010s. This means **a total of 1,033,000 Turkish citizens filed an asylum application** in an industrialised country during the 33 years since the military intervention in 1980. This fact alone is evidence which indicates a link between conflicts and migration outflows. Nevertheless, categories of migration are simply reflecting administrative motives and interests rather than the motives of movers and non-movers. That is to say among the so many millions of Turkish citizens who arrived in Western Europe and elsewhere there were many whose move was motivated not only by various conflicts, but also by their desire for better jobs or education (See Sirkeci, 2006).

It is possible to argue then that migration to and from Turkey has evolved throughout the last century along the lines of incompatible interests, tensions, and conflicts. Despite common emphasis on the flows of labour emigration from the country in the 1960s and 1970s, Turkey has also been a country of immigration for quite a while (Avci and Kirisci, 2006). Significant population flows to modern Turkey date back to the 1910s and the period around the War of Independence following the First World War, when millions were displaced and subjected to compulsory population exchanges. The nationalist character of policies and the period can be blamed for large population losses, particularly among non-Muslim groups. Towards and around the mid-20th Century, these outflows continued with intervals in a rather reactionary fashion in response to events such as *Wealth Tax in*

1942 and the *6-7 September 1955* both are believed to have caused sizeable number of non-Muslims fleeing Turkey.

Similarly, inflows of Turkish and Muslim origin minorities continued to move to Turkey throughout the century. Migrations from Bulgaria have been particularly remarkable in certain periods such as over 400,000 arriving in between 1989 and 1994. Similar large immigration fluxes were also reported from Iran, Afghanistan, Iraq, and most recently from Syria each following respective conflicts in their countries. Although the statistics are poor and often unreliable, since the turn of the century, possibly linked to economic growth and relative political stability in the 2000s, one can expect and find some evidence of increasing immigration to Turkey from Europe –possibly members of the Turkish diaspora- as well as from Middle Eastern, Asian and African countries.

Both past and recent inflows from Middle Eastern and African countries to Turkey have seemingly been moderated by conflicts in countries of origin. Among others in the region, Turkey seems a relatively safer country with a prospering and promising economic environment. However, one should still be cautious here. Despite the evidence for Turkey's continuous economic development, what determines or largely shapes migration decision is not the objective –or evidence based- facts but the perceptions. Hence, in earlier studies we have formulated it as "perceived environment of human (in)security", which is not always based on factual information (Sirkeci, 2006, 2009a). For the Syrians fleeing their homes in fear of persecution in 2012 and for the Kurds who fled Iraq in the 1990s, Turkey must have appeared as an "environment of human security" (Sirkeci, 2005a). Otherwise, some commonly known macro indicators do show us that Turkey's so-called economic boom during the 2000s has not been translated into the desired levels of human development. United Nations' annual Human Development Reports show that Turkey's ranking has not improved much as the country sits on 92nd place among 187 countries despite being one of the top 20 biggest economies in the world (UN, 2012).

Apart from the mass influxes and outflows, individual emigration to and from Turkey was maintained throughout the short history of modern Turkey. Migration literature though mostly focused on the last five decades beginning from the early 1960s when the bilateral labour exchange agreements resulted in mass migration to Germany and other western European countries. Categorisation attempts so far, including my own, tend to align with administrative classifications of migration such as highlighting the dominance of asylum migration, or family reunifications. We can perhaps divide it into two periods, firstly the pre-1960 period: individual outmigration, outmigration of non-Muslim minorities and inflows of Turkish and Muslim minorities from former Ottoman territories dominated the migration from and to Turkey (Sirkeci, 2005b).

Secondly, the post-1960 period, which was dominated by mass emigration linked with rapid urbanisation in Turkey. This second period can be further divided into several periods indicating the fact that from the late 1980s onwards, Turkey has become both a transit and immigration country. Nevertheless, Turkey since the early 1980s remained as one of the leading source countries for refugee and asylum migration in the world. This is mostly due to the Kurdish question which is facilitating emigration in response to an environment of human insecurity. As a result a large Kurdish diaspora emerged in Western Europe originating from Turkey and joined by Kurds from Iraq, Iran and Syria (Sirkeci, 2006).

Turkey's international migration history can also be divided into periods as migration destinations have varied over time. This variation is mostly determined by Turkey's agreements with receiving countries and changes to these circumstances. Whilst during the 1960s, Western Europe was a prominent target destination, during the 1970s and 1980s, Gulf Countries and other Arab countries such as Libya received a substantial number of migrant workers from Turkey. At the same time, Australia began to appear as a destination country. Following the collapse of the Soviet Union, the Russian Federation and Turkic countries of Caucasia and Central Asia were put on the destinations map for Turkish migrants. The United States and Canada attracted perhaps a steady stream of highly skilled migrants from Turkey over the last century. Although some variation has been reported for recent decades, flows to the US have been historically characterised by professionals and postgraduate students (Akcapar, 2009). According to the 2000 US Census, there were 117,575 Turks in the country (Bittingham and de la Cruz, 2004).

Despite the fact that only very few studies are overtly focused on ethnic conflicts and migration (see my earlier work: Sirkeci, 2003, 2005, 2006, 2007), ethnic and minority affairs in Turkey are seemingly a moderating factor for the Turkish international migration regime. Ethnic conflict has almost always coloured the map of migration motivations and it is indirectly evident in, for example, the dominance of refugees, asylum seekers and irregular migrants during the last two to three decades of outflows from Turkey (e.g. Sirkeci, 2006).

Turkish (and Kurdish) diaspora today ranks among the top nationalities among immigrants in the world. This has implications for both determining the destinations for future migration from Turkey but also for the countries of origins of those migrating to Turkey. The total number of Turkish citizens living abroad is estimated to be around 4 million which goes up to 6 million when naturalised Turks and others are included. According to the existing and available data, the largest segments of immigrant population from Turkey are present in Germany, France, the Netherlands, Austria, and Switzerland while the total number of Turkish citizens in 27 EU countries is estimated to be about 2.35 million (Vasileva, 2010). However, one must note that immigration figures are almost always unreliable due to the nature of human mobility, problems and differences in data collection and definitions used.

As immigrants are established in the host countries, it becomes difficult to trace the total volume of immigration-bound minorities. Difficulty in having accurate statistics about these minorities arises from various reasons including; data collection methods used in capturing migration and minority information, classification preferences used in official data collection, difficulty in capturing second and third generations, classification difficulties regarding mixed ethnicities, lack of data on return migration, circular short term mobility, and large number of naturalisations over years. Hence, the number of Turkish citizens in Germany (according to official statistics) seems to decline from over 2,053,000 in 1999 to 1,6 million in 2010 and about one third of those were born in Germany (Vasileva, 2011; Statistische Bundesamt, 2012). The total number of people of Turkish origin (including the Kurds) living in Germany is estimated to be between 2.6 to 4 million once naturalisation and later generations are taken into account (Sirkeci et al., 2012b:36). From 2004 onwards, net migration between Turkey and Germany has been negative (Sirkeci et al. 2012a). A similar declining trend is evident in the Netherlands, France, Austria, and Switzerland –other major destinations for Turkish migrants - but these are all moderated by a number of naturalisations. However, in the UK, the number of immigrants from Turkey seems to have grown between the two censuses in 2001 and 2011.

Table 1 summarises various statistics available on human movements from Turkey to the UK from 1980 to 2011. According to the Annual Population Surveys and Labour Force surveys, the number of residents who were born in Turkey is estimated to be 72,000 (ONS, 2012). This figure was estimated to be 61,000 by 2004[3] (ONS, 2004) and 52,396 born in Turkey along with 75,763 born in Cyprus[4] in the 2001 UK Census. The 2011 UK Census, though, reports 91,115 Turkish born in England and Wales.[5] Nevertheless, the official statistics on asylum seekers, settlement visas[6], and citizenship indicate a much larger population: These three figures suggest **between 140,000 and 180,000 UK residents were born in Turkey**[7] by the end of 2011 while indicating 212,000 admitted at the UK borders despite only about 90,000 visas were issued.

As mentioned earlier the figures are insufficiently accurate to guarantee population size, and are inadequate to help understand the ethnic and religious variety known to exist among the Turkish born minorities in the UK, Germany and elsewhere. Nevertheless, these countries are part of a migration network along which individuals, families, and groups from Turkey and their descendants are likely to move. For example, Germany is both the top source country for immigrants in Turkey and the top destination country for those emigrating from Turkey (Sirkeci, 2009b). In brief, one can guess that the desire to migrate often occurs within a set environment shaped by established networks of mobility.

Migration is more often than not a decision made within households in response to the immediate and wider environment based on the perceptions of individuals, families, and communities (Cohen and Sirkeci, 2011). Minor and major conflicts –i.e. tensions, disagreements, obstacles, clashes, wars- are perceived by

---

[3] Kucukcan (2004:247) cites a figure of 79,000 for 2003 but it is based on Turkish sources and not by the UK statistics/registers.

[4] About 25 to 30 per cent of those born in Cyprus is believed to be of Turkish origin. As an indication we can take that according to the 2001 UK census, 24 per cent of Cyprus born UK residents were Muslim.

[5] According to the UK censuses, from 2001 to 2011, the share of London among Turkish-born declined from 75 per cent to 65 per cent implying a rather dispersed population.

[6] Settlement visas are currently issued after 5 years of permanent residence in the UK. At the end of 6th year of residency, individuals are allowed to apply for British citizenship.

[7] Considering the size of asylum applications over the three decades and the fact that main conflict, therefore main source for fear of persecution, in Turkey has been the Kurdish question and the war between the PKK and Turkish security forces, one can –and should- point that the Kurds from Turkey constitute at least about 40 per cent of Turkish born population in the UK.

people as environments of human (in)security. Thus, migration is a reaction, one of the strategic options to overcome the difficulties perceived by moving (i.e. migrants) and non-moving (non-migrants) actors. Therefore it is no surprise that Gallup World Poll find that sub-Saharan Africa, one of the world's most deprived and conflict-prone regions, stands on top of the league of migration desire as 33 per cent of adults would like to move (Esipova *et al.*, 2011).

Table 1: Asylum, Citizenship, Immigration – from Turkey to the UK, 1980 – 2011[8]

	Asylum application	Citizenship	Grants of settlement	Visas issued	Admitted at border
1980	21	120			
1981	0	175			
1982	38	215			
1983	43	210			
1984	61	340			
1985	27	390			
1986	86	350			
1987	121	485			
1988	337	365			
1989	2,415	445			
1990	1,590	559			
1991	2,110	988			
1992	1,865	541			
1993	1,480	710			
1994	2,045	689			
1995	1,820	706			
1996	1,420	931			
1997	1,445	1,118	4,235		
1998	2,015	2,154	2,360		
1999	2,850	2,913	5,225		
2000	3,990	4,875	5,220		
2001	3,693	4,037	3,310		
2002	3,494	8,040	2,920		
2003	2,992	4,916	4,365		
2004	1,588	4,860	6,060		124,000
2005	951	6,767	5,331	67,652	140,000
2006	426	5,583	3,039	78,698	160,000
2007	208	4,709	2,547	80,016	147,000
2008	193	4,641	3,671	84,020	172,000
2009	187	7,207	3,452	79,739	178,000
2010	155	4,630	5,580	87,818	191,000
2011	170	3,627	3,681	90,316	212,000
TOTAL	39,836	78,296	60,996	568,259	1,324,000

Source: UNHCR, UK Home Office, ONS.

Desire to migrate: Future migration potential

Analyses in this study are based on Gallup surveys 2009, 2010, and 2011. The data was collated from interviews conducted in 2009, 2010, and 2011 as part of the larger Gallup World Poll.[9] In each country, Gallup conducts interviews in the official language. As a result, individuals who do not speak the official language in their country of residence may be under-represented. Of the total sample across 15

---

[8] Asylum applications are reported usually by nationality or citizenship whereas immigrant population is reported by country of birth unless otherwise stated.

[9] Further details of the World Poll methodology can be found in Gallup (2012).

countries, 3% of individuals contacted were unable to participate because of a language barrier. Results are based on aggregated telephone and face-to-face interviews with 401,490 adults, aged 15 and older, in 146 countries from 2009 to 2011. The 146 countries surveyed represent 93% of the world's adult population. Every year, Gallup conduct 1,000 interviews in Turkey (with adults aged 15 and more). Hence, the analyses specific to Turkey are based on 3,000 interviews total.[10]

PNMI (Potential Net Migration Index) is based on data from earlier Gallup surveys (i.e. 2007-2010). Nevertheless, questionnaire is very much the same. Our analyses are drawing upon the responses to a few key questions asked in the Gallup's survey: 1) Ideally, if you had the opportunity, would you like to move permanently to another country, or would you prefer to continue living in this country? 2) (If "would like to move permanently to another country") To which country would you like to move? [Open-ended, one response allowed] (Esipova and Ray, 2010).[11]

Findings and discussion

Perceived environment of human security, as embodied in for example job opportunities and other social development indicators, is determining the destinations (Sirkeci, 2005a and 2009a). The United States then is the top desired destination, with about 23 per cent of potential migrants worldwide wanting to move there (Esipova *et al.*, 2011). It is unsurprisingly followed by Canada, the UK, France, Spain and Australia. Gallup Poll Data is also used to develop the *Potential Net Migration Index* (PNMI) which is simply "the estimated number of adults who would like to move permanently out of a country if the opportunity arose, subtracted from the estimated number who would like to move into it, as a proportion of the total adult population" (Esipova and Ray, 2010). The index scores were based on over 600,000 interviews between 2007 and 2009. Higher positive PNMI scores indicate net migration gains –net adult population gain. Thus countries such as Sierra Leone, Haiti, Zimbabwe and Nigeria are at the bottom of the league with potential adult population losses of up to 56% whilst Singapore, New Zealand, Saudi Arabia, Canada and Switzerland were estimated to face adult population gains between 150% and 219%. Turkey's score in this exercise was -7, in other words, adult population is likely to decline 7% if all desire to migrate materialises. Countries with a similar score were Egypt, Russia, Pakistan and South Korea (Esipova and Ray, 2010). The mid-table ranking of Turkey with a negative score on PNMI scale implies that it will continue to be a source country despite its increasing popularity as an immigration destination.

Evidence shows that Turkey has become a desirable destination for migration

---

[10] This was a serious barrier for more detailed analysis as some cells included very few cases and revealing such figures would be misleading.

[11] In the Gallup World Poll there were additional questions which refer to individuals' level of planning and preparation for migration and available networks in the destination country. However, due to small sample sizes, we were not able to exploit these in our analysis. These questions on migration are: 1) Are you planning to move permanently to another country in the next 12 months, or not? 2) To which country are you planning to move in the next 12 months? (asked only of those who are planning to move to another country in the next 12 months), 3) Have you done any preparation for this move? (For example, applied for residency or visa, purchased the ticket, etc.) (asked only of those who are planning to move in the next 12 or 24 months) 4) Do you have relatives or friends who are living in another country whom you can count on to help you when you need them, or not? (Gallup, 2012).

in her region and beyond (e.g. Sirkeci, 2009b, Sirkeci *et al.*, 2012c). Nevertheless, as mentioned above (i.e. PNMI) it is still likely that Turkey will see net adult population loss in the forthcoming years if the desires are put into practice. To understand the significance of emigration desire in Turkey –i.e. 13 per cent- it is helpful to compare it with some relevant countries around the world. For example, the BRIC countries, which are emerging economies like Turkey.

Turkey has been aspiring to become a full member of the European Union, a desire dates back to September 1959 when she applied for associate membership of the European Economic Community (EEC) (EC, 2012). Therefore, it is not surprising to see 59 per cent of Turkish adults desiring to migrate are likely to be destined for Europe (Table 2). It is then followed by America (possibly mostly USA and Canada) which is again the most popular destination for most migrants around the world.

Table 2. Desire to migrate to and from Turkey, by region, 2009-2011

Desire to emigrate		Desire to immigrate	
Potential Destination	%	Potential Origin	%
Europe	59	Europe	38
Americas	16		
Asia	5	Asia	10
MENA	5	MENA	44
SS Africa	2	SS Africa	8
DK/Refused	13		
Total	100		100

Source: Gallup World Poll

Europe is the dominant source region for those desiring to migrate to Turkey is Europe (Table 2). This is understandable because of the large Turkish immigrant communities presence in several European countries. Overall close relations (economic, political, cultural and historic) between Turkey and Europe can explain why adults from European countries are likely to dominate inflows to Turkey.

Among the adults who want to migrate to Turkey, 20 per cent are from Iran, 12 per cent are from Germany, and 7 per cent from Azerbaijan. Previous studies (Sirkeci, 2009b and Sirkeci *et al.*, 2012c) have shown that the largest group of immigrants in Turkey come from Germany, which has been the main destination for Turkish citizens since the early 1960s. This has resulted in a large network that facilitates migration flows in both directions –to and from Turkey. The large community of Turkish immigrants and their second and third generations in Germany is a reason for Germany being one of the main source countries for adults desiring to migrate to Turkey. Iran and Azerbaijan are the other top source countries for potential migration to Turkey for various reasons. To begin with both countries are geographically and culturally proximate to Turkey. While Azerbaijanis speak Turkish, a large portion of Iran's population is of Azeri origin. Besides, Turkey as a destination has (probably) already an established place within Iranian culture of migration.

Gallup data shows that 13 per cent of Turkish adults desire to emigrate. Again referring to the very same ties between the two countries, the top desired destination for Turkish adults is understandably Germany (25%) and the USA

(12%); the former is historically the top destination for Turks with a large stock of Turkish origin immigrants and the latter is the world's largest immigration country. For 7 per cent of Turkey's adult population, the preferred destination is France among other European destinations (Table 3).

In the World Poll, Turkey is considered as part of South East Europe[12] where 16 per cent of adults want to migrate while in Europe overall 18 per cent of adults are willing to emigrate. In this regard, Turkey's figure stands relatively below the World and European averages. It is important to recognise the fact that Turks, Kurds, and others in Turkey show less interest to move to another country compared to their European neighbours overall and differences are even bigger in individual country cases.

Table 3. Desire to emigrate from selected countries, 2009-2011

Top destinations	%	Immigration countries	%	Troubled countries	%	BRICs	%
Germany	18	USA	10	Iran	15	Brasil	13
UK	30	Canada	10	Iraq	16	Russia	13
Netherlands	17	Australia	7	Syria	27	India	5
France	19			Libya	29	China	6
Greece	21			Egypt	17		
Italy	19						

Source: Gallup World Poll

For example, Liberia (53 per cent) in Africa and Haiti (50 per cent) in Latin America have the highest level of desire to migrate in the world. These countries are not in the same league as Turkey. Turkey's position compared to other countries in more or less similar economic trajectories and within her neighbourhood is not surprising. Two of the four strong emerging economies, namely BRIC countries, have the same level of desire to migrate whilst desire to migrate among Indians and Chinese is half that of Turkish. In Libya and Syria remarkably higher percentages of people are reported to desire moving to another country. However, interestingly in Egypt, Iraq and Iran, the corresponding figures are very close to that of the Turkish sample. Adults in top three immigration countries are understandably less interested in moving abroad. On the European side, all of the four main destination countries for Turkish migrants have much higher levels of desire to migrate. The poll data shows a strikingly higher percentage of adults desiring to leave the UK (30 per cent). This can perhaps be a reaction to the fact the UK's economy is believed to be hardest hit among the strongest economies of Western Europe. Similarly, higher level of desire to migrate among Greeks can be credited to the high level of unrest and economic difficulties Greeks went through during the global financial crisis which began in 2008.

Turkey's continuous economic growth and relative political security and stability over the last decade or so should have played a role in establishing its position as an immigration destination. However this is also a possible reason why desire to emigrate is not much higher among the Turkey's adult population. When

---

[12] South East Europe is composed of Albania, Bosnia and Herzegovina, Croatia, Kosovo, Macedonia, Montenegro, Serbia, and Turkey.

nearly one in three Brits is willing to move abroad, only one in six Turks is interested in doing so. This is perhaps something supporting the argument that Turkey's relatively strong economic performance during the most recent global financial crisis convinced most of the Turkish adults to stay home.

Conclusion

Turkey like other countries in a similar position needs to be prepared for even larger migration inflows likely to occur in the near future. This is not always a burden, there are studies showing the positive impact of immigration on development, innovation and entrepreneurship.

Migration discourses in mainstream media and politics are often overly skewed towards anti-immigration sentiments and therefore pointing to migrants who are to arrive in Europe or elsewhere. However, the reality is that it is not a one way street. More or less, in every country and every economic zone in the World some people move in whilst some others move out. Furthermore, in the long run, the differences between inward and outward migration are likely to fade away. Despite the fact that migration networks and established diaspora play a role in maintaining migration flows between countries, migratory regimes are temporal and tend to shift. For example, in the 1950s, Italians, Greeks and Turks were all 'guest workers'. Five decades on and now Italy is a country of immigration itself, accommodating about 4.5 million migrants.

The conflicts in the neighbouring countries and the region surrounding Turkey, constitute a major context which is likely to facilitate migration to Turkey. The on-going economic crisis and its repercussions in Europe coinciding with discrimination and xenophobia in destination countries are also reasons for likely future migration flows from those countries where established Turkish immigrant populations are present. For example, Germany already tops the list of nationalities among immigrants in Turkey (Sirkeci et al., 2012c).

This preliminary analysis of the data points avenues for further research. For instance, we do not know whether the low level of desire to migrate from Turkey can be linked to negative experiences of migrants abroad. Another interesting line of investigation is the impact of growing far right movements in many traditional immigration countries (in Europe and elsewhere) and the number of attacks on immigrants on migration tendencies. Might have these played a discouraging role for those who may have otherwise considered to emigrate?

Turkish people indicate a lower level of emigration desire compared to World and European averages as well as its neighbouring countries while similar or lower percentages are reported for other emerging markets. That is to say a declining emigration pressure which is expected from a country rapidly becoming a popular immigration destination. This is where Turkey's preparations should target in managing migration in the next 50 years. While Turkey is still expected to lose some population (i.e. PNMI score -7), it is likely to receive a significant number of movers from its European counterparts (e.g. Germany) and neighbours (e.g. Iran and Iraq). Further economic and/or political troubles in neighbouring countries may simply add to the toll. Turkey's significantly low ranking on human development index is a summary indicator of the environment of human insecurity perceived to be present in Turkey which may account for future possible emigration from Turkey.

Further quantitative analysis of the Gallup data and qualitative surveys to supplement are needed for better informed policy making and human mobility management. Analyses focusing particularly on vulnerable groups and ethnic and religious minorities such as Kurds, Arabs, and Alevis are necessary for more accurate estimates of potential migration to and from Turkey. For example, regional distribution of desire to emigration would provide relatively better results indirectly reflecting some ethnic variety. Similarly differences by gender and age groups will also help our understanding. The small cell sizes in the data bars us from further detailed analyses but in forthcoming years accumulating data will make rather sophisticated statistical analyses possible.

Appendix

Figure A1. Asylum seeking, settlement, and citizenship by Turkish born in the UK, 1980-2011

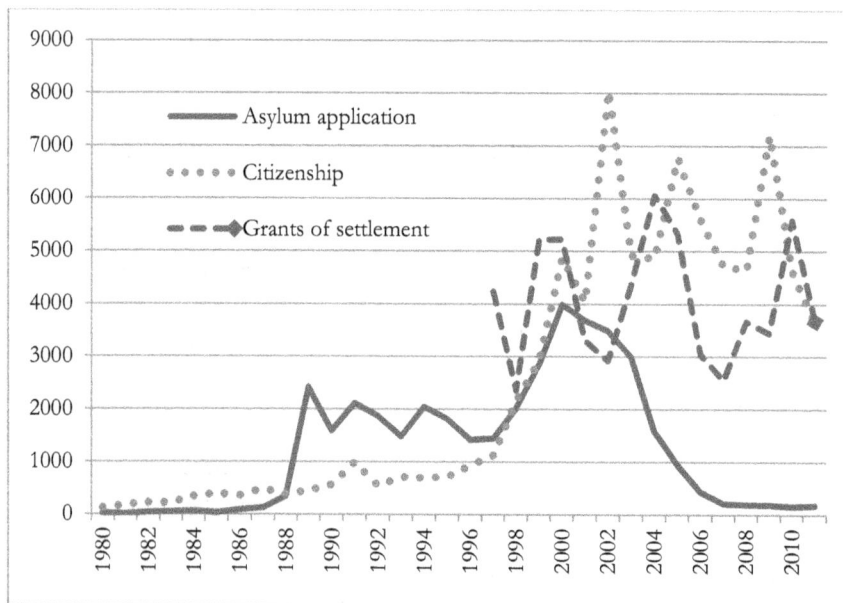

Source: ONS, Home Office, UNHCR.

References

Akcapar, S. K. (2009). Turkish Associations in the United States: Towards building a transnational identity. *Turkish Studies,* 10 (2): 165–193.

Avci, G. and Kirisci, K. (2006). Turkey's immigration and emigration dilemmas at the gate of the European Union. *Migracion Y Desarollo,* Segundo Semestre, pp.123-173.

Bittingham, A. and de la Cruz, C. B. (2004). Ancestry 2000. Census 2000 Brief. US Census Bureau. Available at: http://www.census.gov/prod/2004pubs/c2kbr-35.pdf [Accessed 10 Aug 2012].

Boneva, B., Frieze, I. H., Ferligoj, A., Pauknerová, D., Orgocka, A.(1998). Achievement, power, and affiliation motives as clues to (e)migration desires: A four-countries comparison. *European Psychologist,* 3(4): 247-254.

Borjas, G. (1994). The economics of immigration. *Journal of Economic Literature,* 32(4):1667-1717.

Burrell, K. (2009). *Polish Migration to the UK in the 'new' European Union: After 2004.* Fareham: Ashgate.

Cohen, J. H. and Sirkeci, I. (2011). *Cultures of Migration, the Global Nature of Contemporary Mobility,* University of Texas Press, Austin, USA.

DCLG (Department for Communities and Local Government) (2009). *The Turkish and Turkish Cypriot Muslim Community in England, Understanding Muslim Ethnic Communities.* Volume 2010. London: Change Institute, Department for Communities and Local Government.

DWP (Deparment for Work and Pensions) (2008). National Insurance Number Allocations to Adult Overseas Nationals Entering the UK, 2007/8, London: DWP, available at www.dwp.gov.uk/asd/asd1/tabtools/ nino_allocations_0708.pdf .

Drinkwater S., Eade, J. and Garapich, M. (2006). Poles apart? EU enlargement and the labour market outcomes of immigrants in the UK. *IZA Discussion Paper,* No. 2410. Bonn, Germany: IZA. Available at: http://ftp.iza.org/dp2410.pdf.

Dorigo, G. and Tobler, W. (1983). Push-pull migration laws. *Annals of the Association of American Geographers,* 73: 1–17.

EC (European Commission) (2012). *Turkey 2012 Progress Report.* Brussells, European Commission. Available at: http://ec.europa.eu/enlargement/pdf/key_documents/2012/package/tr_rapport_2012_en.pdf [Accessed 15 October 2012].

Esipova, N. and Ray, J. (2010). Migration could triple populations in some wealthy nations. August 20. Gallup. Available at: http://www.gallup.com/poll/142364/Migration-Triple-Populations-Wealthy-Nations.aspx (Accessed 10 June 2012).

Esipova, N., Ray, J. and Publiese, A. (2011). Gallup World Poll. The many faces of global migration. *IOM Migration Research Series,* No. 43, Geneva, Switzerland.

Gallup (2012). Worldwide Research Methodology and Codebook. April 2012. Gallup.

Kucukcan, T. (2004). The making of Turkish Muslim diaspora in Britain. Muslim Minority Affairs, 24(2):243-258.

McClelland, D.C. (1987). *Human Motivation.* Cambridge, New York, Melbourne: Cambridge University Press.

Martin, P. L. (1991). *The unfinished story: Turkish labour migration to Western Europe: with special reference to the Federal Republic of Germany.* International Labour Organisation, Geneva.

Martin, P. L. (2012). Migration, trade, and development: Comparing Mexico-US and Turkey-Europe. *Migration Letters,* 9(1):11-24. Available at: http://www.migrationletters.com. (Accessed: 2 Oct 2012).

ONS (Office of National Statistics, UK) (2004). Population by country of birth and nationality. Published on 25 Nov 2004. Available:http://www.ons.gov.uk/ons/rel/migration1/population-by-country-of-birth-and-nationality/ 2004/population-by-country-of-birth-and-nationality-2004.zip (Accessed: 2 Aug. 2012).

ONS (Office of National Statistics, UK) (2012). Table 1.3. Estimated overseas born population in the UK by country of birth. Published on 30 August 2012. Available: http://www.ons.gov.uk/ ons/rel/migration1/ migration-statistics-quarterly-report/august-2012/population-by-country-of-birth-and-nationality-datasets.xls (Accessed: 15 Dec. 2012).

Piore, M. (1979). *Birds of Passage: Migrant labour and industrial societies.* New York: Cambridge University Press.

Sirkeci, I. (2003). Migration from Turkey to Germany: an ethnic analysis. *New Perspectives on Turkey,* 2003(28-29):189-208.

Sirkeci, I. (2005a). War in Iraq: Environment of Insecurity and International Migration. *International Migration,* 43(4): 197–214.

Sirkeci, I. (2005b). Diaspora: Turkish. In: M. Gibney and R. Hansen (eds.) *Immigration and Asylum from 1900 to the Present.* Santa Barbara: ABC-CLIO, pp.607-610.

Sirkeci, I. (2006). *The Environment of Insecurity in Turkey and the Emigration of Turkish Kurds to Germany.* New York: Edwin Mellen Press.

Sirkeci, I. (2007). Kurdish speaking Cologne: from guest workers to asylum seekers. In: Guillou, A.Y., S. Tapia, and P.M. Wadbled (eds.) *Migrations turques dans un monde Globalise, Le poids du local.* Rennes, France, Presses Universitaires de Rennes, pp.179-198.

Sirkeci, I. (2009a). Transnational mobility and conflict. *Migration Letters,* 6(1): 3-14.

Sirkeci, I. (2009b). *Improving the Immigration and Asylum Statistics in Turkey – Türkiye'de Uluslararası Göç ve Sığınma İstatistiklerinin Geliştirilmesi.* Nov. 2009, Turkish Statistical Institute, Ankara, Turkey.

Sirkeci, I., Cohen, J. H. and Ratha, D. (2012a). *Migration and Remittances during the Global Financial Crisis and Beyond.* The World Bank, Washington, DC., USA.

Sirkeci, I., Cohen, J. H. and Yazgan, P. (2012b). The Turkish culture of migration: Flows between Turkey and Germany, socio-economic development and conflict. *Migration Letters,* 9(1): 33-46.

Sirkeci, I., Cohen, J. and Can, N. (2012c). Internal Mobility of foreign-born in Turkey. In: Finney, N. and Catney, G. (eds.) Minority Internal Migration in Europe. Farnham: Ashgate, pp.175-193.

Statistiche Bundesamt (2012). Ausländische Bevölkerung. Available at: https://www.destatis.de/ DE/ZahlenFakten/

GesellschaftStaat/Bevoelkerung/MigrationIntegration/AuslaendischeBevolkerung/Tabellen/Geburtsort.html.

Todaro, M. P. (1976). Migration and economic development: a review of theory, evidence, methodology and research priorities. *Occasional Paper* 18, Nairobi: Institute for Development Studies, University of Nairobi, Kenya.

UN (United Nations) (2012). *Human Development Report.* Available: http://hdr.undp.org (Accessed 1 Jan 2012).

UN DESA (United Nations Department of Economic and Social Affairs, Population Division) (2009). *Trends in International Migrant Stock: The 2008 Revision* (United Nations database, POP/DB/MIG/Stock/Rev.2008). Available at: http://esa.un.org/migration/index.asp?panel=1.

UNHCR (2001) Statistical Yearbook. Available at: www.unhcr.org.

Vasileva, K. (2011). "Population and social conditions". *Statistics in Focus.* No. 34/2011. Luxembourg: Eurostat.

Vujicic, et al. (2004). The role of wages in the migration of health care professionals from developing countries. *Human Resources for Health.* 2(3). Available at: http://www.biomedcentral.com/1478-4491/2/3 (Accessed: 1 October 2012).

Zimmermann, K. F. (1996). European migration: Push and pull. *International Regional Science Review*, 19(1/2):95-128.

PART 8: CONTEMPORARY ISSUES

Essential Reading:

Cvajner, M. (2019). International Mobility, Erotic Plasticity and Eastern European Migrations. *Migration Letters*, *16*(4), 513–520.

Sirkeci, I. and Yüceşahin, M. M. (2020). Coronavirus and migration: Analysis of human mobility and the spread of COVID-19. *Migration Letters*, *17*(2), 379-398.

Further Readings

Beqo, G. İ. (2019). Women in Here, Women in There: Changing Roles and Lives of Women Migrants from Turkey in Italy. *Migration Letters*, *16*(4), 531-541.

Carignani, Ş. S., Schlimbach, T., Kmiotek-Meier, E., Diaz, C., Chorne, L. D., Vysotskaya, V., ... & Däubler, M. (2020). Agency and Structure Revisited with Youth Responses to Gendered (Spatial) Mobilities in the EU. *Border Crossing*, *10*(1), 61-78.

Castañer, A. M. A. (2017). Climate change and migration in the rural sector of northern Mexico (Zacatecas and San Luis Potosí). *Migration Letters*, *14*(3), 383-395.

Cvajner, M., & Sciortino, G. (2019). Migration and sexual change. *Migration Letters,* 16(4), 473–480

Dogutas, A. (2019). Gender Based Violence against Syrian Refugee Women in Turkey. *Border Crossing*, *9*(2), 113-124.

Duarte, M. (2020). A Human Right to Relocate: The Case for Climate Migrants. In *Current Challenges in Migration Policy and Law* (pp. 51-64). Transnational Press London.

Fresnoza-Flot, A. (2019). Interacting Legal Norms and Cross-Border Divorce: Stories of Filipino Migrant Women in the Netherlands. *Migration Letters*, *16*(4), 521–529.

Girma, H. (2016). Gender and International Migration: From the Slavery Era to the Global Age. *Migration Letters*, *13*(1), 172.

Mahmutoglu, V. (2020). LONG READ: Performing gender in the diaspora: Turkish women in North London. *Migration Letters*, *17*(6), 837-852.

Naudé, W. (2009). Natural disasters and international migration from Sub-Saharan Africa. *Migration letters*, *6*(2), 165-176.

Pojmann, W. (2007). Organizing women migrants: The Filipino and Cape Verdean women's associations in Rome. *Migration Letters*, *4*(1), 29-39.

Sandal, H. (2020). Radical Queer Epistemic Network: Kurdish Diaspora,

Futurity, and Sexual Politics. *Migration Letters*, *17*(1), 81–90.

Sijapati, B., Mak, J., Zimmerman, C., & Kiss, L. (2019). Nepali Women's Labour Migration: Between Protection and Proscription. *Migration Letters*, *16*(4), 611–624.

Yammine, M. I. (2020). Gendered realities and resilience in displacement: Narratives of Syrian refugee women in Lebanon. *Migration Letters*, *17*(6), 781-798.

CHAPTER 27

International Mobility, Erotic Plasticity and Eastern European Migrations

Martina Cvajner

Introduction

For those who want to study sexual life, international migrations represent excellent strategic research material and allow researchers to study many important problems in innovative ways (Merton, 1987). Exploring the migration and sexuality nexus means dealing with one of the key problems of social science: how do actions and norms change when does the context change? To what degree do adult migrants reproduce in the new location their internalized normative models and their established preferences? To what degree, and under what conditions, is mobility a factor associated with increased erotic plasticity (Baumeister and Stillman, 2006)? Which elements of the available sexual subcultures are appropriated by migrants, and which ones resisted?

In the studies of the migration of women, a large body of research is concerned with the fate of transnational families and the care practices – often mediated by ICTs – necessary to manage the parental relationship spanning two or more locations (Carling et al., 2012; Parrenas, 2015). Another important body of work has explored how the migration of women alters the conjugal norms and practices in both sending and receiving areas, often in an egalitarian direction (Gonzales-Lopez, 2005; Hirsh, 2003). Migrant women, however, do not experience change only as mothers or wives. Their mobility also affects them as "women", lovers and – in the essentialist conception endorsed by many of the women here studied – "females" (Cvajner, 2019). In fact, one of the main drivers of contemporary female migration systems is precisely the increasing number of women who migrate outside of conjugal decision-making, as single, divorced or widowed (Donato et al., 2014; Hofmann and Buckley, 2013)

In this contribution, I will analyze the changes in sexual practices and symbols that have taken place within a group of Eastern European migrant women pioneers during their settlement in North-Eastern Italy. I will argue that the migration experience has had a strong impact on their erotic plasticity, modifying not only the set of practices enacted but also their symbolic association with the image of the sexual good wife. Even if the migrant women here studied were relatively mature at the moment of emigration, their age has not inhibited important and deep transformations, concerning the very same criteria of what is pleasurable and what is not. The women have built during their emigration new types of sexual personhood that have played a role in their integration strategies and the overall outcome of the migration process.

To pursue such analysis, I will use here a triangulation between three different data sources on the Eastern European women pioneers that have arrived from 1998 to 2004-5 in the North-Eastern city I will call here Alpinetown. The first is the field notes of an ethnographic project that started serendipitously in 1999, became professional in 2003 and is still ongoing in various forms. The ethnography has followed the women pioneers from their very first experiences – indeed, days if not hours from their arrival – to their definitive settlement (Cvajner, 2019). A second source is a quantitative survey concerning the sexual attitudes and sexual behaviours of Eastern European women migrants – at the time of the survey and retrospectively - that was carried out in 2007 in Alpinetown (Cvajner, 2008). A third, independent, source is provided by a secondary analysis of the interviews collected in the LIL database, a set of biographical interviews with foreign domestic workers in Italy carried out by several interviewers using a comparable protocol.[1] This analysis has thus clearly all the limitations of a local study, unable to claim a national or global validity. The richness of the data, however, and their triangulation provides an unprecedented wealth of information in a field usually marred by scanty evidence.

The Migration and sexuality nexus

The fact that erotic desire and behaviour - perceived as the most intimate, natural, and authentic human drive - is, in fact, strongly structured by cultural and social cleavages has been claimed since the very origins of contemporary social sciences (Malinowski, 1927). Very early, Alfred Kinsey himself made clear that sexual practices are strongly differentiated among diverse social groups. In his path-breaking research, he highlighted how social groups belonging to different social classes and statuses – what he called "socio-cultural groups" – were differentiated, among many things, by very different sexual mores (Kinsey et al., 1948). Subsequent research has further confirmed both the existence of marked differences between the sexual life in various parts of the world and the existence of a plurality of differentiated – and often opposed - sexual fields within each society (Mulhall et al., 2008; Mackay, 2001; Wellings et al., 2006; Laumann et al., 2005).

Sexual research, however, has also highlighted the fact that internalized models of sexual desire and practice are far from being written in stone. Human sex drives are highly responsive to situational, social and cultural influence (Baumeister, 2000). Although actors usually develop across their life span a stable pattern of desire, practice and preferences, such erotic habitus may be modified in-depth in reaction to social and cultural change (Green, 2008).

Erotic plasticity, however, is essentially a socio-psychological concept (Baumeister, 2000; Benuto and Meana, 2008). It has little to say on how the changes in the internal organization of desire are intertwined with socio-cultural

---

[1]. The LIL database, hosted by the Università di Trento, contains currently 862 interviews, collected in various periods and places. The interviews - collected in 2003-4, 2005-06 and 2015-16 – have been coded in Atlas.ti using a consistent coding system. For more information, see http://www.livingintegrationlaws.it/en/tools/. The LIL database is open to all interested researchers (for access, write to paola.capuana@unitn.it). I will focus here on the 55 (out of a total of 86) interviews of women pertaining to post-Soviet migrants that (a) have arrived or lived in the area of Alpinetown in the «pioneer» period, from the late 1990s to the early 2000; and (b) have talked in the interviews about sexual change.

transformation. To fully understand migration as a driving force for sexual change, we need to complement it, as it is argued in the introduction to the present special issue, with a more systematic socio-cultural framework.

Only then we may ask how the experience of migration and the experience of different ethno-sexual boundaries are part of the broader process of social integration. Very roughly, immigrants may converge toward the mainstream sexual subculture of the new location, participating in the same dating and mating networks of natives; they may converge (or even give birth) to specific sexual subcultures, where their participation is defined at least in part by their migration background. Or they may enforce and maintain a specific and distinctive sexual style, as a form of resistance (Espiritu, 2001).

Eastern European Women Pioneers

The analysis here presented derives from a long-term ethnographic project with a group of women that have migrated from the former territories of the USSR to North-Eastern Italy at the turn of the millennium. Post-soviet women, particularly from Ukraine and Moldova, have been the migration pioneers of one of the largest migration systems involving Italy: until 1998-9, there were basically no recorded migrants in Italy from the territories of the former USSR. Only a few years later, it had become one of the largest groups of migrants in Italy (Sciortino, 2015). The post-soviet migration system has been able to expand – although at a reduced pace – even during the years of the economic crisis. Today, more than two decades later, this migration system maintains its original strong gender imbalance: post-soviet migrants in Italy are mostly women. It is a migration system where settled women sponsor the further arrival of other women (Cvajner, 2018).

The group of pioneers I lived with was in many senses migration's absolute beginners. They migrated towards a country that had no previous history of arrivals from their lands. They had often no previous migration experience, although many of them had practised some form of shuttle trade in the soviet period or in its aftermath. Their migration was remarkably atomized, with very little support from recruitment programs, established migration chains or family networks. Being employed nearly only in live-in care work – usually for elderly people with some disabilities – they lived scattered across the city, with very little opportunities to monitor each other. In this sense, the women experienced a strong decrease in informal social control. Another important element was the demographic profile of the migration pioneers. Above all, they were all middle-aged women, from the mid-thirties to the late fifties. Nearly all of them were mothers, and sometimes grandmothers. They had left their children to the care of their parents or sisters, and become the main breadwinner for their families. They had been, with very few exceptions, de facto or de jure, divorced for years (Vianello, 2009). And they had been, in the years before emigration, excluded from all forms of respectable mating and dating, owing to economic scarcity, insecurity and – above all – their 'old' age.

An important discovery during their emigration was precisely that, in Italy, their age did not disqualify them from romance. Such a discovery has triggered a set of ramified changes in the sexual lives of the women. It has made possible the development of a new sexual field (Green, 2014). In the case of the group here studied, such a field is defined by strongly exogamous sexual stratification that employs unabashedly criteria of race, health and wealth – but not age - to allocate sexual desirability. Moreover, in order to compete in this new and unexpected mating market, the women had to experiment with the perspective of an expanded set of sexual practices desired by the prospective Italian partners (in many cases, it means 'anticipated as desired' by the women themselves).

Dating as an Incorporation Process

Early after their arrival, many women realized that in Italy they were considered – at least by some men – as "women" (Cvajner, 2020). For example, Alina arrived in Italy when she was 44. She considered herself a mother and a mature woman, who after her divorce had resigned herself to a sexless status. Walking in the streets, however, she discovered she was looked at and appreciated. Nadia, smilingly remembered that in Italy *they run after you. You know … when you walk they would [sound] a horn. Especially* [mimicking a shout in the street]: *blonde, blonde! They were insistent!*[2] Emigration, in other words, is undoubtedly an opportunity that allows for experimentation and innovation for those women who succeed in establishing sentimental and sexual relationships in the new context.

In a context marked by a deep sense of downward mobility, loneliness and humiliation, the discovery of potentially participating again in the dating scene was one of the very few bright novelties in their lives.

Moreover, they also discovered that there was an unlikely (but far from negligible) niche of Italian men who could be romantically interested in them. Long-term bachelors, widowers and elderly, divorced males (and quite a few unhappily married). These men were usually less educated and markedly older (but still healthy). Although most of them were working-class natives, they had, nevertheless, important economic resources if compared to the women. Moreover, they were often willing to commit to some kind of stable relationship, as shown by the fact that this is the demographic profile of nearly all the mixed marriages with a Eastern European wife (Guetto and Azzolini, 2015).

After a while, I started noticing that the women were increasingly joking among themselves about the possibility of finding an Italian partner. Sofia, one of the very first Ukrainian women to arrive in Alpinetown, was known for greeting all other women with *did you not find a nice Italiensk yet?*. Sofia was playing on the sense of pressure triggered by two common perceptions they all seemed to hold. First, the women tended to consider sex – more precisely, heterosexual coitus – as a key element of health. Vika, a former Ukrainian teacher, liked to provide me with motherly advice, kept repeating that *without sex… you get ill*. Marika, another woman shocked by the fact I was not yet married at my age, stressed that my headaches were the consequence of my denial of the fact that *the body of a woman needs a man*. A second sense of urgency derived from the fact that the women quickly realized that their dream of leaving live-in care work for working-class elderly would have never

---

[2] Excerpt from the interview n. 724, Living Integration Laws Research.

happened thanks to their education, skills or increased control of the Italian language. Except in very few cases, finding a new partner was the only way to be included in the network of his friends and relatives, access new job opportunities and leave the live-in care work sector. Mating was the way in which Eastern European women could become *signore*. This term, originally used to refer to the (women) employers that gave them orders, had quickly been appropriated by the women to define those of them who could aspire to a somewhat lower-middle-class lifestyle, deemed decent and honourable (Cvajner, 2019).

Gina, a 60-year-old Moldovan grandmother, once explained why these new love opportunities had to be applied in a rigorously exogamous way. She contrasted "our" men – that she labeled depreciatively as *sovok* - with the "Italians". The first was associated only with *alcohol, debts ... he would spend it all [whatever I sent]! I don't need [somebody] like that*. On the contrary, she would now need *somebody who walks [with] me, buys flowers, tells me I'm beautiful. And fucks me, eh*. The strength of such an exogamic norm was such that, at least according to some women, it has become accepted even in the sending communities. Iryna, once explained to me that if *you are in Italy for many years ... it is important that in Moldova it is said that [you] have found an Italian. And if there is no relationship yet, the natural expectation is to assume one wanted it*.

When the women started to feel 'settled' in the new environment, its lovescape became one of the most talked-about elements in their lives. Such a change reverberated also in the ways in which they confronted the frequent stereotypes that stigmatized them: the image of the poor, traditionalist, submissive, devoted woman willing to do literally anything to get and keep a man, and the «Slavic gold-digger» interested only in acquiring as many economic assets as possible, cheating the naïve male partners. Even if still resenting them, they often mentioned them as «proofs» that they were indeed desirable, feared by Italian women as competitive alternatives (Näre, 2014).

Migration and Sexual (re-) socialization

Where do they meet their potential partners? In the beginning, the overwhelming majority met them either at the workplace or thanks to people directly related to it. Some women started a relationship with the elderly they assisted or – more often – with one of their relatives. Some others started something out of random encounters in the street. For a long initial period, the women developed an internal interactional norm: the fact that many of these men were actually married had to be treated as a minor nuisance. Only when the networks had widened enough, and the opportunities for meeting Italian men had increased, did the civil status of the prospective partner became an important piece of information. The interaction with these men, however, brought to light the existence of important sexual differences that the women often discussed among themselves. First, the very first women who had been dating Italian men reported to the group that their new partners were not exclusively focused on the coitus. Rather, Italian males were described as paying quite a lot of attention to foreplay. Moreover, they also took for granted that both receiving and performing oral sex were stable elements of any sexual act[3]. Finally, they expected women to openly look for sexual pleasure. These novelties appeared immediately controversial to the group of migrants. Some women welcomed them as highly positive, evidence of the fundamental kindness of their men that cared – contrary to the *sovok* – about their pleasure. They felt *more cuddled in Italy*[4]. Some others, on the contrary, did not particularly appreciate it. For Vika, a fairly outspoken woman, [one] *had to skip the foreplay and get straight to the meat … he is sweet and always speaks to me when we have sex. …he talks to me and tells me he loves me, that I turn him on … shit fuck me right now bljad.*

None of them, however, considered the possibility of not conforming to the preference of their Italian partners. In fact, the first period was clearly marked by the power asymmetries between Eastern European women and Italian men. The survey carried out in 2006 reveals that, among the women who had had some kind of relationship in Italy after emigration, the number of sexual practices performed had significantly increased. Most of the increase, however, was in practices they had performed even if such were not necessarily desired.

Another change involved the coitus itself. Most women, at least in their retrospective accounts, had mainly practised the missionary position and, rarely, the *more ferarum*. The latter had never been particularly liked, as many women defined it as *beastly* and told candidly that they had done so only at the insistence of their husbands. In Italy, the women discovered that their men practised - on relatively equal terms – at least three positions: the missionary, the *more ferarum* and the so-called *Pompeian* (with the female partner on top). Here the reception of the novelty was more mixed. The use of the Pompeian was highly appreciated as it was seen as a sign of respect. They praised Italian men – again, against the sovok – for having understood their strongly passionate natures. The use of *more ferarum* remained definitely less appreciated but nevertheless practised regularly.

The importance of power asymmetries is also particularly visible in what did *not* change. Most women were living alone, isolated, in conditions of involuntary solitude. Many of them spent six days a week, often around the clock, in strict contact with the reality of physical decay and senescence. They often claimed that they needed sex to say healthy. I consequently expected that the incidence of masturbation in the group would have been high. A first surprise was to discover that they had never masturbated before, not even in the years following their divorce. Actually, they were nearly offended by my question, as they regarded – fully in line with the soviet sexual subculture – masturbation as a filthy and unhealthy habit (Kon and Riordan, 1993). A second surprise was that none of them ever admitted having started in emigration. Here - as there was no request by the partners to anticipate or satisfy the demand of the practice - the strength of the previous erotic habitus could remain strong. The role of power asymmetries, however, is far from permanent. Some of the practices the women were originally sceptical about – such as the extended foreplay – become over time cherished rituals. Other practices were quickly renegotiated. The process of sexual learning,

---

[3]. These elements are highly compatible with the sexual survey of the Italian population carried out in the same years. See Barbagli, Dalla Zuanna, Garelli (2010).
[4] Excerpt from the interview n. 760, Living Integration Laws Research.

although substantial, was rather short, and stabilized quickly in a new sexual style, similar or compatible with the expectation of Italian partners. As in any field, changes have stabilized in a shared definition of the situation, a taken-for-granted evaluation of what is desirable, what is practised and what is expected. Over the years, possibly due to the ageing both of the women and the partners, the migrant women have started stressing much more the dimension of intimacy in comparison to the search for variety and experience.

Conclusion: Strength and Limits to Erotic Plasticity

Until now, I have written of the "women" as they were a unified group going through a universal experience. This would be, of course, completely wrong. As matter of fact, the analyses carried out in the previous pages apply only to the women pioneers – roughly half of the total – that actively looked for or had a relationship in Italy during the first five years of emigration. The other women were dubious about these relationships and tended to question the «real» motives of the prospective Italian partners. They considered sexual experimentation as – at best – a distraction from their sacred duty as mothers and daughters. They could engage – and some of them did – in short term sexual encounters, but they could not conceive of more stable forms of relationships. Over time, the group slowly split in half. The women interested in dating Italian men created their own cliques, participating mostly in events were also friends of the already existing partners could participate. The women who were not interested in dating maintained the traditional sites of makeshift sociability (Cvajner, 2019).

When I tried to grasp the difference between the two groups, I have to surrender to the fact that all obvious explanations were unsatisfactory. The women not interested in dating were not the oldest, nor those in the worst physical shape. They had arrived more or less at the same time of the others, and their families were not particularly troublesome. They were not even more religious than the others[5]. The only significant difference I found was in the migratory project of the women themselves. Those women who dated Italians were usually persuaded they would not return to their homeland or they would return only when very old. They were consequently more willing to undergo new sexual socialization. The women who were not interested, or even opposed, to the birth of sexual liaisons regarded their emigration as strictly temporary (although unable to state a precise deadline for the return). They were not interested in sexual change – indeed in any kind of socio-cultural change – because they regarded emigration in Italy as a period of suspended animation. They perceived themselves as birds of passage, to use Piore's felicitous term (Piore, 1979).

Conclusion

The analyses here presented converge in documenting how migration *may* be a powerful factor in the activation of erotic plasticity. In the sexual lives of the women, there have been several important changes that have taken place even if

---

[5]. On the contrary, the birth of the first small Orthodox and Greek-Catholic churches was made possible not by the presence of a sizeable number of single women. The necessary infrastructure was secured by the women who had been able to mobilize their Italian partners to reach the goal.

the migrants were middle-aged and had already formed a rather solid habitus through an extensive period of sexual socialization in a very different field. The analysis, however, should not be read as offering unqualified support to the thesis of erotic plasticity. First of all, the case of the women who did *not* experience significant sexual change, document how erotic plasticity may be held in check by deeply felt norms or normative projects. If the women migrants think of their emigration as temporary, the pressure to confront the ethno-sexual boundaries is remarkably weakened. To be effective, erotic plasticity, as a psychological concept, has to be integrated with a socio-cultural analysis. As has been seen, moreover, erotic plasticity does not mean that everything changes. As it has been documented, while many things have changed, others have remained rather stable, and even reproduced inter-generationally. It is correct to say that migration may increase the variety and heterogeneity of sexual practices experienced by immigrants. This increase in variety, however, takes place selectively. The enrichment of compatible sexual activity models is functional to the control of the new sexual scripts embedded in the dating and mating networks of the new location.

References

Baumeister FR. (2000) Gender differences in erotic plasticity: the female sex drive as socially flexible and responsive. Psychological Bulletin 126: 347-374. https://doi.org/10.1037/0033-2909.126.3.347

Baumeister RF and Stillman T. (2006) Erotic plasticity: Nature, culture, gender, and sexuality. Sex and sexuality 1: 343-359.

Benuto L and Meana M. (2008) Acculturation and Sexuality: Investigating Gender Differences in Erotic Plasticity. The Journal of Sex Research 45: 217-224. https://doi.org/10.1080/00224490801987465

Carling J, Menjívar C and Schmalzbauer L. (2012) Central Themes in the Study of Transnational Parenthood. Journal of Ethnic and Migration Studies 38: 191-217. https://doi.org/10.1080/1369183X.2012.646417

Cvajner M. (2019) Soviet Signoras. Personal and Collective Transformations in Migration Processes, Chicago: University of Chicago Press. https://doi.org/10.7208/chicago/9780226662428.001.0001

Donato K, Piya B and Jacobs A. (2014) The Double Disadvantage Reconsidered: Gender, Immigration, Marital Status, and Global Labor Force Participation in the 21st Century. International Migration Review 48: S335-S376.

Espiritu YL. (2001) "We Don't Sleep around like White Girls Do": Family, Culture, and Gender in Filipina American Lives. Signs 26: 415-440. https://doi.org/10.1086/495599

Gonzales-Lopez. (2005) Erotic Journeys: Mexican Immigrants and their Sex Lives, Berkeley: University of California Press.

Green A. (2014) Sexual Fields. Toward a Sociology of Collective Sexual Life, Chicago: University of Chicago Press.

Green IA. (2008) Erotic habitus: toward a sociology of desire. Theory and Society 37: 597-626.

Guetto R and Azzolini D. (2015) An Empirical Study of Status Exchange through Migrant/Native Marriages in Italy. Journal of Ethnic and Migration Studies 41: 2149-2172. https://doi.org/10.1080/1369183X.2015.1037725

Hirsh JS. (2003) A courtship after marriage : sexuality and love in Mexican transnational families, Berkeley: CUP.

Hofmann ET and Buckley CJ. (2013) Global Changes and Gendered Responses: The Feminization of Migration From Georgia. International Migration Review 47: 508-538. https://doi.org/10.1111/imre.12035

Kinsey AC, Gebhard PH, Martin CE, et al. (1948) Sexual Behavior in the Human Male, Bloomingdale: IIUP.

Kon I and Riordan J. (1993) Sex and Russian society. Bloomington: Indiana University Press.

Laumann EO, Ellingson S, Mahay J, et al. (2005) The sexual organization of the city, Chicago: UCP.

Mackay J. (2001) How does the United States compare with the rest of the world in human sexual behavior? Western Journal of Medicine 174: 429-433. https://doi.org/10.1136/ewjm.174.6.429

Malinowski B. (1927) Sex and repression in savage society, London: K. Paul, Trench, Trubner & co.

Merton RK. (1987) Three fragments from a sociologist's notebook: establishingbthe phenomenon, specified ignorance, and strategic research materials. Annual Review of Sociology: 1-28. https://doi.org/10.1146/annurev.soc.13.1.1

Mulhall J, King R, Glina S, et al. (2008) Importance of and Satisfaction with Sex Among Men and Women Worldwide: Results of the Global Better Sex Survey. The Journal of Sexual Medicine 5: 788-795. ·

Näre L. (2014) Moral encounters: drawing boundaries of class, sexuality and migrancy in paid domestic work. Ethnic and Racial Studies 37: 363-380. https://doi.org/10.1080/01419870.2012.729669

Parrenas RS. (2015) Servants of Globalization: Migration and Domestic Work, second edition, Stanford: SUP.

Piore MJ. (1979) Birds of passage. Migrant labor and industrial societies, New York: Cambridge University Press.

Sciortino G. (2015) Immigration. In: Jones E and Pasquino G (eds) The Oxford Handbook of Italian Politics. OUP

Vianello FA. (2009) Migrando sole. Legami transnazionali tra Ucraina e Italia, Milano: FrancoAngeli.

Wellings K, et al. (2006) Sexual behaviour in context: a global perspective. The LANCET 368: 1706-1728.

CHAPTER 28

Coronavirus and Migration: Analysis of Human Mobility and the Spread of COVID-19

Ibrahim Sirkeci and M. Murat Yüceşahin

Introduction

COVID-19 / 2019-nCoV or Coronavirus as commonly known, has probably been as terrifying as the Spanish Flu and Swine Flu (Jilani *et al.,* 2019). We have written this article at a relatively early stage of the pandemic. Therefore, the number of cases and death toll were rising[1] but not as shocking as these historic pandemics. However, still reactions, measures, as well as accompanying political discourses vary greatly across the world, while some countries are regionally locked down as was the case in Italy by 21st of February 2020[2], some others claim there is none or a few cases only as was the case in Turkey and Indonesia by 10th of March 2020.

The origin of COVID-19 pandemic, initially, has been linked (i.e. suspected but not yet confirmed) to the cases identified in Wuhan, the capital of Hubei province in Central China.[3] Therefore, it is important to take into account the travel density / volume of passengers carried and routes from Wuhan through connected main regional air travel hubs across China along with the final destinations abroad relating to many of these travellers. The travel volumes are likely to be linked to the Chinese immigrant stock populations in these destination countries following the cultures of migration model, which suggests increasing mobility and traffic between countries of destination and origin over time (Cohen and Sirkeci, 2011).

According to the World Health Organisation (WHO, 2020a), coronaviruses (CoV) are a large family of viruses that cause illness ranging from the common cold to more severe diseases, such as Middle East Respiratory Syndrome (MERS-CoV) (WHO, 2020d) and Severe Acute Respiratory Syndrome (SARS-CoV) (WHO, 2020e). The most recent coronavirus, also known as COVID-19, has not been previously observed in humans, with these types of viruses being known to be transmitted between animals and humans (WHO, 2020f). This was confirmed when the earlier cases were identified in Wuhan, China (Chan *et al.*, 2020). Symptoms of COVID-19 are also known to be similar to common flu, but the spread is much

---

[1] Worldwide number of infected people were 666,211 along with 30,864 deaths by 29 March 2020.
[2] Complete, nationwide, lockdown was announced on 9th March 2020.
[3] According to a World Health Organisation report the source of the virus has not been confirmed yet (https://www.who.int/docs/default-source/coronaviruse/who-china-joint-mission-on-COVID-19-final-report.pdf), while a recent study has established two different strains of the virus: one prevalent in Wuhan, and the other being found everywhere else (https://www.researchgate.net/publication/339461351_Variant_analysis_of_COVID-19_genomes). It should be noted that, whilst the virus was first diagnosed in Wuhan this does not prove that it originated there.

speedier. These symptoms include fever, cough, and breathing difficulties and unfortunately can lead to death (WHO, 2020a). Therefore, the risks to public health are grave and cannot be ignored without serious risk of casualties. In sum, the COVID-19 pandemic is now a major health threat globally (Ferguson *et al.*, 2020: 3). As of 1 April 2020, there have been 905,279 cases and 45,371 deaths confirmed worldwide and the global spread has been extremely rapid (ECDC, 2020).

The purpose of this article is to offer insights using international migration data taking into account a series of basic macro indicators. We argue that monitoring immigrant stock data and travel volume data based on human mobility corridors (i.e. origins and destinations), countries could have been better prepared and taken much earlier measures to contain the spread of COVID-19 or other similar diseases. After introducing the conceptual framework, we explain the data and methods used, following which we discuss our findings, having mapped clusters of countries based on their profiles and numbers of COVID-19 cases. In the subsequent section, we discuss the results of a regression model, which can be used in predicting the potential spread of a pandemic, thereby providing more effective targeted and timely responses to similar outbreaks in the future. Lastly, the limitations of this study and some future avenues for research are presented.

Conceptualising the Spread of Virus and Migration Relationship

We have looked at two sets of literature to gain an understanding the current COVID-19 spread crisis: human mobility/migration literature and studies on the spatial spread of diseases. One of the models in migration literature, namely "cultures of migration", argues that over time, i.e. as migration experiences accumulate in an area and through a route between the origin and destination, mobility continues almost irrespective of changes in the drivers of migration that were in place at the beginning (Cohen and Sirkeci, 2011; Cohen, 2004). Thus, we expect an increasing volume of migration over time through established migration corridors. This can be measured by examining the volume of travel between destinations and place of origin. Therefore, we are expecting a correlation between the travel volume between a country of origin and a destination country and immigrant stock of a group in the latter. Hence, mapping the volume of migration flows from the origin of a disease can be useful in understanding the spread and thus, being equipped to set up appropriate containment measures. In the current COVID-19 crisis, this potential proxy indicator seems to be underestimated despite the mass flight cancellations declared in February and March 2020.

It is argued that the increase in emerging infectious diseases[4] is related to environmental change and to human encroachment into remote areas, which increases the contact between human and non-human species, thereby allowing for cross-species transfers of pathogens (Mayer, 2000; Anthamatten and Hazen, 2011). For example, the emergence of SARS in China in 2003 was linked to close contact between humans and the Himalayan palm civet, sold as meat in Chinese markets

---

[4] COVID-19 is not unique in one respect in that about 30 deadly diseases have been identified since the 1980s (Walters, 2003). If we also consider the new strains of existing diseases, the figures are even higher, whereby 335 infectious diseases emerged between 1940 and 2004 (Jones et al., 2008). HIV-1 and SARS are considered to be completely new to human populations (Anthamatten and Hazen, 2011: 41).

(Klempner and Shapiro, 2004; Anthamatten and Hazen, 2011: 41-42), whilst the most recent case of COVID-19 has been linked to bats (Lai *et al.*, 2020a).

Disease spread patterns are known to be moderated by human activities ranging from agriculture to conflicts, however, further critical insights may be found in spatial approaches to health (Jones *et al.*, 2008: 91; Anthamatten and Hazen, 2011: 42). Spatial approaches help us understand diffusion patterns of emerging infectious diseases. Diffusion refers to the spread of an phenomenon across space. Anthamatten and Hazen (2011) identified three primary types of diffusion (Figure 1).

Figure 1. Three types of spatial-diffusion patterns of viruses and/or contagious diseases

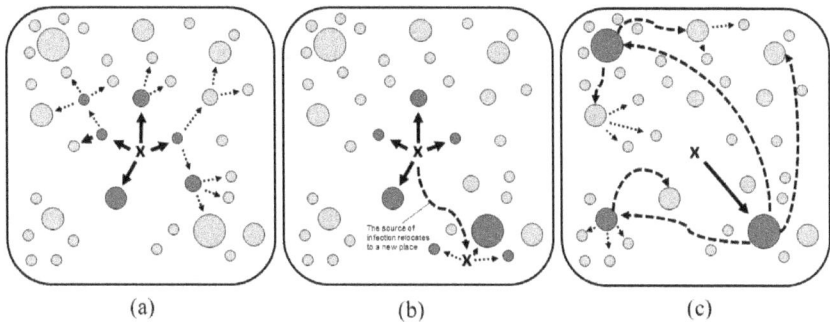

(a)   (b)   (c)

Note: (a) Expansion diffusion; (b) Relocation diffusion; (c) Hierarchical diffusion; The "x" symbolizes the original source of diffusion and the circles symbolize population settlements; larger circles represent larger settlements, and bold circles represent infected settlements.
Source: This figure was prepared based on Anthamatten and Hazen (2011: 44)

Spread of viruses outward from a source is called *expansion diffusion*. Diseases, such as COVID-19, as well as simple head lice, that spread by direct transmission are referred to as contagious diffusion. On the other hand, with *relocation diffusion*, a virus is introduced to a location outside its original range, this often coming with migration, which moves specific cultural practices as well as diseases. A historical example is the introduction of smallpox to the Americas by the conquistadors, whilst a more recent one is the epidemic of cholera that affected Latin America in 1991. This was thought to have been initiated by the release of the cholera pathogen in Peru by a ship arriving from Asia (Mayer, 2000; Anthamatten and Hazen, 2011: 42). It is clear that in the era of super-mobility and ubiquitous connectedness[5], air travel carries pathogens rapidly across the globe (Anthamatten and Hazen, 2011: 42). This was the case in 2003 when SARS quickly spread via air passengers around the world. Pathogens and vectors can be transported rapidly with travel and also by transported goods (Masterton and Green, 1991; Anthamatten and Hazen, 2011: 42). For instance, outbreaks of food poisoning have been traced to shipments of food arriving from abroad. Ho *et al.*, (2002) stated that since 1995, several US outbreaks of cyclosporiasis have been connected to raspberries imported from

---

[5] For connectedness and connected consumers, see Sirkeci (2013).

Guatemala (Anthamatten and Hazen, 2011: 44).

Hierarchical diffusion assumes a spatial hierarchy in the spreading of things. In particular, large metropolitan areas see a much speedier spread of diseases compared to small villages. This is simply due to the sheer number of people and goods travelling in and out of such large settlement areas. Due to population density, among other features, proliferation of diseases in cities is faster as people interact with each other in many public spaces (Anthamatten and Hazen, 2011: 45). The early diffusion of Acquired Immune Deficiency Syndrome (AIDS) in the US is an example of hierarchical diffusion. It had started in a few large cities at first, but over a decade it had spread beyond, first to other cities and then to smaller towns. The spread of HIV in Sub-Saharan Africa saw a very similar pattern[6] (Gould, 1993; Anthamatten and Hazen, 2011: 45).

Data and Method

The chronology of reporting of the COVID-19 cases is important for our analysis. It was first the case that undiagnosed cases marked by pneumonia in people associated with a seafood market appeared in Wuhan, Hubei Province, China, which were reported on 31 December 2019 (e.g. Holshue *et al.*, 2020). Chinese authorities[7] reported this cluster of cases and confirmed the coronavirus for the first time on 11 January 2020 in the Wuhan Municipal Health and Health Commission's Report on Unexplained Viral Pneumonia (NHCPRC, 2020a, 2020b). A local doctor in Wuhan had apparently been alerting others to the potential coronavirus cases as early as mid-December 2019. The development of the symptoms for the COVID-19 seemingly confirms such a start date (Chan *et al.*, 2020). The earliest date for spotting the first COVID-19 case appears as being 17 November 2019, although it was not recognised as such at that time (Ma, 2020) and inadvertently, it was carried to other countries (Lipsitch *et al.*, 2020). This means all countries were exposed to the unchecked spread of the virus between up until mid-January in the case of China, whilst laggard countries failed to take any action until the middle March (e.g. Turkey). Hence, millions of more interactions took place, including trips to and from China and other connected destinations until social distancing and other stricter measures were put in place.

The first case in the USA was diagnosed on 19 January 2020, and the first in Italy was diagnosed on 31 January 2020. For many other countries, reports of the first cases came much later. For example, Turkey announced the first case on 11 March 2020 (McKernan, 2020). In these countries, the number of cases has been rapidly rising since soon after the first one were reported[8], which means the virus has been spreading unchecked for a lengthy period. It has been well documented that, without measures preventing spread, the number of infected people will increase much more rapidly than were this not the case. The United Kingdom has

---

[6] HIV/AIDS rates in rural areas of Ghana were higher than those in urban areas throughout the course of its epidemic (Oppong, 1998; Anthamatten and Hazen, 2011: 45).
[7] Information comes from the official website of the National Health and Health Commission in the People's Republic of China.
[8] For earlier analyses of such a development, see: https://freelonia.org/coronavirus-italian-job/ and https://freelonia.org/gec-kalan-ulkelerde-vaka-sayisi-hizla-artiyor/

been one of the laggard countries, where practically no measures were in place until early March against the spread of COVID-19 (Hunter, 2020).

In our exploration of the spread of the disease, some assumptions were formulated. First, we assumed a normal distribution of the cases diagnosed in Wuhan, Hubei, China. We have calculated the crude rate for COVID-19 cases in Hubei province by dividing the number of cases recorded by the total population and each resident in the province is assumed to have had an equal chance of being infected by this virus. This leads to the second assumption: the same crude rate of COVID-19 spread (CRS) is true for the people who have travelled from Wuhan. Accordingly, we have estimated the CRS for Hubei province, as abovementioned, the region of the origin, in China. The CRS for the province is estimated to be 1.14 per thousand through the formula (1) [i.e. the number of diagnosed cases (c) divided by the total population (p)]:

$$CRS = c/p \times 1000 \qquad (1)$$

This gives us a probable number of people infected who travelled abroad. These numbers of infected travellers are pro-rata distributed to destination countries, according to the volume of travel to each destination. This is the number of infected people that arrived in each country, which should be treated as the minimum number of cases for each destination at the beginning of the pandemic.

We first established the correlation (see Table 1c, Appendix) between migration data and Wuhan's air travel data, as the latter was not available for all countries, to understand the link between human mobility and the spread of COVID-19. We used the 2017 data on immigrant stock in all countries (WB, 2020) as an indicator of travel intensity between countries. In addition, we included some other contextual indicators that may have been moderating the relationship between these independent variables and the dependant variable (i.e. the number of cases of COVID-19 reported by World Health Organisation - WHO). We tested the Gross National Income (GNI) and Human Development Index (HDI) as potential indicators of the macro environment and decided to use HDI as it reflects a much more holistic picture of individual countries. Population size and population density alongside median age were included in our analyses as moderating demographic variables. We also used the Cato Institute's Human Freedom Score (HFS) (CATO, 2020) to control for the possibility of some countries not accurately reporting the COVID-19 cases and related death statistics. We created cross-tabulations summarising the number of cases, the number of deaths according to the WHO (2020a,b,c), airline travellers volumes from Lai *et al.* (2020b: 15) and Chinese migrant stock from WB (2020) in top 30 destination countries along with the probable number of cases in these destinations using the CRS (Tables 1a and 1b, Appendix).

Methodologically, firstly we used correlation analysis to understand the relationship between the number of COVID-19 cases of infection and death as well as potential moderating factors, where the focus is on human mobility drivers (Table 1c, Appendix). Secondly, we ran multivariate regression models to understand the determinants of the number of COVID-19 cases by country. This can also offer a basis for developing a predictive model. Thirdly, we used cluster analysis in order to determine the spatial clustering with the exploratory data from the selected 111 countries[9]. The above described analyses were carried out using the IBM PASW Statistics (Predictive Analytics Software Statistics) program. Cluster analysis was calculated using the k-means algorithm[10]. Cluster analysis is one of the most widely used methods of statistical analysis in social sciences (Rencher, 2002). It considers the similarities of individuals, objects, or spatial units (countries in this study) and groups them into two or more sub-groups (Everitt and Dunn, 1991; Afifi and Clark, 1999; Rencher, 2002; Addio and Ercole, 2005; Yüceşahin and Tulga, 2017). The analysis indicates the spatial units (countries) assigned to the same cluster that are similar in terms of the values of the variables.

Findings and Discussion

We, first, examined the patterns of COVID-19 spread around the world and identified four clusters of countries reflecting their profiles and the volume of cases and deaths along with some key macro indicators as moderating factors. We explored the global data and what has been reported by individual countries and tried to understand the patterns in relation to immigrant stocks from China along with other contextual factors. The following equations were used in the three multivariate regression models run to assess the relative importance of different factors in explaining the total number of COVID-19 cases (TCC), i.e. our dependent variable (Table 1 and 2):

$\hat{y} = \beta_0$ (constant)$+ \beta_1$(TPO)$+ \beta_2$(POD)$+ \beta_3$(MEA)$+ \beta_4$(HDI)$+ \beta_5$(HFS)$+ \beta_6$(ISFC)$+\varepsilon$ (Model 1)

$\hat{y} = 2.313+1.678+8.258+0.026+4.951+0.048+6.852+0.523$

$\hat{y} = \beta_0$ (constant)$+ \beta_1$(TPO)$+ \beta_2$(POD)$+ \beta_3$(MEA)$+ \beta_4$(HDI)$+ \beta_5$(HFS)$+ \beta_6$(ISIC)$+\varepsilon$ (Model 2)

$\hat{y} = 2.543+1.637+6.477+0.023+5.094+0.018+6.725+0.499$

$\hat{y} = \beta_0$ (constant)$+ \beta_1$(TPO)$+ \beta_2$(POD)$+ \beta_3$(MEA)$+ \beta_4$(HDI)$+ \beta_5$(HFS)$+ \beta_6$(HMO)$+\varepsilon$ (Model 3)

$\hat{y} = 2.454+1.765+5.827+0.025+5.112+0.035+6.517+0.517$

Moderating variables in the regression models included total population (TPO), population density (POD), median age (MEA), HDI, HFS, immigrant stock from China (ISFC), immigrant stock in China (ISIC) and human mobility[11] (HMO). The correlation matrix (Table 1) confirms that all the independent variables, except for

---

[9] The selection of 111 countries was data driven, whereby we dropped countries where immigrant stock and/or Covid-19 case statistics were not available.

[10] For the details of and justifications for K-means clustering, please see Afifi and Clark (1999: 395); Bacher (2002: 105); and Rencher (2002: 482).

[11] In order to represent the size of international human mobility, this variable is obtained by multiplying ISFC by ISIC.

the TPO and POD, are significantly correlated with the TCC[12]. However, there are some collinearity problems between the MEA and HDI; the GNI and HDI; and the ISFC and HMO. The correlation coefficient (r) between the MEA and HDI is 0.876; between the GNI and HDI is 0.837 and between the ISFC and HMO is 0.838. To explore the differences and delineate the relationship, three different models were run, as shown in Table 2.

Table 1. Correlation matrix for the exploratory multiple regression analyses (n=111)

	TPO	POD	MEA	HDI	GNI	HFS	ISFC	ISIC	HMO
Total COVID-19 cases (TCC)	0.177	0.064	-0.714**	-0.761**	-0.664**	-0.561**	0.375**	0.313**	0.297**
Total Population (TPO)	1	0.018	-0.056	-0.087	-0.081	-0.106	0.192*	0.213*	0.161
Population density (POD)		1	-0.124	-0.126	-0.323**	-0.097	0.160	0.052	0.034
Median age (MEA)			-1	-0.876**	-0.698**	-0.713**	0.227*	0.124	0.170
Human Development Index (HDI)				-1	-0.837**	-0.751**	0.270**	0.116	0.190*
Gross National Income (GNI)					-1	-0.660**	0.352**	0.086	0.226*
Human Freedom Score (HFS)						-1	0.261**	0.069	0.184
Immigrant stock from China (ISFC)							1	0.456**	0.838**
Immigrant stock in China (ISIC)								1	0.708**
Human mobility (HMO)									1

** Correlation is significant at the 0.01 level (2-tailed)
* Correlation is significant at the 0.05 level (2-tailed)

Regression results confirmed that the total number of cases for each country is significantly moderated by the factors included in our model. In Model 1, the TPO, POD, MEA, HDI, HFS, and ISFC explain 65% of the variance in the number of COVID-19 cases in each county. In this model, in which the ISIC and HMO are excluded because of the high-level correlation among them, both the TPO and HDI are the most significant factors affecting the TCCs. Despite the high-level of correlation between MEA and HDI, we included these two variables in the model since they are conceptually quite different indicators. At the same time, the volume of immigrant stock in destination countries (ISFC) is a statistically significant indicator for the volume of COVID-19 cases (TCCs).

Despite there being no collinearity problem between ISFC and ISIC, we used these indicators in the models 1 and 2 in order to present their explanatory power separately. Similar to the first model, the five variables (TPO, POD, MEA, HDI, HFS, and ISIC) were significant in determining the number of COVID-19 cases and the model 2 also explains 66% of the variance, with HDI being the most significant factor. Moreover, TPO and ISIC are the significant factors in Model 2. Confirming the role of ISIC and ISFC in these two models support our argument that human mobility is a significant determinant of the spread and volume of COVID-19 cases (TCCs) across the world. Therefore, in the third model, instead of ISFC and ISIC, we have included an interaction of the two, i.e. Human mobility

---

[12] We transformed and used logarithmic equivalents (i.e. $Log_{10}TCC$) of the number of cases in the dependent variable, TCC.

(HMO) along with other contextual variables, namely TPO, POD, MEA, HDI, and HFS. These included independent variables explain 64% of the variance in TCCs in each country. The TPO and HDI are the most important indicators for the TCCs. Moreover, human mobility is a statistically significant factor for the TCCs in the countries.

Considering the spread of COVID-19 among 110 countries, for the three models we can argue that countries with larger populations, and higher HDI scores have the highest COVID-19-case levels. Some of these factors are probably more or less self-explanatory. For example, population size is directly related to the pool size for potentially infected individuals. HDI is significant and it shows that relatively poor countries will be affected worse from the COVID-19 pandemic. However, we found no significant relationships between the TCC and population density (POD) and HFS. These results tell us that every one unit increase in the HDI score may mean about five more COVID-19 cases being reported according to these models. In all three models, a one person increase in population size indicates over 1.6 more COVID-19 cases. HFI scores were found to be insignificant in determining the number of cases reported, thus not supporting the negative relationship that was expected.

We have tested the role of migration in three models. In model 1, we have shown that every additional immigrant from China (ISFC) in a given destination country indicates a 6.9 increase in the number of COVID-19 cases. In model 2, every additional immigrant in China (ISIC) from a destination country means 6.73 more COVID-19 cases being found in that country. In model 3, we have used an interaction variable (product of ISFC and ISIC) to show that every one unit increase in HMO leads to 6.52 more COVID-19 cases. Thus, we argue it is not the number of Chinese immigrants, but rather, the totality of human mobility in both directions, i.e. including immigrants in China, that matters.

The volume of migration in each migration corridor linking the countries of origin and destination appears as a strong indicator for the spread of the pandemic. This can be an important proxy to see how countries can predict the scale of and prepare for a pandemic. The role of migration is also explain why similarly large and developed countries have varying numbers of cases emerging. Using migration data alongside the other indicators we have used in the analyses may be helpful for organising the global response to similar pandemics in terms of where to concentrate the resources at early stages so as to contain the spread. This relates to our next question. We discuss in the following passages which countries are more vulnerable and which are more resistant.

We have determined the spatial clustering (i.e. similarities and disparities) of the selected countries using the total number of COVID-19 cases (WHO, 2020a, b, c and ECDC, 2020)[13] along with other all contextual variables. The data for the chosen 10 variables have different units for the 111 focal countries and thus, all have been analysed after logarithmic transformation[14]. As a result of the cluster

---

[13] The total number of COVID-19 cases by country is presented in Tables 2a, b, c, and d in the Appendix.
[14] Logarithmic transformation is a method of standardising data values in log ($\log_{10}$) format. Cluster analysis is a

analysis, the values in log format averages (final cluster centres) of the variables are presented in Table 3. Accordingly, we have assigned 51 of the 111 countries to cluster 1; 35 countries to cluster 2; 15 countries to cluster 3, and 10 countries to cluster 4. The values in log format in Table 3 have been converted into a plot diagram to illustrate clearly the differences between the clusters and the countries in each (Figure 2).

Table 2. Results of multiple regressions for the dependent variable TCCs by country (n=110[b])

Variable[a]	Model 1		Model 2		Model 3	
	β coefficient	t-value**	β coefficient	t-value**	β coefficient	t-value**
(Constant)	-2.313	-4.423***	-2.543	-5.094***	-2.454	-4.747***
Total Population (TPO)	1.678E-09	3.529***	1.637E-09	3.492**	1.765E-09	3.720***
Population density (POD)	-8.258E-05	-1.028***	-6.477E-05	-0.823***	-5.827E-05	-0.726***
Median age (MEA)	0.026	1.709***	0.023	1.525**	0.025	1.588***
Human development index (HDI)	4.951	4.652***	5.094	4.876***	5.112	-4.791***
Human freedom score (HFS)	-0.048	-0.501***	-0.018	-0.196***	-0.035	-0.373***
Immigrant stock from China (ISFC)	6.852E-07	2.383***	–	-**	–	-**
Immigrant stock in China (ISIC)	–	-*	6.725E-06	2.909**	–	-**
Human mobility (HMO)	–	-*	–	-**	6.517E-12	2.004**
Adjusted R²	*0.65*		*0.66*		*0.64*	
F	*34.205*		*35.519*		*33.419*	

Source: Data from ECDC (2020); UN (2019, 2020); WB (2020); Vásquez and Porčnik (2019), authors' calculations.
Significance: ***p < 0.001; **p < 0.01; *p < 0.05.
[a] For further information on some of the variables by countries, see Table 2a, b, c, and d in the Appendix.
[b] Although Myanmar is involved in the Covid-19 case and death list, obtained from ECDC (2020), the case and the death cells have zero. Therefore, the regression analyses omitted this country during the analysing processes. In addition, China is excluded from both the data (Table 2a, b, c, and d in the Appendix) and analyses since this country does not have (Chinese) any migrant stock.

The cluster analysis has shown certain spatial and perhaps socioeconomic patterns across the world. The first cluster (1) is marked by relatively low numbers

---

sensitive analysis for large variables, which can lead to incorrect results because the analysis tries to parse large sets of values. For this reason, the variables to be used in the analysis must either be the same (for example, all percentages) or transformed. Since the units of the variables used in the analysis differ from each other (numbers, years, rates, percentages, scores etc.), they have been standardised and transformed into log (Log₁₀) format. A large log₁₀ value shows that the variable is high in terms of the rate, speed, or score, while a small log₁₀ value shows that they are low.

of COVID-19 cases (Table 3 and Figure 2). In this cluster, total deaths, total population, population density, median age, human development index, gross national income, human freedom score, immigrant stock from China, and immigrant stock in China are also slightly lower than for the countries in other clusters. Most of these countries, if not all, are also considered to be low-income countries, with few exceptions, such as Malta and Brunei Darussalam.

Table 3. Final cluster centres obtained from the cluster analysis (n=111)

		Variables[a]									
		TCC	TDE	TPO	POD	MEA	HDI	GNI	HFS	ISFC	ISIC
	Cluster 1	1.21	0.02	6.61	1.72	1.44	-0.17	3.92	0.84	2.84	2.48
	Cluster 2	2.60	0.67	7.17	1.88	1.54	-0.09	4.32	0.85	3.72	3.01
Log$_{10}$	Cluster 3	2.67	0.98	7.86	2.02	1.54	-0.11	4.24	0.85	4.95	4.36
	Cluster 4	4.11	2.49	7.65	2.31	1.63	-0.04	4.64	0.92	5.16	3.98
Anova Test	*F Value*	*78.39*	*63.82*	*22.29*	*2.88*	*12.02*	*15.17*	*14.20*	*4.84*	*77.17*	*60.92*
	P	***	***	***	*	***	***	***	**	***	***

Source: Data from ECDC (2020); UN (2019, 2020); WB (2020); Vásquez and Porčnik (2019), with authors' calculations

[a] TCC: Total COVID-19 cases;   TDE: Total COVID-19 related deaths; TPO: Total population; POD: Population density; MEA: Median age; HDI: Human Development Index; GNI: Gross National Income; HFS: Human Freedom Score; ISFC: Immigrant Stock from China; ISIC: Immigrant Stock in China.
Significance: ***$p < 0.001$; **$p < 0.01$; *$p < 0.05$

In cluster 2, all the indicators are higher than with the first cluster, whereas the gross national income is higher than for cluster 3; median age is equal to that of cluster 3; and immigrant stock from China and immigrant stock in China from the origin countries are lower than for cluster 3.

In cluster 3, total COVID-19 cases is higher than for cluster 1 and 2. The countries in cluster 3 have higher deaths, population density, median age, immigrant stock from China and immigrant stock in China compared to the countries in the first two clusters. In cluster 3, the total population and immigrant stock in China are higher than the two other clusters. In addition, median age and HFS are equal to cluster 2. In this cluster, 8 countries are located in South and East Asia along with Australia, Canada, New Zealand and Brazil and Russia, two emerging economies.

Cluster 4 comprises the USA, Belgium, Germany, Italy, the Netherlands, the UK, Switzerland, Spain, France, and South Korea, all high-income countries with strong health infrastructures. In this cluster total population is as high as in cluster 3. These countries are marked by a remarkably high volume of COVID-19 cases and large diasporas from China as well as higher population density compared to the other clusters. Remarkably, in this cluster, immigrant stock in China from the other countries is lower than for Cluster 3.

The F values in the cluster analysis show that the most important variables contributing to the clustering regarding the countries' convergence or divergence are, respectively, the total COVID-19 cases (78.39), immigrant stock from China

Figure 2. Clustering of countries and the final cluster centres of the variables

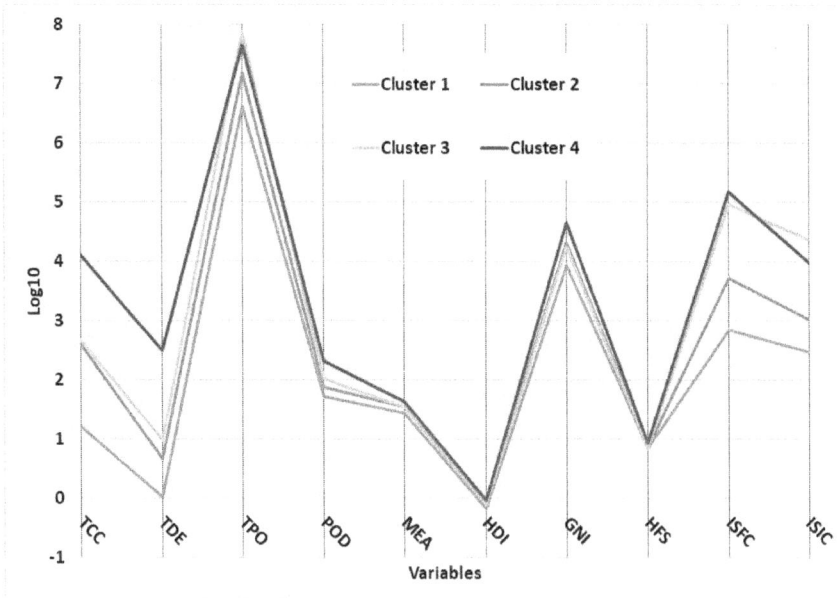

Cluster 1	Cluster 2	Cluster 3	Cluster 4
Azerbaijan, Bahamas, Barbados, Bhutan, Bolivia, Bosnia and Herzegovina, Brunei Darussalam, Cambodia, Central African Republic, Congo, Croatia, Cyprus, El Salvador, Estonia, Fiji, Gabon, Georgia, Ghana, Guatemala, Guinea, Guyana, Haiti, Honduras, Iceland, Kenya, Kyrgyzstan, Latvia, Lithuania, Madagascar, Malta, Mauritania, Mauritius, Moldova, Mongolia, Namibia, Nepal, Papua New Guinea, Paraguay, Rwanda, Serbia, Seychelles, Slovakia, Sudan, Suriname, Timor Leste, Togo, Trinidad and Tobago, Uganda, Uruguay, Tanzania, and Zambia	Argentina, Algeria, Austria, Bulgaria, Chile, Costa Rica, Czechia, Denmark, Dominican Republic, Ecuador, Egypt, Finland, Greece, Hungary, Ireland, Israel, Jordan, Kazakhstan, Lebanon, Luxembourg, Mexico, Norway, Pakistan, Panama, Peru, Poland, Portugal, Romania, Slovenia, South Africa, Sri Lanka, Sweden, Turkey, Ukraine, and Venezuela	Australia, Bangladesh, Brazil, Canada, India, Indonesia, Japan, Malaysia, Myanmar, New Zealand, Philippines, Russia, Singapore, Thailand, and Vietnam	Belgium, France, Germany, Italy, the Netherlands, South Korea, Spain, Switzerland, the UK, and the USA

Note: This plot diagram was prepared by the final cluster centres obtained from the cluster analysis (see Table 3).
Explanation: TCC: Total COVID-19 cases; TDE: Total COVID-19 related deaths; TPO: Total population; POD: Population density; MEA: Median age; HDI: Human Development Index; GNI: Gross National Income; HFS: Human Freedom Score; ISFC: Immigrant Stock from China; ISIC: Immigrant Stock in China.

(77.17), total deaths (63.82), immigrant stock in China (60.92), total population

(22.29), HDI (15.17), GNI (14.20), HFS (4.84), and population density (2.88) (Table 3). The top four most important variables contributing to this clustering are the total COVID-19 cases (TCC) (F=78.39), immigrant stock from China (F=77.17), total deaths (F=63.82), and immigrant stock in China (F=60.92). As can be seen from the red line in Figure 2, ten countries in cluster 4 are in relocation areas of the spatial diffusion pattern of COVID-19. These ten countries are located in three regions: (1) origin-region (China and a neighbouring country, South Korea); (2) first relocation-region (Western Europe); and (3) second relocation-region (USA).

It is important to note that we are examining the predicting power of immigrant populations/diasporas from China and immigrants/diasporas in China for understanding the spread (and volume) of COVID-19 cases, also being in line with the diffusion theories explained at the beginning. However, we are not making a causal relationship, but rather, identifying a proxy to understand the diffusion. Migration relationships or corridors of human mobility established over time as cultures of migration emerge are indicators of developing social and economic relationships between the countries involved. This means more investment and more remittance flows, more holiday trips, and a significant growth regarding other relationships.

Conclusion

The spread of COVID-19 seems to follow a relocation diffusion pattern beyond the neighbouring countries. A hierarchical diffusion pattern was also observed regarding many countries in cluster 4 we have identified. These countries marked by high HDI scores, relatively large populations, high income and sizeable Chinese diasporas have seen the largest volumes of infected populations. However, there was also evidence confirming an expansion to neighbouring countries, as expected, towards Japan and South Korea and other South-East Asian neighbours where initially a significant number of cases were reported.

The statistical models that we have applied clearly show that the COVID-19 spread around the world could have been estimated and mapped out to a substantial degree of accuracy by simply taking into account some macro variables, such as the population size, HDI scores, and immigrant stock from the origin at each destination. We have applied the statistical model at the country level. However, where data are available, this model can be used to identify certain regional or local level concentration of infected individuals. It emerges from the most recent data that large metropolitan areas and global cities, such as London and New York, are taking the lion share of cases in their respective countries. Therefore, further spread from these centres could also be examined using a similar approach. What matters in this model is that viruses relocate to surrounding areas or beyond by transport following the diffusion theory we presented at the beginning of this work.

Our analyses of the data available show that governments around the world could have been more proactive and prepared in responding to the COVID-19 pandemic, if they had utilised model(s) like the one suggested in this article. So far, late and reactionary responses to the crisis have seemingly led to sharp increases in the number of cases and deaths in many countries. We argue that this could have been avoided, if travel data had been used during the early stages of diffusion. By monitoring immigrant stock data and/or travel volume data based on human mobility corridors (i.e. origins and destinations), countries could have been better prepared to tackle the spread of COVID-19. This is one of the lessons that should be learnt for tackling future pandemics more effectively than the present one.

Another important note is that despite some racist exchanges by politicians in early phases of the COVID-19 crisis, the spread of the virus does not have an ethnic origin. We have shown the role of human mobility patterns irrespective of ethnic or national origins. Many other studies by scientists also point that the origin of the viruses have not been confirmed. Given the fact that human settlements more and more expand into living spaces of animals, there is likely to be more transfer of such viruses from animals to humans. Focusing on this latter challenge may mean better use of our resources and energy for future generations.

References

Afifi, A.A. & Clark, V. (1999). *Computer-Aided Multivariate Analysis*. Third ed., London: Chapman and Hall/CRC Press.

Addio, A.C. & Ercole, M.M. (2005). Trends and determinants of fertility in OECD countries: The role of policies. Directorate for Employment, Labour and Social Affairs, *OECD Social, Employment and Migration Working Papers*, no. 27. Cedex.

Anthamatten, P. & Hazen, H. (2011). *An Introduction to the Geography of Health*. London: Routledge Taylor & Francis Group.

Bacher, J. (2002). *Cluster Analysis*. Nuremberg: University Erlangen.

CATO (Cato Institute) (2020). *Human Freedom Index by Cato Institute*. Available at: https://object.cato.org/sites/cato.org/files/human-freedom-index-files/human-freedom-index-2019.xlsx Accessed: 11/03/2020.

Chan, J. F. W., Yuan, S., Kok, K-H., To, K. K-W., Chu, H., Yang, J., Xing, F., Jieling Liu, BNurs, J. L., Yip, C. C-Y., Rosana Wing-Shan Poon, R. W-S., Tsoi, H-W., Lo, S. K-F., Chan, K-H., Poon, V. K-M., Chan, W-M., Ip, J. D., Cai, J-P., Vincent Chi-Chung Cheng, V. C-C., Chen, H., Christopher Kim-Ming Hui, C. K-M. and Prof Kwok-Yung Yuen, K-Y. (2020). A familial cluster of pneumonia associated with the 2019 novel coronavirus indicating person-to-person transmission: a study of a family cluster. *The Lancet*, *395*(10223): 514-523.

Cohen, J. H. (2004). *The Culture of Migration in Southern Mexico*. Austin, TX: University of Texas Press.

Cohen, J. H., & Sirkeci, I. (2011). *Cultures of migration: The global nature of contemporary mobility*. Austin, TX: University of Texas Press.

ECDC (European Centre for Disease Prevention and Control) (2020). *COVID-19 Geographic Distribution Worldwide*. Accessed from https://www.ecdc.europa.eu/sites/default/files/documents/COVID-19-geographic-disbtribution-worldwide-2020-03-23.xlsx, on March 23, 2020.

Everitt, B. S. & Dunn, G. (1991). *Applied Multivariate Data Analysis*. London: Cambridge University Press.

Ferguson, N. M., Laydon, D., Nedjati-Gilani, G., Imai, N., Ainslie, K., Baguelin, M., Bhatia, S., Boonyasiri, A., Cucunubá, Z., Cuomo-Dannenburg, G., Dighe, A., Dorigatti, I., Fu, H., Gaythorpe, K., Green, W., Hamlet, A., Hinsley, W., Okell, L. C., van Elsland, S., Thompson, H., Verity, R., Volz, E., Wang, H., Wang, Y., Walker, P. G. T., Walters, C., Winskill, P., Whittaker, C., Donnelly, C. A., Riley, S., Ghani, A.C. (2020). Impact of non-pharmaceutical interventions (NPIs) to reduce COVID-19 mortality and healthcare demand. *Imperial College COVID-19 Response Team*. DOI: https://doi.org/10.25561/77482. Accessed from https://www.imperial.ac.uk/media/imperial-college/medicine/sph/ide/gida-fellowships/Imperial-College-COVID19-NPI-modelling-16-032020.pdf, on March 20, 2020.

Gould, P. (1993). *The Slow Plague: A Geography of the AIDS Pandemic*. Oxford: Blackwell Publishers.

Ho, A. Lopez, A. Eberhart, M., Levenson, R., Finkel, B. da Silva, A., Roberts, J., Orlandi, P., Johnson, C. and Herwaldt, B. (2002). Outbreak of cyclosporiasis associated with imported raspberries, Philadelphia, Pennsylvania, 2000. *Emerging Infectious Diseases*, 8: 783-788.

Holshue, M. L., DeBolt, C., Lindquist, S., Lofy, K. H., Wiesman, J., Bruce, H., Spitters, C., Ericson, K., Wilkerson, S., Tural, A., Diaz, G., Cohn, A., Fox, C. L., Patel, A., Gerber, S. I., Kim, L., Tong, S., Lu, X., Lindstrom, S., Pallansch, M. A., Weldon, W. C., Biggs, H. M., Uyeki, T. M. and Pillai, S. K. (2020). First case of 2019 novel coronavirus in the United States. *The New England Journal of Medicine*, 382 (10): 929-936.

Hunter, D.J. (2020). Covid-19 and the Stiff Upper Lip — The Pandemic Response in the United Kingdom. *The New England Journal of Medicine*, DOI: 10.1056/NEJMp2005755.

Jilani, T. N., Jamil, R. T., & Siddiqui, A. H. (2019). H1N1 Influenza (Swine Flu). In *StatPearls [Internet]*. StatPearls Publishing. Accessed from https://www.ncbi.nlm.nih.gov/books/NBK513241/, on March 22, 2020.

Jones, K., Patel, N., Levy, M. Storeygard, A., Balk, D., Gittleman, J. and Daszak, P. (2008). Global trends in emerging infectious diseases. *Nature*, 451: 990-993.

Klempner, M. & Shapiro, D. (2004). Crossing the species barrier – one small step to man, one giant leap to mankind. *New England Journal of Medicine*, 350: 1171-1172.

Lai, C. C., Shih, T. P., Ko, W. C., Tang, H. J., & Hsueh, P. R. (2020a). Severe acute respiratory syndrome coronavirus

2 (SARS-CoV-2) and corona virus disease-2019 (COVID-19): the epidemic and the challenges. International journal of antimicrobial agents, 105924. https://doi.org/10.1016/j.ijantimicag.2020.105924. Accessed: 25 March 2020.

Lai, S., Bogoch, I. I., Ruktanonchai, N. W., Watts, A., Lu, X., Yang, W., Yu, H., Khan, K. & Tatem, A. J. (2020b). Assessing spread risk of Wuhan novel coronavirus within and beyond China, January-April 2020: A travel network-based modelling study. *medRxiv (The Preprint Server for Health Sciences)* preprint: 1-25. doi: https://doi.org/10.1101/2020.02.04.20020479, Accessed: March 11, 2020.

Lipsitch, M., Swerdlow, D. L., & Finelli, L. (2020). Defining the epidemiology of Covid-19—studies needed. *New England Journal of Medicine.* Accessed from https://www.nejm.org/doi/full/10.1056/NEJMp2002125, on March 22, 2020.

Ma, J. (2020). Coronavirus: China's first confirmed Covid-19 case traced back to November 17, *South China Morning Post*, 13 March 2020. Accessed from https://www.scmp.com/news/china/society/article/3074991/coronavirus-chinas-first-confirmed-covid-19-case-traced-back, on March 20, 2020.

MacKernan, B. (2020). Turkey announces its first case of coronavirus. *The Guardian, 11 March 2020.* Accessed from https://www.theguardian.com/world/2020/mar/11/turkey-announces-its-first-case-of-coronavirus, on March 16, 2020.

Masterton, R. and Green, A. (1991). Dissemination of human pathogens by airline travel. *Journal of Applied Bacteriology (Symposium Supplement)*, 70: S31-S38.

Mayer, J. (2000). Geography, ecology and emerging infectious diseases. *Social Science & Medicine*, 50: 937-952.

NHCPRC (National Health Commission of People's Republic of China) (2020a). *Outbreak Notification.* Accessed from http://www.nhc.gov.cn/xcs/yqtb/list_gzbd_3.shtml, on March 16, 2020.

NHCPRC (National Health Commission of People's Republic of China) (2020b). *Wuhan Municipal Health and Health Commission's Report on Unexplained Viral Pneumonia.* Accessed from http://www.nhc.gov.cn/xcs/yqtb/202001/1beb46f061704372b7ca41ef3e682229.shtml, on March 16, 2020.

Oppong, J. (1998). A vulnerability interpretation of the geography of HIV AIDS in Ghana, 1986-1995. *Professional Geographer*, 50: 437-448.

Rencher, A.C. (2002). *Methods of Multivariate Analysis.* Second Ed., London: John Wiley & Sons.

Sirkeci, I. (2013). *Transnational Marketing and Transnational Consumers.* London: Springer.

United Nations (UN) (2020). *The 2019 Revision of World Population Prospects.* Accessed from https://population.un.org/wpp/, on March 24, 2020.

United Nations (UN) (2019). Human Development Report 2019: Beyond Income, Beyond Averages, Beyond Today: Inequalities in Human Development in the 21st Century. United Nations Development Programme, New York.

Vásquez, I. and Porčnik, T. (2019). *The Human Freedom Index 2019: A Global Measurement of Personal, Civil, and Economic Freedom.* Washington: Cato Institute, Fraser Institute, and the Friedrich Naumann Foundation for Freedom.

Walters, M. (2003). *Six Modern Plagues and How We are Causing Them.* Washington, DC: Island Press / Shearwater Books.

WB (World Bank) (2020). *Migration and Remittances Data.* Accessed from https://www.worldbank.org/en/topic/migrationremittancesdiasporaissues/brief/migration-remittances-data, on March 15, 2020.

WHO (World Health Organization) (2020a). *Coronavirus.* Accessed from https://www.who.int/health-topics/coronavirus, on March 29, 2020.

WHO (World Health Organization) (2020b). *Coronavirus Disease (Covid-19) Outbreak.* Accessed from https://experience.arcgis.com/experience/685d0ace521648f8a5beeeee1b9125cd, on March 11, 2020.

WHO (World Health Organization) (2020c). *Coronavirus Disease 2019 (Covid-19) Situation Reports.* Accessed from https://www.who.int/emergencies/diseases/novel-coronavirus-2019/situation-reports/, on March 29, 2020.

WHO (World Health Organization) (2020d). *Middle East Respiratory Syndrome Coronavirus (MERS-CoV).* Accessed from https://www.who.int/emergencies/mers-cov/en/, on March 20, 2020.

WHO (World Health Organization) (2020e). *Severe Acute Respiratory Syndrome (SARS).* Accessed from https://www.who.int/csr/sars/en/, on March 20, 2020.

WHO (World Health Organization) (2020f). *Coronavirus Disease (COVID-19) Pandemic.* Accessed from https://www.who.int/emergencies/diseases/novel-coronavirus-2019, on March 20, 2020.

Yüceşahin, M. M. and Tulga, A. Y. (2017). Demographic and Social Change in the Middle East and North Africa: Processes, Spatial Patterns, and Outcomes. *Population Horizons*, 14(2): 47-60.

www.ingramcontent.com/pod-product-compliance
Lightning Source LLC
Chambersburg PA
CBHW050333270326
41926CB00016B/3435